Animals and Religion

What do animals—other than human animals—have to do with religion? How do our religious ideas about animals affect the lives of real animals in the world? How can we deepen our understanding of both animals and religion by considering them together? *Animals and Religion* explores how animals have crucially shaped how we understand ourselves, the other living beings around us, and our relationships with them.

Through incisive analyses of religious examples from around the world, the original contributions to this volume demonstrate how animals have played key roles in every known religious tradition, whether as sacred beings, symbols, objects of concern, fellow creatures, or religious teachers. And through our religious imagination, ethics, and practices, we have deeply impacted animal lives, whether by domesticating, sacrificing, dominating, eating, refraining from eating, blessing, rescuing, releasing, commemorating, or contemplating them. Drawing primarily on perspectives from religious studies and Christian theology, augmented by cutting-edge work in anthropology, biology, philosophy, and psychology, *Animals and Religion* offers the reader a richer understanding of who animals are and who we humans are. Do animals have emotions? Do they think or use language? Are they persons? How we answer questions like these affects diverse aspects of religion that shape not only how we relate to other animals, but also how we perceive and misperceive each other along axes of gender, race, and (dis)ability.

Accessibly written and thoughtfully argued, *Animals and Religion* will interest anyone who wants to learn more about animals, religion, and what it means to be a human animal.

Dave Aftandilian is Associate Professor of Anthropology, member of the leadership team for the Compassionate Awareness and Living Mindfully (CALM) Program, and founding Director of the Human-Animal Relationships (HARE) Program at Texas Christian University.

Barbara R. Ambros is Professor of Religious Studies at the University of North Carolina, Chapel Hill.

Aaron S. Gross is Professor of Religious Studies at the University of San Diego, a past president of the Society for Jewish Ethics, and the founder of the nonprofit organization Farm Forward.

Animals and Religion

Edited by Dave Aftandilian, Barbara R. Ambros, and Aaron S. Gross

Routledge
Taylor & Francis Group

LONDON AND NEW YORK

Designed cover image: Ash, a Broad Breasted White turkey, age 8, was a factory farm survivor who resided at Farm Sanctuary's shelter in Orland, California. Copyright Isa Leshko, from *Allowed to Grow Old: Portraits of Elderly Animals from Farm Sanctuaries* by Isa Leshko, published by the University of Chicago Press.

First published 2024
by Routledge
4 Park Square, Milton Park, Abingdon, Oxon OX14 4RN

and by Routledge
605 Third Avenue, New York, NY 10158

Routledge is an imprint of the Taylor & Francis Group, an informa business

© 2024 selection and editorial matter, Dave Aftandilian, Barbara R. Ambros, and Aaron S. Gross; individual chapters, the contributors

British Library Cataloguing-in-Publication Data
A catalogue record for this book is available from the British Library

Library of Congress Cataloging-in-Publication Data
Names: Aftandilian, David, editor. | Ambros, Barbara, 1968– editor. | Gross, Aaron S., editor.
Title: Animals and religion / edited by Dave Aftandilian, Barbara R. Ambros, and Aaron S. Gross.
Description: Abingdon, Oxon ; New York, NY : Routledge, 2024. | Includes bibliographical references and index.
Identifiers: LCCN 2023041323 | ISBN 9781032348551 (hbk) | ISBN 9781032330181 (pbk) | ISBN 9781003324157 (ebk)
Subjects: LCSH: Animals—Religious aspects.
Classification: LCC BL439 .A558 2024 | DDC 202/.12—dc23/eng/20231127
LC record available at https://lccn.loc.gov/2023041323

ISBN: 978-1-032-34855-1 (hbk)
ISBN: 978-1-032-33018-1 (pbk)
ISBN: 978-1-003-32415-7 (ebk)

DOI: 10.4324/9781003324157

Typeset in Sabon
by Apex Covantage

To all the animals—finned, feathered, furred, scaled, or otherwise—whom we have known and loved, for a moment or a lifetime; and to all the others, too, especially those who have endured suffering due to human action or inaction:

May you be happy.

May you be healthy.

May you be safe.

May you be at peace.

Contents

Illustrations

Figures

Tables

Acknowledgments

First and foremost, we editors would like to thank all of the contributors to this volume for sharing their work with us. While we have known many of you for years, we only just met and came to know some of you in the course of preparing this volume. The depth of your scholarship and compassion for animals shines through in each of your chapters, which you crafted with significant care and effort. Thank you.

For helping us locate potential contributors we are also grateful to the following scholars: Marc Bekoff, Gordon Burghardt, Beth Haller, and Whitney Sanford.

For their editorial assistance in our time of need, thank you to Laura Hobgood and Lina Verchery.

For a generous grant that helped fund the making of this work, we gratefully acknowledge the support of Farm Forward (www.farmforward.com).

For generously donating the use of her powerful photos of rescued elderly farm animals in Barbara Darling's chapter on "The Spiritual Practice of Providing Sanctuary for Animals," as well as kindly allowing us to use one of her images on the cover of this book, we thank Isa Leshko (www.isaleshko.com).

For all their efforts in helping us take this book from idea to print, we deeply appreciate the work of everyone at Routledge. Thanks especially to the editor who first spoke with D.A. about whether we might be interested in creating a book on animals and religion, Rebecca Shillabeer Clintworth. Thanks also to Routledge's Publisher for Religion, Ceri McLardy, who took over for Rebecca while she was on maternity leave. Thank you, thank you, thank you to editorial assistant Ms. Iman Hakimi, who gently nudged us along, waited patiently, answered our questions, and took care of a million details.

For their stimulating research, welcome camaraderie, and heartfelt advocacy on behalf of real animals, we thank all the scholars who have presented papers or participated in roundtables, served as steering committee members or co-chairs, or otherwise contributed their work and ideas to the American Academy of Religion's Animals and Religion Program Unit.

Finally, thank you, the reader, for picking up this book. May it deepen your knowledge, compassion, and care for all the other animals with whom we share this world (and perhaps the next).

On Human-Animal Being

An Opening

Linda Hogan

We are all part of this sacred web of life.

We have respect for the animals. We don't keep them in cages or torture them, because we know the background of animals from the Distant Time. We know that the animal has a spirit—it used to be human—and we know all the things it did. It's not just an animal; it's lots more than that.

—Koyukon elder (Nelson 1983, 24)

For those of us who are Indigenous peoples, native to each continent of the world, our spiritual traditions are based on the ongoing creation of life and the natural world. We live in relationship with the animals, plants, and other lives around us. Our ceremonies and rituals are based on gratitude for this sacred creation and are performed to ensure all life-forms may continue to exist and flourish. For us, the animals, plants, and other life-forms, including all the many sacred sites, are considered a part of *The Great Holy*. This is the simplest way to speak of our spiritual traditions or religions, which are not only elegant but also very complex.

Indigenous Ways of Knowing and Being

We Indigenous peoples have lived on the North American continent for over three millennia. In all these years, we have accumulated large stores of knowledge about our environments and how to understand our place with the land and other living beings, particularly with the great and varied animal intelligences. Some of us prefer to call other than human animal people "beings" or "spirits" since we understand that they have their own sacred place within creation. The Ainu People of Japan consider them "gods." We consider all lives holy in their being. They are of great importance to us. We are grateful for all the many kinds of intelligence they have and all that they have offered us over these thousands of years. We have a reciprocal relationship with them, giving to one another, and have agreements with animal life that are akin to treaties that were kept except for one unusual historical time during strong warfare with European nations.

Animal intelligence balances the whole of knowledge on earth, sky, and in water. This has been evident in our many different creation stories that describe the animal people and water beings as having been brought into life before the humans were. All these beings worked to help the extremely vulnerable humans survive. If any of us might doubt the truth of Indigenous views of animals as persons with their own minds and goals, we

DOI: 10.4324/9781003324157-1

can now read that more and more, the intelligence and lives of animals are being under-stood and revealed through Western science. *Science News, Scientific American, National Geographic*, and other publications explain that the abilities and knowledge the animals have taught us are their own. These give non-Indian readers some sense of the depth of what has been learned through observation and study by our Indigenous scientists and knowledge keepers over the millennia.

From those many thousand years of learning this world, we have learned through our observations and studies the information that Western scientists are only now discover-ing through their own studies. Still, there is joy in finding this seemingly new knowledge coming to light. It offers an opening to change how we all view the world for people from all backgrounds and educations. This new openness can lead all of us to rethink the significance of the animal people and give us hope for sustaining our planet, helping it to thrive ecosystem by ecosystem for the next generations to come.

Some years ago, a small group of researchers found that prairie dogs speak a complex language, complete with syntax and description (see Slobodchikoff, Perla, and Verdolin 2009, 65–92). They were recorded saying a tall male person was passing by their village. Or a short person with a stick (cane). A few years after these first researchers wrote about this recorded prairie dog language, *National Geographic* ran an article on the same topic, as well as the love and care prairie dogs have for one another.

Traditional tribal thinkers had long ago taken this a step farther. Elder Navajo knowl-edge keepers said prairie dogs call down the rain. Puzzling as this sounds at first, we need to consider the water table beneath earth. Water attracts water, and the depth of bur-rows the prairie dogs create is difficult for us to imagine since we only see their surface mounds. Yet it is true; their presence brings the rain. It also attracts the burrowing owls and other predators who feed upon them. Thus, prairie dogs are considered a keystone species, one whose presence is crucial to the well-being of an entire ecosystem.

As for the water and the rain, this attraction of water to itself is also why our planet's richly fertile rain forests attract rain and clouds toward them and even create clouds within themselves. The tragedy of deforestation has resulted in the loss of this water and been accompanied by drought that will last forever in many locations once richly forested, creating numerous losses of birds and forest animals who will remain forever unknown to us. These losses are instances of where the knowledge held by tribal peoples stood strong for thousands of years before the presence of Europeans. The original rain forest peoples predicted the outcome of deforestation, drilling, and mining, including the release of dangerous viruses and the loss of the plants that cure the illnesses caused by these viruses. Our recent COVID-19 pandemic is an example of what can happen when those forests are entered and destroyed for mining or for collecting exotic animals as new and unusual foods or pets.

*

In our present time too many of us lack the reverent observations and deep wisdom of Indigenous cultures about our kinship with other animal lives. Many beliefs in domin-ion over the earth and animals lay behind the colonization that has taken place on this continent and others. The mindset of human dominance and superiority over the natural world has led to the present destruction to our sacred earth life. Instead of a focus on what is most important to our human being, growth, and happiness, we are watching species fall over the edge of life. This way of living has created a feeling of hopelessness about the future for many of us.

Because of this time in history, we human animals seek another map to guide us to a joy-filled and peaceful existence that includes our connection with all other lives. Most importantly, we need a path that honors the animal lives so important to our world. To find such a path, many people are rethinking how they have interpreted religions that have not included animals, plants, water, and other elements, beliefs that have taken the place of Indigenous wisdom traditions.

For the League of Six Nations, a group of tribes primarily in the Northeast who know themselves as the Haudenosaunee, spiritual and personal decisions and ways of life are carried out with a thought toward the future. Each decision, whether political, spiritual, or community-oriented, looks ahead to the next seven generations and does what is best for those seven. It is part of the law of right living or as some of us call it, The Good Red Path.

For them as for many other tribal nations an address of gratitude and thanksgiving is spoken before each gathering of people. In this address, thanks and gratitude are given for every part of our lives, not only for those who walk with two legs upon the earth. Thanks is spoken for the waters: May we keep them clean and unpolluted; For the air we breathe; For the winged insects and birds; For the four-legged animals who walk with us on this sacred ground; For the fish beings; and For the soil, grasses, and trees that give us breath and attract the wildlife. The list of all beings on this planet continues to be thanked. It is our duty as caretakers for all that offers us a life of well-being. It is a loving relationship, one with another.

Living with Leopards

Interestingly, while writing this chapter, I happened to read a *Scientific American* article by Vidya Athreya entitled, "Leopards Are Living among People. And That Could Save the Species" (Athreya 2023). The article describes the small village of Atole in India, where people live with leopards. The leopard is considered a deity and was depicted as holy in ancient cave paintings showing the humans and leopards together. The leopards are still allowed to go among humans, almost always without one harming the other. The leopard is revered.

The two species understand one another and dwell peacefully together, the wild and domestic. They have coevolved and coexisted together from the beginning, so it rarely happens that their lives interfere with one another. Only one man said that he'd had a goat eaten by a mother and son leopard and that it was unusual, but they must have been extremely hungry. He could not punish the leopard who was their god. The article also described how humans saved a young leopard from a well. The young one taken from the abandoned well was related to an older brother leopard who traveled with the mother mentioned earlier.

While many of us see other possibilities in this, it turned out to be a perfect example for what I wanted to say to my brother/sister humans in this chapter. The life around us is part of our own self, our spirit, our being. Perhaps life is beyond our deep knowledge, although we know the spirit lives within and outside us in the incredibly beautiful and fruitful earth. As with the leopards, all of this is a part of the god that is our relationship of living and being. God lives in the bird who sings in the morning and in the grass that knows how to grow back into its shape even after being cut. We humans are meant to be the animal who keeps this world in balance, both the domestic and the wild. We are the caretakers. This is accomplished through ritual and ceremony, through prayer and the giving of thanks, sometimes merely with a song or story, like the one you are reading now.

My Life as a Human Animal

For those of us who are traditionally minded, each animal bears a unique gift. We live together in relationship. That bond is what we offer each other. In my life, I have found it in my heart to care for our world and all it holds. It has been my good fortune to have worked with others who share this love, and we are Native Elders who spend our time caring for what we have the ability to help.

I think of this as I drive to work at the Chickasaw Nation. Yet there are times a person cannot always help a situation, and this is one of those times: On the left side of the road, bulldozers are pushing over all the trees of a rich, green forest, one that has long sheltered deer, birds and their nests, marshes with frogs, and numerous forms of life. I know what is being lost, how they will pile the trees together and soon burn the dead, dry forest so they can bring in cattle. I think the cattle would have liked the shade of trees in the 115-degree Oklahoma summer heat, but that is not taken into consideration.

Before they go to slaughter, the cattle are here for a time, searching for newly planted grasses sprayed with toxins. The cattle are bathed in poison. They are injected with anti-biotics and hormones that act in us as female hormones. This is one reason human males are becoming feminized, and the sperm count is decreasing. The cattle are injected with another poison to fatten them. They eat foods unnatural for cattle, but by now, nothing given them is natural. Their next purpose is to be fattened even more in a feedlot where they lie, sleep, sit, and stand in their toxic manure in order to feed humans. Then they are not slaughtered humanely. All their fear, adrenaline, and anxiety are taken into the humans who eat their flesh.

As for me, I watch the trees pushed over, their dark roots like hands reaching into the sky amid clouds. Soon nothing will remain of the forest but fire and smoke. I will miss the trees with their many birds who lived and sang in those trees and the other animals burned on the forest floor.

Birds

While with my feelings about birds, I know I have been fortunate in this life to do work against destruction of the planet and to the devastation of animal life. I worked with birds of prey for eight years at the Birds of Prey Foundation in Broomfield, Colorado. There I constantly observed the amazing raptors. Each year two Great Horned Owls, a male and a female, served as foster parents for the orphaned young. For most of the orphans, their parent owls were killed by cars, gunshots, electrical wires, or other means. The infant owls were placed with those named for singers, Elton and Nina, in their large flight cages. These foster parent owls took care of the young as the new, softly billowing white feathers flew like clouds around the youngsters. The elder owls groom them but also teach skills that will allow them to fly free one day. As the young grow, they are fed by the parent birds. Those of us who work there marvel at how they feed small pieces of meat to the young, and at the softness of the early feathers we called "chiffon." They look nothing like this before long.

We also laugh at the antics of one adult owl. Elton loves the boot of one of our fellow workers and constantly lands on Dave's boot. Only one. It wants to ride the boot, to love it. We wrote in the bathroom, "For a good time, call Dave."

Soon the infants grow; their chiffon feathers blow away and are replaced with new ones as they mature. The parent owls are given dead mice in a bucket. They become busy lining up the mice on the earth. Once this work is accomplished, they train the young owls, one by one, to fly down, pick up their mouse, and learn to eat. My work is also busy as I pick up the pellets they spit to the earth. The pellets contain hair, bones, little claws, and everything else that can't be digested.

Eventually the young owls learn to catch living mice on their own and how to live with one another, all of their growing not in the presence of humans.

*

I was the first person to work with Sigrid Ueblacker. She was the most amazing healer of birds and designer of the facility, which now includes large flight cages, two intensive care units, and other buildings as it has grown from a single cage in her backyard that housed her first owl. In all our time together, she knew I could kill nothing. It was not in me to take a life. As the facility grew, I was the only person there who didn't have to perform this task to work in intensive care or handling birds.

Sigrid was a true healer. She would have been a rare and valued person in our Indigenous traditions. For example, one afternoon, we waited for a killer bird from the vet school a few hours away. They could not even examine this eagle which was too violent for them, too dangerous, so she was sent to us, hoping we could either handle the bird or euthanize her.

The eagle arrived in a closed cardboard box, not even in a carrier. We understood they could not have forced her into a carrier without being hurt. An eagle can be dangerous. One swipe of a claw across an artery is all it would take to kill a person. But Sigrid was not concerned. As I said, she was a healer and unshaken by the bird's history. For her, they were all souls with intelligence, all gentle. She treated them in this way, and they responded in kind. That afternoon, she opened the box, reached in, and with both hands lifted the bird, a beautiful golden eagle, underfed, thin, with a sunken chest. She leaned the eagle back and, with one finger, caressed each eye as the inner membrane closed slightly then looked at her. She brushed the eagle's feathers into place, then gently held out a wing to see if it was missing many feathers or fractured. "Some killer bird," she said, holding out the wing as they looked gently at one another.

I followed orders, cutting food for the bird to determine if she would eat. The eagle was hungry. She took one bite, then more. It was the other wing that was damaged, so after a time in intensive care, this "killer bird" was placed in the carrier, then a larger cage, and soon with the other eagles, most of them high above us on perches where they watched the world, and we watched them.

Soon this golden eagle who could not fly up to the others found her place in the large flight cage on a tree stump. She would leap up and sit. But she would never fly to up to where the others waited for their release back to air and sky.

Because she remained on that stump most days, we spent our time close to one another. I placed food beneath where she sat. She watched as I cleaned the ground beneath her, always speaking softly or singing a traditional song to her.

I had already learned from birds how to be. *Be.* It is an interesting word with many forms: exist, be present, coexist, life-form, soul. It seemed important in dealing with one another, as well as with other species. I learned that before I entered any of the flight cages or smaller areas, I should stand outside for a while until I was in a good state of being. Calm and at peace. In harmony with the birds. I needed to have an inner silence. I learned this at the beginning of my work.

Soon the golden eagle recognized this love and care and opened her good wing about me, over me, above me. Or she used her beak to straighten up my hair. We learned to *be* together. She would never go back to a life in the sky, gliding in the currents, rising, and landing high above in a great tree to observe the world or look for possible food.

The heartache for me was that she could not stay with us. Federal laws do not consider the human heart. In any case, she would have to be euthanized or sent somewhere else to become an educational bird, and that was where she went. Fortunately, the place where she landed had one of my former students working there. I was overjoyed. At least I could keep up with Grandmother, as I had named her and everyone now called her: *Grandmother*. Barbara called to say that Grandmother arrived without trouble. We stayed in touch about Grandmother.

The love I felt never vanished. Nor did the love I received in return. I could feel it. From her, as from others, I learned. She inspired this poem:

Eagle Feather Prayer
by Linda Hogan

I thank Old Mother
and the golden eagle, the two who taught me to pray
without words. They instilled the part of me
unnamed by anatomy books
They gave to those parts
their own perfect names
and so I stand here now
facing you and the rest of creation
also with secret names.
I send this prayer of gratitude to those who risk their lives
for clean, sweet water,
and once again there is the great silence
of what happened to the buffalo enclosed one night,
as if by some other magic, only dark,
and so hard it is to pray for the shooters
who laughed about hitting the girl with one good shot,
but that is what they said to do.

We love our horses. We love the dogs.
They have helped us.
We love the wildness of buffalo herds.
That is the labor of humans, to love,
but I don't know what happened to the shooters,
their purpose for being.
And with no words,
just with a part of my named self
I hold this fan from Old Mother and the eagle
and with all I have, send a prayer
so very silent.

The animal people often communicate the values and spiritual beliefs of our Native understandings of this world. I think Grandmother was one of those who had the gift our ancestors wanted to pass on in our Indigenous ceremonial and religious practices.

> Whether
> for this we must observe
> the world, lovingly
> > (Unknown author, found written in my diary)

May you all walk in peace and harmony and follow the good path in gratitude.

References

Athreya, Vidya. 2023. "Leopards Are Living Among People. And That Could Save the Species." *Scientific American*, April 1. Accessed June 2, 2023. www.scientificamerican.com/article/leopards-are-living-among-people-and-that-could-save-the-species/.

Nelson, Richard K. 1983. *Make Prayers to the Raven: A Koyukon View of the Northern Forest*. Chicago, Ill. and London: University of Chicago Press.

Slobodchikoff, C.N., Bianca S. Perla, and Jennifer L. Verdolin. 2009. *Prairie Dogs: Communication and Community in an Animal Society*. Cambridge, Mass. and London: Harvard University Press.

Other Recommended Resources

Haudenosaunee Thanksgiving Address. https://americanindian.si.edu/environment/pdf/01_02_Thanksgiving_Address.pdf.

Hogan, Linda. 2020. *The Radiant Lives of Animals*. Boston, Mass.: Beacon Press.

Introduction to Animals and Religion

Aaron S. Gross, Dave Aftandilian,
and Barbara R. Ambros

What Is Animals and Religion, and What Do Scholars of It Study?

When we tell people that we study animals and religion, their first reaction is often confusion—*What is that? Do you mean that you study animal sacrifice? Or the Lamb of God and sacred cows? Or whether dogs go to heaven? Or religious ethics about how to treat animals?*

For most Americans and Europeans, animals and religion simply do not seem to go together, perhaps with the few exceptions just listed. One wouldn't be entirely wrong to think of the domains of religion and animality as non-overlapping because, historically speaking, much of Western thought has tended to *try* to separate them this way. Western thought has often imagined religion as part of a vertical movement above the ordinary, biological, deterministic, and mundane—in a word, the *animal*—aspects of existence. The dominant Western heritage imagined a great chain of being stretching from the inanimate to the animal, and then beyond these, to the higher planes of humanity and, ultimately, divinity; anything that might be called religious was located on these higher planes. Historically, both the vast majority of Christian theologians and, later, most scientifically-minded scholars of religion have argued, or just assumed, that *religion begins where animality ends.* All of us have inherited this curious idea about the nature of religion, which is why the topic of "animals and religion" at first seems strange, *but is this inheritance one we want to keep?* The scholarly subfield of "animals and religion" says no.

It certainly is worth investigating why some religious experts want to insist that religion has little to do with animals, but we need not accept the irrelevance of animals to religion as a truth. Indeed, as this volume introduces it, the animals and religion subfield gains its potency because of an intuition that whatever "religion" is—this volume will not assume a particular answer—it is related to the beings we call "animals." Each chapter reverses the historical distancing of animals and religion by thinking about both together. We believe this leads to a fuller account of religion and a deeper understanding of animals, but you, the reader, must be the final judge.

Challenging Our Ideas About "Religion" and "Animals"

Assuming, as the dominant Western tradition has, that animals have little to do with religion has meant assuming that animals themselves don't engage in religion or anything like it—a topic now very much under debate, as some chapters in this volume show (see Harvey 2006 as well as the opening chapter by Linda Hogan, Chapter 1 by Margaret

DOI: 10.4324/9781003324157-2

Robinson, and Chapter 30 by Barbara Smuts et al.)—but this assumption also has led to an *incomplete picture of the diversity of human religious expression*. That is, setting aside the profound question of how more-than-human animals themselves might engage in religion, let us consider how the idea that "animals and religion don't go together" might confuse our ability to understand religions (see section on "Naming" later for an explanation of what we mean by calling animals "more than human").

Thinking about religion and animals as utterly different domains, for example, has historically led many Christian theologians and scientifically-minded religion scholars alike to assume that activities we share with animals—such as sleeping, eating, or having sex—also couldn't have much to do with religion. In this way of thinking, one might concede, for instance, that a blessing over food—a matter of words, interior experience, and communal gathering—is religious, but eating itself would just be an "animal" act. Does this way of imagining what religion is prove helpful for the person who wants to grasp the full diversity of human religious expression? That is, when we take ideas about religion such as this into the field and start applying them to examples of phenomena we are pretty sure are religious—like the teachings of the so-called world religions (Buddhism, Christianity, Daoism, Hinduism, Islam, Judaism, and so on; for a critique of the category of "world religions," see Masuzawa 2005)—do they help us make sense of the diversity of religions or leave us confused?

The conclusion that animals—and the domains of life associated with them, such as eating—have little to do with the special phenomena we call religion simply does not describe the actual varieties of human religious expression as scholars have come to observe them. For example, diverse studies identify the act of eating—which often enough involves actual animals—playing a central religious role (Norman 2012). Looking at religion on the ground does not support the view that food and eating are peripheral to religious traditions. In fact, some of the *only* religious traditions that radically minimize the religious dimension of eating (or at least claim to) are certain forms of Protestant Christianity. This is not true of all forms of Christianity throughout history. In the Hebrew Bible and Christian Scriptures (what Christians often call the Old and New Testament), for example, we encounter a world where eating seems quite important—even God gets in on the action. Scholars of religion do not agree on what Jesus ate, but most Christian theologians and scholars of religious studies agree that the Christian Scriptures depict Jesus as eating food and that this is a significant part of the Christian understanding of the nature of the divine. For the Christianity of the Bible, God didn't just appear on earth, God became flesh, and God ate. We could say, as some contemporary Christian theologians want to insist, that God not only became human, but also became animal, became a creature (Clough 2012).

If many Westerners tend to think religion has little to do with "animal" activities such as eating, this is not because it is a good description of what religious traditions do but because of the influence of one part of Christianity's vast heritage that has been especially influential in the contemporary West, namely some (not all) streams of Protestant Christianity. Part of what this volume hopes to do is allow readers to make up their own minds about just what this thing we call "religion" is—to help question and place in perspective our own inherited notions. One of the most important aspects of the serious study of religion is simply unlearning common sense notions that worked well enough to get us to the corner store (religions in our local community) but are inadequate now that we want to explore the global village (the full diversity of human religion).

Defining (and Not Defining) Religion

In particular, this volume suggests we need to reconsider the idea that human religious expression—whether inside formal traditions such as Christianity, Hinduism, or Judaism or occurring in less formal contexts that some might want to call "spiritual but not religious"—has little to do with animals or animality. *Religion, we argue, can be more richly, completely, and scientifically described if we assume animals and religion, in fact, go together.*

A point of clarification seems necessary here about how this introduction and most of the chapters in this volume use the word "religion," which is different from our everyday use of the term. For example, in everyday speech, many people want to draw a distinction between *religion*, which is seen as associated with formal institutions, and *spirituality*, which might be seen as something religion-like that doesn't require participation in a formal institution. Some authors in this volume use the word "spirituality" in these everyday ways, for example, following the usage of people they have interviewed (see, e.g., Chapter 20 by Barbara Darling). For the purposes of this introduction and this volume in general, though, we are using the term "religion" as an overarching term that covers the entire terrain of phenomena that some might want to split into religion and spirituality. At the very least, by religion, we refer to both *formal* religious traditions and *informal* practices that seem related to meaning-making in ways that make them more than ordinary; we include, for example, both going to church and a profound experience of awe in nature enjoyed by an atheist as phenomena that can be productively analyzed as religious. Scholars of religion certainly do get around to dividing religion into different categories (the art of taxonomy), but even when we do that, most of us tend not to use the religion/spirituality binary or other seemingly common sense notions because they carry hidden assumptions that get in the way of our seeing whatever example we are considering on its own terms.

Though it may seem just like a simple observation to some of us, assuming that religion is something distinct from spirituality is to partly define religion and therefore narrow our conception of it in ways that might not be justified depending on the religious example we are considering. For example, some people seem to think religion is bad or problematic, but spirituality is good or natural, so we can immediately see that there is an *argument*—not a mere description—coursing underneath the practice of splitting meaning-making human activities into the categories "religious" and "spiritual" (usually an agenda to define what is called spiritual as more natural, purer, or more desirable than religion).

Whatever words are being used, we invite readers to set aside what they think they know about religion (broadly conceived) and learn from the real-life examples presented here. The invitation of this volume is not simply to think through your already preconceived ideas about religion—not just to give you new, animal-filled examples of that same old thing, religion, like showing you different models of a car. Rather, as with all works of religious studies, we hope to blast open the category of religion, reclaim it from imprecise thinking, and try to use it to better understand some of the most interesting aspects of the world around us—especially the interesting aspects we call animal.

In sum, thinking about animals and religion helps us *rethink what religion itself is.* This volume won't tell you what religion is, but it sure is going to give you food for thought. It also won't tell you what animals are or how you should relate to them, but it will present perspectives that might change how you understand more-than-human animals and humans' relationship with them. We do not claim total impartiality. To write about more-than-human animals and religion today with complete neutrality about the state of human-animal and human-nature relations would be strange indeed. We editors and contributors are in part animated by our sense that something is wrong in how we presently relate to the more-than-human world. The goal of this volume, though, is not to share any one idea about how to fix this but to instead invite our readers to join a conversation about more-than-human animals, about religion, and about what we can learn from thinking, feeling, contemplating, and discussing them both in relation to one another.

The "Animals and Religion" Subfield

We have emphasized that there are multiple valid ways of defining religion, but the animals and religion subfield does not argue that all ways of defining religion are equal. Some ways of thinking about religion are more helpful than others. Following the animals and religion subfield as a whole, one of this volume's contributions to the task of thinking helpfully about religion is to suggest that we can't understand the full depth and diversity of religious traditions without attending to more-than-human animals. This argument—that *animals matter to religion*—is fundamental to the whole subfield of "animals and religion." There isn't any time in history that Christian theologians and scientifically-minded scholars of religion didn't write about animals. What is new and exciting in the contemporary animals and religion subfield is not that more-than-human animals are simply mentioned but the further insistence that they matter to religion in significant ways. In the past, talking about more-than-human animals and religion was likely to be a nice aside or a story meant for children (or, more darkly, a vehicle to show the inferiority of someone else's "less civilized"—that is, more animal-like—religion); this volume brings more-than-human animals themselves into the center of our inquiry.

How do more-than-human animals matter to religion? The animals and religion subfield explores this in diverse ways that include asking how animals shape our imagination of religion (already partly explored previously), the roles animals play inside diverse religious traditions, and what ethical concerns emerge from thinking about animals and religion together.

Animals Shape Our Imagination of Religion

Across cultures, the beings we call animals play a crucial role in human self-conception (Gross and Vallely 2012; Aftandilian, Copeland, and Wilson 2007); we use more-than-human animals to think about ourselves and thus use them to think about what we mean by religion. This phenomenon of using animals to imagine humanity and religion has been of great interest to the animals and religion subfield (Gross 2015, Chapter 3). You've surely encountered some form of the question, "What is uniquely human?" Or, "What separates man and animals"? Some religions, especially those that come from civilizations where agriculture is the dominant mode of obtaining food, raise and answer these questions, offering their insights into the nature of humanity or even divinity in part by reflecting on the distinctions between inanimate, animal, human, and divine. All Abrahamic traditions (Christianity, Islam, and Judaism) and Dharma traditions (Hinduism, Buddhism, and Jainism) use animals partly in this way. Other traditions, most notably the religions of Indigenous peoples, tend not to divide the world so starkly into humans and animals but nonetheless imagine animals as fellow sojourners, ancestors, other nations, and in many other ways that define how they think about themselves (and parts of the Abrahamic and Dharma religions do similar things).

All the ways that religious traditions, experiences, or practices help us imagine ourselves and our world through animals—including how we imagine religion itself—are part of the inquiry into animals and religion. In these ways, animals do not so much show up inside already-formed religious traditions but play a role in creating the very space of religion. Indeed, a small number of eminent scholars, including Mircea Eliade, who is generally regarded as a founder of contemporary religious studies, and the influential scholar of classical religions, Walter Burkert, have gone so far as to suggest that the very beginnings of human religion (if they can be recovered), or at least religion's "formative antecedents," might be found in the tensions between humans' empathy for animals and simultaneous use of them in ways that require animal death or suffering, especially in hunting and the process of domestication (Gross 2017, under "Animals as Generators of Religion").

While scholars today tend to be suspicious of any attempt to identify an "origin" of religion, it is undeniable that some of the most ancient human practices for which we have evidence strongly suggest that the importance of animals to human cultures has always had a dimension of deeply felt meaning that is best considered religious. For example, the meticulously detailed paintings of animals from at least 30,000 years ago in Western Europe that Paleolithic peoples created in the resonant depths of caves seem religiously charged. Humans were very seldom depicted, and when we do find humanoid figures, they often appear as human-animal hybrids. These animal images were often placed in areas that were extremely difficult to access and were repainted or painted on top of repeatedly in intricate ways that parallel the robust, communal, and longstanding engagement we associate with religion (for more on cave art see Chauvet, Deschamps, and Hilaire 1996; Clottes 2016; Lewis-Williams 2004). Or we could observe that from its beginnings 5000 years ago, silkworm cultivation (sericulture) in premodern East Asia, performed by women, was bound together with rich narratives and special practices in ways that are arguably religious. These religious dimensions of sericulture ultimately affirmed Confucian gender roles, and by weaving and wearing silk, women became associated with immortals and divinities, partly because the silkworm was thought to transcend death by transforming into a moth, even though the actual silk reeling process killed the insects inside their cocoon (Kuhn 1984; Bray 1997; Como 2005).

Animals Play Important Roles in Religious Traditions

Animals, of course, do not just help define the idea of religion, but they also appear *inside* religious traditions where they play innumerable roles. Animals serve as religious symbols, such as the Lamb of God in Christianity. Animals in religion can themselves be viewed as sacred beings, as Buffalo are by many Native American peoples (see Chapter 28 by James Hatley in this book). Animals can serve as religious teachers, as insects do for Taiwanese Buddhist nuns (Chapter 8 by Lina Verchery), cows do for Hindus (Chapter 21 by Kenneth R. Valpey), and a variety of animals do for participants in the contemporary Council of All Beings ceremony (Chapter 22 by Eric D. Mortensen). Animals also play a role in religious expression through being sacrificed (Chapter 15 by Todd Ramón Ochoa), blessed (Chapter 14 by Laura Hobgood), rescued (Chapter 20 by Barbara Darling), or released and commemorated (Chapters 16 and 23 by Barbara R. Ambros).

Focusing on the roles animals play inside religious traditions can also help us better understand aspects of religions that we thought we already knew, such as the meaning of dominion and stewardship in the biblical book of Genesis (Chapter 10 by Allison Covey), whether animals can count as part of our religious communities (Chapter 13 by Andrea Dara Cooper), and whether religious ethics can extend beyond the human realm (Chapter 9 by Sarra Tlili). In these ways, the study of animals and religion is about uncovering and better understanding the roles that animals have played in specific religious traditions.

Ethical Dimensions of the Animals and Religion Subfield

A final way that scholars of religion consider animals, and one that we editors believe has special importance today, is focusing on animals and religion to help us (re)consider how our religious ideas about animals affect the lives of real animals in the world, and how rethinking those ideas might, therefore, be required of us, for ethical, legal, or religious reasons. Every contributor to this book keeps the impact of their topic on actual animals firmly in mind in their chapters. Indeed, one of the ways the contemporary animals and religion subfield differs from previous discussions of animals in religion is a fierce commitment not to forget animals as real, biological individuals—not to let them become mere symbols or passive objects (Gross 2017, under "A Methodological Commitment to Real Animals"). For this reason, one of the foundational publications in the subfield, the edited volume *A Communion of Subjects*, took its title from a famous quote by Thomas Berry, both a Catholic priest and a scholar of religion, who argued that "the universe is a communion of subjects rather than a collection of objects" (Waldau and Patton 2006, vii).

There is an ethical impulse behind this entire commitment to speak about the actual lives of animals, but the "ought" of how we should treat animals for religious reasons emerges perhaps most clearly in the chapters that cover the eating of animals and their products—or refraining from doing so (Chapters 12, 17, 18, and 19 in Part II by Beth Berkowitz, Vincent Goossaert, Geoffrey Barstow, and Adrienne Krone, as well as Chapters 26 and 27 in Part III by Nerissa Russell and Aaron S. Gross). Other chapters where this ethical concern looms large explore aspects of religious responses to the lives of specific animal populations, such as companion animals (Chapter 25 by Laura Hobgood) or marine and urban wildlife (Chapter 11 by Dave Aftandilian and Chapter 29 by Seth B. Magle and Dave Aftandilian).

The Animals and Religion Subfield, "Animal Studies," and Interdisciplinarity

The animals and religion subfield is not only an internal development in Christian theology or religious studies but also increasingly a fluid part of a broader interdisciplinary conversation and field known by various names, including animal studies, critical animal studies, human-animal interactions, or human-animal studies (e.g., DeMello 2021; Gruen 2018; McCance 2013; Waldau 2013). Scholars regularly gather to discuss "animal studies" at national and international conferences; several academic journals and university presses publish studies in this area; and more and more colleges and universities are creating interdisciplinary programs to teach students about animal studies. (For a helpful list of degree programs, journals, institutes, and other resources in animal studies, visit the Animals & Society Institute's HAS Links website at www.animalsandsociety.org/

resources/resources-for-faculty/has-links/.) This volume's consideration of the "animals and religion" subfield works under the same assumption as animal studies more broadly about the value of using diverse disciplinary approaches.

For example, if we are starting from the standpoint of the validity of modern science and want to investigate the question raised earlier about whether other animals might themselves engage in practicing religion, we probably will want to know whether other animals can think and feel and whether they have a consciousness of self and other. For such reasons, we can benefit from studies by scholars working in the natural sciences who study animal cognition and consciousness. We might also do well to know whether scientists who study wild animals in the field have ever observed behaviors that might plausibly be called religious (the answer to this question is "yes," as Barbara Smuts and her colleagues explain in the last chapter in this book). Of course, science, as we define it in Western contexts, is just one way of knowing animals; we can also come to know animals in a myriad of ways, such as through personal experiences and close observations of them, making art or stories about them, working in partnership with them, and, of course, through other academic disciplines outside the natural sciences.

To help readers engage in interdisciplinary inquiry with animals, we have sought out contributors who specialize not only in religious studies but also scholars who work primarily in anthropology, biology, philosophy, and psychology. You will also find that the scholars who write from a religious studies point of view in this book work from an interdisciplinary perspective. Religious studies does not advocate a particular methodology of its own in the way most academic disciplines do (history advocating a historical method, sociology advocating a sociological method, and so on) but instead utilizes a range of approaches from the humanities, social sciences, and, more rarely, the life sciences to explore the topic of religion.

Because of the special value we see in interdisciplinary approaches, it is helpful to understand how particular discourses adjacent to the "animals and religion" subfield are also part of the larger "animal turn" that has taken place in many humanities and social sciences disciplines over the past several decades (see, e.g., Chen 2023; Ritvo 2007; Sherman 2020; Weil 2010). Cultural anthropology and geography form part of the theoretical background that guided our selection of chapters, so let us briefly consider how these disciplines have created their own subfields, giving special attention to animals, including animals and religion.

Cultural anthropology, as its name suggests (*anthropos* is the Greek word for "human"), is a discipline that has traditionally focused almost exclusively on studying humans and their cultures. Yet beginning in the mid-2000s, anthropologists created a new mode of writing and research called multispecies anthropology; scholars in this field focus on "studying the host of organisms whose lives and deaths are linked to human social worlds" and "how a multitude of organisms' livelihoods shape and are shaped by political, economic, and cultural forces" (Kirksey and Helmreich 2010, 545). Among other tools, multispecies anthropologists have been using participant observation, an experiential method first developed to study human cultures, as a way to incorporate other animals into anthropological research (Hurn 2012, 207–208). For example, in his study of elephants and their handlers in Nepal, Piers Locke learned how to do this job himself, taught as much by the mother elephant whom he worked with, Sitsama—whom he came to recognize as a person with whom he needed to build a reciprocal social relationship, just as she did with him—as by his Nepalese hosts (Locke 2017). And to understand the "multispecies commons" built collaboratively around the Ethiopian city of Harar by humans and hyenas, Marcus Baynes-Rock had to research both kinds of persons—hyena persons and human persons—and learn how each species came to recognize members of the other as persons (Baynes-Rock 2013, 2015). Studies in multispecies anthropology such as these have much to offer scholars of animals and religion who focus on personhood (local religious traditions also played important roles in shaping the human-animal relationships that both of these anthropologists studied).

Similarly, cultural geographers developed a new animal geography in the mid-1990s that has studied "the complex entanglings of human-animal relations with space, place, location, environment and landscape" (Philo and Wilbert 2000, 4). Moreover, this new animal geography has paid attention to the agency of other than human animals (Philo and Wilbert 2000, 24). Zoogeography, the study of the geographic distribution of animal species, has been an established subfield of geography (within biogeography) since the nineteenth century and is considered the first wave of animal geography. During the second wave of animal geography in the mid-twentieth century, cultural geographers began to study human relationships with wildlife and livestock. For example, Frederick and Elizabeth Simoons's *A Ceremonial Ox of India* (1968) is one seminal work from this time. With the rise of the animal rights movement in the 1980s and 1990s, the new animal geography emerged as a third wave. Key works from this period include Yi-Fu Tuan's *Dominance and Affection* (1984), Jennifer Wolch and Jody Emel's *Animal Geographies* (1998), Chris Philo and Chris Wilbert's *Animal Spaces, Beastly Places* (2000), and Julie Urbanik's *Placing Animals* (2012). The new animal geography decenters the human as the focus of study. It includes all kinds of other than human animals (not just wildlife and livestock but also working, companion, and feral animals) in all sorts of places, including urban landscapes. Moreover, it considers the subjectivity of other than human animals rather than treating them only as objects of human control (Urbanik 2012, 26–38).

While we do not have space to consider the animal turn in every adjacent field informing this volume, as the cases of cultural anthropology and geography demonstrate, this volume comes at a time when numerous disciplines are taking up "the question of the animal" in a new way. This volume draws on all these rich streams to provide a gateway to questions about more-than-human animals and religion—including which names we ought to use for animals.

Naming Animals So That They Matter

> Then the Lord God said, "It is not good that the man [Adam] should be alone; I will make him a helper as his partner." So out of the ground the Lord God formed every animal of the field and every bird of the air, and brought them to the man to see what he would call them; and whatever the man called every living creature, that was its name. The man gave names to all cattle, and to the birds of the air, and to every animal of the field.
>
> (Gen. 2:18–20, NRSV)

When I (D.A.) was a kid, and the other kids would call me mean names at school, I would come home crying to my mom. She would hug me and tell me that "names don't matter." Though her words made me feel better at the time, since then, I have learned that names *do* matter (which, of course, my mom also knew!).

When we call another human demeaning names based on what makes them different from us, whether that be their race or gender or ability or religion, we harm them not just emotionally but also physically; constant daily microaggressions like this can add up to shorter lifespans and lower qualities of life for those who are victimized (Casey et al. 2019; Jadotte, Salmond, and Allread 2022; Kattari 2020). To help readers visualize what microaggressions feel like in their sequential art story "Wives," Native American authors Darcie Little Badger and Tara Ogaick depict the cruel words and glances that two women who are married to each other receive throughout their day as arrows that others shoot into the women (Little Badger and Ogaick 2017).

Especially when naming means placing diverse animal individuals in a single category, it may also be a way to demonstrate one's power over other beings. In the earlier quote from the Garden of Eden story, the one who names, Adam, has power over the ones who are named, metaphorically placing humanity in general, and men in particular, in a position of power over all the other creatures. In a now classic text of animal studies, *The Animal That Therefore I Am*, philosopher Jacques Derrida reflects on this biblical passage and argues that the power to name animals that God gave Adam functions here to "mark his ascendancy, his domination over them, indeed, his power to tame them" (Derrida 2008, 15). In this sense, we see how the names that we give to animals can function as a way that we separate ourselves from them and as a means to put them in their supposedly God-given place. Recognizing this power of naming from the opposite direction, in her powerful short story "She Unnames Them," Ursula K. Le Guin imagines Eve unnaming the animals, telling them instead that they can choose their own names, and finding that "They seemed far closer than when their names had stood between myself and them like a clear barrier" (Le Guin 1987, 195).

Yet, other kinds of naming, like bestowing an individual name upon a particular animal, can also help bring them closer to us. Think of how giving a dog or cat or parrot or another companion animal a name helps make us feel like they are more a part of our family (even if not necessarily an equal partner with the human family members). Giving such a name to an animal recognizes them as a unique individual, different from others of their species, with whom we might be able to engage in a meaningful, person-to-person relationship.

The names we call animals, then, affect how we see them and who they are in relationship to us and, therefore, suggest how we ought to treat them. Referring to an animal as "it" or "which" tends to make us think of them as an object or thing or a piece of property, whereas referring to them instead as "she" or "he" or "they," "who" or "whom," helps us see them as more like human persons, as subjects of a life with agency and emotion. This is why the primatologist Jane Goodall and many other eminent scientists, academics, and animal advocates sent a letter to the Associated Press in 2021 asking that they revise their Stylebook for journalists on how they should refer to animals so that

> When gender is known, the standard guidance should be, *she/her/hers* and *he/him/his*, regardless of species. When it is unknown, the gender-neutral *they, he/she,* or *his/hers* should be used. It is also preferable to use *who* rather than *that* or *which* when describing any individual nonhuman animal.
>
> (Goodall et al. 2021)

Throughout this book, the contributors have done their best to follow this advice when referring to other animals, describing them as "she" or "he" or "they" or "who."

And what should we make of the most common word used to describe more-than-human species, *animal*? Since "animal" derives from the Latin word *anima*, which means "breath" or "soul," we could argue that anyone who breathes is an animal—including in one category us humans alongside other animate species. The word "animal," then, could be a way to help refocus our attention from how we differ from other animals to what we share with them instead (which Matthew Calarco describes as an "indistinction" approach in Chapter 7). Yet, as we began this introduction by emphasizing, this is not how most humans think about animals—instead, the word "animal" encourages us to see them as fundamentally different than us: lower on the evolutionary scale or great chain of being than humans. Terms like *nonhuman animals* also seem to derive from hierarchical, less-than-us notions like this, or at least from a dualistic sense of "them" (all other animals) versus "us" (humans).

For this reason, several alternative names to identify animals have been proposed. The philosopher Lisa Kemmerer, for instance, has suggested the term *anymal*, which she explains "is a contraction of 'any' and 'animal,' and is a shortened version of the concept, 'any animal who does not happen to be the species that I am'"; she adds, "This term encourages people to think about how they use the word, animal, and why and perhaps even about how our actions affect rats and rabbits, cattle and chickens—the rest of the animal world" (Kemmerer 2006, 10, 13). For similar reasons, Derrida playfully coined the term *l'animot*, combing the common French words for animal, *animale* (female) and *animal* (male), with the French suffix *-mot*, which means word. In French, the pronunciation of *l'animot* would be the same as the pronunciation of the normal French plural of animal/e, *animaux*. The way *l'animot* confuses singular and plural invites readers to pause over the violence implicit in reducing so many diverse species to a single word. The suffix -mot also helps us remember the importance of words in relation to animals, as well as our common (mis)understanding of animals as lacking the capacity to use language (Derrida 2008, 47–48).

In this volume, while we cannot avoid sometimes simply using the term "animal(s)," we will most often refer to *other than human animals* or *more-than-human animals*. Some of us prefer "more-than-human animals" because it turns our usual hierarchical views of other animals on their head, suggesting that they have many physical abilities and understandings of the world and even sacredness that humans lack. This way of referring to those whom we usually just call animals also fits better with Indigenous conceptions of animals (see the opening chapter by Linda Hogan and Chapter 1 by Margaret Robinson). And while "other than human animals" still implies a dualism—a binary distinction between other animals and humans—it does not necessarily label them as lesser because of this (which "nonhuman" may imply by focusing our attention on what animals supposedly lack). Indeed, feminist philosopher Marti Kheel, an early pioneer of the animals and religion subfield, used the phrase other than human animals precisely "as a reminder of our kinship" with animals (Kheel 2008, 21).

In closing this section on naming, it is worth noting that we usually do not know the names that animals would prefer to call themselves, whether referring to an individual within their own species or to a different kind of animal. In my (D.A.'s) family, we are pretty sure that the sister and brother cats we live with call each other "Stinky Brother" and "Mean Sister," but of course, we have nothing to base that on except our observations of how they treat each other (and our senses of humor!). Quite seriously, though, as you will read in Robert W. Mitchell and Mark A. Krause's chapter on animal consciousness and cognition, many animals do have senses of "self" and "other," so it is entirely possible that animals might have some name-like labels they use to identify different kinds of beings. We might imagine—and indeed have some biological evidence to support—that such names, if they exist, could relate to how each kind of animal engages with the world around them (see Safina 2020, 49–52 and 147 on individual-identifying calls among sperm whales and parrots). For whales, perhaps one's name might be a few specific note phrases in a song, and for dogs, who depend so much on their sense of smell, maybe one's name is a specific individual scent. (For a literary imagining of what African elephants might call themselves and members of other species, based on what is known from studies of their behavior in the wild, see Barbara Gowdy's novel, *The White Bone* [2000].) In any case, for the foreseeable future we are stuck naming more-than-human animals ourselves, and as we consider animals and religion together, we would do well to be aware of just how much the names we use shape how we think, feel, and act toward our fellow living beings.

How This Book Is Organized, and Why

Animals and Religion begins with a chapter by honored Chickasaw (Native American) elder, writer, and animal rescuer Linda Hogan that invites us to look at animals as Indigenous peoples around the world do: as sacred beings—as thinking, speaking subjects of their own lives with whom humans ought to strive to develop caring relationships of respect, reciprocity, and coexistence. These themes are also expressed in other religious traditions, though unfortunately, often not so commonly or so deeply, and you will see them running through many, if not all, of the chapters in this book.

We have organized the rest of *Animals and Religion* into three sections or sets of chapters. The first section (Part I) focuses on issues of religion and identity, answering questions such as, "Who are the other animals in relation to us humans?" Or, as the final chapter in this section by Matthew Calarco puts it (Chapter 7), how are humans and other animals similar to, different from, and indistinct from one another? What boundary lines have we drawn between animals and ourselves, for example, in terms of personhood (Chapter 1 by Margaret Robinson), consciousness and cognition (Chapter 2 by Robert W. Mitchell and Mark A. Krause), and emotion (Chapter 3 by Donovan O. Schaefer), and how have different religious and scientific understandings of animals tended to blur those boundaries as we have examined them more closely? Finally, how do our own positionalities in terms of gender and sexuality (Chapter 4 by Katharine Mershon), race (Chapter 5 by Christopher Carter), and disability (Chapter 6 by Alan Santinele Martino and Sarah May Lindsay) affect how we view ourselves in relation to other animals? Such questions help us get to the heart of what we mean by "religion" and what it means to be human, animal, and both.

In the middle section (Part II), we present a range of religious practices toward and with animals that have emerged in various religious traditions over time. We also consider how these practices have helped believers become more present to and/or distanced from real animals. Organizing such a rich diversity of topics into a single order is no easy feat, and we encourage the reader to explore them as best fits their own interests (or assignments). But from our perspective, this section begins with two chapters that explore how becoming more attentive to other animals, to their capabilities and needs, can help us come to care about them more deeply—even little-loved animals like insects (Chapters 8 and 9 by Lina Verchery and Sarra Tlili). The next set of chapters explores animals from the points of view of theology, personhood, and kinship (Chapters 10 through 13 by Allison Covey, Dave Aftandilian, Beth A. Berkowitz, and Andrea Dara Cooper), as well as how practices such as blessings of pets, sacrifice, and animal releases translate those theological understandings into concrete actions that affect the lives of real animals in the world, often in unexpected ways (Chapters 14, 15, and 16 by Laura Hobgood, Todd Ramón Ochoa, and Barbara R. Ambros). Three chapters examine the issue of eating animals, or not, from different religious perspectives (Chapters 17, 18, and 19 by Vincent Goossaert, Geoffrey Barstow, and Adrienne Krone). And the last four chapters in this section examine different religious practices that can offer new ways to care about and for animals, ranging from providing sanctuary to animals (Chapters 20 and 21 by Barbara Darling and Kenneth R. Valpey) to representing their grievances against humans through a Council of All Beings (Chapter 22 by Eric D. Mortensen) to memorializing their lives in ways that may equate them with, or set them apart from, our own beloved human dead (Chapter 23 by Barbara R. Ambros).

The chapters in the final section (Part III) delve deeply into religious responses to animal lives, especially to the challenges that animals face in a human-dominated world. We begin by discussing how contemplative practices can help practitioners connect more closely with animals, thus healing some of the separation and alienation from other living beings that many humans feel (Chapter 24 by Dave Aftandilian). The next three chapters focus on animals who are often viewed as closest to humans and how we behave toward them in religious and ethical senses: companion animals and other animals we have domesticated to provide us with food, labor, and other benefits (Chapters 25, 26, and 27 by Laura Hobgood, Nerissa Russell, and Aaron S. Gross). In the next two chapters, the authors explore who we are in religious, philosophical, and lived relationship to wild animals, both those that settler-colonialists have almost driven extinct, such as the Buffalo of North America (Chapter 28 by James Hatley), and those who live next door to us in our cities and suburbs (Chapter 29 by Seth B. Magle and Dave Aftandilian). Finally, the last chapter introduces us to what science and personal experience can teach us about the religiosity of—what the authors consider as the "spirituality" of—animals, both wild and domestic (Chapter 30 by Barbara Smuts, Becca Franks, Monica Gagliano, and Christine Webb). The authors of this chapter make a passionate (and persuasive) plea that we should do scientific studies of animals differently in ways that allow for the possibility of seeing animals as spiritual beings and viewing our encounters with them as sacred.

Most chapters include a final section of "Other Recommended Resources." Readers can discover new perspectives on topics related to each chapter's main themes through these books, articles, websites, or videos.

The reader will also notice that the chapters in *Animals and Religion* are organized by topic rather than by religious tradition (e.g., Buddhism and Animals or Judaism and Animals). A topical arrangement fits better with the interdisciplinary nature of our approach, but in case it might be helpful to some readers and instructors, Table 0.1 provides a list of whole chapters or parts of chapters that cover various religious traditions:

Table 0.1 Chapters organized by religious tradition

Religious Tradition	Chapter(s)
Indigenous Religions (Native North American)	On Human-Animal Being: An Opening 1: L'nuwey Views of Animal Personhood 24: Contemplative Practices 25: Companion Animals 28: Meditations on Living with Ghosts
Black Atlantic Religions	15: Sacrifice
Buddhism	8: Learning to Walk Softly 16: Refraining from Killing and Releasing Life 17: Vegetarianism, Prohibited Meats, and Caring for Animals 18: The Difficult Virtue of Vegetarianism 23: Commemorating Animals 24: Contemplative Practices

(Continued)

Table 0.1 (Continued)

Religious Tradition	Chapter(s)
Christianity	5: Race, Animals, and a New Vision
	10: Animal Theology
	11: Blue Theology and Water Torah
	14: Blessings of Pets
	23: Commemorating Animals
	25: Companion Animals
	29: Urban Wildlife: Religious Responses
Confucianism & Daoism	16: Refraining from Killing and Releasing Life
	17: Vegetarianism, Prohibited Meats, and Caring for Animals
	23: Commemorating Animals
Hinduism	21: Cow Care in Hindu Animal Ethics
	25: Companion Animals
Islam	4: Gender and Sexuality
	9: Islamic Case for Insect Ethics
	25: Companion Animals
Judaism	11: Blue Theology and Water Torah
	12: Animal Families in the Biblical Tradition
	13: The Cat Mitzvah: Jewish Literary Animals
	14: Blessings of Pets
	19: Veganism as Spiritual Practice
	23: Commemorating Animals
	25: Companion Animals
	27: The Ethics of Eating Animals
	28: Meditations on Living with Ghosts
Neolithic	26: Domestication and Religion
New Religious Movements	19: Veganism as Spiritual Practice
	20: Spiritual Practice of Providing Sanctuary
	22: The Council of All Beings

References

Aftandilian, Dave, Marion W. Copeland, and David Scofield Wilson, eds. 2007. *What Are the Animals to Us? Approaches from Science, Religion, Folklore, Literature, and Art.* Knoxville: University of Tennessee Press.

Baynes-Rock, Marcus. 2013. "Life and Death in the Multispecies Commons." *Social Science Information* 52 (2): 210–27.

_____. 2015. *Among the Bone Eaters: Encounters with Hyenas in Harar.* University Park: Pennsylvania State University Press.

Bray, Francesca. 1997. *Technology and Gender: Fabrics of Power in Late Imperial China.* Berkeley: University of California Press.

Casey, Logan S., Sari L. Reisner, Mary G. Findling, Robert J. Blendon, John M. Benson, Justin M. Sayde, and Carolyn Miller. 2019. "Discrimination in the United States: Experiences of Lesbian, Gay, Bisexual, Transgender, and Queer Americans." *Health Services Research* 54: 1454–66.

Chauvet, Jean-Marie, Eliette Brunel Deschamps, and Christian Hilaire. 1996. *Dawn of Art: The Chauvet Cave, the Oldest Known Paintings in the World.* New York: Harry N. Abrams.

Chen, Huaiyu. 2023. "The Animal Turn in Asian Studies and the Asian Turn in Animal Studies." In *Animals and Plants in Chinese Religions and Science*, 145–67. London and New York: Anthem Press.

Clottes, Jean. 2016. *What Is Paleolithic Art? Cave Paintings and the Dawn of Human Creativity*. Translated by Oliver Y. Martin and Robert D. Martin. Chicago, Ill. and London: University of Chicago Press.

Clough, David. 2012. *On Animals: Volume I, Systematic Theology*. London: T&T Clark.

Como, Michael. 2005. "Silkworms and Consorts in Nara Japan." *Asian Folklore Studies* 64: 111–31.

DeMello, Margo. 2021. *Animals and Society: An Introduction to Human-Animal Studies*. 2nd ed. New York: Columbia University Press.

Derrida, Jacques. 2008. *The Animal That Therefore I Am*. Edited by Marie-Louise Mallet. Translated by David Wills. New York: Fordham University Press.

Goodall, Jane, Marilyn Kroplick, Debra Merskin, Carrie P. Freeman, Marc Bekoff, Stephen Wells, Steven M. Wise, et al. 2021. "Joint Open Letter to the Associated Press Calling for a Change in Pronouns: Animals Are a Who, Not a What." www.idausa.org/OpenLetterAP.

Gowdy, Barbara. 2000. *The White Bone: A Novel*. New York: Picador.

Gross, Aaron S. 2015. *The Question of the Animal and Religion: Theoretical Stakes, Practical Implications*. New York: Columbia University Press.

———. 2017. "Religion and Animals." In *Oxford Handbook Topics in Religion*. https://academic.oup.com/edited-volume/41330/chapter/352334897.

———, and Anne Vallely, eds. 2012. *Animals and the Human Imagination: A Companion to Animal Studies*. New York: Columbia University Press.

Gruen, Lori, ed. 2018. *Critical Terms for Animal Studies*. Chicago, Ill. and London: University of Chicago Press.

Harvey, Graham. 2006. "Signs of Life and Personhood." In *Animism: Respecting the Living World*, 99–105. New York: Columbia University Press.

Hurn, Samantha. 2012. *Humans and Other Animals: Cross-Cultural Perspectives on Human-Animal Interactions*. London: Pluto Press.

Jadotte, Yuri, Susan Salmond, and Virginia Allread. 2022. "A Population Health Perspective on Racism and Racial Microaggressions." *Orthopaedic Nursing* 41 (2): 148–57.

Kattari, Shana K. 2020. "Ableist Microaggressions and the Mental Health of Disabled Adults." *Community Mental Health Journal* 56: 1170–79.

Kemmerer, Lisa A. 2006. "Verbal Activism: 'Anymal.'" *Society & Animals* 14 (1): 9–14.

Kheel, Marti. 2008. *Nature Ethics: An Ecofeminist Perspective*. Lanham, Md.: Rowman & Littlefield.

Kirksey, S. Eben, and Stefan Helmreich. 2010. "The Emergence of Multispecies Ethnography." *Cultural Anthropology* 25 (4): 545–76.

Kuhn, Dieter. 1984. "Tracing a Chinese Legend: In Search of the Identity of the 'First Sericulturalist'." *T'oung Pao, Second Series* 70 (4/5): 213–45.

Le Guin, Ursula K. 1987. "She Unnames Them." In *Buffalo Gals and Other Animal Presences*, 194–96. Santa Barbara, Calif.: Capra Press.

Lewis-Williams, J. David. 2004. *The Mind in the Cave: Consciousness and the Origins of Art*. London: Thames & Hudson.

Little Badger, Darcie, and Tara Ogaick. 2017. "Wives." In *Deer Woman: An Anthology*, edited by Elizabeth LaPensée and Weshoyot Alvitre, 39–49. Albuquerque, N.M.: Native Realities Publishing.

Locke, Piers. 2017. "Elephants as Persons, Affective Apprenticeship, and Fieldwork with Nonhuman Informants in Nepal." *Hau: Journal of Ethnographic Theory* 7 (1): 353–76.

Masuzawa, Tomoko. 2005. *The Invention of World Religions*. Chicago, Ill.: University of Chicago Press.

McCance, Dawne. 2013. *Critical Animal Studies: An Introduction*. Albany: State University of New York Press.

Norman, Corrie E. 2012. "Food and Religion." In *The Oxford Handbook of Food History*, edited by Jeffrey M. Pilcher, 409–27. Oxford and New York: Oxford University Press. https://doi.org/10.1093/oxfordhb/9780199729937.001.0001.

Philo, Chris, and Chris Wilbert. 2000. *Animal Spaces, Beastly Places: New Geographies of Human—Animal Relations*. London and New York: Routledge.

Ritvo, Harriet. 2007. "On the Animal Turn." *Daedalus* 136 (4): 118–22.

Safina, Carl. 2020. *Becoming Wild: How Animal Cultures Raise Families, Create Beauty, and Achieve Peace*. New York: Henry Holt.

Sherman, Phillip. 2020. "The Hebrew Bible and the 'Animal Turn.'" *Currents in Biblical Research* 19 (1): 36–63.

Simoons, Frederick J., and Elizabeth S. Simoons. 1968. *A Ceremonial Ox of India: The Mithan in Nature, Culture and History*. Madison: University of Wisconsin Press.

Tuan, Yi-Fu. 1984. *Dominance and Affection: The Making of Pets*. New Haven, Conn.: Yale University Press.

Urbanik, Julie. 2012. *Placing Animals: An Introduction to the Geography of Human—Animal Relations*. Lanham, Md.: Rowman & Littlefield.

Waldau, Paul. 2013. *Animal Studies: An Introduction*. Oxford and New York: Oxford University Press.

_____, and Kmberley Patton, eds. 2006. *A Communion of Subjects: Animals in Religion, Science, and Ethics*. New York: Columbia University Press.

Weil, Kari. 2010. "A Report on the Animal Turn." *Differences: A Journal of Feminist Cultural Studies* 21 (2): 1–23.

Wolch, Jennifer, and Jody Emel, eds. 1998. *Animal Geographies: Place, Politics, and Identity in the Nature—Culture Borderlands*. London and New York: Verso.

Other Recommended Resources

Aftandilian, Dave. 2021. "Teaching Animals and Religion." *Worldviews* 25: 48–71.

Animals & Society Institute, Human-Animal Studies (HAS) Links. www.animalsandsociety.org/resources/resources-for-faculty/has-links/

Smith, Jonathan Z. 1998. "Religion, Religions, Religious." In *Critical Terms for Religious Studies*, edited by Mark C. Taylor, 269–84. Chicago, Ill. and London: University of Chicago Press.

Part I
Religion and Identity

1 L'nuwey Views of Animal Personhood and Their Implications

Margaret Robinson

The L'nuk (also known as the Mi'kmaq)[1] are an Indigenous people whose unceded territory of Mi'kma'ki lies on the northeastern coast of North America. Archaeological evidence suggests that L'nuk have lived in Mi'kma'ki for over 12,000 years, which places our ancestors in the territory around the time of the last glacial retreat and the decline and extinction of megafauna such as the giant beaver (Lewis 2016, 180; Paul 2007).

L'nuk have traditionally relied on other animals for food, clothing, and shelter. Before the colonial occupation of our territories, up to 90% of the L'nuwey diet was comprised of animals who lived in or near the water systems of Mi'kma'ki. Lnu'k traveled freely across our territory, spending warm seasons fishing in coastal rivers where food was plentiful and moving inland during cold seasons to hunt animals such as moose or caribou. Seasonality is still a feature of subsistence hunting among L'nuk, despite the centralization policy of the 1940s in which the settler government attempted to forcibly consolidate L'nuk onto isolated reserves. In L'sitkuk (also called Bear River First Nation), for example, Lacia Kinnear (2007) reports that people fish in the summer, hunt in the fall, trap in the winter, and use the by-products of subsistence hunting (e.g., animal claws, teeth, and feathers) to produce craftwork throughout the year.

Seasonal living patterns mean that L'nuwey culture developed in harmony with the life cycles of animals in the territory and the surrounding ecosystem. Close association with other animals is also embedded in the language of the L'nuk, which embodies and expresses our cultural worldview. Half of the names for months of the year, for instance, refer to animals (e.g., July is Peskewiku's, Animal Fur Thickens Time, and October is Wikewiku's, Animal Fattening Time; Johnson 1991, 27).

There is no single Indigenous view of other animals. Although Canada categorizes L'nuk as a First Nations people,[2] Indigenous nations each have distinct cultures, languages, histories, and spiritualities, so the views of L'nuk cannot be assumed to apply to other nations. The L'nuwey value of non-interference discourages pressuring others to conform, but encourages modeling of good behavior. Traditions of consensus-building urge discussion until agreement is reached. But the same value may be expressed in different ways. Therefore, the details in this chapter about the relation of L'nuk to other animals highlight themes in belief and practice, but do not apply to all L'nuk everywhere.

L'nuwey Perspectives on Other Animals

L'nuk generally view other animals as like humans in essential ways. A study conducted in L'sitkuk found that community members viewed animals to be equally important as human beings, and some animals held special meaning for families or individuals due to

DOI: 10.4324/9781003324157-4

longstanding engagement with them (Kinnear 2007, 95). This special association can be seen in the use of animal symbols to represent individuals, families, or matrilineal clans. Such animal imagery was traditionally painted on canoes or other items of importance and also appears as symbols of individual L'nu who signed treaties with Europeans (Government of Canada 2012).

L'nuk spirituality posits that all beings were created by Kji-Niskam (Great Spirit; Union of Nova Scotia Indians, Native Council of Nova Scotia, and Confederacy of Mainland Mi'kmaw n.d.) and therefore possess their own spirits and have their own relationships to the Creator. Animal behaviors tend to be attributed to intelligence rather than instinct, since many animals exhibit social traditions and an understanding of their environment by preparing for winter, expressing emotional bonds with one another, or using objects as tools. One member of L'sitkuk describes this view of animals as resulting from close observation over time:

> So, in doing so [spending time with animals], you'll learn so much about that animal. You'll learn about their habits, you'll learn about where they sleep, when they rest, you'll learn about their relationship with . . . family, with their other counterpart [may refer to the animal's mate], you'll . . . learn about their spirituality: not much different than yours and mine.
>
> (Kinnear 2007, 65)

Kinnear describes the views of participants in her study as like those found in deep ecology, ecofeminism, or social ecology, albeit with different origins and legal standing (2007, 59).

L'nuk recognize animals as having spirit, but also see spirit in beings that others may view as inanimate, including rocks, water, plants, weather, and fire. Animals (including human beings) are all part of a large inter-reliant web of created life. According to L'nu scholar Patricia Doyle-Bedwell and colleague Fay Cohen, the similarities between humans and other spirited beings mean that "all creation is sacred, all creation is equal" (2001, 183).

Animals play a significant role in the cultural life and traditional government of the L'nuk, which is strongly rooted in subsistence hunting and fishing. Each district was presided over by a Saqamaw, who oversaw hunting and fishing and ensured fair distribution of food in their district (Pictou 2021, 3). District Saqamaq would gather in spring or autumn to discuss issues of common interest, and for issues of national significance, a Grand Council (Santé Mawiómi) would be called, overseen by a Grand Chief. Contemporary L'nuwey governance closely resembles this traditional structure, although elected officials now represent specific communities rather than districts, and women serve as Saqama'sgw (female chiefs).

Cultural worldviews and practices are passed from one generation to the next through the teachings of elders and knowledge keepers, through stories, and by modeling good behavior. Beliefs about animals are often shared when teaching a skill, such as how to hunt or fish. As one man in the community of L'sitkuk describes,

> My father always took us trout fishing and he always taught me just take what you need for today. And sometimes I'd say, "Dad why don't we get a few more?" And he'd always say, "No, we have to wait for the next time because we have what we need for today." So, he always taught me about conserving.
>
> (Kinnear 2007, 73)

The refusal to kill more animals than one needs to live expresses an L'nuwey value called *netukulimk*. This term refers broadly to subsistence harvesting, cultivating, hunting, and fishing. The Native Council of Nova Scotia defines *netukulimk* as a spiritual practice of using "the natural bounty provided by the Creator for the self-support and well-being of the individual and the nation" (1993, 7). Anthony Davis and colleagues suggest that *netukulimk* can be translated as "avoiding not having enough" (2010, slide 6). An emphasis on avoiding scarcity distinguishes subsistence practices from commercial hunting and fishing to accumulate profit. It also distinguishes subsistence from hunting or fishing for sport, which is viewed as immoral (Kinnear 2007, 77). Some view the concept of *netukulimk* to entail a duty to protect the animals on whom L'nuk rely for food (Prosper et al. 2011).

Many animals hold significance to the L'nuk, and matrilineal clans have been associated with animals living in the territory such as the beaver, crow, deer, eagle, fox, or lobster, and with insects such as the bee, mosquito, ladybug, or butterfly (Government of Canada 2012). The eagle is viewed as spiritually significant, often described as carrying prayers to the Creator. Kinnear notes that the sacredness of the eagle is expressed through protocols governing the use of their feathers:

> According to one interview participant, an eagle feather should never be sold for crafts or any purpose. Another community member said an eagle feather must never touch the ground and it must be securely placed in an area where it will not fall. One young female interview participant emphasized that an eagle feather, received as a gift, must never be on display within one's home.
>
> (Kinnear 2007, 97)

Eagle feathers are sometimes used in talking circles, a ceremonial communication in which people sit in a circle and express their views sequentially, passing a sacred item that identifies the authorized speaker. Eagle feathers are also awarded to individuals in recognition of significant accomplishments. While many L'nuk hold the eagle in high esteem, some speculate that this practice was adopted from Indigenous nations further west.

L'nuk are knowledgeable about animal species across their territory, including species identified as at risk or endangered. A study led by Anne Benoît of the Canadian Wildlife Service and L'nuk colleagues (2010) found that elders and knowledge keepers in communities across Mi'kma'ki could identify nearly half of 71 endangered animals and plants, including species not typically found in their district. The authors suggest that ecological knowledge is supported and spread by the movement of L'nuk across districts. Community members accurately identified all species of mammal but did less well on some birds, molluscs, and reptiles (Benoît et al. 2010, 6), which shows that some types of animals are more familiar than others. The ability to recognize species at risk is impressive given longstanding efforts to assimilate L'nuk into settler culture. Forcible incarceration in residential schools, for example, separated L'nuk children from their families and prevented them from speaking their language or practicing their traditions (Knockwood 2015).

Animals in L'nuk Stories

Traditional L'nuk stories feature animals prominently, often as protagonists. When stories are shared verbally, details will vary and may be tailored to the audience, their stage of life, and their learning needs. Stories that have been written down are helpful for preserving L'nuwey culture,[3] yet the creation of a fixed text risks losing the flexibility that makes oral storytelling a valuable teaching tool. In addition, some stories recorded by settlers have undergone an editorial process that makes them less accurate in how they reflect L'nuwey ways of thinking and speaking.

A story shared by Clifford Paul, coordinator of the Moose Management Initiative with the Unama'ki Institute of Natural Resources, describes the shift from megafauna to the animals we know today. The tale features Kluskap, a cultural hero, and begins in a time when humans feared other animals due to their enormous size:

> The bear was too big, gigantic in fact, as was the wolf, the beaver, the wild cat. Even the squirrel was too big! The people were in fear of doing what they had to do in the forest—the necessary activities to take care of themselves and their families.
>
> Kluskap recognized the problem and since he loved the Mi'kmaq people, he endeavoured to find a solution. The answer came quick. He told the people that he would stroke the animals, lovingly pet them until they got to the size his people are comfortable and safe with. So he held the bear and petted it until it reached its present size. He did the same with the wild cat, wolf, beaver, and yes, even the squirrel, until all the animals were brought to their present size.
>
> (Paul 2007, 1)

Paul speculates that the story communicates metaphorical truth about evolution (2007, 1). Also notable is that the solution to human fear is not violence toward animals, but loving care. Kluskap's gentle petting nurtures animals into a smaller form and enables humans to pursue *netukulimk*.

L'nu legal scholar Tuma Young shares a tale that expresses the L'nuwey belief in animal reincarnation. In this story, two young men on a journey come across a house occupied by a man and his grandmother. The youth are welcomed, fed, and invited to stay the night. "I have my grandmother living with me," the man tells them. "She has been with me since the world was made" (Young 2016, 88). In this regard, the man is reminiscent of Kluskap, who is sometimes described as living with his grandmother. Once the sun has gone down, the man keeps time on a drum of birchbark and begins to sing:

> I am Waisisk Ketu'muaji Ji'nm, I am Man Singing For Animals. I am singing for the animals, for all the animals, the waisisk, to come alive, to come back to life, from all those parts of them, all those wings, heads, feet, all those bones, meat, marrow, all those parts of them that have not been eaten by the People, all those parts of them that have not been eaten by other animals, all those parts of them that have been thrown away.
>
> (Young 2016, 88)

The man sings through the night and shares a teaching about the importance of not wasting any parts of animals killed for food (Young 2016, 88). In the morning the man leads the youth to the shoreline and plays a whistle made from shell. In response to the music fish arrive, visible through the clear water. "These are my fish," says the man. "They have come from all those parts of fish which the People throw away on the shore. I sing for them and they come back" (Young 2016, 89). Every night, the man repeats his song and live animals emerge from the animal bones over which he sings, with moose, caribou, mink, beaver, and bear mentioned specifically.

Young describes the story of "Man Singing to Animals" as "a classic L'nu teaching story," aimed at instilling L'nuwey protocols to treat animals respectfully and to honor them when they sacrifice themselves to feed L'nuk. Failure to do so will result in the animal remembering the mistreatment and being unwilling to self-sacrifice in the future. Young suggests that the story of "Man Singing to Animals" illustrates an L'nuwey principle that sees the whole animal as encapsulated in each of its parts, "meaning . . . that if a piece of bone or material is still present, the animal can be restored" (Young 2016, 89). Elder and poet Rita Joeòq shares a teaching that animal bones should be returned to their habitat (e.g., fish bones placed back into the water) so that the spirits may awaken in their home when they reincarnate (Joe and Choyce 1997, 34). Such stories and practices express and reinforce a belief in reincarnation, detailing how diligent ceremonies of love and respect support animal return and preserve the species on which L'nuk rely for food.

Implications for the Lives of Animals

Mi'kmaw kinship systems include multiple generations of human beings related by blood or marriage, but concepts of kinship also include animals. In prayer, ceremony, hunting, and other contexts, we use the phrase *M'sit No'kmaq* (all my relations) to recognize animals as our relatives (Pictou 2021, 2). Robin Cavanaugh and Alfred Metallic note that in Listuguj First Nation "people refer to the salmon as their brother" (2002, 25), a kinship expressed primarily through subsistence fishing and its associated protocols:

> The salmon determines which family will have the honour and prestige of sharing the salmon with others in the community. The families pay respect to the salmon by celebrating through a feast and recognizing the contribution of the salmon to the family's physical and spiritual sustenance.
>
> (Cavanagh and Metallic 2002, 25)

In this biospiritual economy, animals sacrifice themselves to feed the people, who express their gratitude through ceremonies, protocols, and activities that honor and respect the animals.

One of the ways L'nuk demonstrate gratitude and respect for animals is through ceremonial offerings. Offerings may include sacred plants, such as sweetgrass, sage, cedar, or tobacco. Participants in Kinnear's study report offering traditional medicines, but also gold or other valued items. Some offer prayers to the spirit of the animal who had been hunted, others pray to the Creator, and others pray to both animals and the Creator (Kinnear 2007, 80). Similar practices are reported in relation to harvesting plants, which are also seen as spirited beings.

Some L'nuk develop special relations with a specific animal or species, viewing them as guides or teachers. Spiritual relations with animals feature in traditional stories. A story called "The Invisible Boy" features a hunter able to transform into a moose. This connection leaves him vulnerable to injury; when a moose femur in his home is thoughtlessly smashed, the hunter's own leg breaks (Robinson 2014). In some cases, specific families become associated with an animal, which some describe as matrilineal clan groupings. A traditional story about a boy raised by bears identifies the boy as an ancestor of the Sylliboy family, noting "his relatives belong to Bear" (Parsons 1925, 97).

Activism for Animal Protection

In recent years many L'nuk have begun to describe themselves as "rights holders." L'nuk possess "Aboriginal rights," which include rights to territory, to subsistence, to practice culture, to speak their language, and to self-govern (Hanson 2009). Such rights reflect the nationhood, culture, and territorial governance of Indigenous peoples prior to colonial occupation. While Aboriginal rights are enshrined in Section 35 of the Canadian Constitution and in Section 25 of the Canadian Charter of Rights and Freedoms, those documents only acknowledge these rights, they do not confer them (Hanson 2009). In Mi'kma'ki, L'nuk also possess rights recorded in a series of Peace and Friendship Treaties with the British Crown, signed between 1725 and 1779. These treaties do not surrender territory or water systems (which are viewed as essential sources of livelihood) but affirm the right of L'nuk to hunt and fish.

In 1999 a landmark court case upheld these treaty rights (*R. v. Marshall* 1999, 3 S.C.R. 456). Donald Marshall, Jr. of Membertou First Nation, known in his community as "Junior,"[4] was charged under Canada's Fisheries Act for catching, possessing, and selling eels out of season and for fishing without a license issued by the government of Nova Scotia. Marshall's defense argued that the Peace and Friendship Treaties recognize Marshall's right to hunt and fish and to sell caught produce to obtain a moderate livelihood. The Supreme Court of Canada decided the Peace and Friendship Treaties of 1760–1761 did confirm a right for the L'nuk to hunt, fish, and gather for food and ceremony, and to trade such goods for necessaries such as food, clothing, and housing. This was viewed as a victory for L'nuk.

Responding to anger from white settlers, a subsequent ruling (*R v. Marshall* 1999, 3 S.C.R. 533) elaborated that treaty rights may be regulated by settler governments to preserve public interests, such as conservation. Despite the second ruling, the Department of Fisheries and Oceans Canada did not propose a system for acknowledging a moderate livelihood fishery for L'nuk. As a result, a number of First Nations in Mi'kma'ki developed their own treaty fisheries, although conflict over whether this is within the boundaries of the Supreme Court ruling is ongoing. L'nuk fishers exercising their treaty rights were often met with sabotage and violence from settler fishers. In 2020, the largest holder of shellfish licenses in Canada, Clearwater Seafoods, announced the company had been purchased by a coalition of Mi'kmaw First Nations partnering with Premium Brands of British Columbia.

In 2005 the Supreme Court of Canada ruled that L'nuk must demonstrate regular and physical occupation of their territories before they can claim a right to that area's resources (Lewis 2016, 180). Given L'nuwey principles of doing minimal damage to the environment, seasonal movement across our territory, and the historic use of portable housing, establishing regular use to settler satisfaction remains a challenge. L'nuk archeologists are working to meet this need by excavating ancient piles of discarded shells whose high calcium content preserves dateable artifacts.

The 2005 Supreme Court ruling may have shaped the actions of L'nuk protecting the Sipekne'katik River from plans by Alton Gas to develop an underground high-pressure hydrocarbon storage facility. L'nuk involved in the protest built a treaty post near the construction site and traded earrings, set eel traps, and shared teachings related to eel fishing. As one activist explains, "we did it symbolically but purposefully . . . [to] exercise our right of trade," and "show traditional land use" (Pictou 2021, 22).

While authority over hunting and fishing was traditionally held by Saqamaq (District Chiefs) and the Kji' Saqamaw (Grand Chief), L'nu knowledge keeper Muin'iskwoq notes that a council of grandmothers was consulted in "decisions that affected the course of the nations" (Augustine-McIsaac 2016). The governance role of grandmothers is evident today in activism to protect animal habitats and waterways from destruction caused by settler resource extraction industries. L'nu scholar Dr. Sherry Pictou, the first woman to be elected District Chief of the Confederacy of Mainland Mi'kmaq, conducted research with Grandmothers and Water Defenders. One participant critiqued the environmental assessment that was supposed to determine the potential impact of the project on the river and the animals that rely on it:

> They didn't look at the right time of year to count the tommycod. We saw so many flaws in their research, in their environmental assessment, how they got that science. One of their boats got stranded! They didn't know when the tide was going out, when the tide was coming in! They just didn't have any real knowledge of the river.
>
> (Pictou 2021, 20)

Among those supporting the protests against extraction was then Chief Rufus Copage of Sipekne'katik First Nation. One participant in Pictou's study described Chief Copage as opposed to the project for reasons that are at once economic, cultural, and relational: "he fishes there and his whole family fished in that river. They had connections to that river for generations" (Pictou 2021, 17). Some participants in Dr. Pictou's study perceived Kwilmu'kw Maw-Klusuaqn Negotiation office (KMKNO; a research body working for the Assembly of Nova Scotia Mi'kmaq Chiefs) as in favor of the Alton Gas project (Pictou 2021, 14), a claim Kwilmu'kw Maw-Klusuaqn has denied, stating they always had concerns about the impact of the project on the environment and on the rights of the L'nuk (KMKNO 2019).

Cultural Resistance

Under colonial occupation, relations with animals have ruptured, but have also endured and reemerged. L'nuk had traded with European fishers and travelers long before Europeans settled in our territory, but the size and scope of the European fur trade eclipsed previous trading practices. The fur industry that emerged in the seventeenth century and continued through to the mid-nineteenth century commercialized animal bodies on a massive scale, driving some animals, such as the beaver, near extinction. New alliances with French traders began to eclipse the friendship role that other animals held in the lives of L'nuk (Robinson 2014). The fur trade funded and was closely entwined with Christian missionary efforts, and supported the emergence of settler colonies, as Europeans fought for control over our territories and resources. Canada's residential school system and similar settler-run day schools endorsed objectified views of animals and reinforced such views as divinely ordained.

The Shubenacadie Indian Residential School, for example, which operated from 1930 through to 1967, forced students to operate a 130-acre dairy farm (Thomson-Millward 1997). Dairy farming entails repeatedly impregnating cows then taking calves from their mother, which causes visible and enormous emotional distress to cow and calf. As mammals, cows form close bonds with their offspring, and mother cows are reported to bellow and cry for days when their calves are taken, the males to be killed for veal (Gaard 2013). Once a cow recovers, she is impregnated again and has each subsequent calf taken

(Gaard 2013). Such practices contradict L'nuwey values of non-interference in animal life and respect for animal motherhood. Scholars note the dairy industry has been integral to settler colonialism in North America, with land being cleared of Indigenous nations and animals to make way for imported cows and the crops needed to feed them (Deckha 2020; Eisen 2019). The word for cow in Mi'kmaq, *wenjitia'm*, means "French moose" (Mi'kmaq Online n.d.), which may reflect a view of cows as essentially foreign to our territory.

Settler occupation and resource extraction has impacted Mi'kma'ki considerably, polluting waterways and stripping the area of many of its old-growth forests. Many animals are now at risk or endangered as a result; the moose, for example, has been considered extinct in mainland Nova Scotia since the 1930s. As a result of loss of animal habitat, proximity to animals is sometimes problematized. Some members of L'sitkuk First Nation, for example, note that bears (traditionally symbols of maternal protection) may pose a threat to children when they seek food in human settlements (Kinnear 2007). Protocols of respect for other animals assume we live in close daily contact with animals and have access to sacred plants, making some traditions challenging for L'nuk in urban centers to learn or practice. L'nu scholar Travis Wysote notes that changes in our kinship relation with other animals also shape treaty practices:

> What happens when keystone species are hunted to near extinction for their furs, or to compensate for poorly-planned and unsustainable colonial settlements? What peace and friendship is possible then?
>
> (Wysote and Morton 2019, 496)

Political activism in Mi'kma'ki has often taken up the question of human responsibility to other animals and their habitats. A flyer promoting a 900km Water Walk around the Bay of Fundy emphasizes the spiritual over the political, quoting the late Josephine Mandamin, an Anishinaabe grandmother and founding member of the water protection movement in Canada: "We walk to honour all Water, Nibi, Samqwan, and to speak to the water spirits so that there will be healthy rivers, lakes, and oceans for our ancestors and the generations to come." Environmental protection movements are not limited to Indigenous people, and settler allies regularly join in protests and conservation efforts. As the effects of climate change become increasingly evident, L'nuk teachings and practices are being adopted by settler allies, and some have come to see values such as *netukulimk* to be a way forward for all residents of Mi'kma'ki, in a spirit of reconciliation.

L'nuwey concepts of animal personhood have yet to be incorporated into settler legal frameworks in which holding status as a person confers rights. However, international developments seem promising. Writing about the U.S. context, Colin Dayan (2018) argues that legal personhood can be extended to animals because U.S. law assigns personhood rather than framing it as determined by species or requiring a capacity for moral action. Indeed, Dayan notes that some legal statutes assign personhood to corporations and similar bodies. In Aotearoa/New Zealand, Mount Taranaki and the Whanganui River hold status as persons under law, with the intention of protecting them from assault (Roy 2017). Such an approach may be useful in Mi'kma'ki, where Kluskap Mountain (a sacred mountain known to settlers as Kellys Mountain) is threatened by mining interests (LeBlanc-Smith 2017). While a mountain is a different sort of person than a bear or a salmon, developments in Aotearoa/New Zealand can suggest how personhood might extend beyond an assessment of capacities for thought, communication, or suffering.

Mary Midgley proposes that the quality of persons that demands "moral consideration" is their capacity for feeling, "expressed by the forming of deep, subtle, and lasting relationships" (2005, 132–43). For the L'nuk, I suspect the quality that makes both a mountain and a bear capable of sustaining relations with humans is our mutual grounding in spirit, a topic with which settler legal frameworks are poorly prepared to grapple. While legal personhood may offer grounds for protecting sacred sites such as Kluskap's Mountain, I hesitate to assume it must inevitably do so. One need only consider the position of L'nuk rightsholders, who are legally people yet still suffer violent treatment at the hands of the state and its representatives.

Arian Wallach and colleagues argue that human exceptionalism "has legitimated the historic and ongoing exploitation of the more-than-human world" (2020, 1104). L'nuwey views of all being as rooted in spirit rejects human exceptionalism, coming closer to what Dayan describes as empathy for the "vulnerable and the violated" that urges us "to appreciate the creatureliness of all things" (2018, 277). Dayan's approach resonates with me, calling to mind the time my father recruited my brother and I to save a batch of frog eggs from a swiftly drying puddle (Robinson and Corman 2017). Rather than folding other animals into our concept of humanity, which Lori Gruen (2014) argues relies on sameness to justify rights, I agree with Dayan that expanding our concept of animality to embrace human beings may be a more productive strategy (2018, 277; see also Matthew Calarco's Chapter 7 on "Same, Other, Indistinct" in this volume). L'nuwey views of life as rooted in spirit push us further, to see vulnerability in a mountain or river, and to endorse rights for beings beyond the animal kingdom.

Notes

1 Previous writing about our people sometimes used the spelling Micmac. Today people often refer to us as the Mi'kmaq, and use the adjective Mi'kmaw (e.g., a Mi'kmaw scholar and activist). Those who speak Mi'kmaq (also called Lnuísimk) may self-identify as L'nu, meaning "the people." I have seen L'nuk used as the plural form.
2 In Canada "Aboriginal" refers to three groups—First Nations, the Métis, and Inuit—whose rights are federally recognized.
3 Some written stories were collected by settler scholars, and Canadian copyright law views such work as the property of the settler collector rather than the L'nu storyteller or their community.
4 Donald Marshall, Jr. was the son of Donald Marshall, Sr., Kji Saqamaw (Grand Chief) of the Mi'kmaq, who served from 1964 until his death, in 1991.

References

Augustine-McIsaac (Kaqtukwasisip Muin'iskw), Jean. 2016. "Mi'kmaw Daily Life-Organization." *Mi'kmaw Spirit*, March. www.muiniskw.org/pgCulture1b.htm.

Benoît, Anne, Andrea Dykstra, Cheyenne Francis, John James Gould, Michelle Knockwood, Patricia Knockwood, Franklin Levi, Adele Levi, Catherine Paul, and Brian Prosper. 2010. *Mi'kmaq Knowledge of Species at Risk in New Brunswick, Nova Scotia and Prince Edward Island*. Technical Report Series No. 510, Canadian Wildlife Service, Atlantic Region.

Cavanagh, Robin, and Alfred Metallic. 2002. "Mi'gmewey 'Politics': Mi'gmaq Political Traditions." Report prepared for the Mi'gmawei Mawiómi. www.aboutourland.ca/sites/default/files/files/resources/Mi'gmewey%20Politics%20Mi'gmaq%20Political%20Traditionsfinal.pdf.

Davis, Anthony, J. Jane McMillan, and Kerry Prosper. 2010. "Seeking Netukulimk: Mi'kmaq Knowledge, Culture and Empowerment." www.msvu.ca/wp-content/uploads/2020/05/NAISA20edited20version2020102.ppt.

Dayan, Colin. 2018. "Personhood." In *Critical Terms for Animal Studies*, edited by Lori Gruen, 267–79. Chicago, Ill. and London: University of Chicago Press.

Deckha, Maneesha. 2020. "Veganism, Dairy, and Decolonization." *Journal of Human Rights and the Environment* 11 (2): 244–67.

Doyle-Bedwell, Patricia, and Fay Cohen. 2001. "Aboriginal Peoples in Canada: Their Role in Shaping Environmental Trends in the Twenty-First Century." In *Governing the Environment, Persistent Challenges, Uncertain Innovations*, edited by Edward A. Parson, 169–206. Toronto: University of Toronto Press.

Eisen, Jessica. 2019. "Milked: Nature, Necessity, and American Law." *Berkeley Journal of Gender, Law & Justice* 34: 71–115.

Gaard, Greta. 2013. "Toward a Feminist Postcolonial Milk Studies." *American Quarterly* 65 (3): 609–13.

Government of Canada. 2012. "Mi'kmaq History Month, Eastern Woodland Print Communications." https://novascotia.ca/abor/docs/mikmaq-history/HistorymonthPoster20123B.pdf.

Gruen, Lori. 2014. "Should Animals Have Rights?" *The Dodo*, January 20. www.thedodo.com/should-animals-have-rights-396292655.html.

Hanson, Erin. 2009. "Aboriginal Rights." First Nations and Indigenous Studies Program, University of British Columbia. https://indigenousfoundations.arts.ubc.ca/aboriginal_rights/.

Joe, Rita, and Lesley Choyce, eds. 1997. *The Mi'kmaq Anthology*. Lawrencetown Beach: Pottersfield Press.

Johnson, Eleanor. 1991. "Mi'kmaq Tribal Consciousness in the Twentieth Century." In *Paqtatek, Vol. 1: Policy and Consciousness in Mi'kmaq Life*, compiled by Stephanie Heather Inglis, Joy Mannette, and Stacey Sulewski, 21–33. Halifax: Garamond Press.

Kinnear, Lacia. 2007. "Contemporary Mi'kmaq Relationships between Humans and Animals: A Case Study of the Bear River First Nation Reserve in Nova Scotia." Master's thesis, Dalhousie University.

KMKNO (Kwilmu'kw Maw-klusuaqn Negotiation Office). 2019. "Statements Made About KMKNO on Alton Gas Are False." April 11. https://mikmaqrights.com/?p=2875.

Knockwood, Isabella. 2015. *Out of the Depths: The Experiences of Mi'kmaw Children at the Indian Residential School at Shubenacadie, Nova Scotia*. 4th ed. Halifax: Fernwood Publishing.

LeBlanc-Smith, Yvonne. 2017. "Protest Planned as Cape Breton Mountain Becomes Focus of Mining Group." *CBC News*, November 25. www.cbc.ca/news/canada/nova-scotia/kelly-s-mountain-sean-kirby-protest-mining-mi-kmaq-1.4418614.

Lewis, Roger. 2016. "The Journey of a L'nu Archaeologist in a Mi'kmaw Place." In *Being and Becoming Indigenous Archaeologists*, edited by George Nicholas, 178–83. London and New York: Routledge.

Midgley, Mary. 2005. "Is a Dolphin a Person?" In *The Essential Mary Midgley*, edited by David Midgley, 732–43. London and New York: Routledge.

Mi'kmaq Online. n.d. www.mikmaqonline.org/servlet/dictionaryFrameSet.html.

Native Council of Nova Scotia. 1993. *Mi'kmaq Fisheries: Netukulimk, Towards a Better Understanding*. Truro: Native Council of Nova Scotia.

Parsons, Elsie Clews. 1925. "Micmac Folklore." *The Journal of American Folklore* 38 (147): 55–133.

Paul, Clifford. 2007. "Kluscap's Science." *Unama'ki Institute of Natural Resources*, March 16. www.uinr.ca/kluscaps-science/.

Pictou, Sherry. 2021. *Wolastoqiyik and Mi'kmaq Grandmothers-Land/Water Defenders Sharing and Learning Circle: Generating Knowledge for Action*. Research Council of Canada, Social Sciences and Humanities. www.kairoscanada.org/thank-you-mikmaq-grandmothers-for-protecting-land-and-water-through-indigenous-self-determination.

Prosper, Kerry, L. Jane McMillan, Anthony A. Davis, and Morgan Moffitt. 2011. "Returning to Netukulimk: Mi'kmaq Cultural and Spiritual Connections with Resource Stewardship and Self-Governance." *International Indigenous Policy Journal* 2 (4): 1–19.

Robinson, Margaret. 2014. "Animal Personhood in Mi'kmaq Perspective." *Societies* 4 (4): 672–88.
_____, and Lauren Corman. 2017. "All My Relations: Interview with Margaret Robinson." In *Animal Subjects 2.0: A New Ethical Reader in a Posthuman World*, edited by Jodey Castricano and Lauren Corman, 229–48. Waterloo: Wilfrid Laurier.
Roy, Eleanor Ainge. 2017. "New Zealand Gives Mount Taranaki Same Legal Rights as a Person." *The Guardian*, December 22. www.theguardian.com/world/2017/dec/22/new-zealand-gives-mount-taranaki-same-legal-rights-as-a-person.
Thomson-Millward, Marilyn Elaine. 1997. " 'Researching the Devils': A Study of Brokerage at the Indian Residential School, Shubenacadie, Nova Scotia." www.nlc-bnc.ca/obj/s4/f2/dsk3/ftp04/nq24763.pdf.
Union of Nova Scotia Indians, Native Council of Nova Scotia, and Confederacy of Mainland Mi'kmaw. n.d. *Mi'kmaw Resource Guide*. Eastern Woodland Publishing. www.mikmaweydebert.ca/home/wp-content/uploads/2015/06/Pg94DOCMikmawResourceGuide.pdf.
Wallach, Arian D., Chelsea Batavia, Marc Bekoff, Shelley Alexander, Liv Baker, Dror Ben-Ami, Louise Boronyak, et al. 2020. "Recognizing Animal Personhood in Compassionate Conservation." *Conservation Biology* 34 (5): 1097–106. www.ncbi.nlm.nih.gov/pmc/articles/PMC7540678/.
Wysote, Travis, and Erin Morton. 2019. " 'The Depth of the Plough': White Settler Tautologies and Pioneer Lies." *Settler Colonial Studies* 9 (4): 479–504.
Young, Tuma. 2016. "L'nuwita'simk: A Foundational Worldview for a L'nuwey Justice System." *Indigenous Law Journal* 13: 75–102.

Other Recommended Resources

Barsh, Russel Lawrence. 2002. "Netukulimk Past and Present: Mikmaw Ethics and the Atlantic Fishery." *Journal of Canadian Studies* 37 (1): 15–42.
Confederacy of Mainland Mi'kmaq. 2007. *Kekina'muek: Learning About the Mi'kmaq of Nova Scotia*. Eastern Woodland Publishing. https://native-land.ca/wp-content/uploads/2018/06/MikmaqKekinamuek-Manual.pdf.
Daniel, Ian, and Elliott Page, directors. 2019. *There's Something in the Water*, Film, 73 mins. Collective Eye Films. www.collectiveeye.org/products/theres-something-in-the-water.
Jeffery, Elaine. 2007. "After 12,000 Years of Yesterdays: Where Will Debert Be After 12 Years of Tomorrows? The Impact of Mi'kmawey Debert on the Culture, Economy, and Environment of the Mi'kmaq." https://library2.smu.ca/bitstream/handle/01/22097/jeffery_elaine_masters_2007.PDF?sequence=1.
Lelievre, Michelle A., Alyssa Abram, Cynthia Martin, and Mallory Moran. 2021. "All Our Relations: Re-Animating the Mi'kmaw Landscape on Nova Scotia's Chignecto Peninsula." In *The Far Northeast: 3000 BP to Contact*, edited by Alexandre Pelletier-Michaud, 285–314. Ottawa: University of Ottawa Press.
MacDonald, Lindiwe. 2001. "The Process of Mi'kmaq Community-Based Development: A Case Study of the Bear River Mi'kmaq Npisunewawti'j (Medicine Trail) Project." Master's thesis, Department of Environmental Studies, Dalhousie University. www.nlc-bnc.ca/obj/s4/f2/dsk1/tape2/PQDD_0018/MQ57305.pdf?is_thesis=1&oclc_number=1007001170.
McLellan, L. Hudson. 2015. "Contemporary Settler Colonialism: Media Framing of Indigenous Collective Action in Elsipogtog, Mi'kma'ki." Honours thesis, Department of Sociology and Social Anthropology & Department of Environmental Sustainability and Society, Dalhousie University. https://dalspace.library.dal.ca/bitstream/handle/10222/56853/H%20McLellan%20Sociology%20Honours%20Thesis.pdf?sequence=1&isAllowed=y.
Obomsawin, Alanis, director. 1984. *Incident at Restigouche*, Film, 45 mins. www.nfb.ca/film/incident_at_restigouche/.
Pictou, Sherry M. 2015. "Small 't' Treaty Relationships without Borders: Bear River First Nation, Clam Harvesters, the Bay of Fundy Marine Resource Centre and the World Forum of Fisher Peoples." *Anthropologica* 57 (2): 457–67.

_____. 2017. "Decolonizing Mi'kmaw Memory of Treaty: L'sitkuk's Learning with Allies in Struggle for Food and Lifeways." PhD diss., Department of Philosophy, Dalhousie University. https://dalspace.library.dal.ca/bitstream/handle/10222/72811/PICTOU-SHERRY-IDPHD-APRIL_2017.pdf_.pdf?sequence=1&isAllowed=y.

Wysote, Travis, and Daniel Salee. 2016. "'Don't Touch Me. I'm Sovereign': The Blockade in Mi'gmaq Perspective." Unpublished article, Concordia University. https://concordia.academia.edu/TravisWysote.

2 Animal Consciousness and Cognition

Robert W. Mitchell and Mark A. Krause

What Is Consciousness?

We begin this chapter by defining the term "consciousness," which is by no means easy. A simple dictionary definition, unfortunately, will not suffice for our purposes. Consciousness is multifaceted, and its complexity is a barrier to attaining consensus among those who research the cognitive abilities of all animals. For our purposes, we are not referring to just one species, such as humans, in this chapter. For comparative psychologists, any organism with a nervous system is fair game for the study of consciousness, and we wouldn't expect all species to conform to any single theory of what consciousness entails.

Any delving into animal consciousness relies on understanding consciousness in our own case. What do we mean when we say we are conscious? First we assume that any form of consciousness is tied in some way to a material living body. In its simplest form, consciousness means some form of reactivity by living creatures (often called "awareness" to distinguish it as having arisen earlier in evolution or being less complex than other forms of consciousness). More elaborately, consciousness commonly refers to perception and perception-like processes experienced by animals. When we say we are conscious, it normally means we are able to perceive something, whether it be experienced as something outside the self, feelings internal to the body such as emotions or pain, or perception-like phenomena such as visual or auditory mental images. We see, smell, hear, taste, and touch; we are upset, feel pain in particular locations on our body, are happy, sad, or indifferent; and we dream in visual and auditory imagery, talk to ourselves without making any sounds, sign to ourselves without making any movements, and imagine ourselves and others doing things.

Consciousness covers a lot of ground! As Peter Godfrey-Smith writes, "I see 'consciousness' as a mixed-up and overused but useful term for forms of subjective experience that are unified and coherent in various ways" (2016, 97). Having one form of consciousness (e.g., hearing) need not indicate that you have another form (internal speech). Therefore, when discussing the evolution of consciousness, we cannot exclude other than human animals just because they may not possess some specific capacity such as a naturally occurring symbolic language. Nervous systems are wired to sense and perceive the world. Organisms are highly diverse in the types of stimuli they can perceive, and this serves as an important reminder that humans likewise are adapted to sense their surroundings within constraints. We may not see what other organisms see, hear what they hear, or smell what they smell because our or their capacities are limited or different. Studying other species and understanding their behavior requires that we consider how *they* experience the world.

DOI: 10.4324/9781003324157-5

The Inner Worlds of Animals

Perception (a conscious process) is often distinguished from sensation. Sensation concerns whether something is "detected" by the organism's nervous system, whereas perception refers to whether what is detected is experienced as something *by* the organism. The difference between sensation and perception can be difficult to discern. For example, some plants that have tendrils that attach to twigs as they grow account for the circumference of the twig prior to attaching to it and modify their tendrils' aperture. How these plants do this raises interesting questions about whether the modification occurs through perceptual experience or sensory responsiveness (Castiello 2021), though, because they do not have a nervous system with which to perceive, plants' activities seem likely to be explained better by sensory responsiveness.

Questions about consciousness in animals begin by asking if they have the requisite receptors and nerves connected to a nervous system because sensations and perceptions depend on these (Braithwaite 2010). Some animals, such as the jumping spiders in the genus *Portia*, show remarkably sophisticated hunting skills to catch prey—enticing a spider by plucking on its web until it responds, imitating the effect on the web of a just-blown breeze, detouring to arrive at a desired location even when it is out of view, and organizing these skills in novel contexts. These skills are supported by extensive chemoreceptive, visual, and other receptors, with multiple eyes on their body that convey extensive arrays of information (Cross et al. 2020; Harland and Jackson 2004). Given their complex capacity to organize information and respond so flexibly to their environment, it would seem strange to deny consciousness of some sort to *Portia*.

The behavior of *Portia* indicates how some aspects of consciousness seem already organized, or ready to be organized, by experience. This observation is not unique to *Portia*. Animals develop in bodies (including their sensory and motor systems) that allow them to sense and perceive aspects of their environment. According to Jakob von Uexküll ([1934] 2010), the influential German philosophical biologist, by observing animals and performing experiments with them, we can discover how their world appears to them. Whereas von Uexküll acknowledges that some creatures (like sea urchins) are merely reflexive systems, he argues that when there is coordination among diverse forms of information, animals have an *Umwelt*, an "environment" that is their perceptual world (as opposed to simply their surroundings). This *Umwelt* consists of "all the features accessible to the subject" (43). Von Uexküll's idea of *Umwelt* allows us to understand animals' conscious experience through observing them and experimenting with their responsiveness to diverse things in their environment. His famous example of a tick waiting on a branch for a mammal to walk beneath the tick illustrates his ideas: butyric acid from the mammal's sweat induces the tick to let go, the tick's tactile collision with the mammal activates the tick to move about on the mammal, and the warmth of the mammal's skin induces the tick to puncture the skin and thereby get blood. He describes the tick's world as "impoverished" because it is so limited in the number of things that influence it, but it is a world ("environment") nonetheless, and one that is distinguished from all the possible environments that could be available via other sensory and neural apparatuses. William James ([1892] 1961) earlier wrote in ways similar to von Uexküll about animals' attention to particular aspects of their surroundings but not others (258–266) as well as about diversity in human experience when he discussed "habits of attention" (39; cf. von Uexküll [1934] 2010, 133–135).

Von Uexküll's ideas take "the standpoint of the animal" ([1909] 1985, 223), describing "a subject that lives in its own world" ([1934] 2010, 45). He describes animals as operators of their machine-like bodies: an animal is a *"subject* who uses these aids [its bodily machinery], who affects and perceives with them" (42). He suggests that, in some cases, animals' nervous systems allow them to develop representations (ideas about what is external) that integrate their perceptions. He calls this their "counterworld," based on schemas that represent their surroundings in ways that are useful to the animals. In the counterworld, the animal can come to understand objects as such, rather than just responding to stimuli (von Uexküll [1909] 1985, 234–235). A counterworld is dependent on the animal's perceptual systems because these are internalized for the animal to use as tools for acting in its surroundings. Whereas normally some animals can perceive, now they can imagine these perceptions internally, without the objects of these perceptions being present. Animals such as ticks are unlikely to experience a counterworld, given their limited *Umwelt* and nervous system.

Von Uexküll's focus on understanding animals by observing them is merely describing what many of us do already: we see what animals do in the contexts they are in and make judgments about their intentions and experiences (Mitchell and Hamm 1997). We become especially adept at this when we have multiple encounters with the same animals; studies concerned with an animal's development can reveal changes in the intentions and experiences we judge this animal to have, based on their bodily changes, activities, and learning (e.g., Miles 1994). However, observational analyses of animal behavior in context can become problematic when we assume (contrary to von Uexküll's ideas) that animals' intentions and experiences are just like our own. This is criticized as anthropomorphism: putting animals into the shape (*morph*) of humans (*anthropos*). In essence, this means we are imposing our viewpoint on them, instead of taking their viewpoint.

Anthropomorphism vs. Mental State Attribution

Anthropomorphism is the attribution of human characteristics to nonhuman entities. In relation to developing a scientific understanding of the natural world, anthropomorphism raises two concerns.

The first is seeing purposiveness in nature when evidence supports a simpler explanation. Many believe that the human brain is wired to interpret phenomena in terms of purpose and intentionality. The complex patterns we perceive in the external world are interpreted through a social and psychological lens. It is our default state (Caporael and Heyes 1997; see also Guthrie 1993). We see plants striving to orient toward the sun to soak up light and ants organizing themselves in a flowing stream of busy bodies working to keep their colony provisioned and, without training, simply assign purpose.

Scientists are taught to inhibit their natural inclination to ascribe purposiveness to the behavior of their subjects. Scientifically, we view plants' movement toward light mechanistically, not as something plants strive to do. Ants may be tiny machines mindlessly guided by chemical cues. This does not mean that we are always incorrect when we interpret animals as acting intentionally. We just have to make sure that we have evidence to support our interpretations. Those who conduct scientific studies of animals learn methods to recalibrate their default state to a more distanced setting, where the seemingly complex may (or may not) get explained in simpler terms, and where we don't presume that what we observe in nonhuman animals is fundamentally the same as in humans (though, of course, we may discover that it is quite similar).

This relates to the second concern regarding anthropomorphism: interpreting animals' mental states in terms of human ones. Experimental work with animals at times avoids the use of mental state terms in understanding animal behavior. Take, for example, applying the terms "fear" and "pain" to the experience of rodents used in aversive conditioning experiments. One experimental procedure involves delivering an electric shock to the subjects' feet at the same time as a brief burst of white noise is played through a speaker. The animals subsequently freeze when they hear the white noise because it elicits fear of the pain-inducing shock that was previously paired with it. But for behavioral psychologists, "fear" and "pain" are thought to add nothing to a scientific account of what is called aversive conditioning: the acquisition of a behavior (freezing) in response to an aversive event (shock). The argument is made that animal subjects' behavior can be fully *described* in physical terms (ceasing movements) instead of mentalistic ones (e.g., fear, pain). Rodents are a common model species used in studies of aversive conditioning by researchers who want to translate their findings into knowledge that will help us better understand human anxiety disorders, such as post-traumatic stress disorder (PTSD). But using them as a model for humans assumes that rodents experience something like the fear in PTSD: why would we bother using rodents in these experiments if they were completely unlike us?

Scientists who study animal behavior also adopt a Darwinian (evolutionary) view of behavioral and mental continuity among species (Darwin 1896), which assumes that humans and other animals share aspects of their psychology to some degree. Thus, there exists a tension in dominant scientific thought: on one side of this tension is methodological and interpretive rigor, which cautions us not to ascribe human characteristics to nonhumans. On the other side, scientists understand that all living organisms are fundamentally linked through evolutionary processes, so there is reason to think that, for example, rodents and humans both experience some common forms of pain.

As scientists, we can ask questions about the mental states of animals: Can dogs intend to deceive? Do elephants mourn their dead? Can monkeys be jealous? Can reptiles play? Can most cats see red? Scientists answer questions of these types via observation of and experimentation with animals, but early in the history of the scientific study of animal psychology, researchers simply attributed many of these internal states to animals, assuming that, with various corrections, we can apply *our* experiences of *our own* mental states to understand those of animals (Burghardt 1985). That is, these early researchers engaged in a problematic form of anthropomorphism. Problems with such anthropomorphism are not only potential misattributions of states to nonhumans, but also the incorrect assumption that humans are all essentially alike in their perceptions of the world (see what follows).

As an aside, we should acknowledge that early researchers presented diverse perspectives on anthropomorphism and its mirror image, zoomorphism (attributing other than human animal characteristics to humans). Some psychologists, often using an evolutionary gloss, presented particular human groups as somehow less than human and more like animals (using white males from Western European societies as the standard); some presented species, including apes, dogs, and ants, as very similar to humans in intelligence; and others presented some nasty characteristics presumed to be true of "beasts" (e.g., uncontrolled violence) as present in humans as part of our "animal" nature. Although some of their publications make for amusing reading today, others that demonized and denigrated human groups were racist and, even when not, had terrible consequences for those described (for example, enforced sterilization for people considered "feeble-minded," or low in intelligence; see Richards and Stenner 2023, 30–37). The contemporary scientific community rejects racism and other denigrations of human groups.

Scientists are now quite cognizant of the fact that not all humans experience the world in the same way. We know this by observing, interacting with, and experimenting with them, just as we do with animals. There are cultural differences and even sensory differences (e.g., color blindness) between humans, and within and across animal species. Yes, humans can tell us something about their experiences, but these communications are always limited: much of how we describe our internal states derives from what we *take* to be intersubjective (shared) experiences about external things that are describable in language (see Richards and Stenner 2023, 7). Consider that most color-blind people assume they see the world similarly to others only to discover their color blindness because people tell them they see some aspects of the world differently. One man, Adam Reisman, writing on quora.com, had customers in the clothing store where he worked "shriek at me when I tried to match clothing for them." Tests indicated that he was color-blind. He wrote, "Before that, I literally had no idea. I just thought I had bad taste." (Failures of intersubjectivity may be easier to determine than successes!) It seems likely that there is great variability in what appears linguistically as the "same" experience so that what we expect to be the same may not be (Jerolmack 2009). We may both be experiencing pain, but our experience of it may not be the same. You and your significant other may love each other, but you each may have different feelings related to love.

The evolutionist Leonard Trelawny Hobhouse long ago argued that, although we cannot use our own experiences to understand nonhuman animal consciousness, we can use such experiences to come up with terms to *name* actions and mental states that seem to be similar to those of humans to indicate their shared *function*, but not their identity in experience or reality (1901, 89–90, 131). When we say that animals see or hear, for example, we are not assuming that they are having exactly the same experience as a human does or one that is just like that experienced by all humans, but rather than they function similarly.

The term "anthropomorphism" implies that we learned to use mental words only to describe humans, and then only later applied them to animals. But we learn to use mental words to apply to all animals, including humans, at the same time: "children readily approach animals as minded actors, individuals with intentions and desires whose actions are intelligible from their mental states" (Melson 2001, 93). Thus, using psychological terms to describe animals is not anthropomorphism but is instead an ordinary use of mental terms (Mitchell 2012a). It is only later that we may develop ideas about whether or not animals, including at times other humans, experience the world in the same way that we do. At that point, we may begin to recognize that mental state terms are most often based on observable aspects of animal (including human) behavior in context that usefully allow us to understand that behavior (Hobhouse 1901; Hebb 1946). Experimenting with and long-term observations of animals to understand their psychology can, of course, lead us to new ways of thinking about them that deviate from our original interpretation.

The question remains as to why we expect others to have experiences that are in some sense like our own—an expectation so common it may take a moment to realize how dubious it is. The answer seems to be that we have no choice if we are to have a sense of our experiences *as* our own. Peter Frederick Strawson (1963) argued against the idea that we extrapolate from our own case to understand how others are psychologically like us because if we are to do so, we would have to have an idea of *our own experience* designated as such, and that this is impossible unless one already has the idea that someone else has experiences. If I'm the only one whose experiences I'm aware of, then I would not think of these experiences as my own, as there would be no other experiences to compare them to that would allow me to distinguish them as distinctly mine; as a result, I would simply have experiences that are not designated as *mine*. The problem for Strawson was to provide an answer to how one gets the idea that one has experiences designated as "my own." His answer was that in order to have experiences that are designated as one's own, one needs to have a primitive concept of the person, which uses two criteria for evidence of experiences: my experiencing consciousness, and my observations of others' bodily activities. In Strawson's argument, you need both if you are to come to an understanding that you have conscious experiences. Using others' bodily activities as evidence of consciousness means that you can recognize other subjects of experience and thus recognize that you also have experiences that are distinct to you. Essentially, this provides you with a sense of having personal experience, as well as recognizing that others do, too.

Complex Cognition in Nonhuman Species: Implications for Consciousness

Strawson further posits that language allows for this primitive concept of a person, by providing a structure that puts the subject (I, you, they, she) in the same relation to the predicate (at its simplest, a verb) whether the subject is you or someone else (the so-called subject-predicate linguistic structure): I see, you see, they see, she sees. In this view, animals without language may be subjects of experience without being aware of other subjects, as von Uexküll believed for most organisms.

But some animals do seem to have something like language. For example, a variety of animals have been taught to produce and/or comprehend some human language or language-like phenomena: apes (orangutans, gorillas, chimpanzees, and bonobos) have been taught human sign language or the use of a keyboard with images representing words, and have employed these to engage in meaningly communicative exchanges with humans and, in some cases, other apes (Krause and Beran 2020). In some cases, apes sign to themselves, indicating what they are doing or planning to do (see, e.g., Miles 1994; Lyn, Greenfield, and Savage-Rumbaugh 2006). The African gray parrot Alex (Pepperberg 2008) was taught to speak and understand some English sentences about objects and actions, and bottlenose dolphins (Herman 2012) and sea lions (Schusterman and Gisiner 1997) were taught gestural signs (and the dolphins, also acoustic signals) for objects and actions that they were requested to act upon and do, respectively. A few dogs have also been trained to understand an extensive array of nouns and actions (for example, Chaser: see Pilley and Reid 2011), and a few dogs without training learn names for new toys with apparent ease (Fugazza et al. 2021).

But other animals, such as prairie dogs, seem to have their own vocal language that designates various aspects of potential predators, such as size, color, and shape; distinguishes coyotes from similar looking dogs; and can even be used to create novel sounds for novel objects (Slobodchikoff, Perla, and Verdolin 2009). The linguistic or quasi-linguistic demarcation of objects and actions by some of these animals suggests that they may be capable of the subject-predicate linguistic structures (e.g., I move, you eat) that Strawson envisions for developing an understanding of self and other minds, though at present, there is no evidence of potentially subject-representing vocalizations by them (e.g., I, you). Other animals, such as vervet monkeys, use a more limited linguistic structure, employing what amount to nouns: they use three different alarm calls to designate three different types of predators (each of which requires different responses to avoid danger; Seyfarth, Cheney, and Marler 1980).

Another method by which nonlinguistic creatures could become persons, in Strawson's sense, is cross-modally matching their kinesthetic sense of their own body's spatial position and movement with a visual experience of their own or others' similar movements, as happens (respectively) when they recognize themselves in mirrors or recognize being imitated or imitating others, all activities which some members of a few species (such as apes and cetaceans) have exhibited (Mitchell 2012b). This kinesthetic-visual matching allows the matcher to know what the other experiences kinesthetically when the matcher sees the other, and to know how it feels when it matches the other's movements. As with language, this provides the matcher with two criteria which are both used to recognize subjects of experiences: their own experience when engaged in action, and observation of the other's matching actions. Minimally, I see you as sharing a kinesthetic experience that matches my kinesthetic experience.

Once that is known, the matcher may begin to develop some perspective-taking skills that allow greater insight into their world. They might be able to imagine the other and themselves as actors in visual imagery, and use this imagination to further develop their understanding via diverse means (see Malle 2005; Mitchell 2012b). Indeed, as the kinesthetic-visual matching model suggests, chimpanzees' skills at mirror self-recognition and recognizing that they are being imitated tend to be present in the same individuals, and some of these individuals show some skill at a form of perspective taking (Krachun et al. 2019).

Recognition of others' perspective derived from kinesthetic-visual matching and language do not allow us to understand everything about *how* the world feels or looks like to others—what are called their "qualia" (Nagel 1974). But we can make educated guesses about some aspects of their conscious experience, as we can via other means as well (Allen 2016; Radner 1994). For example, scientists now think that some insects create something like mental snapshots of the areas they are leaving, and then replay these backwards to get back to the original nest (e.g., Durier, Graham, and Collett 2003).

Some scientists prefer to avoid using mental state terms in relation to animals (including humans), arguing that they are pre-scientific folk psychology. Clive Wynne proposes that such "mentalism" fails because it "uses ultimately non-material causes to attempt to explain behavior," and because mental states are "intrinsically private and thus by definition subjective, not objective" (2007, 132). Such arguments are easily countered (see Burghardt 2007): one can assume that our nervous system is organized to produce intentions, thoughts, and other mental states that are material processes occurring through and in our bodies (see, e.g., Millikan 1997; Burghardt 2007); and one can assume that, however private and subjective mental states can be (and many, such as intentions and emotions, are not in that they are essentially tied to bodily activities and reactions), they are very likely to influence their possessor's activities. Wynne proposes that "we must ask about the sensory, perceptual and responsive worlds of the lion qua lion" (e.g.) based on convergent information from the animal's behavior, its physiology, and experimental research (2007, 132)—exactly what von Uexküll had proposed to understand the *Umwelt* of an organism. Indeed, in referring to the animal's "perceptual and responsive worlds," Wynne incorporates these mental states into his argument against their existence. As Ruth Millikan wrote,

What is really needed in order to understand nonpropositional animal cognition is not a translation into English, but explicit description of the *kinds* of representational systems such animals in fact use, and their ways of using them. The ultimate goal will be to construct and test models of the cognitive system of each of the various animal species, much as human psychologists . . . construct and test models of human information processing. The ultimate confirmation of such models will lie in the minute physiologies of the various species.

(1997, 197)

The fields of comparative psychology and ethology (including cognitive ethology) were developed to understand animals' worlds by observing their behavior and responses in diverse contexts (Mackenzie 1977). Ethology has been described as the study of behavior in naturalistic contexts and comparative psychology in experimental contexts. But, in fact, early researchers in both fields held both foci; cognitive ethology is one name for a recent merger of the two fields.

More recent developments have shown a variety of elaborate descriptions of cognitive and other mental states in diverse species of animals. For example, there is much interest in the question of whether some nonhuman animals have what is called "episodic memory," which refers to the ability to remember a specific event (what happened), a place (where it happened), and its time (when it happened). Pet owners sometimes respond with an incredulous "yes, obviously!" when they discover that comparative psychologists have spent so much time trying to figure this out.

But think further about what episodic memory entails. The individual needs to store a mental representation of the event. They need to recall the specific place it occurred, but keep in mind that an organism may wander across a vast number of places on a daily basis. They need to recall when that specific event occurred, which could be at any point of their lifetime. Binding these three elements together into a single episodic memory, and doing so for many different and distinguishable experiences, is a rather complex mental feat. Laboratory experiments with a diverse array of distantly related species, such as rats, blue jays, and apes, indicate that they have episodic (or episodic-like) memory capacities (Clayton 2017; Krause and Sanz 2019). We suspect that scientists will discover even more about the conscious experiences of animals as they continue to study them. As Gordon Burghardt wrote, the scientific study of consciousness in animals is "worthwhile, timely, and fascinating" (1997, 276).

References

Allen, Colin. 2016. "Animal Consciousness." *Stanford Encyclopedia of Philosophy*. Accessed December 4, 2016. https://plato.stanford.edu/entries/consciousness-animal/.

Braithwaite, Victoria. 2010. *Do Fish Feel Pain?* Oxford: Oxford University Press.

Burghardt, Gordon M. 1985. "Animal Awareness: Current Perceptions and Historical Perspective." *American Psychologist* 40 (8): 905–19.

_____. 1997. "Amending Tinbergen: A Fifth Aim for Ethology." In *Anthropomorphism, Anecdotes, and Animals*, edited by Robert William Mitchell, Nicholas Simonds Thompson, and Helen Lyn Miles, 254–76. Albany: SUNY Press.

_____. 2007. "Critical Anthropomorphism, Uncritical Anthropocentrism, and Naïve Nominalism." *Comparative Cognition and Behavior Reviews* 2 (1): 136–38.

Caporael, Linda R., and Celia Heyes. 1997. "Why Anthropomorphize? Folk Psychology and Other Stories." In *Anthropomorphism, Anecdotes, and Animals*, edited by Robert William Mitchell, Nicholas Simonds Thompson, and Helen Lyn Miles, 59–73. Albany: SUNY Press.

Castiello, Umberto. 2021. "(Re)claiming Plants in Comparative Psychology." *Journal of Comparative Psychology* 135 (1): 127–41.

Clayton, Nicola S. 2017. "Episodic-Like Memory and Mental Time Travel in Animals." In *Handbook of Comparative Psychology: Perception, Learning, and Cognition*, Vol. 2, edited by Josep Call, 227–43. Washington, D.C.: American Psychological Association Press.

Cross, Fiona R., Georgina E. Carvell, Robert R. Jackson, and Randolph C. Grace. 2020. "Arthropod Intelligence? The Case for *Portia*." *Frontiers in Psychology* 11 (568049): 1–17.

Darwin, Charles. 1896. *Descent of Man and Selection in Relation to Sex*. New York: D. Appleton.

Durier, Virginie, Paul Graham, and Thomas S. Collett. 2003. "Snapshot Memories and Landmark Guidance in Wood Ants." *Current Biology* 13: 1614–18.

Fugazza, Claudia, Shany Dror, Andrea Sommese, Andrea Temesi, and Ádám Miklósi. 2021. "Word Learning Dogs (*Canis familiaris*) Provide an Animal Model for Studying Exceptional Performance." *Scientific Reports* 11 (14070).

Godfrey-Smith, Peter. 2016. *Other Minds: The Octopus, the Sea, and the Deep Origins of Consciousness*. New York: Farrar, Straus and Giroux.

Guthrie, Stewart Elliott. 1993. *Faces in the Clouds: A New Theory of Religion*. New York: Oxford University Press.

Harland, Duane P., and Robert R. Jackson. 2004. "*Portia* Perceptions: The *Umwelt* of an Araneophagic Jumping Spider." In *Complex Worlds from Simpler Nervous Systems*, edited by Frederick R. Prete, 5–40. Cambridge, Mass.: MIT Press.

Hebb, Donald O. 1946. "Emotion in Man and Animal: An Analysis of the Intuitive Processes of Recognition." *Psychological Review* 53: 88–106.

Herman, Louis M. 2012. "Body and Self in Dolphins." *Consciousness and Cognition* 21: 526–45.

Hobhouse, Leonard Trelawny. 1901. *Mind in Evolution*. New York: Macmillan.

James, William. (1892) 1961. *Psychology: The Briefer Course*. Notre Dame, Ind.: University of Notre Dame Press.

Jerolmack, Colin. 2009. "Humans, Animals, and Play: Theorizing Interaction When Intersubjectivity Is Problematic." *Sociological Theory* 27 (4): 371–89.

Krachun, Carla, Robert Lurz, Lindsay M. Mahovetz, and William D. Hopkins. 2019. "Mirror Self-Recognition and Its Relation to Social Cognition in Chimpanzees." *Animal Cognition* 22 (6): 1171–83.

Krause, Mark A., and Crickette M. Sanz. 2019. "The Evolution of Human Learning and Memory: Comparative Perspectives on Testing Adaptive Hypotheses." In *Handbook of Cognitive Archaeology: Psychology in Prehistory*, edited by Tracy B. Henley, Matt J. Rossano, and Edward P. Kardas, 174–95. New York: Routledge.

Krause, Mark A., and Michael J. Beran. 2020. "Words Matter: Reflections on Language Projects with Chimpanzees and Their Implications." *American Journal of Primatology* 82 (10): e23187.

Lyn, Heidi, Patricia Greenfield, and Sue Savage-Rumbaugh. 2006. "The Development of Representational Play in Chimpanzees and Bonobos: Evolutionary Implications, Pretense, and the Role of Interspecies Communication." *Cognitive Development* 21: 199–213.

Mackenzie, Brian D. 1977. *Behaviourism and the Limits of Scientific Method*. Atlantic Highlands, N.J.: Humanities Press.

Malle, Bertram F. 2005. "Three Puzzles of Mindreading." In *Other Minds: How Humans Bridge the Divide Between Self and Other*, edited by Bertam F. Malle and Susan D. Hodges, 26–43. New York: Guilford Press.

Melson, Gail. 2001. *Why the Wild Things Are: Animals in the Lives of Children*. Cambridge, Mass.: Harvard University Press.

Miles, Helen Lyn. 1994. "Me Chantek: The Development of Self-Awareness in a Signing Orangutan." In *Self-Awareness in Animals and Humans: Developmental Perspectives*, edited by Sue Taylor Parker, Robert William Mitchell, and Maria L. Boccia, 254–72. Cambridge: Cambridge University Press.

Millikan, Ruth. 1997. "Varieties of Purposive Behavior." In *Anthropomorphism, Anecdotes, and Animals*, edited by Robert William Mitchell, Nicholas Simonds Thompson, and Helen Lyn Miles, 189–97. Albany: SUNY Press.

Mitchell, Robert William. 2012a. "Inner Experience as Perception(like) with Attitude." In *Experiencing Animals: Encounters Between Human and Animal Minds*, edited by Julie A. Smith and Robert William Mitchell, 154–69. New York: Columbia University Press.

———. 2012b. "Self-Recognition in Animals." In *Handbook of Self and Identity*. 2nd ed., edited by Mark R. Leary and June Price Tangney, 656–79. New York: Guilford.

———, and Mark Hamm. 1997. "The Interpretation of Animal Psychology: Anthropomorphism or Behavior Reading?" *Behaviour* 134: 173–204.

Nagel, Thomas. 1974. "What Is It Like to Be a Bat?" *The Philosophical Review* 83 (4): 435–50.

Pepperberg, Irene. 2008. *Alex and Me*. New York: Harper.

Pilley, John W., and Alliston K. Reid. 2011. "Border Collie Comprehends Object-Names as Verbal Referents." *Behavioral Processes* 86: 184–95.

Radner, Daisie. 1994. "Heterophenomenology: Learning About the Birds and the Bees." *The Journal of Philosophy* 91: 389–402.

Richards, Graham, and Paul Stenner. 2023. *Putting Psychology in Its Place: Critical Historical Perspectives*. New York: Routledge.

Schusterman, Ronald J., and Robert C. Gisiner. 1997. "Pinnipeds, Porpoises, and Parsimony: Animal Language Research Viewed from a Bottom-Up Perspective." In *Anthropomorphism, Anecdotes, and Animals*, edited by Robert William Mitchell, Nicholas Simonds Thompson, and Helen Lyn Miles, 370–82. Albany: SUNY Press.

Seyfarth, Robert M., Dorothy L. Cheney, and Peter Marler. 1980. "Vervet Monkey Alarm Calls: Semantic Communication in a Free-Ranging Primate." *Animal Behaviour* 28: 1070–94.

Slobodchikoff, Constantine N., Blanca S. Perla, and Jennifer L. Verdolin. 2009. *Prairie Dogs: Communication and Community in an Animal Society*. Cambridge, Mass.: Harvard University Press.

Strawson, Peter Frederick. 1963. *Individuals: An Essay in Descriptive Metaphysics*. Garden City, N.Y.: Anchor Books.

von Uexküll, Jakob. (1909) 1985. "Environment [*Umwelt*] and Inner World of Animals." Translated by C.J. Mellor and D. Gove. In *Foundations of Comparative Ethology*, edited by Gordon M. Burghardt, 222–45. New York: Van Nostrand Reinhold.

———. (1934) 2010. *A Foray into the Worlds of Animals and Humans, with a Theory of Meaning*. Translated by Joseph D. O'Neil. Minneapolis: University of Minnesota Press.

Wynne, Clive D.L. 2007. "What Are Animals? Why Anthropomorphism Is Still Not a Scientific Approach to Behavior." *Comparative Cognition and Behavior Reviews* 2: 125–35.

Other Recommended Resources

Books

Andrews, Kristin. 2020. *The Animal Mind: An Introduction to the Philosophy of Animal Cognition*. 2nd ed. New York: Routledge.

Lazareva, Olga F., Toru Shimizu, and Edward A. Wasserman, eds. 2012. *How Animals See the World: Comparative Behavior, Biology, and Evolution of Vision*. Oxford: Oxford University Press.

Mitchell, Robert William, ed. 2002. *Pretending and Imagination in Animals and Children*. Cambridge: Cambridge University Press.

———, Nicholas Simonds Thompson, and Helen Lyn Miles, eds. 1997. *Anthropomorphism, Anecdotes, and Animals*. Albany: SUNY Press.

Smith, Julie A., and Robert William Mitchell, eds. 2012. *Experiencing Animal Minds: An Anthology of Animal-Human Encounters*. New York: Columbia University Press.

Yong, Ed. 2022. *An Immense World: How Animal Senses Reveal the Hidden Realms Around Us*. New York: Random House.

Videos

Gordon Burghardt discussing *Umwelt*. www.youtube.com/watch?v=_vVoLQJ4iiY.

Various experts explain ideas relevant to animal consciousness and cognition in the Animals and Society Video Series. Alexandra Horowitz discusses *Theory of mind*; Robert W. Mitchell, *Anthropomorphism*; Ken Shapiro, *Kinesthetic empathy*; Maneesha Deckha, *Personhood*; Sarah E. McFarland, *Animal agency*; and Jonathan Balcombe, *Sentience*. Go to: www.animalsandsociety.org/resources/resources-for-scholars/defining-human-animal-studies-an-asi-video-project/.

3 Emotion

Donovan O. Schaefer

Introduction

The most stunning feature of the Scottish capital city of Edinburgh is a stretch of road called the Royal Mile. Running on a slope down from the imposing Edinburgh Castle at the top to Holyrood Palace at the foot, the Mile is studded with churches, impressive government buildings, and statues commemorating famous figures from Scottish history. But stroll a few blocks south of the splendid structures and you'll find a much more humble statue: a bronze dog—a shaggy terrier, about life-size—perched on top of a granite fountain, his soulful eyes looking out from beneath furry eyebrows, his nose rubbed to a shine by passersby (see Figure 3.1).

Figure 3.1 The Greyfriars Bobby Fountain in Edinburgh, U.K., sculpted by William Brodie in 1873
Source: Photo by the author

DOI: 10.4324/9781003324157-6

This is Greyfriars Bobby. He was a real dog who lived in the nineteenth century and who, so the local story goes, followed the casket of his deceased master to the nearby Greyfriars Kirkyard, then stood vigilantly near the dead man's grave for fourteen years. In fact, in addition to the statue, the church has a tombstone for Bobby, with the inscription, "Let his loyalty and devotion be a lesson to us all." If you ever visit, you should bring a stick and add it to the pile left by other guests who have paid their respects to Bobby at this spot.

The philosopher Jeremy Bentham once wrote about the question of whether animals should be considered as subjects of our moral concern: "The question is not, Can they reason?, nor Can they talk? but, Can they suffer?" (Bentham 1879, 311 fn. 1). Bentham's insight was that even though questions about animal welfare are often linked to scientific and philosophical investigations into how smart animals are, our real concern should be with the extent to which animals can *feel* pain. No matter how intelligent an animal is, the fact that they feel pain should be our primary moral concern.

This chapter is about emotions. It looks at how some scientists and philosophers have understood animal feelings, and considers what this might mean for animals and religion. But as illuminating as Bentham's summary of the situation is, the story of Greyfriars Bobby shows us that there's much more to be said about animal feeling. Animals aren't just little jars of potential suffering that need to be morally respected because of their capacity to feel pain. They have complicated emotional lives and a rich capacity to feel and connect with the world around them—including with humans and other animals. Not only that, the feelings of animals, when we pay attention to them, are powerful *for us*. Human beings are drawn to animals when we realize that they experience profound emotions. We even recognize some of these feelings as religious, such as Bobby's epitaph characterizing his behavior as devotion.

There has been a lot of research on animal feelings, and we can't cover the whole terrain in a single chapter. For this reason, we'll focus on a few key thinkers—some well-known, others less so—who provide important perspectives on humans, animals, and our shared feelings. We'll start with Charles Darwin, who spent half a lifetime looking at the question of how humans and other animals are related. As we'll see, Darwin placed a strong emphasis on emotion as a common property of humans and other animals—especially other mammals, our closest kin. We'll then turn to Jakob von Uexküll and his influential concept of the lifeworld—the collection of things found in the environment that matter to animals. Finally, we'll see what this all means for religion—and whether animals have even more in common with us on this score than we might think.

The Darwinian Revolution

Charles Darwin remains one of the most important scientists in human history. His research became the foundation for the entire field of biology. Almost every discovery in biology over the past 150 years can be successfully connected to the basic blueprint Darwin charted for how life on earth plays out. But as famous as Darwin is, his views are often misrepresented or simplified. So let's take a closer look at what Darwin wrote, especially on our core topics of animals, emotions, and religion.

Darwin is most closely associated with the theory of evolution. But it's important to understand that many people before Darwin had come up with the idea that organisms were related to each other by lines of development. These pre-Darwinian evolutionary ideas took a number of different forms. Darwin's own grandfather, Erasmus Darwin, wrote a long scientific poem about the way early particles on Earth developed into other organisms over time. A book published anonymously in 1844 told a similar story—fifteen years before Darwin's *On the Origin of Species* (Secord 2000). The French scientist Jean-Baptiste Lamarck believed that organisms could change themselves during their lifetime (by becoming good runners, for instance) and pass those changes on to their offspring—and that over time these changes would lead to new species.

Many of the people interested in evolutionary ideas were very excited about their political implications, too. People we would now think of as anti-racists, feminists, and advocates for workers' rights believed that the idea of evolution—rather than eternal hierarchies—would help knock down oppressive structures. ("Darwinism" as a scientific paradigm is often confused in the twenty-first century with "social Darwinism," a later invention that sought to apply a simplistic version of Darwinian biology to society, paving the way for later horrors like the eugenics movement. Darwin himself was opposed to this and was deeply committed to the abolition of race-based enslavement [see Desmond and Moore 2009].)

"Evolution" (which earlier thinkers called "transformism" and Darwin called "descent with modification") was an idea that had been around for a while in Darwin's time. But it was also not very popular. Even the best scientists of the day didn't think it was convincing. Darwin's important 1859 book *On the Origin of Species* changed that. What was distinct about Darwin's approach was his emphasis that evolution entailed a combination of *variation* and *selection*. Organisms were varying all the time. Even the most similar ears of corn were, to the expert eye of a farmer, just a little bit different. Sometimes these differences helped that organism to survive and reproduce. Over long periods of time, those changes would add up and new species would emerge. This was the mechanism of natural selection. Another crucial difference was that many early evolutionists believed that a spirit was driving evolution forward and that more evolved species were simply superior. Darwin, on the other hand, saw variation as random and was more cautious about ranking species in a simple hierarchy. In fact, in an early journal, Darwin wrote a reminder to himself: "Never say 'higher' or 'lower'" (Gould 1996, 137).

Darwin on the Emotional Continuity of Humans and Animals

Darwin's ideas inspired scientists, activists, and religious people to begin exploring the new evolutionary landscape he had created. But there were also many skeptics. Darwin spent the rest of his life fighting these skeptics. Some of them disagreed with him on scientific grounds. The theory was new and still had gaps in it, as Darwin himself realized. But others had a knee-jerk reaction to the idea that humans were not specially created and the sole beneficiaries of a unique destiny. One of Darwin's former teachers was so angry about *Origin* that he told a friend Darwin had turned into "a teacher of that which savours of rankest materialism, and of an utter rejection of the highest moral evidence, and the highest moral truth" (Sedgwick 1890, 361). Darwin had to meet this resistance with more evidence that humans were related to other animals.

Origin doesn't discuss the relationship between human beings and evolution at all. Darwin knew exactly how upset the claim of human connection with other animals would make some of the people in his society. Unlike some others who believed the political implications of evolution were important to end oppressive systems, Darwin was generally quiet about those issues. His focus was on the science, and he didn't want to offend people while his theory was just getting off the ground. But in 1871, he published

The Descent of Man, a book in which he laid out his arguments for human continuity with other animals in full.

Descent starts with a series of thoughtful observations about animals and humans. Darwin points out, first of all, the obvious fact of the similarities between humans and other mammals—the same number of fingers and toes, the same basic skeletal structure, the same facial layout, and similar arrangements of our internal organs. He points out that humans and animals sometimes get sick from the same diseases. And he reminds his readers that drugs like nicotine and alcohol that work on humans have similar effects on other mammals. We have similar reproductive systems and similar developmental stages *in utero*. Even where organisms are different, there are rudimentary forms that seem to reflect an earlier common ancestor. Humans don't have tails, for instance, but we do have tailbones (called the coccyx). That's all just in the first chapter. Darwin goes on to explore his ideas for how humans and other animals might be related throughout the rest of the book.

Darwin originally wanted to dedicate a few chapters of *Descent* to emotion as a way of illustrating animal and human continuity. But by the time he finished working, he had *so many* ideas about this topic that he decided to write a whole new book. This turned into a "sequel" to *Descent* called *The Expression of the Emotions in Man and Animals*, which was published just a year later. In this book, Darwin reviewed many different kinds of human bodily emotional responses—from facial expressions to the way our hair stands on end when we're scared or excited—and showed that they were similar to responses found in other animals. This, he argued, could be no accident. There must be a biological relationship between humans and other animals, and our emotional similarity (especially with those organisms most like us, other primates and other mammals) was some of the best evidence of this fact (Darwin 1872 [2009]).

Darwin also, in these two books, speculated about the nature of religion. In *Descent*, he observed that all human societies seem to have beliefs in spirits, often attached to specific objects, places, or natural formations. Darwin suggested that this, too, could be seen in animals. He told a story about his dog who, lying on the grass on a hot day, became agitated by a nearby parasol that was waving in the wind. The dog, having "reasoned to himself . . . that movement without any apparent cause indicated the presence of some strange living agent," barked at the mysteriously animated object (Darwin 1882, 95). Darwin proposed that this was a possible point of origin for belief in spirits.

He also came at religion from another direction, exploring how it related to emotions like awe or love. Darwin was very interested in the idea that the gestures and expressions people use in religious activity, such as praying, were ways of displaying emotions. "The feeling of religious devotion," he wrote, "is a highly complex one, consisting of love, complete submission to an exalted and mysterious superior, a strong sense of dependence, fear, reverence, gratitude, hope for the future, and perhaps other elements" (Darwin 1882, 95). The fullest expression of religion, he says, requires a high degree of intellectual development, but he also adds that there are clear parallels between these feelings and those found in other animals. He even quotes another scientist who observed that "a dog looks on his master as on a god" (Darwin 1882, 96). Here the love of dogs for their human companions is related to religion.

What we see in Darwin's work, then, is a very powerful argument for the continuity of humans and other animals on the register of emotion. Because we are biological kin, we have many of the same feelings. This is both evidence of Darwin's overall theory and the foundation of a new way of looking at human-animal relationships. Moreover, this becomes the foundation of a framework for thinking about *religion* that focuses on feeling, and suggests that humans and animals have common religious orientations by virtue of sharing the same *emotional* make-up.

Building on Darwin: The Idea of the "Lifeworld"

Later thinkers developed Darwin's ideas further. The German biologist Jakob von Uexküll, for instance, tried to understand in even more detail how humans and our animal kin experience the environment around us. For von Uexküll, every animal has a "lifeworld" that surrounds it. This lifeworld is defined by the presence of things that really matter to the organism, which shine out like bright lights and draw us toward them. He starts with a very simple organism—a tick—and notes that the lifeworld of a tick includes just a few of these powerful beacons: the smell of animal sweat, motion (which means they've landed on a mammal's body—and makes them scurry around), and warmth (which makes them burrow into a mammal's body). The rest of the world, for the tick, is dim and uninteresting. But these beacons lance out through the darkness and fill the tick's lifeworld with importance (von Uexküll 1957, 12).

More complicated animals, von Uexküll explains, have more elaborate lifeworlds. Humans experience not just a few beacons, but many—all overlapping and blinking on and off at us simultaneously. These include different aspects of our environments—water, food, shelter—as well as other animals—predators, prey, and possible mates or companions. For von Uexküll, humans are the most complicated organisms on the planet—so our lifeworlds are complicated, too. But still, they're organized around a consistent set of things that are important to us: food, safety, companionship, music, sports, stories, colors, places, and interesting objects.

There are three other important features of lifeworlds. First, these lifeworlds are partly evolved *and* partly learned. Von Uexküll talks a lot about how different people—scientists or artists, for instance—create different lifeworlds that allow them to appreciate different things. Humans are hardwired to learn languages, but which language we learn depends on our environment (Cheney and Seyfarth 2007, 7). Similarly, domestic dogs form very powerful bonds with their human companions. But *which* human they become attached to will depend on their surroundings—which is why Greyfriars Bobby stayed near the graveyard rather than going home with any other nearby human.

Second, these don't all have to be needed for survival. A tick may not have this luxury, but more complex organisms like birds and mammals have lifeworlds rich in elements that are beautiful or exciting—not just necessary to stay alive. Finally, von Uexküll understood the relationship between an animal and their lifeworld in terms of feeling. Excitement, pleasure, and joy define the way we encounter beacons in our lifeworlds—as well as their converse, such as fear when we see a predator or grief when we lose a companion. Like Darwin, von Uexküll realized that even though humans and animals have different lifeworlds—what matters to you may be different than what matters to your dog—we're fundamentally the *same kind of creatures*. We all navigate our lifeworlds by feeling our way along.

Von Uexküll was a founder of a science called "ethology." Ethology means "the study of character," and it is a way of understanding animals that is different from the laboratory method. In laboratories, ethologists believe we don't get a chance to study how animals really are. If we were to base all of our understanding of humans on people who were trapped in solitary confinement, we would have a very distorted view of how human beings actually work. This is because the natural environment of human beings is not a prison cell. In fact, the natural environment of human beings includes other human beings! Similarly, ethologists believe that we can't use laboratory studies to understand how animals work. Like prisoners, laboratory animals have been traumatized by the experience of captivity. Instead, we have to observe animals in their natural lifeworlds—which, as with humans, often include other animals of their own species (and of other species).

However, von Uexküll's ethological approach was out of fashion for much of the twentieth century. A different way of looking at things, called "behaviorism," was for a long time the dominant scientific approach. Behaviorists believed that rather than looking at emotions or even thoughts, the only way to study animals (and, for some, humans as well) was to look at observable behavior. This led to an ideology that saw animals as machines that could be broken down into different parts and studied.

Behaviorism also produced many violent experiments to examine how animals behaved. For instance, in the 1970s, a primatologist traveled to Madagascar to do an experiment in which he slashed the pupils of newborn macaques with a scalpel (Berkson 1973). He then returned the blind infants to their mothers and watched how the other monkeys in the community reacted to them. (His finding was that the other macaques in the group would give extra care to the blinded infants and help them to survive.) Science has largely moved past this view, but in many ways, legal and folk understandings of animals are still defined by behaviorism. Many of us see animals as unfeeling stimulus-response machines rather than as beings with rich emotional relationships with the world around them. This is where taking scientists like Darwin and von Uexküll *more* seriously can give us a much clearer picture of how animals interact with their lifeworlds.

Defining Religion

To further explore how Darwin's ideas bear on religion, we need to consider how religion has been defined differently in different times and places. We often think of religion as exclusively focused on beliefs—a set of things we think are true that can be put into words. But William James—a nineteenth-century psychologist who was very influenced by Darwin—called religion "the feelings, acts, and experiences of individual men in their solitude, so far as they apprehend themselves to stand in relation to whatever they may consider the divine" (James 1961, 42). James was mostly interested in humans, but he also opened the door to a broader understanding of what makes religion what it is by focusing on *emotion* rather than just ideas.

Religion has been defined in many ways, and it doesn't make sense to arbitrarily select a single correct interpretation. But it's important to recognize how different definitions of religion elevate different aspects of it and therefore help us see different aspects of reality. This is why scholars of religion generally regard the fact that religion can be productively defined in different ways as inevitable and unproblematic. For example, James's definition brings feeling into the foreground. This is consistent with how many people think about religion in their everyday experience. It's why some places or objects become "sacred" even if they're not about supernatural beings. Or why something might seem "holy" to us even if it's not part of our "religion"—it evokes powerful feelings. James, interestingly, believed that religion could be associated with many different feelings and many different objects.

Religion is present in moments of great joy (like weddings or baptisms) and moments of profound grief (like funerals). Although we sometimes think of religion as separate from society or politics, the presence of things like battle standards or war memorials in churches gives us a clearer picture of how closely related religion is to seemingly secular concerns. Not only that, but religion is also closely associated with food, art, music, architecture, natural beauty, and community. Even the Christian Eucharist, which includes the ritual consumption of communion wafers during a church service, likely started out as a meal that early Christians would share together. In other words, religion is something that seems to piggyback on the lifeworlds we already have as human beings. The emotions and objects that matter to us are brought together in our practices of worship. Belief may play a part here, but it's really only one corner of a much bigger picture.

Religion for Humans and Other Animals?

Many ethologists since von Uexküll have noticed animals in their natural environments carrying out practices that, if we observed them in humans, would likely be considered religious (see Chapter 30 on "The Connection We Share: Animal Spirituality and the Science of Sacred Encounters" by Barbara Smuts et al. in this volume). For instance, primatologists have noticed that chimpanzees respond in unusual ways to features of the natural landscape such as storms, waterfalls, high wind, and even wildfires. The chimpanzee expert Jane Goodall has observed this behavior among chimpanzees and called it the "dance of awe"; she believes that this dance is a way of expressing emotions that could be seen as religious (Goodall 2006). The baboon expert Barbara Smuts described an unusual encounter she had in which a baboon group she was traveling with spontaneously sat and meditated for half an hour beside a rushing river at sunset (Smuts 2001).

Another place where animals seem to express religious behavior is in the way they respond to the dead. Elephants are known to travel to the locations of their dead relatives and to caress the bones there with their trunks. Elephants have also been seen placing branches and fronds over the bodies of the recently deceased (Moss [1988] 2000). The scientist who blinded infant monkeys with a scalpel in Madagascar observed that one of the babies died, but was then carried by its mother for several days afterwards (Berkson 1973). Greyfriars Bobby also seemed to be mourning the death of his human companion by remaining at his graveside until the end of his own life. As we know, a lifeworld can include other people and animals. We respond powerfully to our own dead, just as some animals seem to do with theirs. This can even extend across species (Pribac 2021).

The truth is that we just don't know very much about animals in their natural habitats. Many of our observations of animals are made in artificial circumstances, such as with domesticated livestock or pets. The ethological project of learning about what animals do when we're not looking is still in an early phase. New technology has made this easier and enabled new discoveries. For instance, up until Jane Goodall first began studying chimpanzees in the 1960s, it was assumed that humans were the only animals able to use tools. But Goodall immediately observed chimpanzees crafting branches and blades of grass to catch termites. In the 2010s it was learned that chimpanzees will sometimes return to the same specific trees, over and over again, and throw rocks at them (Kühl et al. 2016). This discovery was only made because of the new use of trail cameras.

The evolutionary biologist E. O. Wilson has said something similar, that different species each have their own "spirits" that become more elaborate as they develop. "Civilized termites," he writes, "would support cannibalism of the sick and injured, eschew personal reproduction, and make a sacrament of the exchange and consumption of feces. The termite spirit, in short, would have been immensely different from the human spirit—horrifying to us, in fact" (Wilson 1993, 38). In our closer relatives, however, we see spirits that resonate with us in powerful ways. Chimpanzees dancing at the base of a waterfall, or elephants tenderly treating their dead, inspire us with the power of their expression. We recognize an emotional symmetry. It feels like religious reverence.

And that's what all these things have in common. In drawing on lifeworlds, they build on the emotional connection between animals and their environments. Jane Goodall in her work mentions emotion in describing both her own religious experiences—like finding herself overcome with awe while visiting the Notre Dame Cathedral in Paris—and those of the chimpanzees she studies (Goodall with Berman 1999). In both cases, the lifeworld is saturated with feeling. Powerful beacons blaze up, becoming the raw material of experience. And this, for many, is religion.

Conclusion

The primatologist Frans de Waal has written that if the basic supposition of all evolutionary biology—that humans and animals are related in the long arc of deep time—is true, then "there must at some level be continuity between the behavior of humans and that of other primates." He adds that "No domain, not even our celebrated morality, can be excluded from this assumption" (de Waal 1997, 1). As Darwin saw, humans and other animals—especially other mammals—have similar emotional blueprints. Von Uexküll came up with an even more comprehensive explanation for how humans and animals build lifeworlds in fundamentally the same way. As we've seen in this chapter, even religion is something that seems to cross the species barrier. In this view, religion draws on emotional templates common to many animals—patterns of feeling that are activated by lifeworlds.

What's interesting about this picture is that it tells the story of both continuity and difference across species. Different animals have different lifeworlds. We might even say they have different religions. The Harvard professor Kimberley Patton has interpreted this theologically. She writes about how important it is—for many religious traditions—that different animals are allowed to experience these emotional potentials. A rabbit, for instance,

> reveals something *unique* about who God is, some dimension of His being that is, in a word, rabbity. For no apparent reason other than joy, rabbits leap high into the air, twist their furry bodies, and kick out their feet in abandon. There is an aspect of God's Self that at creation expressed itself as a rabbit, and nothing can better reveal that particular aspect of the divine nature than a real, living rabbit. In some ways, we can compare this to Eastern ideas: the rabbit is more than just a rabbit, but is instead a metaphysical participant on the great playing field of the cosmos.
>
> (Patton 2000, 427)

Many religious traditions, from Islam to Catholicism to Indigenous Mvskoke Creek and Cherokee traditions, consider it obvious that animals, like humans, have their own ways of praising the divine (Schaefer 2012). Considering how religion and emotion relate with respect to different animals highlights both similarities and differences in religious practices across species.

It's not necessarily productive to try to pinpoint which parts of a lifeworld are religious and which are not religious. Are fans at a football game—decked out in the same colors, singing traditional songs, united in moments of intense feeling—religious? Are monks who brew and sell beer *not* religious? "Religion" is a complicated, imprecise word. But what we *can* say is that what gets called religion is often *emotional*. Religion seems to appear when humans—and other animals, too—do things that are emotionally rich for them.

This also has implications for animal ethics. We've already talked about experimentation on animals. It's important to remember that even animal tests that are *not* violent still involve lifelong confinement for the animals involved. This is also the fate of many animals trapped in the global factory farm system. Like prisoners, they live their lives cut off from sources of joy and other rich emotions. Seeing animals as religious, then, is a way of reaffirming that animals have their own value and their own horizons of experience and feeling. This may prompt us to reassess the harm that is done to them not just in killing, but in keeping them confined for their entire lives.

References

Bentham, Jeremy. 1879. *An Introduction to the Principles of Morals and Legislation.* Oxford: Clarendon Press.

Berkson, Gershon. 1973. "Social Responses to Abnormal Infant Monkeys." *American Journal of Physical Anthropology* 38: 583–86.

Cheney, Dorothy L., and Robert M. Seyfarth. 2007. *Baboon Metaphysics: The Evolution of a Social Mind.* Chicago, Ill.: University of Chicago Press.

Darwin, Charles. 1876. *The Origin of Species by Means of Natural Selection, or the Preservation of Favoured Races in the Struggle for Life, 6th Edition, with Additions and Corrections.* London: John Murray.

_____. 1882. *The Descent of Man and Selection in Relation to Sex.* 2nd ed. London: John Murray.

_____. (1872) 2009. *The Expression of the Emotions in Man and Animals.* new ed. Edited by Joe Cain and Sharon Messenger. London: Penguin Books.

Desmond, Adrian, and James Moore. 2009. *Darwin's Sacred Cause: Race, Slavery, and the Quest for Human Origins.* Chicago, Ill.: University of Chicago Press.

Goodall, Jane. 2006. "Epilogue: The Dance of Awe." In *A Communion of Subjects: Animals in Religion, Science, and Ethics,* edited by Paul Waldau and Kimberley Patton, 651–56. New York: Columbia University Press.

_____ with Philip Berman. 1999. *Reason for Hope: A Spiritual Journey.* New York: Soko Publications.

Gould, Stephen Jay. 1996. *Full House: The Spread of Excellence from Plato to Darwin.* New York: Harmony Books.

James, William. 1961. *The Varieties of Religious Experience: A Study in Human Nature.* New York: Collier Books.

Kühl, Hjalmar S., Ammie K. Kalan, Mimi Arandjelovic, Floris Aubert, Lucy D'Auvergne, Annemarie Goedmakers, Sorrel Jones, et al. 2016. "Chimpanzee Accumulative Stone Throwing." *Scientific Reports* 6: 22219. www.nature.com/articles/srep22219.

Moss, Cynthia. (1988) 2000. *Elephant Memories: Thirteen Years in the Life of an Elephant Family,* with a New Afterword. Chicago, Ill.: University of Chicago Press.

Patton, Kimberley C. 2000. "'He Who Sits in the Heavens Laughs': Recovering Animal Theology in the Abrahamic Traditions." *Harvard Theological Review* 93 (4): 401–34.

Pribac, Teya Brooks. 2021. *Enter the Animal: Cross-Species Perspectives on Grief and Spirituality.* Sydney: Sydney University Press.

Schaefer, Donovan O. 2012. "Do Animals Have Religion? Interdisciplinary Perspectives on Religion and Embodiment." *Anthrozoös: A Multidisciplinary Journal of the Interactions of People & Animals* 25 (Supplement 1): 173–89.

Secord, James A. 2000. *Victorian Sensation: The Extraordinary Publication, Reception, and Secret Authorship of Vestiges of the Natural History of Creation*. Chicago, Ill.: University of Chicago Press.

Sedgwick, Adam. 1890. *Life and Letters of the Reverend Adam Sedgwick*, Vol. II. Edited by John Willis Clark and Thomas McKenny Hughes. Cambridge: Cambridge University Press.

Smuts, Barbara. 2001. "Encounters with Animal Minds." *Journal of Consciousness Studies* 8 (5): 293–309.

von Uexküll, Jakob. 1957. "A Stroll Through the Worlds of Animals and Men: A Picture Book of Invisible Worlds." In *Instinctive Behavior: The Development of a Modern Concept*, edited by Claire H. Schiller, 5–80. New York: International Universities Press.

Waal, Frans B.M. de. 1997. *Good Natured: The Origins of Right and Wrong in Humans and Other Animals*. Cambridge, Mass.: Harvard University Press.

Wilson, Edward O. 1993. "Biophilia and the Conservation Ethic." In *The Biophilia Hypothesis*, edited by Stephen R. Kellert and Edward O. Wilson, 31–41. Washington, D.C.: Shearwater/Island Press.

Other Recommended Resources

Goodall, Jane. 2005. "Primate Spirituality." In *The Encyclopedia of Religion and Nature*, edited by Bron Taylor, 1303–06. London and New York: Continuum.

Guthrie, Stewart. 2002. "Animal Animism: Evolutionary Roots of Religious Cognition." In *Current Approaches in the Cognitive Science of Religion*, edited by Ilkka Pyysiäinen and Veikko Anttonen, 38–67. London and New York: Continuum.

Kennedy, Keebe. 2006. *Animals Like Us: Animal Emotions*, Video, St. Thomas Productions, 49 mins. www.youtube.com/watch?v=laod4t3woeU&list=PLTOUyQcU3JG38kwqjUnxhn0zFRHA5dB09&index=1.

King, Barbara J. 2007. *Evolving God: A Provocative View on the Origins of Religion*. New York: Doubleday.

———. 2014. *How Animals Grieve*. Chicago, Ill.: University of Chicago Press.

Rollin, Bernard. 1988. *The Unheeded Cry: Animal Consciousness, Animal Pain and Scientific Change*. Oxford: Oxford University Press.

Schaefer, Donovan O. 2015. *Religious Affects: Animality, Evolution, and Power*. Durham, N.C.: Duke University Press.

Yong, Ed. 2022. *An Immense World: How Animal Senses Reveal the Hidden Realms Around Us*. New York: Random House.

4 Gender and Sexuality

Katharine Mershon

Introduction: Personal Connections

My scholarship in animals and religion, alongside gender and sexuality, started in an unexpected way: when I adopted a dog named Zoe. She had a blocky head, a muscular body, long gazelle-like legs, and short fur with a brown patch over her right eye. Under "breed," she was listed as a "pit bull." Through the adoption process, I learned that dogs like Zoe were the most common type in animal shelters—and the fact that most shelters were packed with pit bulls was not an accident. In the 1980s, the American media began stereotyping pit bulls as "dangerous dogs," associating them with Black, brown, and male-dominated spaces, projecting racist associations about "inherently violent" people onto dogs. Not long after I adopted Zoe, I started volunteering at a local city animal shelter, where I saw the effects of these stereotypes firsthand.

As I became more involved in animal rescue, I grew increasingly uncomfortable with the godlike power humans hold over animals, deciding which ones are worthy of life or death. Most of those who ended up at the shelter where I volunteered came from the city's most systematically disenfranchised neighborhoods, areas that were also predominantly Black and brown. This movement of dogs away from Black and brown spaces made me worry about how a "good home" was often code for a white, middle-class nuclear family, complete with a white picket fence. I started to wonder if rescue was a form of "civilizing" the dogs—one that bore uncomfortable resonances with early American settler colonialist projects (whose goal was to strip Indigenous peoples of their culture and convert them to European Christian beliefs and norms). While I had previously been focused on how only certain kinds of dogs were deemed worthy of rescue, I began thinking about my underlying assumptions about the kinds of people who were deserving of dogs in the first place. For whom were these dogs being rescued? And from what, exactly?

While struggling with these ethical quandaries, one day at the shelter, I heard an announcement over the loudspeaker calling an employee to the front desk for a "dog redemption." I looked around to see if anyone else thought this announcement was strange. They did not. Their lack of response makes sense, given that redemption is essential to the work of animal shelters in the contemporary United States. As institutions, animal shelters are not usually defined by their relation to religion, nor do they have explicitly religious missions. However, the language of redemption structures their most foundational practices.

When an owner reclaims a lost animal, shelters call this a "redemption." Dog redemption initially appears to be a matter merely of an economic exchange. In order to redeem a dog, the person must show proof of ownership, since animals are legally considered

DOI: 10.4324/9781003324157-7

property; they must also pay a fee to the shelter for the costs of housing and feeding. This literal usage reflects the etymology of the word "redemption." Its original Latin root describes an economic process in which something or someone is "bought back" or "regained." This term, which emerged in the context of Roman slavery and was used in the institution of chattel slavery in the United States, reappears in animal shelter language (e.g., Fessenden 2006; Emberton 2013).

At the same time, the process of redeeming a dog from the shelter takes on a religious dimension, bearing structural similarity to Christian conversion narratives, in which someone is saved from the prospect of death or sin, and thereby "born again." This religious meaning of redemption is often extended from the dog to the human rescuer through stories that describe an experience of personal healing, moral satisfaction, and unconditional love. (For more on the central role of redemption narratives in shaping American identity, see Tuveson 1968; Shulman 2008; McAdams 2013.)

As the example of dog rescue shows us, religious terms and practices cannot be separated from their broader historical and social contexts. Similarly, the study of gender and sexuality is incomplete without addressing other categories central to identity formation, such as race, class, and colonialism. Through two case studies that will take us from "the crazy cat lady" as portrayed in the long-running popular American television show, *The Simpsons*, to a 2016 Turkish documentary about the cats and humans of Istanbul (*Kedi*), we'll see how gender, sex, and religious norms determine one's inclusion and positionality in human communities. While these examples cover different cultures and genres, they both emphasize ecofeminist forms of knowledge that privilege emotions, embodiment, and community. In the process, we will learn how religious beliefs and practices define the stories people tell about animals and, by extension, one another.

Gender, Sexuality, and Other Than Human Animals

Ecofeminism and Feminist Care Ethics

The transdisciplinary field of ecofeminism can help us understand how the study of animals connects to gender and sexuality studies. Ecofeminism emerged in the late 1970s and early 1980s from feminist scholarship and movements for social justice and environmentalism. Figures such as Carol J. Adams, Josephine Donovan, Marti Kheel, Alice Walker, Greta Gaard, Lori Gruen, and many others have worked to challenge uncritical assumptions about gender and animality (having animal-like qualities). Feminist scholar Susan Fraiman provides a summary of the kinds of simplistic and harmful stereotypes that ecofeminism seeks to expose and resist:

> Broadly speaking, these [stereotypes] include the notions that women and animals are linked together as avatars of nature; that they are similarly debased by their shared association with body over mind, feeling over reason, object rather than subject status; that men are rational subjects, who therefore naturally dominate women and animals alike; that masculinity is produced in contradistinction to the feminine, animal, bodily, emotional, and acted upon; that degree of manliness is correlated to a degree of distance from these and other related categories—physicality, literalness, sentimentality, vulnerability, domesticity, and so on.
>
> (Fraiman 2012, 99)

In other words, the qualities understood as the most valuable in the history of Western thought—intellect and reason—have been associated with men and, by extension, what it means to be human. In contrast, "inferior" characteristics such as emotion and embodiment have been associated with women—and in turn, with animals. In her classic work *The Death of Nature: Women, Ecology, and the Scientific Revolution*, ecofeminist historian of science Carolyn Merchant describes the implicit sexism embedded in directly associating women with nature. In one example, Merchant cites the figure of "Mother Earth," who is understood as "a kindly beneficent female who provides for the needs of mankind in an ordered, planned universe" (Merchant [1980] 1990, 2). In this instance, the connection between women and nature depends on assumptions about women being natural nurturers and caregivers. Ecofeminists seek to expose these value judgments and challenge their underlying logic by demonstrating how much we can learn through forms of knowledge accessed through the emotions, the body, and life outside the human (see, e.g., Adams and Gruen 2014).

Now let's turn to some concrete examples that show how applying an ecofeminist lens can make us more aware of the implicit and explicit ways that anthropocentric (human-centered) ideas about gender and sexuality are projected on to the bodies of animals. In turn, we will also see how gendered ideas about the right kinds of relationships we should have with animals are used to decide who should or should not belong in human communities.

Case Study: Cat Ladies

As a means of showing how the insights of ecofeminism, religion, gender, and sexuality can help us better understand everyday cultural phenomena, let's talk about one of my favorite figures: the "cat lady." In her chapter on cats, folklore, and the supernatural, folklorist Lynne S. McNeill describes how one constant among the massive amount of cat stories told around the world is "this sense of something mysterious or indefinable" and even "supernatural" about cats that lives on today (McNeill 2007, 6). As McNeill notes, topics in world feline folklore align with popular stories about supernatural creatures, including the following recurring themes:

> required formality at encounters (the devil himself often requests formal treatment), power over fertility and death (women thought to be witches were often blamed for—or asked in secret to assist with—situations pertaining to both these issues), and ability to provide luck both good and bad (a common aspect of fairy encounters as well).
>
> (McNeill 2007, 6)

In McNeill's account, what's also particularly interesting about cats is that, unlike other supernatural beings, humans invite cats into all parts of our lives, despite their potentially dangerous powers. Like all things supernatural, McNeill concludes, cats are also liminal creatures. As anyone who shares space with a cat can attest, they are "betwixt-and-between" categories—neither wild nor domestic, neither fully independent nor dependent (McNeill 2007, 9).

Just as cats' "oddly independent" nature was a factor in their connection to witches, "cat ladies" become "crazy" when they develop too much autonomy and therefore threaten the patriarchal order. To undermine their power, cat ladies are usually represented as pathetic, unmarried women who choose to live with cats rather than human family members. The "crazy cat lady" archetype only works because it draws on deeply entrenched stereotypes about women as "hysterical," which is another way of saying they "have too many feelings" and as a result, should not be taken seriously. Crazy cat ladies thus occupy a liminal space in the human social order: "it is even possible to connect the discomfort that many people feel toward both cats and women (and especially 'cat ladies') to a perception that they are similar in their impermanence between domesticity and wildness" (McNeill 2007, 12). Put differently, cat ladies are threatening to the dominant patriarchal order because they reject traditional gender norms and therefore cannot be controlled by men.

Why is the cat lady so threatening, and how can the tools of religion, gender, and sexuality studies help us understand her enduring potency? As described earlier, cats and women are associated with witches, a trope that continues today. Part of what makes witches so terrifying in American culture (think of the Salem Witch Trials) is their potential to disrupt and perhaps even change who belongs in the dominant (read: white, male, and Christian) community. The crazy cat lady stereotype continues to have cultural resonance because it allows us to dismiss women before they disrupt patriarchal social structures:

> it [the crazy cat lady trope] is a reminder of the historical, cultural association between mature women, animals, and the irrational; that not only are our relations with animals sentimental (read: "trivial"), but they are also made possible by having a shared status of mindless irrationality and animality.
>
> (Probyn-Rapsey 2018, 176)

By linking women to animals, and therefore suggesting they are unreasonable and overly emotional, then we can simply laugh at them instead of question the patriarchal social order that they threaten.

Arguably the most famous example of the crazy cat lady in U.S. culture is Dr. Eleanor Abernathy, a character on the long-running American animated television series *The Simpsons* (Kirkland and Sheetz 2007; Probyn-Rapsey 2018, 176). Episode 13 of Season 18 (2007) describes how Dr. Abernathy was once a smart and ambitious young feminist who wanted to be both a doctor and a lawyer "because a woman can do anything." At the young age of 24, she had earned both an M.D. from Harvard Medical School and a J.D. from Yale Law School, representing her entrée into the most elite realms of society. By the age of 32, however, the stress and isolation of her career started to wear on her. As a means of dealing with the burnout, Dr. Abernathy turned to alcohol and to her cat, Buster, whom she described as "a real comfort." Although not overtly stated, the implication is that Dr. Abernathy is alone with her cat because she focused on her career at the expense of finding human companionship. The dangerous and deviant nature of a single, successful woman is further spelled out when Dr. Abernathy adds that she "might even get a second cat." The crazy cat lady, which Dr. Abernathy is on the verge of becoming, "not only loves cats too much, she loves them 'more than people,' instead of a husband, and, quite literally, in place of heteronormative domesticity" (McKeithen 2017, 124).

And this is exactly what happens. Immediately after Dr. Abernathy makes that seemingly casual statement, the show cuts to a scene in which she is utterly transformed. All the previous indicators of her social and economic success are gone. Dr. Abernathy no longer lives in her tidy condominium with her single cat but instead is surrounded by cats in a dark, dirty space. It is as if the cats brought the alley with them, reflecting how cats transgress the boundaries between private and public spheres. Dr. Abernathy's tailored pink pantsuit and lipstick are also gone, and she has aged approximately forty years. She is no longer her previously articulate Ivy League-educated self but has become a mentally ill woman who speaks in incoherent screeches and stutters. Because she has lost all vestiges of her authority—her career, economic stability, voice, and youth—the cats represent the only power she has left. As a result, she uses them as weapons to discourage humans from getting close to her (she literally throws them at people).

In other episodes featuring Dr. Abernathy, her body is always crawling with cats, whether she is in a movie theater, at someone else's home, or walking down the street. This kind of intimacy not only violates norms about cross-species physical contact but also clearly violates standards about where animals belong. The implicit message behind Dr. Abernathy's story is that her downfall is a result of her feminist-motivated ambition and independence. Stripped of all markers of "acceptable" female ways of behaving, Dr. Abernathy becomes akin to a feral animal herself—in other words, she is liminal: neither fully human nor animal. While she appears as a comedic figure in the show, applying the tools from the study of religion, gender, and sexuality demonstrates that the story of Dr. Abernathy is deeply misogynistic (rooted in the hatred of women). As this example reveals, the crazy cat lady trope must be taken seriously because it uses humor to mask a dangerous political purpose: to cast threatening women (read: smart, educated, ambitious, unmarried) out of communities.

Case Study: The Cats of Istanbul

Whereas the case of Dr. Eleanor Abernathy is an extreme example of what happens to women who love "improperly" (by choosing cats over human companions, the streets instead of the home), the Turkish film *Kedi* (Torun, Wuppermann, and Fontana 2017) transports the viewer to Istanbul, a Muslim-majority city where the act of caring for street cats is portrayed as a religiously and socially-supported activity for people of all genders. Unlike most Western contexts in which animal care is coded as feminine and therefore marginal, cisgender men in *Kedi* proudly proclaim their abiding devotion to Istanbul's cats. By analyzing this documentary alongside the *The Simpsons*, we will see how gender norms related to more-than-human animals are shaped by religion and nationality. Put differently, *Kedi*'s celebration of the male rescuers' love for cats cannot be separated from Islamic teachings about the animals, as well as the historic role of cats in shaping Istanbul's identity.

From the outset, *Kedi* situates cats as symbols and citizens of Istanbul, Turkey. The film opens with the following narration:

> Cats have lived in what is now Istanbul for thousands of years. They have seen empires rise and fall and the city grow and shrink. Though cared for by many, they live without a master. And whether adored, despised, or overlooked, they are undeniably a part of everyone's life (00:32–00:42).

Unlike hierarchical understandings of pet keeping based on ownership, these cats seemingly have full autonomy over where they live, what they eat, whom they see, and where they go. Many people help them, but they have independent lives.

As part of their autonomy, the cats of Istanbul transgress human-created boundaries, appearing in shops, markets, cafes, boats, and so on. Instead of having one owner, the cats develop relationships with different humans to meet specific needs. For instance, according to the documentary's narrative, a spirited tuxedo cat named Gamsiz ("care-free" in Turkish) has an entire community at his command. Gamsiz is a bit of a trouble-maker, getting into scrapes with other cats and requiring frequent veterinary attention. Because he doesn't have a single owner, his care is supported by the community. "There's a bunch of us in the neighborhood," a male restaurateur/Gamsiz devotee explains. "We have an open tab at pretty much every vet. We also collect donations, which help fund these expenses. Whatever is in our tip box goes to the cats" (49:35). Through community-funded efforts, everyone in the neighborhood cares for Gamsiz and other street cats.

This scene exemplifies Istanbul-based literary scholar Kim Fortuny's claim that "[i]n Istanbul, as in other metropolises in other parts of the world, the relationship between urban animals and urban people has not been thoroughly civilized and privatized. In other words, it has not been commodified" (Fortuny 2014, 278). As opposed to the model of individual animal ownership more common in the U.S., the community members pool together their resources to support Gamsiz's care, creating a structure akin to mutual aid.

Notably, most of Gamsiz's caregivers are men who are not biologically related but are bound through a shared commitment to the cats. The film doesn't comment on the gender of the caregivers—it's just normalized. In an interview about the film, however, director Ceyda Torun speaks to the culturally-specific gender dynamics:

> In Turkey, you're not supposed to express your emotions, you're supposed to be tough, especially if you're a guy. Being passionate is excused, that's a different thing, but when it comes to something serious like having a mental breakdown or being forced to find a purpose in life, talking about cats is a great icebreaker for people, a way for them to express their emotional needs more easily.
>
> (Catster 2016)

Even though Turkish men are traditionally expected to be strong and stoic, caring for street cats allows them to express their emotions. We see this clearly in the embodied ways the men encounter the animals—petting, brushing, kissing, and holding them. Because of "the general love for cats in Turkey," male cat caregivers are not seen as social outcasts—in fact, quite the opposite (Calafato 2021, 72). Instead, they are viewed as doing crucial work to preserve the city's sacred creatures.

The spiritual dimension of caring for street animals runs deep in Turkish culture:

> Many contemporary Turkish people, religious or otherwise, refer to the street dog as a living soul: it is often observed to me that "*Onu da Allah yaratti*" (God created him too); or that "*O da bir can*" (He's a living soul too). His status as a living being, and this includes black dogs, is what leads many in the general public to set out food for him and not refer him to the municipality that may take him away to worse conditions than the streets, or more likely extermination.
>
> (Fortuny 2014, 276)

While Fortuny's article focuses on Istanbul's street dogs, *Kedi* suggests that this responsibility also extends to cats. In one scene, the camera lingers on a sign in front of food and water bowls that reads: "These cups are for cats and dogs. If you don't want to be desperate for a cup of water in the next life, don't touch these cups" (14:00). These signs reflect the fact that people don't just have an ethical responsibility to animals because helping them is a good thing. Their responsibility is also *theological*: you won't just be a bad person if you mess with the animals' food and water—you'll be punished in the afterlife by being treated like a deprived animal.

Indeed, the film emphasizes that cats have a unique relationship with God. Early in *Kedi* one male feline caregiver says, "It is said that cats are aware of God's existence, but that dogs are not. Dogs think people are God, but cats don't. Cats know that people are middlemen to God's will. They're not ungrateful—they just know better" (14:29–45). Not only do humans have a God-given responsibility to cats, but unlike dogs who mistake the source of ultimate authority, cats recognize that people are channels to the divine. While this statement may be slightly tongue-in-cheek, it has major theological stakes. In this account, cats have a concept of religion. (For other examples of animals being viewed as spiritual or religious, see Patton 2000; Pribac 2021; Schaeffer 2012.)

In highly stylized aerial shots, the specifically Muslim character of Istanbul comes to the fore. The film features Istanbul's iconic Blue Mosque throughout, and the call to prayer is a regular part of its sonic background. Cats are shown as part of the rhythm of the city's religious life—sitting on the steps of mosques or depicted as striking silhouettes against an orange sky as the call to prayer resounds throughout the city (1:05). In another scene, the director interviews a male artist who talks about how as a child, he and his brother created a cemetery for the street cats they loved who often died too soon:

We would bury them with great ceremony. And because we'd seen crosses in cowboy movies . . . and because we weren't about to engrave tiny gravestones, we'd make crosses out of twigs. Then one day, our father saw us and freaked out over the crosses. Immediately, he sent us to Qur'an school so that we wouldn't suddenly turn Christian (44:44–45:14).

Instead of being angry about *whom* his children were honoring, the father objects to *how* they mourned. The problem isn't that his kids were participating in religious observances for cats but that they weren't practicing Muslim forms of observance.

And there are indeed multiple Islamic teachings that describe cats very positively. For example:

Turkey is not unique among predominantly Muslim countries for honouring its cats, which are considered ritually clean animals in Islam. In the hadith, the collected sayings and actions of Muhammad, there are numerous examples of the Prophet's fondness for cats. By one account, Muhammad cut off his sleeve when he had to rise for prayers so as to not disturb a feline that had curled up on his robe for a nap. In another tale, the pet cat of Abu Hurayrah (literally "father of the kitten") saved Muhammad from an attack by a deadly serpent. Muhammad purportedly blessed the cat in gratitude, giving cats the ability to always land on their feet. Cats were considered guardians in other respects for the Islamic world: they defended libraries from destruction by mice and may have helped protect city populations from rat-borne plagues.

(*The Economist* 2017)

Supporting this Muslim view of cats as ritually clean animals (unlike dogs), Cyril Glassé reports that cats are "allowed to roam freely inside mosques, including the Grand Mosque of Mecca. Stories of cats that seek out persons who are praying, and of cats sensitive to the presence of grace, are common" (Glassé 2008, 114).

Muslims likely consider cats to be ritually clean partly because of their impeccable personal hygiene. In his early 20th-century natural history of animals, Muhammad ibn Musa Damiri writes, "[The cat] is graceful and elegant, and cleans its face with its saliva; when any part of its body is dirty, it cleans it" (Damiri 1906, 85). Donald Engels adds that unlike medieval Western Christians, Muslims of that era "emphasized cleanliness, washing, and bathing. Hence they seem to have appreciated the cat, in part, for this reason" (Engels 1999, 150–151). Thus, contact with cats did not compromise a Muslim's purity for prayer, unlike contact with dogs; in fact, a cat's drinking water could even be used for ritual ablutions if needed (ibid.).

Ceyda Torun, *Kedi*'s director, expresses similar sentiments about the centrality of cats to Islamic teachings, as well as the duty of faithful Muslims to care for cats. In the same interview cited earlier she said,

> There's also a religious factor. There's a belief, for example, that the streaks on the forehead of the tabby come from where the Prophet Mohammed stroked his tabby cat [see also Engels 1999, 150]. Many people I interviewed told me, if you're a true Muslim, you're a lover of all animals. And cats in particular have free rein because of stories like this from Islam; people can use them to justify allowing themselves to love an animal so much.
>
> (Catster 2016)

In this case, the religious importance of cats in Islam is used to permit the presence of "big feelings" in men. It's OK for men to be affectionate or emotional because they are participating in Allah's work. One could argue that they are even acting as "true Muslims" by treating cats with respect and kindness, following the example of the Prophet Muhammad himself. (There are also historical precedents for Muslim cat rescue; for example, Donald Engels notes that the Sultan Beybars in Cairo founded charitable organizations to feed and shelter homeless cats; see Engels 1999, 151.)

Unlike the "crazy cat lady," the cats of Istanbul are seen as redemptive forces who help reintegrate people back into society. In a particularly powerful scene, a middle-aged man describes his experience with cat rescue as follows:

> I had a nervous breakdown in 2002. That's when I got more involved with cats. Doing this cured me. I was really caught up; I was really lost. This truly is therapy. . . . No drugs were able to save me. . . . I believe I got healthy by taking care of cats (1:01:32–1:01–42).

Cats play an important redemptive role for many people by giving them a purpose in the community: "several people [interviewed in *Kedi*] talk frankly about having felt broken in some way, and about how taking care of homeless cats feels redemptive" (D'Angelo 2017). Instead of humans being the people doing the redemptive work (as I experienced at the animal shelter), the cats are the ones doing the redeeming by reintegrating humans back into the community. This is the opposite of what we saw in *The Simpsons*, where cats served as both a sign of Dr. Abernathy's mental illness and physical barriers between her and other people.

The fact that the cats are mostly not spayed or neutered in *Kedi* also leads to conversations about the cats' own genders and sexualities, as well as to how human beings fit into these feline social structures. For example, we meet a female cat dubbed "the psychopath" because she's a fierce fighter in the neighborhood and rules over her "husband," as one interviewee fondly calls him (29:15–29:41). She's described as "a jealous housewife, who doesn't leave her husband alone. And she doesn't let anyone near him, either" (38:38–39:00). These are instances where people project human understandings of gender and sexuality onto the cats, to great comedic effect. But at the same time, these observations are rooted in deep knowledge of these feisty felines, gained through daily interactions and close observations. These cats clearly have social hierarchies and connections; their observers serve as translators to other people. This isn't to say that the cats are living in a feline utopia, despite how it may look. Instead of addressing whether or not there *should* be spay and neuter policies, the film skirts the issue—just as it glosses over the other forms of violence the cats undoubtedly face (being hit by cars, etc.).

Other reports on the cats of Istanbul confront this issue directly, noting that there still are not enough resources to care for the cats. As Hilary Sable, a cat rescuer in Istanbul, notes,

> There's such a big problem with stray animals and homeless animals in this country primarily because there isn't much of a culture for spaying and neutering. The life of a street cat is not very long. It's between 3–6 years if you're very, very lucky. But still, the population is growing not diminishing.
>
> (BBC 2016)

There are free adoption services for people living in other countries who want to adopt a street cat from Istanbul, but these are also not discussed in the film (Fortuny 2014, 283).

Instead of questioning whether or not there should be so many kittens, pregnant cats or mothers (the language the film uses) are taken as a given. Early on, we meet a male fisherman who is caring for orphaned kittens too young to eat solid food. This is an incredibly labor-intensive, round-the-clock job. Instead of being embarrassed about occupying a stereotypically "feminine" role, the man is proud of his deep knowledge about kitten care while also recognizing his limits. "Of course, I can't take the place of their mother, but I do what I can," he says (18:13). While he knows that he's not their parent, he's content offering the kittens care outside of traditional family and species structures. The fisherman is also not alone in this care work, since a male cat has moved in with the kittens: "He keeps them warm. Both a father and a mother," the fisherman explains (19:36–20:26). Unlike the human supporting partner, the male cat takes on a role only possible for another cat. Together with the help of his human counterpart, the kittens survive, representing a remarkable moment of multispecies care.

This is the idealized image of Istanbul that the film wishes to project—one in which humans and cats live together in harmony, free of more formal forms of intervention. This moment embodies what's both beautiful and challenging about the film. On the one hand, it takes up Josephine Donovan's ecofeminist ethic that is grounded in "an emotional and spiritual conversation with nonhuman life-forms" and "a women's relational culture of caring and attentive love" (Donovan 1990, 375). On the other hand, it neglects to address the broader structures that lead to the overwhelming population of orphaned kittens in the first place. While these individual acts of care are moving, we should question whether or not a solution based on individual goodwill is the best answer to an overwhelming cat population in a city where even the humans face potential displacement from gentrification.

By avoiding a discussion of these material realities, this relational form of multispecies care is instead portrayed as Allah's work. Earlier in the film, the fisherman tells a story about how his brand-new boat sank in a storm. Later that same day, he saw a wallet on the ground with a cat next to it, seemingly pointing toward it. He ignored the cat, but this image stayed with him. He went back later that day, and the wallet was still there. When he opened it, he found precisely the amount of money needed to recoup the cost of the boat. For him, this was a "godsend." After this encounter, he began caring for the cats (19:36–20:36). We see him happily tending to the animals, and we hear his voice in the background: "God says, 'I test people.' God brings us closer to Him in different ways. For me, it was these animals. I guess I was worthy of His love" (1:13–30). Just as the cats were previously described as seeing people as God's middlemen, here we have a human who finds God through cats, representing a form of redemption that transcends species.

While emotionally and visually appealing, we need to recognize that this is a sanitized depiction of animal rescue. Even when we see cats suffering, we don't find out their fate. We don't learn about whether or not the rescuers actually pay off their hefty vet bills. The city's official policies toward the cats are not discussed at all. Instead, it seems that the film's primary concern is to offer a counternarrative to Western viewers who associate Islam with violence, and in the process, the violent side of animal rescue is brushed aside in favor of stories of redemption.

Conclusion: Losing Sight of Animals in Rescue

As we wrap up, I want to return to where we started: with animal rescue and my concerns about how the language of rescue and redemption prioritized the immediate relief of suffering at the expense of a long-term plan to help animals thrive. As feminist scholar Harlan Weaver incisively argues, these feel-good rescue stories mask a history of violence that they risk reenacting through the bodies of dogs:

> The sense of emotional satisfaction that lends [white] saviorist storytelling its charge and allure emerges from a specific history: colonization. Most relevant to this issue is settler colonialism (the displacement and genocide of Indigenous people and their culture by Eurocentric people), a key component of which is its "civilizing mission." The promise of salvation plays out on a spiritual level in the form of Christianity and on a material level in the transformation of the colonized into the "civilized." Colonization has occurred through the transfer of worship practices to Christian churches and the concomitant erasure of Indigenous cosmologies and ways of knowing across the globe. This "salvation" in the name of Christianity both undergirds and parallels the labor and claims specific to rescued dogs taken from the streets or the shelter—spaces of supposedly certain death—into the domestic space of the family home. Saviorist storytelling [in animal rescue] literally would not make sense without this narrative of settler colonialism and Christianity.
> (Weaver 2021, 49)

If we follow Weaver in seeing these two seemingly distinct practices—assisting (rescuing) suffering animals in the contemporary context and the historical reality of Europeans suppressing or destroying Indigenous cultures in the name of civilizing (rescuing) them—as deeply related in unexpected ways, there are several practical implications. For example, let's return to my time at the animal shelter. Weaver's insights should encourage predominantly white, middle-class, and female animal rescue workers like me to pause and consider, for example, our biases about what we think constitutes a "good home." This isn't to say that animal rescue is inherently harmful or that animal rescuers are bad people. Instead, we need to hold together two complex ideas simultaneously—to *both* recognize that religion and colonialism have played a role in shaping the culture of animal rescue *and* use that knowledge to protect humans and dogs by avoiding impulsive acts of rescue motivated by white saviorism. It's not enough to have good intentions; the outcome matters more than a fleeting feel-good story. Instead, we need to ask what's best for each individual animal, which requires the forms of knowledge celebrated by the feminist writers we've discussed—that which is contextual, particular, and embodied.

Acknowledgments

This chapter is dedicated to Zoe Mershon (2010–2020), the dog of my heart and my greatest teacher. I also want to thank Sarra Tlili for her help finding sources on cats in Islam.

References

Adams, Carol J., and Lori Gruen, eds. 2014. *Ecofeminism: Feminist Interactions with Other Animals and the Earth*. New York: Bloomsbury Academic.
British Broadcasting Corporation (BBC). 2016. "Why Are There So Many Stray Cats in Istanbul?" November 7. Accessed March 31, 2023. www.bbc.com/news/av/world-europe-37880274.
Calafato, Özge. 2021. "A Wooden Box, Tripod, and Cloth: The Role of Alaminüt Photography in the Making of Modern Turkey." In *The Camera as Actor: Photography and the Embodiment of Technology*, edited by Amy Cox Hall, 57–77. New York: Routledge.
Catster. 2016. "Istanbul's Charismatic Street Cats in Focus in New Film 'Kedi.'" Interview with Ceyda Torun, June 6. Accessed February 11, 2023. www.catster.com/lifestyle/istanbuls-charismatic-street-cats-in-focus-in-new-film-kedi.
Damiri, Muhammad Ibn Musa. 1906. *Ad-Damîrí's Hayāt al-hayawān, a Zoological Lexicon*. Translated by A.S.G. Jayakar. London: Luzac & Co.
D'Angelo, Mike. 2017. "*Kedi* Might Look Like a Glorified Cute Cat Video, But It Has Plenty to Say About People, Too." *AV Club*, February 8. Accessed February 11, 2023. www.avclub.com/kedi-might-look-like-a-glorified-cute-cat-video-but-it-1798190398.
Donovan, Josephine. 1990. "Animal Rights and Feminist Theory." *Signs* 15 (2): 350–75.
The Economist. 2017. "Istanbul's Love of Street Cats." February 9. Accessed March 31, 2023. www.economist.com/prospero/2017/02/09/istanbuls-love-of-street-cats.
Emberton, Carole. 2013. *Beyond Redemption: Race, Violence, and the American South after the Civil War*. Chicago, Ill.: University of Chicago Press.
Engels, Donald. 1999. *Classical Cats: The Rise and Fall of the Sacred Cat*. London and New York: Routledge.
Fessenden, Tracy. 2006. *Culture and Redemption: Religion, the Secular, and American Literature*. Princeton, N.J.: Princeton University Press.
Fortuny, Kim. 2014. "Islam, Westernization, and Posthumanist Place: The Case of the Istanbul Street Dog." *Interdisciplinary Studies in Literature and Environment* 21 (2): 271–97.

Fraiman, Susan. 2012. "Pussy Panic versus Liking Animals: Tracking Gender in Animal Studies." *Critical Inquiry* 39: 89–115.

Glassé, Cyril. 2008. *The New Encyclopedia of Islam.* 3rd ed. Lanham, Md.: Rowman & Littlefield.

Kirkland, Mark, and Chuck Sheetz, directors. 2007. *The Simpsons*, Season 18, episode 13, "Springfield Up." Aired February 18, 2007, on Fox.

McAdams, Dan P. 2013. *The Redemptive Self: Stories Americans Live By.* rev. and expanded ed. New York and Oxford: Oxford University Press.

McKeithen, Will. 2017. "Queer Ecologies of Home: Heteronormativity, Speciesism, and the Strange Intimacies of Crazy Cat Ladies." *Gender, Place, & Culture* 24 (1): 122–34.

McNeill, Lynn S. 2007. "The Waving Ones: Cats, Folklore, and the Experiential Source Hypothesis." In *What Are the Animals to Us? Approaches from Science, Religion, Folklore, Literature, and Art*, edited by Dave Aftandilian, Marion W. Copeland, and David Scofield Wilson, 5–19. Knoxville: University of Tennessee Press.

Merchant, Carolyn. (1980) 1990. *The Death of Nature: Women, Ecology, and the Scientific Revolution*, with a New Preface. San Francisco, Calif.: Harper & Row.

Patton, Kimberley C. 2000. " 'He Who Sits in the Heavens Laughs': Recovering Animal Theology in the Abrahamic Traditions." *Harvard Theological Review* 93 (4): 401–34.

Pribac, Teya Brooks. 2021. *Enter the Animal: Cross-Species Perspectives on Grief and Spirituality.* Sydney: Sydney University Press.

Probyn-Rapsey, Fiona. 2018. "The 'Crazy Cat Lady.' " In *Animaladies: Gender, Animals, and Madness*, edited by Lori Gruen and Fiona Probyn-Rapsey, 175–85. New York: Bloomsbury.

Schaeffer, Donovan O. 2012. "Do Animals Have Religion? Interdisciplinary Perspectives on Religion and Embodiment." *Anthrozoos* 25: S173–89.

Shulman, George. 2008. *American Prophecy: Race and Redemption in American Political Culture.* Minneapolis: University of Minnesota Press.

Torun, Ceyda, Charlie Wuppermann, and Kira Fontana. 2017. *Kedi.* Istanbul: Termite Films. Distributed by Oscilloscope Laboratories.

Tuveson, Ernest Lee. 1968. *Redeemer Nation.* Chicago, Ill.: University of Chicago Press.

Weaver, Harlan. 2021. *Bad Dog: Pit Bull Promises and Multispecies Justice.* Seattle: University of Washington Press.

Other Recommended Resources

Boisseron, Bénédicte. 2018. *Afro-Dog: Blackness and the Animal Question.* New York: Columbia University Press.

Callan-Jones, Christie, and Jeannette Loakman. 2009. *Cat Ladies.* Toronto: Chocolate Box Entertainment. Distributed by TVF International. https://youtu.be/GdMIUYqochI.

Cats of Istanbul (Istanbul Kedileri) Facebook Page. Accessed March 15, 2023. www.facebook.com/CatsofIstanbul/.

Rogers, Katharine M. 2006. *Cat.* London: Reaktion Books. Rereleased in 2019.

Waal, Frans de. 2022. *Different: Gender Through the Eyes of a Primatologist.* New York: Norton.

5 Race, Animals, and a New Vision of the Beloved Community

Christopher Carter

Introduction: The Politics of Protest

For those of us born after the civil rights movements of the 1960s, the summer of 2020 may well be remembered as the summer of protest. The murders of George Floyd and Brianna Taylor by police officers and the murder of Ahmaud Arbery by white male vigilantes protecting their neighborhood shook American households. Videos of these tragic deaths were shared on social and mainstream media and ignited widespread protests across the United States. While many, if not the majority, of these protesters understood themselves to be participating in peaceful demonstrations for racial justice, the response these protests generated from local police forces would lead one to believe otherwise. Images from protests in Minneapolis, Los Angeles, Detroit, and New York reveal a heavily armed and militarized police presence ready to confront and control the protesters. This photo of Black Lives Matter (BLM) activists in Lafayette Park on June 1, 2020 (Figure 5.1) was taken moments before the police used tear gas and their shields to forcibly remove peaceful protesters. Clearing out these protesters made it possible for then President Donald Trump to have his picture taken, while holding a Bible, in front of St. John's Episcopal Church.

The image of the BLM protesters with their hands raised, physically embodying the anti-police violence chant "hands up—don't shoot" stands in stark contrast to the "mask mandate" protests during that same summer. As the COVID-19 pandemic continued to tear through the U.S., the Centers for Disease Control and Prevention suggested that properly wearing a mask would help reduce the spread of the virus. The images from the protest at the state capitol in Lansing, Michigan, my home state, stand out (see Figure 5.2). Unmasked white men who were standing mere inches away from law enforcement were seen yelling at officers. Other unmasked white men were carrying a variety of guns, from assault rifles to handguns, inside of and around the capitol building. Notably, the police officers were not dressed in body armor, nor were they pictured carrying assault rifles themselves.

By now you are probably wondering what all of this has to do with animals or race! In this chapter I will argue that the different police responses to these protests have everything to do with the way the term "animal" has been racialized. The fear that police officers have of Black bodies and other bodies of color is tied to an understanding of the human, a flawed theological anthropology that has falsely associated blackness *with* animality. With theological anthropology I am referring to the Christian theological understanding of Black, Indigenous, and other people of color as subhuman that emerged during the era of coloniality as a means to theo-ethically justify genocide and

DOI: 10.4324/9781003324157-8

Figure 5.1 Protesters kneel in front of riot police moving to clear demonstrators out of Lafayette Park and the area around it for President Donald Trump to be able to walk through for a photo opportunity in front of St. John's Episcopal Church, during a rally against the death in Minneapolis police custody of George Floyd, in Washington, D.C., June 1, 2020

Source: Photo by Ken Cedeno for Reuters. Reprinted with permission

Figure 5.2 Protesters try to enter the Michigan House of Representatives chamber after the American Patriot Rally organized by Michigan United for Liberty protest for the reopening of businesses on the steps of the Michigan State Capitol in Lansing, Michigan, April 30, 2020

Source: Photo by Jeff Kowalsky/AFP via Getty Images. Reprinted with permission

enslavement. The fear of the "wild animal" and the "savage" Black African is the ideological foundation upon which *white body supremacy* has been built. I use the phrase "white *body* supremacy" to draw attention to the ways in which the ideology of white supremacy renders all non-white bodies, be they human or other than human, as objects.

To be sure, even animal rights organizations have fallen prey to reinforcing an idea of the animal that flattens important distinctions between human and other than human animals. In so doing they undermine support for collective liberation for people of color because their suffering is seen as similar to or just like other than human suffering. All suffering need not be the same for all suffering to matter. Given this, I will conclude this chapter by outlining a way forward for individuals and organizations that aim to help build an anti-oppressive world where both humans and nonhuman animals can break free from the grip of white body supremacy and begin to heal from our collective traumas.

The Human/Nature Binary

In their book *The History of the World in Seven Cheap Things*, Raj Patel and Jason Moore offer a compelling argument that the Western world has been built on the logic of cheapening. Of the seven cheap things they identify, two of them are useful in our quest to understand the relationship between race and the animal: cheap nonhuman nature and cheap nonhuman lives.

By "cheap," they do not mean that nature and lives are low-cost, though that is a part of their argument. Instead they understand the cheapening of nature and lives as a "strategy, a practice, a violence that mobilizes all kinds of work—human and animal, botanical and geological—with as little compensation as possible" (Patel and Moore 2017, 22). In this way, something is able to be cheapened once we are able to create relational distance from it. Moreover, our distance from "it" allows us to turn a potential subject into an object; we cheapen it by making it into a thing. It is our inability to recognize and accept our relational responsibilities toward all life that enable human beings to cheapen animal subjects into objects.

Given this, I do not agree with the authors' conclusions that the cheapening of nature and life can be attributed primarily to capitalism, though capitalism plays an important role. Rather, I suggest that capitalism as a structural economic system is a symptom of a deeper malady that plagues the ideological foundations of modern Western thinking about *what counts as life* and *whose lives actually count*. The ideology of coloniality— that is, the mindset and knowledge system that preceded, accompanied, and made possible colonial encounters—is the foundation upon which the logic of cheapening is built. Capitalism is the product of a colonial worldview.

Coloniality, as a way of thinking, emerged during sixteenth-century European encounters with the Indigenous peoples of what would later become known as the Americas. This encounter marks the beginnings of Euro-American empires that played the primary role in ushering us into our current geological age, which some refer to as the Anthropocene. Empire making of this magnitude has historically required the cheapening of certain lives for the benefit of those elite few in power. To be sure, empire making was not new. Coloniality is what sets Euro-American empire apart from others empires that emerged from Western civilization. Coloniality enabled nonhuman life and certain human bodies—Black and other non-white, poor, and female bodies—to be policed in new ways that would render them perpetually cheap by placing and subjugating them within oppositional binaries, particularly the binary of society and nature.

Our modern understanding of the word "society" is a product of colonial thinking. "Beginning in the middle of the 16th century, society came to mean not just the company that we keep, but also a bigger whole of which individuals are a part" (Patel and Moore 2017, 46). Human beings have seemingly always given names to establish boundaries between social groups: Christendom, Sunni or Shia, or the Middle Kingdom, among others. But our modern notion of society has a historically unique antonym: nature. One is either a part of society or they are a part of nature; you are either a human fit for society or you are a savage fit for the wild. Once nature and society take on these new distinctions, they allow for a new way of organizing and structuring human beings and human encounters with the Earth that enable certain lives to be cheapened and rendered merely as things.

The Nature of Race

The idea of race operating today begins to be built upon this nature/society split. Whiteness, as a basis for one's identity, renders one's relationship to the land as a secondary factor in their social identity. This disconnection reinforces the nature/society split. Prior to the colonial encounter, Europeans identified themselves by their religious tradition and their country of origin, that is, English, French, Spanish, Portuguese, and so on. In this way the earth itself, the landscape of one's country of origin, was an important signifier of one's social identity. The idea of race that developed required removing place as the central marker of one's identity and replacing place with the pigmentation of one's body. One could be French, English, Spanish, or Portuguese, but for the idea of race to stick, the landscapes of their white bodies needed to take precedence over the landscapes of their home countries as the primary means of classifying and organizing the human body. As theologian Willie Jennings notes in his book *Christian Imagination: Theology and the Origin of Race*, the idea of whiteness rendered any narrative of self-identity bound to geography, trees, or animals as unintelligible (Jennings 2011, 57):

> With the emergence of whiteness, identity was calibrated through possession of, not possession by, specific land. . . . People would henceforth (and forever) carry their identities on their bodies, without remainder. From the beginning of the colonialist moment, being white placed one at the center of the symbolic and real reordering of space.
>
> (Jennings 2011, 58)

By de-linking notions of self-identity from the earth and tying them to human bodies, the idea of race can be understood as both a sociocultural and ecological event. Ecologically race normalizes the human/nature oppositional binary. No longer are human beings understood as a part of creation; rather, fully human beings ought to become creators in their pursuit to control and tame nature. The idea of race in turn allows for the creation of different classes of humans. The white men who created and perpetuated the idea of race measured the humanity of other non-white human beings against their own, and since they saw themselves as the ideal human form, they determined that those humans who were most unlike them were closer to nature, closer to the animal.

Sociologists Michael Omi and Howard Winant have examined the history of new and emerging racial identities and categorization in the West, and their work is helpful in our analysis of the relationship between the idea of race and animals. In the West, race should be understood as a "master category—a fundamental concept that has profoundly shaped and continues to shape, the history, polity, economic structure and culture" (Omi and Winant 2014, 106). In this way, we understand how coloniality, the enslavement of Africans, and the genocide of Indigenous peoples in North America were fundamental to race, making and categorizing the people who constituted the modern world. Race, just like nature, just like the animal, becomes a template of both difference and inequality that is measured against humanness—which is code for whiteness.

As one of two master categories of social organization (with gender being the second category), race became one of the dominant ways of identifying and classifying human bodies. As social beings, we categorize the world to make sense of it. Human classifications can help us discern our friends from our enemies, place ourselves within accepted social hierarchies, and guide us in our interactions with the individuals and groups we encounter (Omi and Winant 2014, 105). However, the very act of defining racial groups has produced both intended and unintended consequences, as our conceptions of race have shifted, producing new and emerging racial identities. In this way, race can be understood as an "unstable and decentered" web of social meanings that are continually being transformed through political struggle (Omi and Winant 2014, 110).

Race and Religion

Although our contemporary common sense understanding of race invokes biologically based human characteristics such as skin pigmentation, we must remember that the selection of biological features used in classification is always a social and historical process. During the early stages of European colonialism, Prince Henry the Navigator and Christopher Columbus become central figures in defining the European *Christian* man as the human ideal and non-European human beings as others. In the wake of his voyage around the southern tip of Africa, Prince Henry claimed that Europeans were culturally and religiously superior to Africans. Henry asserted that African cultural and religious practices were demonic, made aesthetic judgments based on Africans' skin color, and inaugurated the transatlantic slave trade based upon those judgments (Carter 2014, 176). Christopher Columbus built upon the work of Prince Henry by applying the same concepts to the Indigenous peoples of North and South America. Carter notes that Columbus's logs describe the newly "discovered" lands as *terra nullius* (lands of no one) and their inhabitants as less than or insufficiently human due to their physical appearance as well as cultural and religious practices that deviated from Eurocentric norms (Carter 2014, 176).

By understanding and contextualizing his imperial mission through a religious (Christian) lens, Columbus created the framework necessary for Christian European white men to view themselves as imperial God-men. Theologically, Euro-American Christians openly wondered whether Africans and Indigenous Americans bore the imprint of the *imago Dei*. Were they created in the image of God, as all humans are understood to be based on the Genesis creation narratives? And if so, did they reflect the image of God to the same degree as European men? By suggesting that Black, Indigenous, and other non-white bodies were not quite as human as European bodies were, European Christian men felt no moral obligation to treat enslaved Africans as they would other human beings.

In this way, it is no coincidence that colonialism and chattel slavery emerged during the period when European Christian men were able to claim that Africans and Indigenous

American people were evil and savage because they were either non-Christian or "too close to nature" and "like animals," and therefore distant from God. For the church, hierarchy is weaponized as a way to theo-ethically justify the immoral and unjust domination of others by white people in general and white men in particular. In so doing, religious orders sought to normalize oppressive practices as either divinely ordained or worthy of reward in the afterlife. As civil rights pioneer and Black theologian Howard Thurman noted in regards to the white oppression of people of color, if the oppression is viewed as normal, then it is correct; if correct, then moral; if moral, then religious (Thurman 1996, 33).

By fashioning their theological anthropology—that is, the understanding of the God-human encounter—through the lens of coloniality and white dominance, white clergy and religious leaders have been able to weaponize the cheapening of non-white human life in ways that have enabled them to maintain political power that is tied to empire. With theological anthropology I am referring to the normative claims that influence the way in which Christians understand and embody the God-human encounter, and how Christians have come to know themselves as fully human. Your interpretation of this encounter situates how you understand yourself in relation to others: God-human, human-human, and human-nonhuman nature. Indeed, the modern understanding of what it means to be human, to be an "Anthropos," is an event grounded in and supported by Western white Christian norms and ideologies. As such, slavery, colonialism, segregation, and the logic of capitalist development that emerged from colonialism can all be understood as a problem of a particular white Christian theological anthropology. This theological anthropology not only defined Black and other non-white bodies as others, but it also helped to concretize the othering rationale onto nature itself.

Race, Religion, and the Creation of "The Animal"

Most activists of color who do anti-racist or human rights work have touched upon "the animal question" in some way. A thorough analysis of racism or coloniality usually calls attention to the degree to which non-white people are animalized or referenced as behaving "like animals" (Ko and Ko 2017, 45). That is, those who seek to maintain (or create) an oppressive dynamic between two groups often describe the marginalized group as falling outside of the realm of "human" as a way to legitimize behaviors toward them that would otherwise be considered immoral at best and evil at worst. However, the analysis done by most anti-racist activists on the relationship between anti-racism and animalization tends to stop at this point, followed by the claim that people of color "are humans too" and should be treated as such, rather than being treated "like animals."

I agree with Black feminist Syl Ko's claim that this way of thinking requires "an *open acceptance* of the negative status of 'the animal' which . . . is a *tacit acceptance of the hierarchical racial system of white supremacy in general*" (Ko and Ko 2017, 45, emphasis added). The human/animal binary, which follows the logic of the society/nature binary, is a critical component of the ideological foundation that upholds white supremacy. This means that *our modern delineation of human/humanity and animal/animality was constructed along racial lines*. As such, the negative notion that many human beings have of the animal is the anchor of the system of white colonial logic and the ideology of white body supremacy (Ko and Ko 2017, 45).

Psychologist and post/de-colonial theorist Franz Fanon makes this clear in *Wretched of the Earth* when he writes,

> In plain talk, [the colonial subject] is reduced to the state of an animal. And conse-quently, when the colonist speaks of the colonized he uses zoological terms. Allu-sion is made to the slithery movements of the yellow race, the odors from the "native" quarters. . . . In his endeavors at description and finding the right word, the colonist refers constantly to the bestiary.
>
> (Fanon 2005, 7)

Anti-racist activists have understood these connections since the time of African enslavement by whites. What I am suggesting here is that the strategy of claiming that people of color "are humans too" will be ineffective unless anti-racist activists and ani-mal rights activists also attend to the racialized structure of the human/animal binary.

To be sure, when someone states that a group of human beings are animalistic, they do not necessarily mean that the group of people fall outside of the scientific category of *Homo sapiens*. Rather, they are stating that these human beings do not look, live, worship, or reason normally, where "normal" is understood as Eurocentric white male norms. In other words, when one does not *act white* or when one behaves in ways that challenge white body supremacy and the hierarchy of white supremacy, they are seen as an animal. Depending upon how well some of the less human animals can replicate the social and behavioral norms that white men dictated as human norms, certain non-white human animals could be treated *like* humans, even if they could not really *be* fully human. In this way, the white racial imagination's conception of the animal—developed within a culture of Christian white male supremacy—is the conceptual vehicle that mor-ally and ideologically justifies violence against subhuman (e.g., people of color) and non-human (animal) others (Ko and Ko 2017, 46).

To summarize, the core message embedded within colonial Western understandings of the human person are that in order to be seen as a full human being, one must be either white or accept the hierarchy of human beings that protects the image of the heterosexual white male as the image of God on earth, the pinnacle of creation. Contrary to the anti-critical race theory propaganda that is espoused by political conservatives, I do not mean to say that Americans have *explicitly* been taught that being raced as white and inter-preting the world through the white/non-white human/nature binaries is ideal. Rather, I argue Americans are socialized to accept the idea that human beings exist separate and apart from nature, and the white racial imagination and racism ensure that our vision of the ideal human is understood to be white.

Human/Animal Rights

Having reached the concluding portion of this chapter, it will be helpful for you, the reader, to know a bit about my social location as it informs my argument regarding com-monly used language among animal rights activists. I am a Black man who grew up in small town in West Michigan. I spent a lot of time outdoors and grew up loving nature, but not having any strong relationships with animals other than humans. I now real-ize that my immediate family dealt with the trauma of racist animalization by avoiding association with animals. For the first half of my life, I was rather neutral about animals (if one considers eating animals and animal products a neutral act). During this period of my life I adhered to the traditional society/nature division and felt that a nonhuman animal's value was tied to the value they provided human beings. For the second half of my life, I have been partnered with a woman who eventually became a veterinary oncologist—needless to say that, at minimum for the sake of my marriage, my perspectives on other than human animals have shifted and are no longer tied to the value they provide human beings, for food or otherwise.

This evolution of thought was not without tension. As I began to understand the connections between the oppression of nonhuman animals and people of color, I also experienced the language that people used to describe this connection as dismissive of the distinct traumas that people of color have experienced in America. Attending animal rights conventions and having conversations with animal rights people was a painful experience. I often felt that my very humanity, as a person of color, was under attack. The dominant way of framing the oppression and exploitation of nonhuman animals hinged on the term "speciesism."

The concept of speciesism was popularized by Peter Singer in his book *Animal Liberation*. Speciesism is a belief that different species of animals are significantly different from one another in their capacities to feel pleasure and pain and live an autonomous existence, usually involving the idea that one's own species has the right to rule and use others (Singer 2009). In his book, Singer argues that speciesism is problematically subjective in ways similar to racism and sexism. According to this reasoning, what makes speciesism like racism and sexism is that an identifying category that should be morally arbitrary such as race, gender, or species becomes the basis upon which moral decisions are made. Following this reasoning, the majority of animal advocates argue that in ethical deliberations, considering one's species—especially the idea that being human can be the basis for positive moral regard—is no different than arguing that being white or male can be the basis for positive moral regard.

This understanding of speciesism highlights the tension that arises between animal activists and anti-racist activists. Animal rights activists seek to dismantle structures of power that have prioritized human needs and desires over the needs and desires of other species by decentering the human as a basis for positive moral regard. Although not logically necessary, this often leads to the related idea that *just* because someone is human doesn't *necessarily* mean that they deserve to be treated in any particular way. The logic that Singer hopes will lead to an expansion of ethics can lead to a contraction of concern, and here is where the tension with anti-racist work begins. Anti-racist activists have sought to dismantle structures of power that prioritized the needs and desires of those racialized as white over those racialized as people of color by decentering whiteness as the methodological starting point for evaluating one's humanness. However, for anti-racist activists the argument that humanness as such is the basis for positive moral regard is essential in their fight for human rights for people of color that have been denied due to white body supremacy and the racist belief that they are less human than whites.

These seemingly incompatible worldviews are among the primary reasons why animal rights groups are predominantly white and why racial justice groups are predominantly people of color. The animal rights group seeks to decenter the human and the anti-racists seek to recenter a more inclusive human. However, as I suggested at the beginning of this chapter, both groups are seeking to dismantle two expressions of the same primary form—*white body supremacy*. If we are going to make sustainable strides toward an anti-oppressive society, one that is both anti-racist and takes seriously the rights of animals, we will need to build solidarity between and among racial justice and animal rights activists. Solidarity requires a common vision of what injustice we are fighting and a common language to use to describe our efforts.

Animal rights groups do not need to decenter the human to build a strong argument for animal rights, and anti-racists must avoid recentering the human as it exists within the society/nature binary, since that binary is the product of coloniality and white supremacy. In their essay "Re-Centering the Human" Syl Ko and Lindgren Johnson describe what such an approach would entail (Ko 2021).

For animal rights activists, solidarity asks them to no longer evaluate moral regard for humans or nonhuman animals from a primarily "objective" or "scientific" position. This approach attempts to evaluate human injustices from an external perspective such that they can examine traits, properties, and capacities about human beings in the same ways they would any other animal (Ko 2021). This approach also allows animal activists to argue that there is no trait, property, or capacity that other animals do not share in some way. From this "objective" position, the notion that being human itself can be reason alone for rights or moral regard is a matter of prejudice—speciesism.

The problem with this approach is that it is built on the assumption that humans understand themselves primarily from the external perspective and that it is from this external perspective that they primarily make their moral decisions. This is clearly not true, particularly with respect to racial discrimination. If all it took to dismantle white body supremacy was a convincing argument that the external appearance of people of color proves that they are human and should be treated as such, the American anti-racist struggle would have ended after the Civil War and during reconstruction when racial discrimination was illegal.

Racism is structured around external factors such as appearance, but the arguments made by racists are based on perceived internal differences between white people and people of color, that is, white people are smarter, more trustworthy, work harder, etc. The longstanding strength of white body supremacy is that it denies the subjective realities of beings who are not racialized as white and gendered as male. This is why using "speciesism" as a term to describe animal injustice is unhelpful for creating solidarity because the oppressions experienced by humans and nonhuman animals are fundamentally unlike one another in important ways. The longstanding trauma of racism on people of color includes the pain, anguish, and suffering that we have endured due to centuries of dehumanization. Within the objectivist approach that relies on the language of speciesism, there isn't room to take seriously the internal experience of the suffering and oppression of people of color. Thus, a thinker like Singer may embrace anti-racism on the surface by speaking against sexism, racism, and speciesism, but his arguments indirectly support racialization by imagining the ethical task in a way that alienates people of color by failing to take seriously the reality of human situatedness. Developing responses to suffering and oppression that are unique to those who are oppressed asks us to develop empathic and compassionate responses based on the subjective experience of those who are marginalized.

For example, when people of color complain about their mistreatment by law enforcement, the common response within a white supremacist culture is that people of color should "behave in compliance with the officers." A response coming from a place of solidarity should push white people to ask themselves how they would feel if they believed they were being mistreated by law enforcement. Anti-racism asks us to give a moral heaviness to the internal and subjective experiences of people of color—it asks us to view these internal and subjective experiences as true and real. This requires unlearning ideologies that have normalized and moralized racist attitudes, beliefs, and assumptions that prompt us to question the truth of their experience.

Similarly, a strong moral argument can be made for animal rights if we prioritize the subjective experience of the other than human animal. This approach does not ask us to decenter the human; rather, it asks us to respect the subjective experience of the animal in the same way that we would respect the subjective experience of a person of color. A subjectivist approach recognizes that substantial moral regard for other than human animals necessitates appreciating that other animals have species-specific ways of subjectively existing in the world. Given this, other than human animals should have the space and freedom to set up and participate in their own forms of life without our interference, or at least with only minimal interference in cases where it cannot be prevented or contributes to mutual flourishing and enrichment (Ko 2021).

That the subjective experience of other than human animals carries moral weight that helps dismantle white body supremacy is a crucial point for anti-racist activists. Failure to respect the subjective experience of other animals would allow for the maintenance of the subjective experience hierarchy that currently upholds white supremacy. There is no anti-oppressive way to deny the subjective life experience of another animal, human or otherwise. As we have discussed, the reasoning that upholds coloniality and the society/nature binary is built upon denying subjectivity to women, nonhuman nature, nonhuman animals, and non-white people.

Conclusion

I began this chapter by describing the distinctions between the law enforcement response to protesters who were mostly people of color and those who were white. As this chapter makes clear, law enforcement's violent response toward racial justice protesters is rooted in colonial assumptions that are projected onto bodies: white bodies are ideal and must be protected, non-white and other than human-animal bodies are tools whose subjective experience must be minimized to uphold the logics of coloniality.

I am, by nature and profession, an optimist, and I believe that understanding the connections between white body supremacy and the exploitation of animals is crucial if our goal is to end white body supremacy and dismantle coloniality. However, I am not naïve to the fact that what I am asking law enforcement to do, and what I am asking you the reader to do, is to upend your worldview and restructure your default assumptions around the subjective experiences of people of color and other than human animals. This is no small task because it requires you to decenter whiteness as the primary frame of reference for interpreting the world, and it asks you to value the subjective experiences of other that human animals for their own sake, without comparing them to human beings.

This is why I believe that a solidaristic movement between animal rights groups and anti-racist activists is essential. Both groups desire to dismantle white body supremacy and the colonial worldview that white supremacy helps to uphold, a worldview that denies the subjective experiences of people of color and other than human animals. There is much that each group could learn from the other, but for this learning to be sustainable, it requires a new *decolonial* sociocultural understanding of the human person. Decolonization is the twin process of identifying and dismantling colonial assumptions about the human person and the nonhuman world in all their forms. Decolonization requires seeking out both the obvious and the hidden aspects of these objectifying assumptions that are used to normalize colonial thinking.

Martin Luther King Jr. was by no means a decolonial thinker. However, throughout his all too brief life, his speeches, sermons, and writings demonstrated that as he aged, he grew more and more aware of the ways Black American oppression was tied to a larger structural worldview. In one of his final sermons, "Beyond Vietnam," he articulates his stance against the Vietnam war by describing how white body supremacy is an interlocking system of oppression tied to consumerism and militarism (King 2016). Given the trajectory of King's thinking, I want to conclude this chapter by building upon his vision for a beloved community that is inclusive of the more-than-human world. The beloved community is a descriptive term popularized by King, and it captures the essence of what he believed was necessary to create an anti-racist world. I stretch King's vision to include the more-than-human world to cast a vision of an anti-oppressive society, a society that affirms the subjective experiences of people of color and more-than-human animals. This vision is an invitation to imagine the kind of community that anti-racist and animal rights activists can only build together.

For Dr. King, the beloved community was not a utopian goal to be confused with the rapturous image of the Peaceable Kingdom in which lions and lambs coexist in idyllic harmony. Rather, the beloved community is a realistic, achievable goal that can be attained by a critical mass of people committed to living in solidarity with one another and extending an empathic compassion toward human and more-than-human animals. Living into the beloved community means holding ourselves accountable to doing the work in the present of building a future in which all people can share in the abundant resources of our planet. The beloved community is a place where more-than-human animals are no longer exploited or seen as objects to be used merely for the benefit of human beings. The subjective experience of more-than-human animals matters not only because we recognize their suffering, but also because we recognize that our survival as a human species depends upon their flourishing. The beloved community is a place where poverty, hunger, and homelessness are unacceptable outcomes that spur change because we live in solidarity with one another, and we know in our bones the suffering of others is our own. Our compassion for them moves us to do what we can to help alleviate it. As members of the beloved community, our tables are open to all who would sit or roost.

In the beloved community racism and all forms of discrimination, bigotry, and prejudice will be replaced by an inclusive spirit where the plurality of human experience will be recognized as fully human. Anti-ecological and extractivist thinking will be replaced with an understanding of the interdependence and interconnectedness of all life (cf. the Earth Charter's call for "a new sense of global interdependence and universal responsibility"; available at https://earthcharter.org). In the beloved community love and trust triumph over fear and hatred; peace with justice prevails over war and military conflict because we have de-linked our minds from oppressive hierarchical values that have placed a "certain kind of human" as the pinnacle of evolution and in its place, we have developed an understanding of the human person that is rooted in love, solidarity, and an interdependent flourishing.

To be sure, the beloved community is not devoid of interpersonal, group, or international conflict. As justice-oriented activists, we recognize that conflict is an inevitable part of the human experience. However, we also believe that conflicts can be resolved peacefully, and adversaries can be reconciled through a mutual, determined commitment to nonviolence and restorative acts of compassion. All conflicts in the beloved community should end with reconciliation of adversaries cooperating together in a spirit of radical compassion.

Imagine a world where animal rights and racial justice activists can live into this vision and invite others to do the same. Now imagine yourself helping to build this world, using the skills and talents that are unique to you. And finally, go and do your best to help breathe life into this imaginative existence.

References

Carter, J. Kameron. 2014. "Humanity in African American Theology." In *Oxford Handbook of African American Theology*, edited by Katie G. Cannon and Anthony B. Pinn, 175–83. New York: Oxford University Press.

Fanon, Frantz. 2005. *The Wretched of the Earth*. Translated by Richard Philcox. New York: Grove Press.

Jennings, Willie James. 2011. *The Christian Imagination: Theology and the Origins of Race*. New Haven, Conn.: Yale University Press.

King Jr., Martin Luther. 2016. *The Radical King*. Edited by Cornel West. Boston, Mass: Beacon Press.

Ko, Aph, and Syl Ko. 2017. *Aphro-Ism: Essays on Pop Culture, Feminism, and Black Veganism from Two Sisters*. New York: Lantern Books.

Ko, Syl. 2021. "Re-Centering the Human." #*Coroseum And Choas On The Table. Um Museum*. www.mooniperry.com/text/re-centering-the-human-syl-ko-and-lindgren-johnson/view/4921017/1/4921217.

Omi, Michael, and Howard Winant. 2014. *Racial Formation in the United States*. 3rd ed. New York: Routledge.

Patel, Raj, and Jason W. Moore. 2017. *A History of the World in Seven Cheap Things: A Guide to Capitalism, Nature, and the Future of the Planet*. Oakland: University of California Press.

Singer, Peter. 2009. *Animal Liberation: The Definitive Classic of the Animal Movement*. New York: Harper Perennial Modern Classics.

Thurman, Howard. 1996. *Jesus and the Disinherited*. Boston, Mass.: Beacon Press.

Other Recommended Resources

Carter, Christopher. 2021. *The Spirit of Soul Food: Race, Faith, and Food Justice*. Urbana, Ill.: University of Illinois Press.

Cone, James H. 2000. "Whose Earth Is It Anyway?" *Cross Currents* 50 (1/2): 36–46.

Harris, Melanie L. 2017. *Ecowomanism: African American Women and Earth-Honoring Faiths*. Maryknoll, N.Y.: Orbis Books.

Johnson, Lindgren. 2017. *Race Matters, Animal Matters: Fugitive Humanism in African America, 1840–1930*. New York: Routledge.

Nibert, David A. 2002. *Animal Rights/Human Rights: Entanglements of Oppression and Liberation*. Lanham, Md.: Rowman & Littlefield.

6   From Inspirational Beings to "Mad" Veg/ans

Tensions and Possibilities Between Animal Studies and Disability Studies

Alan Santinele Martino and Sarah May Lindsay

The Intersections of Disability Rights and Other Than Human Animal Rights

Around the time this chapter was written, a TikTok clip of a woman carrying a peacock onto an airplane, claiming them to be her emotional support animal, went viral (*The Sun* U.K. Edition, May 10, 2022). The clip shows the woman carrying the bird onboard, then seated with the peacock on her lap, their long plume of feathers extending into the aisle and head high and alert above the woman. At the center of this story lie human interpretations of disability and other than human animals, raising questions such as: Why is a peacock an unusual support animal? What is an emotional support animal? Why is it acceptable to use other than human animals as supports? Did this woman really need this peacock? Was she disabled the right way or enough? What about the well-being of the peacock?

To help answer these questions, this chapter introduces research looking at the intersections of critical disability studies and critical animal studies (e.g., Jenkins, Montford, and Taylor 2020; Santinele Martino and Lindsay 2020; Taylor 2017). Together, these fields explore the idea that the forms of oppression experienced by disabled people (ableism) and other than human animals (speciesism) are highly interconnected and reproduce each other. Oppression is about the suppression of the rights and freedoms of particular social groups in our society. This oppression is sometimes "justified" through a process of "othering" these social groups, perpetuating a notion of "us versus them." Whom we view as the "other" is contextual and volatile. At the margins, for example, we find social actors, such as "the service dog, the pathologized animal activist or animal lover, the disabled more-than-human animal, and the animalized disabled human" (Jenkins, Montford, and Taylor 2020, 1). These are precisely the "voices" we choose to highlight in this chapter.

Tensions and Debates

Before we proceed, it is important to acknowledge the tensions that, at times, have blocked discussions bringing together ableism and speciesism. We, ourselves, have faced some resistance from scholars in both of our fields who said that talking about disability and animal rights jointly is simply "unethical," "too dangerous," or a "disservice to the field." Certainly, despite some shared views and aims, ableism is observable in some animal studies, and speciesism exists in some disability scholarship. Disability studies scholars have, for example, pointed out the ableism in the work of animal studies scholar and utilitarian philosopher Peter Singer, who postulated that parents should be allowed to euthanize their disabled children (Carlson and Kittay 2010; Vehmas 1999). According

DOI: 10.4324/9781003324157-9

to Singer, the experience of disability (especially more severe impairments) often, if not always, comes accompanied by suffering, and thus, to end the lives of disabled infants could be seen as a "compassionate" act (see Booth 2018). Such a view of disability, however, denies the multifaceted, complex experiences of disability, the intrinsic value of disabled people's lives, and the possibility of them having a satisfying life.

Historically, disabled people have been devalued and dehumanized through comparisons with other than human animals (Jenkins, Montford, and Taylor 2020); disabled people have been told that they have "frog legs, penguin waddles, seal limbs, and monkey arms" because of their bodies' appearance (Taylor 2011, 192). As Taylor notes, "these comparisons have an element of truth that isn't negative—or, I should say that *doesn't have to be negative*" (192, emphasis added). Yet, by being compared to animals, the lives of disabled people are seen as having less value than those of other humans and animals. This tension between the two fields is captured well by Stephen Drake (2010):

> Aside from Peter Singer, there is a scary amount of support in our society for killing old, ill and disabled people—especially when significant cognitive disability is involved. Often such killing is justified by making comparisons between the killing of old, ill and disabled people and the comfortable myths we have about the euthanasia of pets (namely, the myth that all or most pets are killed because they are dying and in unrelievable suffering). When disabled people are equated with animals, it never works out well for us.
>
> (para. 17)

Animal rescuers and activists, as well as vegetarians and vegans, have also been critiqued for supposedly prioritizing the well-being and lives of other than human animals over those of humans. Yet, one should ask, why are humans more important than other animals? These hierarchies are not helpful if they fail to acknowledge how humans' and other animals' lives are interconnected. What is in question here is the notion that humans are inherently more important than animals and, consequently, should receive better treatment. This ideology is both speciesist and anthropocentric. Speciesism refers to a belief that one species of animal is superior to another (Ryder 1989), whereas anthropocentrism means "human-centered." Anthropocentrism is more than just a point of view; rather, it is a false orientation toward human supremacy, and a belief in our "right" to seek fulfillment of our "needs" via the dominance and use of all other animal species, as well as the environment more generally.

Above all, the fact that animal comparisons are treated as insults demonstrates the worth we attribute to nonhuman animals (Hurn 2012, 14). Within any given culture, some other than human animals are revered and untouchable while others are demonized.

Species and breeds are human social constructions (DeMello 2021, 9–11). Of course, it can aid our understanding to try to organize and classify the enormous quantity of other than human animals and other beings in our midst. Objectively, there are observable differences between, say, a granite boulder and a mouse, an eagle and an iguana, or a cat and a human. However, other than human animals are organized and categorized in a hierarchy of worth based on their perceived use, threat, or value to humans. As Sutton and Taylor (2019) note in their discussion of problem species, nonhuman animals who are viewed as "risky" or "undesirable" are seen as being in need of control or elimination.

Other than human animals and disabled humans are similarly problematized or, at least, often viewed as both a social liability and as unproductive. There are discussions about what makes lives worth living, and what counts as livable lives. At the same time, according to Sunaura Taylor (2011), current disability studies scholarship "can no longer exclude other species" (198). Nik Taylor and colleagues (2018) call for a species-inclusive approach, since the societies we live in include a multitude of species. Similarly, multi-species anthropologists have turned interspecies relations from a peripheral topic in the field to one worth pursuing to "change the way we think about other humans and other animals" (Hurn 2012, 10). There are innumerable examples that show how much we can benefit from conversations between animal studies and disability studies scholars. In the rest of this chapter, we will use several current and past real-world examples to illustrate some of the most central discussions around the intersections of disability and animality.

Shared Themes

Speaking for or with the "Voiceless"

While many of us use our voice to communicate with others in our everyday lives, the question of voice goes beyond that. Having a voice also means having power and agency to express ourselves and share our own perspectives. When voices are expressed differently from normative ways—for example, through assistive devices, body gestures, facial expressions, movements, grunts, or snarls—however, they tend to be silenced. Disabled people, especially those who communicate in non-normative ways, have historically been quieted and are rarely given the chance to speak for themselves in research. Instead, family members and other social actors tend to speak on their behalf (Santinele Martino and Fudge Schormans 2018).

Yet rather than passively being given a voice by nondisabled people, disabled people have claimed their own "voice" and forms of mobilizing. In fact, rather than viewing it as a hindrance, disabled activists have highlighted the power of mobilizing in the "disabled way" (O'Toole 2015). As an example, Corbett O'Toole (2015) tells us about a sit-in by disabled activists in a San Francisco federal building in 1977. When communication from inside the building was cut off, activists used sign language via one of the windows to communicate with others on the outside.

In a similar manner, some human activists in animal rights claim to be "the voice of the voiceless," supposedly advocating on behalf of nonhuman animals who are unable to express their own interests and needs (Suen 2015). Being reduced to the status of the "voiceless" or "powerless" hides forms of agency among other than human animals (and disabled people). Moreover, the notion of "giving a voice" can be seen as both paternalistic and a colonialist practice, one that suppresses the autonomy and the voices of certain social groups supposedly for their "own good." Rather than being "passive victims of human depredations," other than human animals exert agency and are "active participants in human-animal relations" (Carter and Charles 2013, para. 2).

Forms of active resistance by animals are illustrated by orcas in amusement parks who fight back against their captivity (Cowperthwaite 2013) or lambs in New Zealand who flee from farms by unlatching gates (Masson 2003, 132). In some cases, these "brave" escapees become celebrities and are "rewarded" by being sent to animal rescue organizations or sanctuaries. For example, a baby cow who attracted media attention for escaping a slaughterhouse in New York City later found sanctuary in a rescue center (Place 2021).

Yet these examples of resistance often go unheard (Nibert 2013). Most often, other than human animals who resist are recaptured or killed purposely or accidentally. Resistance is problematized; expressing agency is not permissible (or useful). Moreover, cases such as these are also stark reminders of the cognitive dissonance that plagues our society: we cheer and weep for the cow who jumped off the slaughterhouse truck while we continue to consume the bodies of other cows in our hamburgers.

Though well-intentioned, the notion of "giving voice to the voiceless" is also imbued with potentially harmful, if unintended, consequences for both disabled people and other than human animals (Alper 2017). First of all, there is a risk that rather than "speaking" with, silenced groups are instead spoken for. This notion also fails to acknowledge structural inequalities that created those different positions of power in the first place. It is crucial to challenge the very understandings of voice and agency that are based on ableism and speciesism.

Inspirational Beings

Countless videos now circulate the Internet sharing the stories of inspirational disabled humans and animals alike (Birke and Gruen 2022). Images show disabled children hearing or seeing colors for the first time, or disabled dogs and chickens who can now walk on their own due to apparatuses made by humans. The struggles, and supposed courage, of disabled people and animals in overcoming disability and obstacles, as well as the "miraculous" inventions that aid disabled bodies, are commonly foregrounded in these viral representations (Birke and Gruen 2022).

Disabled activists have long questioned what has been called "inspiration porn." This term, as Stella Young ([2012] 2022) explained in her famous TEDx talk, refers to "an image of a person with a disability, often a kid, doing something completely ordinary—like playing, or talking, or running, or drawing a picture, or hitting a tennis ball—carrying a caption like 'your excuse is invalid' or 'before you quit, try.'" In essence, these images are meant to inspire nondisabled people at the cost of objectifying disabled bodies/minds. In a similar manner, images of disabled nonhuman animals show these beings partaking in "normal" activities while being labeled as inspirational. For example, in a *Buzzfeed* article entitled, "28 Animals That Don't Give a Crap about Their Disabilities," the subheading reads: "These fur balls were dealt crappy hands, but they're still smiling, purring and wagging their little tails. That's what I would call totally inspirational!" (Stewart 2013).

Recently, videos and images of disabled other than human animals have proliferated on social media (Taylor 2017, 2020). Take, for instance, Chris P. Bacon [*sic*], a pig who had a wheelchair made for him to support his impaired back legs, or Waddle, a duck who was given a prosthetic foot, or Henry Kim from Seoul, South Korea, a goldfish who uses a wheelchair to swim in his aquarium (Hamilton 2017). In this particular context, the audience is inspired by both the disabled animal and the humans who helped "fix" them. It is nondisabled people who come to the rescue.

Even if unintentionally, these stories reproduce the notion that nondisabled bodies/minds are normal, the norm, and desirable (Davis 1995); interestingly, as these cases show, even other animals are meant to strive toward nondisabled bodies/minds. Additionally, what these inspirational stories fail to demonstrate is how many disabled animals are euthanized because they cannot be used for breeding, are seen as a burden, or are too costly to care for; essentially, they are disposed of if they are not economically viable (Bruges 2018; see also Barbara Darling's Chapter 20 on "The Spiritual Practice of Providing Sanctuary for Animals" in this volume). At the same time, inspirational stories of disability distract us from disabling forms of inequality.

"Mad" Veg/ans

In some parts of contemporary Western cultures, veganism is popular and associated, at least if it is performed in particular ways, with health and environmental benefits. The term "vegan" has become an important marketing term used to attract buyers in certain demographics. However, in other situations, those who do not follow a "normal" Western diet of animal flesh, eggs, milks, and the like are often seen as deviant "outsiders." According to Howard Becker (1963), deviance is that which is successfully cast as such, and those behaving outside established norms, such as by choosing a plant-based diet, may be variously cast as extreme, odd, unhealthy, or defiant. In our social world, vegetarians and vegans are sometimes perceived as being "radical," "fanatic," and "crazy" (Aguilera-Carnerero and Carretero-González 2021); psychiatric labels have even been applied to their eating practices, such as "anti-vivisection syndrome," "selective eating disorder," or "orthorexia nervosa" (Jenkins, Montford, and Taylor 2020, 1). The use of "madness," in this context, serves as a tool to discredit these groups and their practices. Not only that, it also relies on sanist (the oppression of people with a history of mental health experience) and stigmatizing language (e.g., "crazy") to achieve that aim (Poole et al. 2012). This marginalizes both veg/ans (vegetarians and vegans) and people with diverse mental health experiences, as well as those with both lived experiences.

An interesting connection to normalcy is the case of the growing number of celebrities and athletes who highlight, varyingly, the importance of "going veg" to combat climate change, maintain weight, improve overall health, or draw attention to and reject the use (and abuse) of other than human animals. High-profile celebrities such as Beyoncé, Madonna, and Zac Efron have been considered freaks of nature for their beauty, talent, endurance, and/or strength. A celebrity's exceptional status is perhaps further amplified by their open adoption of a veg/an diet, which is still often viewed as unusual in North America and Europe (Lund et al. 2016). Similarly, adopting a veg/an diet is often seen to mark someone as exceptionally pious in various religious traditions (see, e.g., Geoffrey Barstow's Chapter 18 on "The Difficult Virtue of Vegetarianism in Tibetan Buddhism" in this volume). In this way, celebrities advertising their "new lifestyle" may further set them apart from the norm, confirming veg/anism as another unreachable aspect of their fame.

Veg/anism is also sometimes seen as just a fad that will eventually fade like other social trends (Cole and Morgan 2011). However, the adoption of veg/anism by powerful and influential social actors is a reminder that deviance is not always negative, since, at its base, it simply refers to difference. For many disability and animal studies scholars (see, for example, Taylor 2017), it is what we do with this observed difference that matters.

What Is a Life Worth Living?

A core concern at the intersection of critical animal studies and disability studies is the malleable and powerful concept of worth and what this means for the lives of those considered. The right to life debate is weighty. Take, for example, the case of "domestic" cats. In Australia, as in many other countries, cats are cherished family pets. But there are also "feral" cats, who live alone or in colonies, instead of in the home. The latter are viewed as "pests," so much so that the Australian government undertook

> a massive "5 Year Action Plan" . . . [with] the aim of killing 2,000,000 'feral' cats nationwide by 2020 in the name of conservation. Compliance with such undertakings is based, in part, on the idea that the nonhuman animals involved are "pests," "dangerous" to existing native flora and fauna.
>
> (Sutton and Taylor 2019, 379)

Conversely, cats kept as pets in the household are excluded from this targeted, "conservatory" act. The case of the Australian cats draws attention to how species, as a construction, is powerful, contextual, and malleable. Here, cats inhabit a "border" position, being a species both valued and reviled (Sutton and Taylor 2019). Deviance, as shown in this case, can lead to drastic policies aimed at control or elimination. Above all, it is noticeable how some other than human animals are revered and untouchable while others are "demonized."

In a similar manner, because disabled bodies/minds are often understood to be "questionably human, as aberrant, abhorrent, as an unfortunate existence" (Taylor 2013, para. 2), the lives of disabled people are sometimes seen as not worth living. According to Joel Reynolds (2022), the notion that "some lives are not worth living results from the ableist conflation of disability with pain and suffering" (4). Disability is viewed as undesirable. This can be seen, for instance, in films such as *Me Before You* (2016), in which the main character, a man who becomes paralyzed, dies by suicide after being faced with the possibility of living the rest of his life as a disabled person. For some disabled viewers, the message seemed to be that suicide was preferable to living with a disability. In response to the film, disabled activists on Twitter started the hashtag #MeBeforeEuthanasia. Despite the increasing visibility of disabled people, their lives continue to be open for social and political debate about what counts as a life worth living.

(Un)Productive Bodies

The idea that some lives are not worth living is also highly tied to notions of productivity. The idea that disabled people are unproductive, dependent, or idle has been around for a long time (Rose 2017). Less attention, though, has been paid to how disabled people are exploited and excluded from employment opportunities and social policies. From a historical perspective, the notion that some social groups, including disabled people, are leeches draining the public coffers has led disabled people to disproportionally experience the influence of eugenics, including forced sterilization and institutionalization (Grekul, Krahn, and Odynak 2004).

These judgments around productivity also affect animal lives. For example, in our examination of websites from animal shelters and municipal animal control agencies in Ontario, Canada, we found blatant speciesist language, such as the need "to protect people from animals" and "solve the overpopulation problem." These websites frequently portrayed companion animals as dangerously overpopulated and unable to manage their own lives responsibly, thereby becoming a potential "burden" on society, and thus being in need of sterilization (i.e., spaying and neutering). Moreover, sterilization was framed as a medical procedure that not only helps address a "serious overpopulation problem," but that also "promotes animal health."

Expectations for "farmed" animals' productivity are often the opposite, although this is similarly guided by their perceived "use value." For example, female cows are "artificially inseminated," forced into perpetual milk production, and their babies are taken from them and forbidden to nurse. Some male calves are kept for reproductive purposes only (to make sperm), while many others are killed or kept for veal. If these beings are unable or refuse to fulfill these expectations, they are murdered or left to die. In a similar manner, female chicks may be kept to produce eggs, whereas male chicks are often discarded by the egg industry, since they are seen as useless and unproductive liabilities. Female laying chickens are kept as long as they are useful for egg production; afterward they are either discarded or eaten.

This tendency to evaluate and devalue individual other than human animal lives by given value, appearance, and productivity, coupled with an insistence on the need for their surveillance and management, parallels how disabled humans have historically been the target of similar judgment and social control.

Service Animals: Helpers or Exploited?

Wearing their easily recognizable colorful vests, service animals, usually dogs, are visible examples of the link between human disability and other animals in society. Service animals are trained to provide physical and psychiatric supports to disabled people (Oliver 2016). They engage in a variety of activities, such as turning lights on and off, alerting humans about sounds like smoke alarms, or being a calming force in times of anxiety (DeMello 2021, 201–202). To become a service animal, dogs need to go through an extensive amount of training, typically from an early age, which can cost up to $60,000 per dog (DeMello 2021, 201). The demand is higher than the number of service animals available to work with disabled people (DeMello 2021; MacPherson-Mayor and van Daalen-Smith 2020). In some countries, laws allow disabled people to bring service animals into public and private spaces with the intention of making community participation accessible. Speciesism (and sometimes, breedism) is evident here, however, since only certain animal species are considered to be "eligible" service animals; this is often based on their particular use to disabled humans (Abdulkareem 2021). There is also ableism at play, since visible disabilities (such as using a wheelchair) are privileged in disability legislation; this legislation guides who may use a service animal and where the human and animal must be accommodated in society.

Unfortunately, within these relationships, service animals can sometimes be reduced to their value or functionality for humans (Oliver 2016, 242). There are distinctions made, legally and access-wise, between a companion (or pet), service, support, or therapy animal, based on how humans use them. No one, whether human or animal, should be assigned value because of their supposed utility and functionality. Instead, inspired by an ethics of care, it is worth looking at the important and unique roles and supports that other than human animals bring to human lives and, conversely, humans' moral duty to ensure a quality of life for other animals through our relationships and interactions (Engster 2006).

Service dogs eventually "retire" and become "pets" with their current humans or join another family. Sunaura Taylor's (2017, 219) discussion of her experiences with a "service" dog highlights the fragility and changeability of these type of relationships. Taylor, who is disabled, chose to train her service dog, Bailey, herself to help with tasks such as reaching her keys and accompanying her on outings. In an ironic twist, Bailey fell ill and consequently became disabled as well, thus becoming unable to serve as a service animal. For Taylor, their relationship was built on mutual care. Instead of rejecting or disposing of Bailey when he was no longer reliable for his intended purposes, Taylor embraced a caretaker role, carrying Bailey outside to go the bathroom and back into the house, for instance. Importantly, Taylor describes both a mutual caring and Bailey's enhanced role as a source of emotional and psychiatric support. Taylor, in fact, refers to this relationship as one involving two "vulnerable, interdependent beings of different species learning to understand what the other needs. Awkwardly and imperfectly, we care for each other" (2017, 223). In a similar manner, Birke and Gruen (2022) speak to these bonds formed between disabled humans and other animals. For instance, they mention the cooperative relationship between Della, a blind dog, and Dan, a person with a disability, whose relationship "was meaningful, helping each to overcome obstacles" (38).

On the other hand, it has also been claimed that service animals are "enslaved" by humans (Vegan Feminist Network 2015). There is concern that service animals will disproportionally serve the needs of their disabled human companions and, potentially, become "disposable" later in their lives. While some might claim that this is always a one-sided relationship of care, others have argued that it does not need to be that way by suggesting that relationships of care can be reciprocal (MacPherson-Mayor and van Daalen-Smith 2020; Oliver 2016). Nevertheless, as Devon MacPherson-Mayor and Cheryl van Daalen-Smith (2020) importantly note, "The 'use' of one party in order to emancipate another, is therefore fraught with necessary cautions. There are shared oppressions and rights *at both ends of the service dog leash*" (73; emphasis is in original).

But What Has Religion Got to Do with It?

Many religious traditions articulate a moral and ethical commitment not to inflict suffering onto others, including animals. Take, for instance, Jain monks who sweep the ground gently with a broom as they walk to avoid stepping on insects (Cherry and Sandhu 2013). At the same time, some religious traditions still perpetuate an understanding of human superiority over other animals and justify animal suffering in the name of protecting and feeding humans (Caruana 2020).

The authors of this chapter are not scholars of religion; however, we are deeply engaged in holistic equity work. We locate the key constructions of species and disability as powerfully (and empoweringly) linked to morality, care, ethics, and peace; we know we can learn from religion and religion from us.

More work needs to be done to connect the dots when it comes to the intersections of religion, animality, and disability. For example, consider the current debates about the access of service animals versus emotional companion animals to religious spaces like churches. By aligning to policies that grant special status to service animals, specifically dogs, we run the risk of reproducing a human-created hierarchy of categories of animals, one that shapes animals' access to spaces and their relationships with humans.

A Much-Needed Alliance

At the core of our discussion, at the intersection of disability and species, is a question that is also an opportunity: What can we learn from each other? To work in a deliberately inclusive and collective way, we must address the constructs of species and disability and the impacts these ideologies have on equity-driven issues and the lives of those involved. Why is it offensive to be called an "animal" or "disabled"? Consider first that humans *are*, by the very scientific taxonomy that we ourselves created, animals. Second, "disability" is not a synonym for worth; and, if it is, we are the species constructing this. Species and disability need not be divisive. Difference need not be hierarchical nor problematic.

The work of both critical disability studies and critical animal studies is, at its core, justice-seeking. Many in the field would agree that our end goals are reciprocity, inclusivity, interdependence, coexistence, and justice. Problematic notions such as sentience, intelligence, and dependency are used to justify the marginalization of both other than human animals and disabled humans. Both fields have lessons to teach one another. This is seen, for example, in disability studies discussions about "interdependence, creative ways of mobilizing, and making space for non-normative ways of voicing lived experiences," along with critical animal studies' more "holistic approach, which considers all beings and our environments, through our social relationships and unavoidably interdependent existences" (Santinele Martino and Lindsay 2020, 2–3). We should move away from treating other than human animals as tools and focus on our duties toward one another. Above all, this dialogue between disability and animal rights points to the importance of not measuring one's worth based on notions of utility and productivity nor inequitable and divisive constructions such as species and ability.

References

Abdulkareem, Yusuf. 2021. "Service Animals and Emotional Support Animals: A Distinction That Privileges Physical Disabilities Over Mental and Emotional Disabilities." Master's thesis, Faculty of Law, University of Manitoba.

Aguilera-Carnerero, Carmen, and Margarita Carretero-González. 2021. "The Vegan Myth: The Rhetoric of Online Anti-Veganism." In *The Routledge Handbook of Vegan Studies*, edited by Laura Wright, 354–65. London and New York: Routledge.

Alper, Meryl. 2017. *Giving Voice: Mobile Communication, Disability, and Inequality*. Cambridge, Mass.: MIT Press.

Becker, Howard. 1963. "Outsiders." In *Outsiders: Studies in the Sociology of Deviance*, 1–18. London: Free Press.

Birke, Lynda, and Lori Gruen. 2022. "Mutual Rescue: Disabled Animals and Their Caretakers." *Animal Studies Journal* 11 (1): 37–62. http://dx.doi.org/10.14453/asj/v11i1.2.

Booth, Katie. 2018. "What I Learned About Disability and Infanticide from Peter Singer." *Big Think*, January 11. Accessed January 31, 2023. https://bigthink.com/health/what-i-learned-about-disability-and-infanticide-from-peter-singer/.

Bruges, Trudi. 2018. "Are Disabled Animals Fetishized on Social Media?" Accessed June 14, 2022. https://criphumanimal.org/2018/12/11/disabled-animals-fetishized/.

Carlson, Licia, and Eva Feder Kittay. 2010. "Introduction: Rethinking Philosophical Presumptions in Light of Cognitive Disability." In *Cognitive Disability and Its Challenge to Moral Philosophy*, edited by Eva Feder Kittay and Licia Carlson, 1–24. Malden, Mass.: Wiley-Blackwell.

Carter, Bob, and Nickie Charles. 2013. "Animals, Agency and Resistance." *Journal for the Theory of Social Behaviour* 43 (3): 322–40. https://doi.org/10.1111/jtsb.12019.

Caruana, Louis. 2020. "Different Religions, Different Animal Ethics?" *Animal Frontiers* 10 (1): 8–14. https://doi.org/10.1093/af/vfz047.

Cherry, Ron, and Hardev Sandhu. 2013. "Insects in the Religions of India." *American Entomologist* 59 (4): 200–02. https://doi.org/10.1093/ae/59.4.200.

Cole, Matthew, and Karen Morgan. 2011. "Vegaphobia: Derogatory Discourses of Veganism and the Reproduction of Speciesism in U.K. National Newspapers." *The British Journal of Sociology* 62: 134–53. https://doi.org/10.1111/j.1468-4446.2010.01348.x.

Cowperthwaite, Gabriela, director. 2013. *Blackfish*, DVD. Atlanta: CNN Films and Manny O. Publications.

Davis, Lennard J. 1995. *Enforcing Normalcy: Disability, Deafness, and the Body*. London: Verso.

DeMello, Margo. 2021. *Animals and Society: An Introduction to Human-Animal Studies*. 2nd ed. New York: Columbia University Press.

Drake, Stephen. 2010. "Connecting Disability Rights and Animal Rights—A Really Bad Idea." Accessed August 1, 2022. https://notdeadyet.org/2010/10/connecting-disability-rights-and-animal.html.

Engster, Daniel. 2006. "Care Ethics and Animal Welfare." *Journal of Social Philosophy* 37: 521–36. https://doi.org/10.1111/j.1467-9833.2006.00355.x.

Grekul, Jana, Arvey Krahn, and Dave Odynak. 2004. "Sterilizing the 'Feeble-Minded': Eugenics in Alberta, Canada, 1929–1972." *Journal of Historical Sociology* 17: 358–84. https://doi.org/10.1111/j.1467-6443.2004.00237.x.

Hamilton, Anna. 2017. "What's Up with the Internet's Fascination with Disabled Animals?" Accessed June 14, 2022. https://annaham.net/2017/05/11/whats-up-with-the-internets-fascination-with-disabled-animals/.

Hurn, Samantha. 2012. *Humans and Other Animals: Cross-Cultural Perspectives on Human-Animal Interactions*. London: Pluto Press.

Jenkins, Stephanie, Kelly Struthers Montford, and Chloe Taylor, eds. 2020. *Disability and Animality: Crip Perspectives in Critical Animal Studie*s. London and New York: Routledge.

Lund, Thomas B., Dorothy E.F. McKeegan, Clare Cribbin, and Peter Sandoe. 2016. "Animal Ethics Profiling of Vegetarians, Vegans and Meat-Eaters." *Anthrozoos* 29 (1): 89–106. https://doi.org/10.1080/08927936.2015.1083192.

MacPherson-Mayor, Devon, and Cheryl van Daalen-Smith. 2020. "At Both Ends of the Leash: Preventing Service-Dog Oppression through the Practice of Dyadic-Belonging." *Canadian Journal of Disability Studies* 9 (2): 73–102. https://doi.org/10.15353/cjds.v9i2.626.

Masson, Jeffrey Moussaieff. 2003. *The Pig Who Sang to the Moon: The Emotional World of Farm Animals*. New York: Ballantine Books.

Nibert, David A. 2013. *Animal Oppression and Human Violence: Domesecration, Capitalism, and Global Conflict*. New York: Columbia University Press.

Oliver, Kelly. 2016. "Service Dogs: Between Animal Studies and Disability Studies." *Philosophia* 6 (2): 241–58. https://doi.org/10.1353/phi.2016.0021.

O'Toole, Corbett J. 2015. *Fading Scars: My Queer Disability History*. Fort Worth: Autonomous Press.

Place, Nathan. 2021. "Cow That Escaped from New York Slaughterhouse Gets New Life in Animal Sanctuary." Accessed August 1, 2022. www.independent.co.uk/news/world/americas/cow-escape-new-york-animal-sanctuary-b1983566.html.

Poole, Jennifer, Tania Jivraj, Araxi Arslanian, Kristen Bellows, Sheila Chiasson, Husnia Hakimy, Jessica Pasini, and Jenna Reid. 2012. "Sanism, Mental Health, and Social Work/Education: A Review and Call to Action." *Intersectionalities: A Global Journal of Social Work Analysis, Research, Polity, and Practice* 1: 20–36. https://journals.library.mun.ca/ojs/index.php/IJ/article/view/348.

Reynolds, Joel M. 2022. *The Life Worth Living: Disability, Pain, and Morality*. Minneapolis: University of Minnesota Press.

Rose, Sarah F. 2017. *No Right to Be Idle: The Invention of Disability, 1840s–1930s*. Chapel Hill: University of North Carolina Press.

Ryder, Richard D. 1989. *Animal Revolution: Changing Attitudes towards Speciesism*. Oxford and Cambridge, Mass.: Blackwell.

Santinele Martino, Alan, and Sarah M. Lindsay. 2020. "Introduction: The Intersections of Critical Disability Studies and Critical Animal Studies." *Canadian Journal of Disability Studies* 9 (2): 1–9. https://doi.org/10.15353/cjds.v9i2.623.

Santinele Martino, Alan, and Ann Fudge Schormans. 2018. "When Good Intentions Backfire: University Research Ethics Review and the Intimate Lives of People Labeled with Intellectual Disabilities." *Forum Qualitative Sozialforschung/Forum: Qualitative Social Research* 19 (3). https://doi.org/10.17169/fqs-19.3.3090.

Stewart, Shannon. 2013. "28 Animals That Don't Give a Crap About Their Disabilities." Accessed June 14, 2022. www.buzzfeed.com/shanrstew/28-animals-that-dont-give-a-shit-about-their-disa-7x1g.

Suen, Alison. 2015. *The Speaking Animal: Ethics, Language and the Human-Animal Divide.* London and New York: Rowman & Littlefield.

Sutton, Zoei, and Nik Taylor. 2019. "Managing the Borders: Static/Dynamic Nature and the 'Management' of 'Problem' Species." *Parallax* 25 (4): 379–94. https://doi.org/10.1080/13534645.2020.1731006.

Taylor, Nik, Zoei Sutton, and Rhoda Wilkie. 2018. "A Sociology of Multi-Species Relations." *Journal of Sociology* 54 (4): 463–66. https://doi.org/10.1177/1440783318816214.

Taylor, Sunaura. 2011. "Beasts of Burden: Disability Studies and Animal Rights." *Qui Parle* 19 (2): 191–222. https://doi.org/10.1080/13534645.2020.1731006.

_____. 2013. "Vegans, Freaks, and Animals: Toward a New Table Fellowship." *American Quarterly* 65 (3): 757–64. https://doi.org/10.1353/aq.2013.0042.

_____. 2017. *Beasts of Burden: Animal and Disability Liberation.* New York: The New Press.

_____. 2020. "Animal Crips." In *Disability and Animality: Crip Perspectives in Critical Animal Studies*, edited by Stephanie Jenkins, Kelly Struthers Montford, and Chloë Taylor, 13–34. London: Routledge. https://doi.org/10.4324/9781003014270.

Vegan Feminist Network. 2015. "A Feminist Critique of 'Service' Dogs." Accessed January 31, 2023. http://veganfeministnetwork.com/a-feminist-critique-of-service-dogs/.

Vehmas, Simo. 1999. "Discriminative Assumptions of Utilitarian Bioethics Regarding Individuals with Intellectual Disabilities." *Disability & Society* 14 (1): 37–52. https://doi.org/10.1080/09687599926361.

Young, Stella. (2012) 2022. "I'm Not Your Inspiration, Thank You Very Much." *TEDx-Sydney*, online video, 9:03. www.ted.com/talks/stella_young_i_m_not_your_inspiration_thank_you_very_much?language=en#t-539335.

Other Recommended Resources

Alaimo, Stacy. 2017. "Foreword." In *Disability Studies and the Environmental Humanities: Toward an Eco-Crip Theory*, edited by Sarah Jaquette Ray and Jay Sibara, ix–xvi. Lincoln: University of Nebraska Press.

The Dodo. www.thedodo.com/search?q=disability.

Donaldson, Sue, and Will Kymlicka. 2011. *Zoopolis: A Political Theory of Animal Rights.* Oxford: Oxford University Press.

The Ecoability Collective. www.criticalanimalstudies.org/eco-ability-collective/

KALW Public Media. 2018. "What Are the Connections Between Animal Liberation and Disability Liberation?" Accessed August 21, 2022. www.kalw.org/show/your-call/2018-02-27/what-are-the-connections-between-animal-liberation-and-disability-liberation#stream/0.

Kirksey, Eben. 2015. *Emergent Ecologies.* Durham, N.C. and London: Duke University Press. https://doi.org/10.1215/9780822374800.

Lindsay, Sarah May. 2022. "The 'Problem' of Multispecies Families: Speciesism in Emergency Intimate Partner Violence (I.P.V.) Shelters." *Social Sciences* 11 (6): 242. https://doi.org/10.3390/socsci11060242.

Matsuoka, Atsuko, John Sorenson, T. Mary Graham, and Jasmine Ferreira. 2020. "No Pets Allowed: A Trans-Species Social Justice Perspective to Address Housing Issues for Older Adults and Companion Animals." *Aotearoa New Zealand Social Work* 32 (4): 55–68. https://doi.org/10.11157/anzswj-vol32iss4id793.

Nocella, Anthony J. II, Judy K.C. Bentley, and Janet M. Duncan, eds. 2012. *Earth, Animal, and Disability Liberation: The Rise of the Eco-ability Movement*. New York: Peter Lang.

Nocella, Anthony J. II, and Amber E. George, eds. 2022. *Vegans on Speciesism and Ableism: Eco-ability Voices for Disability and Animal Justice*. New York: Peter Lang.

7 Human Beings and Animals

Same, Other, Indistinct?

Matthew Calarco

Introduction

One of the chief aims of this volume is to encourage more careful consideration of the nature of animals and our interactions with them. This is a crucial task, for how we think about and interact with animals has profound implications for our lives and theirs. As the chapters in this section in particular demonstrate, our standard, common sense ideas about the nature of animals have been challenged by a variety of religious and cultural traditions, critical theoretical frameworks, and developments in contemporary science. In addition, these chapters and the ones that follow investigate some of the problems that attend our standard ways of interacting with animals, whether in the form of eating them, hunting them, using them in religious rituals, or employing them as objects of scientific research.

Now, if it is widely agreed among animal studies scholars that our standard ideas about animals and how to treat them are unsatisfactory, it is far less obvious what set of alternative ideas and practices should replace them. My aim in this chapter is to introduce the reader to three general trends that have emerged in the interdisciplinary field of animal studies in recent years that offer a way of responding to this query. The title of my contribution names the basic rubrics under which those three approaches are presented: Are animals the *same* as human beings? Are animals something fundamentally *other* than human beings? Are human beings and animals ultimately *indistinct*? In what follows, I introduce each of these approaches and highlight its respective strengths and weaknesses.

I will not, however, argue that one of the approaches is the correct one and that the other two should be abandoned. Rather, I suggest viewing each framework as having its own value and importance, despite whatever shortcomings it might have. Furthermore, I believe it is important not just to *think* about these various approaches and make judgments about them at an intellectual level; it is far more important to *inhabit* them, to live with and inside them for a while, and to learn to see the world using the lenses they provide. For these approaches are not just abstract conceptual frameworks—they point us toward another way of life that, if adopted, would have far-reaching implications for our everyday actions and decisions and for the lives of animals.

In order to appreciate the positive contributions and aims of each of the approaches discussed here, it will be helpful first to say a bit more about the common sense ideas about human beings and animals against which they are reacting. I mentioned in the opening paragraph that much of the work in this book and in other recent writing on animals has challenged our standard ideas about animal existence and the practices that

DOI: 10.4324/9781003324157-10

reflect and grow out of these ideas. But what, precisely, are these standard ideas? Here we will have to simplify things somewhat, but we will not be far off the mark if we describe standard conceptions of how human beings and animals relate as being *binary* and *hierarchical* in nature.

"Binary" denotes a strict opposition in which human beings are located on one side of a line or boundary and all animals reside on the opposite side of that limit. Thus, in trying to differentiate human beings from animals, it is common to claim that human beings have a number of traits, properties, and abilities that animals generally lack, including such things as the ability to use language, the presence of culture, an awareness and understanding of death, the capacity for empathy, and so on. In particular religious traditions, the differentiator may be a uniquely human kind of proximity to the divine (for example, the biblical concept of only humans having been created in the image of God) or a unique ability to achieve a transcendent state (for example, the Buddhist notion that only a human being can achieve enlightenment or spiritual awakening).

"Hierarchical" indicates that these sorts of oppositions between human beings and animals are thought to justify ranking human beings over animals, with human beings being understood to possess more (or possibly exclusive) value, importance, and significance in a variety of registers. The violent treatment of animals is often justified by using such hierarchical claims. For example, in the contemporary Western philosophical tradition, it is commonly argued that killing animals is not an ethical or legal issue because animals are supposedly not aware of or do not understand what death is, and hence their deaths do not matter in the same way that human deaths do.

Same

If we bear in mind some of the main ideas examined thus far in the previous chapters, we will be primed to respond that this way of opposing human beings to animals and ranking the former over the latter is rather untenable. For one thing, it is not altogether clear that animals can be cleanly and clearly differentiated from human beings along the lines of language, culture, awareness of death, self-consciousness, and other markers suggested by the Western philosophical tradition; in many cases, animals appear quite clearly to manifest some of these capacities and characteristics (and in some cases, to an astonishingly high degree). This counter-proposition is the central contention of those thinkers and activists who stress the relative *identity* or *sameness* of human beings and animals, an approach that dominates in the fields of animal law and animal ethics. The basic argumentative strategy here is to establish continuity between human beings and animals in ways that are ethically and legally salient, and then to develop arguments that show how such human-animal sameness should, in principle, lead to providing animals with the same ethical standing and legal protections that human beings have. In an explicit religious context, this kind of argument might point to different criteria for identity—say, being creatures of the same God instead of sharing sentience—but would take the same basic form of arguing for continuity, sameness, and likeness as grounds for concern.

According to this approach, what we referred to earlier as binary and hierarchical thinking about animals is an instance of *speciesism*, a prejudice that leads us to believe that members of the species *Homo sapiens* have more moral worth than other animals. The term speciesism gains its "ism" from its resemblance to other, similar discriminatory "ism"s, such as racism, sexism, ageism, ableism, and so on. All of these "ism"s are prejudices against a group based on unjustified and unpersuasive criteria that suggest members of that group should have lesser or no normative standing compared to non-members.

Theorists and activists who critique speciesism often trace its origins back to ancient Greek thought and the early Christian tradition, both of which emphasize human exceptionalism and human rank over animals in a "great chain of being" that places divine beings and humans at the top of the chain and animals, plants, and other nonhuman beings at the bottom (Lovejoy [1936] 1964). While theorists who critique speciesism acknowledge the existence and influence of a handful of pro-animal thinkers throughout history, a thoroughgoing and persuasive challenge to speciesism is often understood to emerge only with the Darwinian revolution in modern biology (for a contrasting account, see Preece 2011). By establishing a fundamental continuity between the evolution of human and animal life through both theoretical and empirical means, Darwin and modern evolutionary theory undercut one of the chief pillars of speciesism, namely, the idea that there are absolute breaks in kind between invariant species. In an evolutionary context, traditional claims about purportedly unique human characteristics and uncrossable boundaries between human beings and other animal species are replaced by a framework that emphasizes shared anatomical, physiological, and cognitive roots and that admits differences between human beings and animals only in terms of degree. The image of human beings we receive from evolutionary theory is thus one in which human beings fit squarely within and at the very late edge of a multipronged branch on the tree of life. In biologist Stephen Jay Gould's illustrative phrase, human beings should be seen as a "tiny, late-arising twig on life's enormously arborescent bush" (Gould 1994, 91).

Once the evolutionary continuity of human beings and animals is established, the door is then swung open for reconsidering the normative status of animals. For if human beings and animals can be shown to be identical (or even roughly similar) in relevant ways, then logic necessitates that they should receive identical (or at least roughly similar) consideration. This logical principle, often called the *principle of equal consideration*, has been used to combat discrimination and unequal treatment in a variety of human institutions and practices (Francione 2002; for an examination of the significance of these ideas in a Christian theological context, see Deane-Drummond 2014; Johnson 2014). Sameness theorists aim to extend this principle to our interactions with animals, arguing that there is no compelling reason to override the principle of equal consideration and to exclude animals who are relevantly similar to human beings from the moral and legal community. But as pro-animal thinkers point out, this is precisely what we do on a regular basis in such contexts as factory farming and medical experimentation, where the interests of animals are routinely overridden in favor of our own (sometimes trivial) interests. Thus, we kill animals for food when we could feed ourselves equally well on non-animal foodstuffs; we sometimes perform painful, invasive experiments on animals that lead to little or no benefit for human or animal welfare, and so on. Identity theorists believe that once we begin to see the utterly arbitrary and outmoded nature of most of our attitudes and practices involving animals, we might—indeed ought to—begin to think about how best to revise them.

Although the sameness framework is sometimes characterized by critics as being extreme or radical, it is, in fact, fairly conservative in its stance toward the ethical and legal norms that guide the dominant culture. Theorists and activists who employ this approach are not attempting to revolt entirely against traditional norms but are instead suggesting that the norms to which most of us are *already* committed logically entail their being extended to animals (Engel 2003). This approach does not call, then, for a fundamental change in our ethical or legal beliefs, only consistency in how they are applied. And consistent application of these norms, the sameness approach argues, leads inevitably to the conclusion that animals should be included within the boundaries of the moral community in more or less new ways.

But which animals? And what are the criteria animals must meet in order to be categorized as relevantly similar and receive similar normative consideration? The answers to such questions vary depending on which variant of the sameness approach is adopted. For philosophers like Peter Singer ([1975] 2002) and Gary Francione (2002), the most important criterion for inclusion in the moral community is sentience, or the capacity to experience and feel pain and pleasure and to be able to express preferences for one state over the other. For others such as philosophers Tom Regan (1983) and Paola Cavalieri (2001) or legal theorist Steven Wise (2000), the criterion is subjectivity and includes such capacities as acting intentionally and being self-aware. Depending on the framework at issue, then, the kinds of animals who will be considered full members of the moral community will differ slightly, for not all animals exhibit sentience, subjectivity, and other such traits in a visible or verifiable way.

The merits of the sameness approach are evident at both the intellectual and the practical level. First, there is a logical persuasiveness to the idea that like beings should be given like consideration. And with the extensive body of empirical information we have about the rich subjective lives of various species of animals (see Chapter 2 on "Animal Consciousness and Cognition" by Robert W. Mitchell and Mark A. Krause in this volume), it does seem blatantly unjust and arbitrary to deny them the same consideration we would typically grant our fellow human subjects. Second, the sameness approach is not just intellectually compelling, but it is also practically effective in many ways. Almost all mainstream animal rights and animal welfare organizations are founded on some version of the sameness approach, and their campaigns often appeal to the sorts of principles and ideas surveyed here. This is especially visible in the longstanding legal struggle for animal rights, which is premised on the notion that many animals fulfill the criteria for legal personhood and should thus be liberated from having property status. Notably for this volume, sameness based legal arguments presented by Steven Wise and the Nonhuman Rights Project in their efforts to establish legal personhood for animals through the defense of an elephant named Happy currently in captivity were supported not only by an amicus brief from philosophers but ones from Christian theologians and Jewish Studies scholars as well (Nonhuman Rights Project n.d.). In these ways and others, the sameness approach has been a crucial, widely employed, and influential way of thinking about human and animal existence and relationships.

These evident strengths also carry with them, however, some potential problems. Depending on which criteria are determined to be normatively relevant, the sameness approach can also be used to *deny* moral standing to a broad swath of animal species. For example, the criteria for having standing as a legal person are fairly demanding and include such things as having desires, being able to act intentionally, and possessing a conscious sense of self (Wise 2000). While some animal species, such as primates and cetaceans, arguably meet these standards, many animal species probably do not—which effectively would reinforce and justify their status as property rather than persons. Similarly, with ethical frameworks that seek to establish animal rights, the common criterion used to determine moral belonging—that of being a subject-of-a-life—is also not universally present in uncontroversial ways among many animal species. Regan himself, who is the most influential advocate of the rights approach, acknowledges that only mammals one year of age and older clearly meet the standard of being a subject-of-a-life with intrinsic value and rights (Regan 1983, 78).

It might be the case that the sameness approach is strategic—that is, it might be hoped that by extending rights to a select group of animals who are very close to human beings in relevant ways, such rights will continue to cascade like falling dominoes across the rest of the animal kingdom. Perhaps that is a good strategy, and maybe something like this broad extension of rights and consideration might take place in the decades to come. But at some point, the sameness strategy reaches a critical limit, for there will always be animals who are so far different from human beings in the relevant ways that they will never meet the criteria for moral inclusion. Furthermore, the exclusive focus on bringing animals into the boundaries of the moral community fails to consider the rest of the non-animal, more-than-human world, leaving these other entities in the position of being no more than property under the law and outside the scope of moral consideration.

Other

These kinds of concerns about differences are at the heart of the second approach we will examine: the approach that sees animals as "other." Like the sameness approach, theorists and activists concerned with difference and otherness seek to challenge traditional binary and hierarchical accounts of human and animal relations, but the respective strategies are rather different. Of primary importance for theorists who focus on otherness is rejecting the hierarchical aspects of traditional ways of thinking about and interacting with animals.

If we consider the idea of hierarchy more carefully, there do not seem to be any very compelling reasons for why differences per se among beings should lead to one group or individual having higher ranking or more value over another group or individual. For example, we can make a fairly clear distinction between people who have brown hair and those who do not, or between those who are at least five feet tall and those who are not. We would presumably find it rather arbitrary, though, if someone argued that people who have brown hair or who are taller than five feet count more than those who lack these traits; there should be some compelling reason given for *why* such differences entail having more value.

We could, of course, make the same point about many animals. Although sameness theorists persuasively argue that some animals and human beings share important traits, animals remain in many ways rather different from human beings. For example, we presumably experience the world in ways that are very different from the way most animals do; similarly, human beings engage in all sorts of activities that animals for the most part do not or cannot engage in (and vice versa). But such differences need not lead us to denigrate animals or see them as having lesser worth; such differences could, instead, be seen as something to be affirmed, even admired and celebrated. Indeed, such differences might be viewed in a theological register as evidence of the richness of God's creation or as different aspects or modes of God's existence. Much as the biodiversity and richness of life is understood as being essential to planetary flourishing, this approach would have us see the multiplicity of human and animal lives as generally being a good thing. In brief, then, difference thinkers do not want to erase differences between human beings and animals, or reduce these two groups to a unified biological kingdom (*Animalia* or *Meta-zoa*), where all beings are effectively the same, similar, or identical. On this approach, differences are generally to be respected and engaged with rather than denied (even if they are not affirmed and embraced in every instance). The ethical task here is to learn to respect and affirm others in their differences from us, not just in the ways they resemble us or are identical with us.

But how, precisely, one might ask, are we to understand otherness and differences here? Are animals other at the level of individuals? At the level of communities? At the level of species? As with the sameness approach, the answer to such fine-grained questions will depend on the particular theorist or tradition examined. Among Western thinkers who stress the otherness of animals, philosopher Jacques Derrida is perhaps the most influential (Derrida and Roudinesco 2004; Derrida 2008). His work belongs to a line of philosophers who tend to stress the radical otherness of individual human beings. For these philosophers, the main idea is that each human individual is an experiencing subject with their own point of view on the world, a center of experience that remains inaccessible in principle to every other subject. In other words, I will never see or experience the world in precisely the way you do (and vice versa); your subjective existence is, in principle, inaccessible to me and remains unique to you. Ethical life, then, must begin from the fact that despite our common belonging to the human species, a particular nation, a shared region, or other such set, we remain irreducibly singular beings and should be respected and cared for as such.

One of the significant features of Derrida's work is to consider the implications of extending this sort of ethical respect for singularity to animals. What if we were to think about and relate to animals not just as "animals" or even as "cats," "dogs," "crows," "octopuses," and so on, but as singular animals with their own unique subjective lives and who are something more than members of and representatives of their species? Such an approach would suggest that we need to consider more carefully the ways in which general categories are used both to justify violence toward animals as well as the limits of talking about animal rights in general (rather than our responsibilities to this particular other living being).

Now, if the differences between individuals (whether human or animal) who have their own, unique subjective experiences of the world give rise to radical differences, how should we think about otherness and difference at the collective level—for example, between different species or between the human species and other animal species? Let us, again, consider Derrida's approach. Derrida argues that traditional oppositional distinctions between human beings and animals are too clunky to be workable (Derrida and Roudinesco 2004, 63–64). To speak about all animals as if they have some shared essence leads to reducing the richness and variety of animal life and encourages thinking about animals as if they were unrelated to human beings in any meaningful way. We could make the same point about referring to all human beings as if they shared some simple essence that makes them human; such a way of speaking—while important in some contexts as a means of contesting interhuman forms of discrimination—tends to gloss over the richness and variety among human beings, say along the lines of gender differences or differences in lived experience, and so on.

Now, this way of thinking about difference and otherness might seem to imply that it is untenable to talk about a distinction between human beings and animals, which is precisely Derrida's conclusion. But he still maintains that there are significant differences (in the plural) between human beings and animals (Derrida and Roudinesco 2004, 66). Here, though, the borders that run between and among human beings and the wide variety of animals who inhabit the earth are understood to be multiple and complex and require us to develop correspondingly rich and varied concepts to negotiate that terrain. For Derrida and other theorists who take a similar approach, the theoretical task is not to eliminate the difference between human beings and animals but to refine, complicate, and multiply difference*s* (again, in the plural) so as to do justice to the richness of both human and animal life (Derrida 2008, 31). Notably, Derrida finds the resources for this task in a wide range of Western philosophical and religious sources, and he engages in an extended analysis of the biblical book of Genesis in developing his position.

At the level of practice, the focus on the otherness of animals is compatible with a number of ethical and political strategies. Some theorists and activists, especially in the pro-animal feminist tradition, emphasize the importance of developing care and empathy for animals and learning to love and respect them in their otherness (Donovan and Adams 1996). Other theorists focus on developing maximal respect for animals and interrogating the contradictions involved in extending human-oriented rights to animals (Wolfe 2003). Whatever the concrete strategies pursued might be, the chief strength of the otherness approach is that it challenges simple oppositional distinctions between human beings and animals without allowing that stance to collapse into a reductive view of the identity of human beings and animals. These theorists maintain, no doubt correctly, that animal otherness and differences do not constitute a barrier to caring for and respecting them. To the contrary, any ethics and politics worthy of the name must learn to extend concern across differences and to engage with others—whether human or animal—on their own terms.

Indistinct

Despite its theoretical and ethical sophistication, the otherness approach leaves us with a lingering problem: it still appears committed to the idea that human beings are fundamentally different from animals. Thus, even though this approach would have us note that animals are not to be thought of as belonging to a single homogeneous group, it still seems to maintain that human beings are different enough from all other animals to warrant maintaining *something* of a distinction between these groups. Thus, Derrida can state that he is unsatisfied with a simplistic distinction between human and animal but still insists in a rather traditional way that "the gap between the 'higher primates' and man is . . . abyssal" (Derrida and Roudinesco 2004, 66). In this way, the difference approach risks leaving us largely on the same terrain as that of the tradition: namely, that of trying to discern what it is that is supposed to make us uniquely human, but now in a more subtle, complicated, and refined way (for a fuller reading of Derrida on this issue, see Still 2015).

What if, however, we turned away entirely from this project of trying to determine what makes humans distinctive (Agamben 2004)? What if, instead, we were to turn our attention to thinking about sameness and otherness, identities, and differences, along other axes and toward other ends (Calarco 2015)? Such refusal and redirection are the quintessential gestures of the indistinction approach to thinking about human beings and animals. This approach asks us to give up our investment in the longstanding project of distinguishing human beings from animals and turn our attention elsewhere.

Furthermore, it asks us to reconsider the ways in which animals are aligned with human beings in the sameness framework. As noted previously, many pro-animal thinkers argue that progress in human-animal relations depends on demonstrating that animals are "like us," which is to say that animals show evidence of possessing quintessentially human capacities and traits like subjectivity and self-awareness. But, why, we might ask, should our thinking always proceed in this direction, starting from human traits and then moving outward? Why not proceed in the opposite direction and examine the various ways in which human beings are, in surprising and profound ways, *like animals*? Here, of course, the alignment with animals is not intended to be degrading to human beings, as in those contexts where marginalized human beings are called "animals" in an attempt to dehumanize and devalue them (Boisseron 2018; Jackson 2020; Taylor 2017). Rather, indistinction theorists seek to affirm linkages between human beings and animals that have been traditionally disavowed or denied: our shared mortality, our similar forms of embodiment, our common vulnerability, and our shared exposure to passions and affects (emotional responses) such as love and joy. Such things belong exclusively neither to human beings nor animals but to "the whole creation . . . groaning together," as the Apostle Paul describes it (Rom. 8:22); they indicate our shared condition as earthbound beings who are exposed to what necessity and fate bring our way. To affirm human-animal indistinction is thus a matter of saying "yes" to this shared condition and seeing a worthwhile life as one built through experimenting with the myriad relations that constitute this condition.

This affirmative and experimental stance is another one of the key characteristics of the indistinction approach. Here the emphasis is placed not just on abstaining from practices that cause animals pain or death (which, to be sure, is an important goal) or respecting the otherness of animals (which is also a laudable practice); instead, the goal is to reconstitute healthier, more interesting, and more beautiful relations with our animal kin. To this end, many theorists and activists who adopt this orientation see pro-animal discourse and practice as something closer to an ethological field experiment for living anew and in common with animal life (Buchanan, Bastian, and Chrulew 2018). Such experiments can take a range of forms, from the long-term experiences of Joe Hutto living with a herd of wild mule deer (Hutto 2014), to Craig Foster's remarkable friendship with an octopus (Ehrlich and Reed 2020), to Donna Haraway's notoriously complicated relationship with her dog companion Cayenne (Haraway 2003), to Thom van Dooren's studies of bird species that are on the brink of extinction (van Dooren 2014), or (more basically) with the wide variety of domestic, liminal, and wild animals we might encounter in our own milieus (Donaldson and Kymlicka 2011; Wolch 1998). The ultimate point of this sort of ethological practice is not primarily to accumulate scientific knowledge about the animals encountered but to re-form our relations with them, and to allow those relations to transform our sense of who we are at the individual, collective, and environmental levels. It is here, along these other axes of relation formed in experimental contexts, that new categories and novel ideas about sameness and otherness emerge—concepts that help us reorient ourselves in the world and that do so in view of doing justice to our relations with our more-than-human kin.

There are, however, potential problems involved in adopting this approach to thinking about and transforming human-animal relations. The theorists and activists who take up such projects, while typically intending to develop better relations with animals, neither carry with them nor proffer clear normative guidance; consequently, ethological experiments of this sort can easily go awry, unwittingly repeating practices of domination or exclusion (Giraud 2019). Furthermore, there are fundamental limits to the sorts of encounters and relations we might form with certain animals (despite the fact that our actions clearly affect the entire planet in a variety of direct and indirect ways). Not only are there many animals who remain inaccessible and entirely unknown to us, but there are countless species and individuals who flourish best when we refrain from going near them and grant them their relative independence from us. Thus, even if we acknowledge that there are no fixed and ready-made distinctions between us and other animals, making certain differentiations in view of our co-flourishing might be required. The ultimate point of the indistinction approach, though, is that the relative forms of sameness and otherness that are salient to the project of co-flourishing are not pre-fixed along some imaginary, invariant human/animal axis but can only be discerned in and through the process of inhabiting experiments in living well with our planetary kin.[1]

Note

1 I thank Dave Aftandilian and Aaron Gross for their many helpful and substantive suggestions on an earlier draft of this chapter.

References

Agamben, Giorgio. 2004. *The Open: Man and Animal.* Translated by Kevin Attell. Stanford, Calif.: Stanford University Press.

Boisseron, Bénédicte. 2018. *Afro-Dog: Blackness and the Animal Question.* New York: Columbia University Press.

Buchanan, Brett, Michelle Bastian, and Matthew Chrulew. 2018. "Introduction: Field Philosophy and Other Experiments." *Parallax* 24 (4): 383–91.

Calarco, Matthew. 2015. *Thinking Through Animals: Identity, Difference, Indistinction.* Stanford, Calif.: Stanford University Press.

Cavalieri, Paola. 2001. *The Animal Question: Why Nonhuman Animals Deserve Human Rights.* New York: Oxford University Press.

Deane-Drummond, Celia. 2014. *The Wisdom of the Liminal: Evolution and Other Animals in Human Becoming.* Grand Rapids, Mich.: Eerdmans.

Derrida, Jacques. 2008. *The Animal That Therefore I Am.* Edited by Marie-Louise Mallet. Translated by David Wills. New York: Fordham University Press.

_____, and Elisabeth Roudinesco. 2004. *For What Tomorrow . . .: A Dialogue.* Translated by Jeff Fort. Stanford, Calif.: Stanford University Press.

Donaldson, Sue, and Will Kymlicka. 2011. *Zoopolis: A Political Theory of Animal Rights.* New York: Oxford University Press.

Donovan, Josephine, and Carol Adams, eds. 1996. *Beyond Animal Rights: A Feminist Caring Ethic for the Treatment of Animals.* New York: Continuum.

Ehrlich, Pippa, and James Reed, directors. 2020. *My Octopus Teacher*, Film, Netflix. www.netflix.com/title/81045007.

Engel, Mylan. 2003. "The Immorality of Eating Meat." In *The Moral Life: An Introductory Reader in Ethics and Literature*, edited by Louis Pojman, 856–90. New York: Oxford University Press.

Francione, Gary L. 2002. *Introduction to Animal Rights: Your Child or the Dog?* Philadelphia, Pa.: Temple University Press.

Giraud, Eva H. 2019. *What Comes After Entanglement? Activism, Anthropocentrism, and an Ethics of Exclusion.* Durham, N.C.: Duke University Press.

Gould, Stephen Jay. 1994. "The Evolution of Life on Earth." *Scientific American* 271 (4): 84–91.

Haraway, Donna J. 2003. *Companion Species Manifesto.* Chicago, Ill.: Prickly Paradigm Press.

Hutto, Joe. 2014. *Touching the Wild: Living with the Mule Deer of Deadman Gulch.* New York: Skyhorse.

Jackson, Zakiyyah Iman. 2020. *Becoming Human: Matter and Meaning in an Antiblack World.* New York: New York University Press.

Johnson, Elizabeth A. 2014. *Ask the Beasts: Darwin and the God of Love.* London: Bloomsbury.

Lovejoy, Arthur O. (1936) 1964. *The Great Chain of Being: A Study of the History of an Idea.* Cambridge, Mass.: Harvard University Press.

Nonhuman Rights Project. n.d. "Client: Happy." Accessed June 7, 2022. www.nonhumanrights. org/client-happy/.

Preece, Rod. 2011. *Animals and Nature: Cultural Myths, Cultural Realities.* Vancouver: University of British Columbia Press.

Regan, Tom. 1983. *The Case for Animal Rights.* Berkeley: University of California Press.

Singer, Peter. (1975) 2002. *Animal Liberation.* New York: Ecco.

Still, Judith. 2015. *Derrida and Other Animals: The Boundaries of the Human.* Edinburgh: Edinburgh University Press.

Taylor, Sunaura. 2017. *Beasts of Burden: Animal and Disability Liberation.* New York: The New Press.

van Dooren, Thom. 2014. *Flight Ways: Life and Loss at the Edge of Extinction.* New York: Columbia University Press.

Wise, Steven M. 2000. *Rattling the Cage: Toward Legal Rights for Animals.* Cambridge, Mass.: Perseus.

Wolch, Jennifer. 1998. "Zoöpolis." In *Animal Geographies: Places, Politics, and Identity in the Nature-Culture Borderlands,* edited by Jennifer Wolch and Jody Emel, 119–38. London: Verso.

Wolfe, Cary. 2003. *Animal Rites: American Culture, the Discourse of Species, and Posthumanism.* Chicago, Ill.: University of Chicago Press.

Other Recommended Resources

Balcombe, Jonathan. 2010. *Second Nature: The Inner Lives of Animals.* New York: Palgrave Macmillan.

Cullen, Jason. 2021. *Deleuze and Ethology: A Philosophy of Entangled Life.* New York: Bloomsbury Academic.

Despret, Vinciane. 2021. *Living as a Bird.* Translated by Helen Morrison. Medford, Mass.: Polity.

Fowler, Karen Joy. 2013. *We Are All Completely Beside Ourselves.* New York: Putnam.

Haraway, Donna J. 2008. *When Species Meet.* Minneapolis: University of Minnesota Press.

Herzog, Werner, director. 2005. *Grizzly Man,* DVD. Santa Monica, Calif.: Lions Gate Home Entertainment.

Marchesini, Roberto, and Marco Celentano. 2021. *Critical Ethology and Post-Anthropocentric Ethics: Beyond the Separation between Humanities and Life Sciences.* Cham: Springer.

O'Connell, Caitlin. 2021. *Wild Rituals: 10 Lessons Animals Can Teach Us About Connection, Community, and Ourselves.* San Francisco, Calif.: Chronicle Prism.

Plumwood, Val. 2000. "Being Prey." *Utne Reader,* July–August: 56–61.

Part II
Religious Practices and Presences

8 Learning to Walk Softly

Intersecting Insect Lifeworlds in Everyday Buddhist Monastic Life

Lina Verchery

從朝寅旦直至暮，一切眾生自迴護。若於足下喪其形，願汝即時生淨土。
From dawn until dusk, all living creatures seek to protect their lives.
Should you be crushed under my foot, may you be instantly reborn in the Buddha's Pure Land.
　　　　—verse recited to insects when walking in tall grass or driving on country roads

The Problem with Shoes

In his classic work on compassion training, the eighth-century C.E. Buddhist monk Śāntideva asks, "Where is there hide to cover the whole world? The wide world can be covered with hide enough for a pair of shoes alone" (Śāntideva 1995, 35). As we move through life, we bump up against things that hurt us, both physically and emotionally. Since there is not enough fabric to make the whole world soft, we simply must protect our own two feet.

But the problem with shoes is they sometimes protect *too* well. The thick soles that prevent injury and discomfort also render us impervious to what lies underfoot. As the Buddhist nuns during my fieldwork would remind me, this applies not just in the literal sense to the countless plants and insects we unknowingly crush with each step but also to the way we move through life in general. In the interest of self-preservation, we protect ourselves from whatever might frighten or hurt us, but in so doing we often frighten and hurt that which—and those whom—we encounter. We are thus faced with a dilemma: should we care for others at risk to ourselves or care for ourselves at the risk of others?

In this chapter, I propose a third option, inspired by fieldwork research I conducted while living with a group of Buddhist nuns in Taiwan. Rather than choose between the pain (to oneself) of walking barefoot through life, so to speak, and the harm (to others) of wearing shoes, we might instead learn to walk softly. Virtuosic rock climbers offer a vivid image of what this might look like. As they scale impossibly craggy vertical cliffs, their feet do not imperviously strike the rock but wrap around it. Gripping like hands, they mold and adapt to the contours underfoot. This is not painless; rock climbing shoes have deliberately thin soles, allowing climbers to feel every sharp edge, hard lump, or awkward crevice. This is far from the comfort of an ordinary shoe, but the sensitivity it enables creates a relationship with the ground. Being able to *feel* is what makes this connection possible.

This chapter explores how a group of Buddhist nuns aspire to walk softly alongside insects over the course of a typical day at the monastery. Rather than focus on how doctrinal ideas *about* animals shape Buddhist practice, we instead look at how actual

DOI: 10.4324/9781003324157-12

insect encounters force the nuns to stretch, challenge, and deepen their embodied moral practice by cultivating skills like patience, attention, and generosity. Undergirding these encounters is a recognition of difference. Rather than force bugs to fit into the human world, the nuns adjust their world to make space for bugs. Like a rock climber who adapts her foot to the terrain, walking softly can involve compromise, discomfort, and vulnerability, but in so doing it also enables connection.

Intersecting Insect Lifeworlds

In a famous essay, Thomas Nagel (1974) argues that humans cannot know what it is like to be a bat. That is, an animal's subjective experience of the world—what Giorgio Agamben (2004), drawing on the work of Baltic German biologist Jakob von Uexküll, calls their "lifeworld" (*Umwelt*)—is shaped by the unique elements that are important for that particular creature. Although a tick inhabits the same world as we do, her subjective experience of that world—that is, her *lifeworld*—is vastly different from our own. Whereas we humans pay attention to things like sounds, colors, or words, the tick's lifeworld is dominated by smell (specifically, the smell of butyric acid excreted by mammals), touch (strands of fur help her sightlessly navigate to her food source), and temperature (thirty-seven degrees Celsius indicates she has found blood). A tick's lifeworld is so radically different from our own that we will never experience the world quite as she does, nor vice versa.

But the fact that lifeworlds are different does not mean they are disconnected. Consider the spider and the fly:

> The spider knows nothing about the fly, nor can it measure its client as a tailor does before sewing his suit. And yet it determines the length of the stitches in its web according to the dimensions of the fly's body, and it adjusts the resistance of the threads in exact proportion to the force of impact of the fly's body in flight. . . . The two perceptual worlds of the fly and the spider are absolutely uncommunicating, and yet so perfectly in tune.
>
> (Agamben 2004, 41–42)

Although the spider has no access to the lifeworld of the fly, nor the fly to that of the spider, the web is a place where their lifeworlds *intersect*. The web is a kind of wordless contact point, like the interface of the rock climber's sole and the surface of the rock.

Over the course of a typical day at the monastery, the nuns take pains to notice such points of intersection. Observing their practice—not merely through the lens of the human lifeworld but through the lens of where human and insect lifeworlds meet—helps us notice the many insights that arise from living alongside and attending to insects. The practice of walking softly, the nuns insist, not only brings benefit to the insects but also to the humans; according to the nuns, walking softly helps one learn to walk better.

A Day in the Life(Worlds) of Buddhists and Bugs

The Buddhist monastic day begins in the middle of the night. Although the official wakeup is around 3:15 am, in my experience, it was not unusual to be awoken even earlier by a strange breeze wafting a few inches from my face. I would groggily open my eyes to find one of my dorm-mates standing above me, swinging large arcs in the air with a billowing net of specially crafted gauze. Whenever a flying insect got into the dorm, this net was used to gently catch and release them. The rigorous monastic schedule provisioned less than five hours for sleep each night, and I marveled at the devotion of my dorm-mates who readily interrupted those precious few hours to ensure that bugs trapped inside found their way back out.

This paled in comparison, however, to the effort required a few hours later. Each morning, we drove up a steep and winding mountain path leading from the dormitory to the Buddha Hall, where morning ceremonies would begin at 4:00 am. Especially in winter, we often faced pouring rain, which flooded this path with worms, slugs, and insects of all kinds. It would ordinarily be impossible to drive without crushing these creatures, but the monastery residents devised a clever solution. Each day, one person would serve as vanguard, walking ahead of the car with a strong flashlight to inspect the road. If she spotted a bug, she gave a signal, and two others promptly jumped out of the vehicle wielding a soft broom and dustpan with which to gingerly relocate the creature to the side of the road. This painstaking process would continue for the whole journey up the mountain, with the car lurching behind at a snail's pace.

Mid-morning in the Buddhist monastery is dedicated to preparing lunch—the only meal of the day—and whenever one deals with food, one must also deal with bugs. It was not uncommon to discover mealworms in the rice, moths in the flour, or tiny worms burrowed inside the fruits and vegetables. All such insects were removed one by one and carefully released outside, with consideration given to whether they might prefer low grass or a leafy tree, sun or shade, moisture or dry soil, and so on.

Before any food can be consumed, moreover, it must first be ritually offered on the Buddha altar. But this, too, presented a problem. The fresh foods that adorn these altars—saucy stir-fries, steaming rice, and sweet, juicy fruit—naturally attract ants. The latter, cleverly anticipating the timely daily delivery of these delicacies, would lay pheromone trails leading right up to the altar and could quickly infest the whole area, making it impossible to clean without injuring them. But the nuns developed an ingenious method to deter the ants of their own accord. Each offering was placed above a shallow dish of water, creating a natural moat. After a bit of searching, the ants would realize they could not cross the moat and turned back, leaving their pheromone trail to naturally dissipate behind them.

Afternoons in the monastery are for outdoor labor, especially gathering firewood to heat the evening's bath water. Residents avoid breaking branches off trees, lest they disturb the insects who live there, and instead gather wood that has naturally fallen to the ground. But before this wood can be burned, each piece must be meticulously inspected for insects. While assisting the nuns with this task, I noticed how years of practice had fine-tuned their eyes. Where I saw nothing, they routinely detected a tiny hole on a branch, a tunnel burrowed just below the bark, or some fine silk-like threads in a tiny crevice woven by a moth. Such pieces would be carefully returned to the forest, even if it meant a bit less hot water for us that evening.

Each monastic day ends with chanting and meditation. As dusk descends, it is not uncommon for mosquitoes to venture into the meditation hall, perhaps delighted by the unusual stillness of the humans sitting inside. Rather than see mosquitoes as a nuisance, however, the nuns regard them as helpful for meditation training. If your mind and body can remain undisturbed while a mosquito buzzes in your ear, it is a sure sign of advanced meditative concentration! The nuns also see such encounters as an opportunity to practice compassion. Rather than recoil at a mosquito's bite, they willingly offer their blood to the hungry insects. They would encourage each other to generate compassion while watching the mosquito's tiny belly fill with red blood and to make a wish that this meal might provide her the sustenance needed for her own journey toward liberation.

Learning to Walk Softly

While some of these practices may seem extreme, I suggest they contain insights we all might learn from, even if we never set foot in a Buddhist monastery. First, walking softly accepts and accommodates difference. Because insect lifeworlds are so radically different from our own, compassion sometimes requires creating distance, like making a moat to deter ants. Supporting separation can thus paradoxically be an act of connection; giving creatures the space they need to thrive is, in fact, an act of compassionate relation.

Second, walking softly requires observational skill. Through their daily practice, the nuns learn to pay attention to tiny details; this is how they saw bugs I had overlooked in the firewood. Attending closely to the microcosmic world allows one to see dimensions of life we ordinarily ignore. Developing this kind of observational skill, however, takes patience and practice (Tishman 2017). The painstaking attention required to sweep insects off the road, for instance, might strike us as impractical. But the nuns see such efforts as not only benefiting others but also benefiting themselves. Expressed differently, it is not that we pay attention to those we care about, but that we care about those to whom we pay attention. By going out of their way to pay attention to insects, the nuns strengthen their capacity for compassionate care. Attention, in other words, is not an *expression* of compassion; it is a *method* of developing it.

Finally, walking softly is not perfect or painless; it involves compromise, discomfort, and sometimes disappointment. One cannot save every worm on the road, detect every bug in the firewood, or tolerate every kind of stinging insect. But walking softly is less about aspiring for perfection than about enabling relationship. There is no connection without risk. But like the rock climber who chooses to wear thin-soled shoes, walking softly means sacrificing a little bit of comfort and convenience to enable a deeper and more intimate connection with the world and its creatures. And that, I suggest, is of benefit to both nonhuman and human animals alike.

References

Agamben, Giorgio. 2004. *The Open: Man and Animal.* Translated by Kevin Attell. Stanford, Calif.: Stanford University Press.

Nagel, Thomas. 1974. "What Is It Like to Be a Bat?" *The Philosophical Review* 83 (4): 435–50.

Śāntideva. 1995. *The Bodhicaryāvatāra.* Translated by Kate Crosby and Andrew Skilton. Oxford and New York: Oxford University Press.

Tishman, Shari. 2017. *Slow Looking: The Art and Practice of Learning Through Observation.* New York and Abingdon: Routledge.

Other Recommended Resources

Heirman, Ann. 2020. "Protecting Insects in Medieval Chinese Buddhism: Daoxuan's Vinaya Commentaries." *Buddhist Studies Review* 37 (1): 27–52.

Kyabje Lama Zopa Rinpoche. 1977. "The Mosquito is the Cause of Our Enlightenment." *Lama Yeshe Wisdom Archive.* Accessed June 13, 2022. www.lamayeshe.com/article/mosquito-cause-our-enlightenment.

Nuridsany, Claude, Marie Pérennou, and Jacques Perrin. 2017. *Microcosmos: Le Peuple de L'herbe*, DVD Video. New York: Kino Classics.

Oreck, Jessica, Maiko Endo, and Akito Kawahara. 2010. *Beetle Queen Conquers Tokyo*, DVD Video. Brooklyn, N.Y.: Factory 25.

Small, Ernest. 2019. "In Defence of the World's Most Reviled Invertebrate 'Bugs.'" *Biodiversity* (Nepean) 20 (4): 168–221.

9 An Islamic Case for Insect Ethics

Sarra Tlili

The moral standing of insects raises unique challenges for ethics. Animal rights theorists and welfare laws have tended to exclude this class of animals from moral consideration under the pretext that all or most invertebrates are neither sentient nor conscious. However, the last few decades have witnessed the emergence of a body of research demonstrating the opposite. While these findings dictate that the interests of insects need to be taken more seriously, they also raise new empirical and methodological complications. Some insects consume human crops, some can infect us with diseases, and others can destroy humans' property. How to balance human and insect interests is now a question that mandates more ethical scrutiny not only because of its environmental ramifications but also because of our duties toward fellow sentient beings. The new findings about insects' cognition and ability to feel pain and other stressors (nociception) also raise legitimate concerns about the methodologies of current animal ethics theories. So far, the inclusion of certain animals into the circle of moral consideration has been enabled by the exclusion of others, most notably insects. By extending moral consideration to all forms of animal life, such boundaries become untenable, giving rise to a new set of questions. For example, considering the number of insects killed during vegetable farming, do we need to reevaluate vegetarian and vegan diets' cost to animal life? What about the idea of shifting to insect-based diets (entomophagy)? Similarly, substituting vertebrates with invertebrates in animal experimentation may be a false remedy for our ethical concerns.

While some of these questions are unique to the modern context, the question of insect welfare is nothing new. In this chapter, I will explore an answer proposed by the Muslim jurist Aḥmad ibn Ghānim al-Nafrāwī (1634–1714), with a view toward its applicability to modern challenges. To this end, I will first offer a brief overview of recent debates on insect welfare. Second, I will introduce the Islamic scriptural background for al-Nafrāwī's views. Third, I will describe, analyze, and evaluate al-Nafrāwī's engagement with this issue. In conclusion, I will consider how these views may inform modern animal ethics debates.

Recent Debates on Insect Ethics and Welfare

The exclusion of insects from the circle of moral consideration reminds us of the time when all nonhuman animals were excluded from this circle under the pretext that they were insentient and unconscious. In both cases, this exclusion is motivated by longstanding anthropocentric (human-centered) and self-serving biases rather than concrete evidence that animals lack sentience and consciousness. Given how little research has been done on the subject (Gjerris, Gamborg, and Röcklinsberg 2015, 349), the main argument

DOI: 10.4324/9781003324157-13

invoked in support of insect insentience is the degree to which they differ from humans. It is, therefore, by placing humans at the center and treating them as the standard in defining consciousness that insects are denied these capacities.

Indeed, this stance was for a long time deliberately adopted as the default scientific approach to the nonhuman animal world, as shown, for example, by the Morgan Canon. C. Lloyd Morgan developed the axiom that "an animal's behavior was only to be considered 'conscious' if there was no simpler explanation" (Matthews and Matthews 2010, 25). This stance has also proven self-servingly useful in some areas. Irina Mikhalevich and Russell Powell note that because of invertebrates' presumed insentience and unconsciousness, many scientific funding agencies encourage scientists to replace vertebrates with invertebrates to promote ethically sounder research (2020, 2). (Invertebrates are animals who do not have a backbone or spine, including but not limited to insects.) The view that invertebrates lack morally significant capacities thus allows scientists to pursue animal experimentation while easing the ensuing guilt and evading public pressure.

Contrary to prevalent perceptions, however, Mikhalevich and Powell affirm that "over the last several decades . . . a growing body of research is pointing to sophisticated cognitive abilities in a number of invertebrate lineages" (2020, 2; see also Horvath et al. 2013 and Klein and Barron 2016). David Baracchi and Luigi Baciadonna cite many cognitive capacities that have been shown by insects such as bees, ants, and wasps, including the abilities to count, categorize things, and to communicate using sophisticated symbols. "Bees, in particular," they write, "seem to master mental representation of space and time, which are among the main hallmarks of consciousness" (Baracchi and Baciadonna 2020, 2).

While the growing evidence in support of insects' sentience and consciousness dictates that they be included in the circle of moral consideration, current animal ethics theories do not seem to be well equipped to address this situation. John Hadley and Elisa Aaltola pertinently point out that the field of animal ethics is "by and large, a site for 'moral extensionism,'" whereby moral and political theory is extended across the species barrier to nonhuman animals (2015, 2). Through an appeal to the principle of consistency, animal theorists from various schools of thought argue that "One cannot consistently grant moral standing to all humans without granting it to at least some animals" (Monsó and Osuna-Mascaró 2020, 2).

Yet by their very nature, extensionist animal ethics theories remain dependent on the principle of exclusion. Thus far, extensionism has been an elite system that used to be strictly limited to humanity but whose rules have been somewhat relaxed to admit species that are more like us into the moral club. To include insects—who represent 85% of all forms of animal life (Karp 1996, 67)—in this club means that all boundaries must be erased and the very club mentality be abandoned. While this does not necessarily mean that the moral interests of a fly must be given the same weight as those of a cow, invoking cognition and the ability to feel pain in defense of excluding some animals from moral consideration is no longer a compelling justification.

Insects in Islamic Scriptural Sources

The first nonhuman animal mentioned in the Qur'an is an insect. The verse in question says, "Indeed, God does not disdain to use the example of a gnat or anything above it" (2/al-Baqara: 26). Muslim scholars have inferred from this verse both that in God's sight, an animal's size is irrelevant to its status and, more generally, that the human criteria for assigning status are irrelevant to the Qur'an's worldview. In humans' eyes, gnats may appear insignificant, but in God's sight, they are as worthy as any other creature. Moreover, many interpret the phrase "above it" to mean anything larger or smaller than the gnat. This interpretation disrupts anthropocentric preconceptions in yet another way since it places gnats rather than humans at the center of creation and measures everything against them.

Moreover, both the Qur'an and the hadith (prophetic tradition) ascribe agency and interiority (sense of self) to arthropods. In the Qur'an, the bee receives divine inspiration (16/al-Naḥl: 68), and an ant is portrayed as a wise leader, articulating lucid instructions and protecting fellow members of her community from destruction (27/al-Naml: 18–19). The hadith not only reiterates the Qur'anic theme that insects, like other animals, are God-conscious but also treats this capacity as the main reason why they should be accorded moral consideration. In one narrative, Muhammad reportedly relates that a prophet (believed to be Moses) burned an anthill in reaction to an ant's bite, for which God reprimanded him for destroying a whole community that worshipped God. Relatedly, when some of Muhammad's companions set an anthill afire, he ordered them to immediately put the fire out and prohibited Muslims from burning any animal alive. Muhammad also gave specific instructions not to kill ants and bees.

However, while these instructions show that the hadith is not oblivious to insect welfare, compared to teachings about larger animals, one also notes that instructions pertaining to insects are not as strict as those concerning larger animals. For example, the hadith states that the wanton killing of a sparrow or any larger animal is punishable in the hereafter, thus seemingly leaving out arthropods, most of which are smaller than the sparrow. This relative silence, however, should be read against another hadith, which states that the killing of the members of four or five harmful species, called *fawāsiq* (animals such as scorpions and mice), incurs no blame. The fact that members of this group are singled out as the only ones that may be killed without incurring blame seems to imply that the unjustified killing of other animals—including insects—may incur blame. Thus, while the relative silence of the hadith seems to indicate that humans do not have the same responsibilities toward insects as they do toward larger animals, when read against the reports about the *fawāsiq*, this silence may imply at least tacit discouragement from killing insects.

Al-Nafrāwī on Insect Welfare

Moving to Islamic juridical sources on insects, al-Nafrāwī's legal discussion is part of his commentary on the treatise of the early authority ibn Abī Zayd al-Qayrawānī (d. 996). This early jurist describes the killing of lice and bedbugs with fire as detestable and does not object to killing ants if they cause intolerable harm—despite the Prophet's instruction to the opposite, though he still prefers that they not be killed (ibn Abī Zayd 1986, 287–88). One already notes some discrepancy between scriptural teachings and these legal injunctions, given that the Prophet's instruction to burn no animal alive is translated into discouragement rather than outright prohibition. In legal terms, this means that killing insects with fire is not punishable, although refraining from it entails a reward in the hereafter. Moreover, the Prophet's command not to kill ants is somewhat relaxed.

Al-Nafrāwī expounds on ibn Abī Zayd's views by spelling out the principles underlying these legal stipulations. The detestability of killing insects with fire, he explains, is informed by the general prohibition of inflicting pain on animals (*al-nahy 'an ta'dhīb al-ḥayawān*) as well as the Prophet's command not to kill any creature with fire. In line with ibn Abī Zayd's views, however, al-Nafrāwī is careful to stress that these prophetic injunctions imply only detestability and not outright prohibition. Because lice and bedbugs can cause harm, it is permissible to kill them. Al-Nafrāwī also explains that if bedbugs are exceedingly numerous, it is permissible to kill them even with fire since it is difficult to kill each insect individually. Furthermore, although ants form a special category due to the Prophet's specific instructions about them, if they become exceedingly harmful, it is permissible to kill them, even with fire. Accommodation of human needs thus seems to take precedence over the interests of insects.

While making these dispensations, however, al-Nafrāwī also stresses that ants worship God, hence the Prophet's instruction to Muslims not to kill them. In conclusion, he writes, "If ants cause no harm, it is impermissible to kill them; if they cause intolerable harm, one is free to either spare or kill them; and if they cause tolerable harm, it is better not to kill them." Interestingly, al-Nafrāwī extends this reasoning even to the members of the *fawāsiq* category (e.g., scorpions and mice), whose killing, he affirms, becomes impermissible if they pose no threat.

On the surface, al-Nafrāwī's divergence from prophetic teachings is twofold. He departs from prophetic teaching in his authorization to kill insects even with fire and his prohibition to kill the members of the five harmful species (*fawāsiq*). However, a closer look shows that he has discerned and applied the underlying principle of these teachings. The permissibility of killing the five harmful animals is due to their threat to humans' lives, health, or property. Interestingly, another scholar, al-Ṣāwī (d. 1825), applies this principle even to humans. He says, "Even humans who cause harm, such as those who shed blood, dispossess people of their properties, and violate sacred rights, (may be harmed)" (al-Dardīr 1986, 4: 771).

Conclusion

While expanding scriptural strictures to accommodate human needs, al-Nafrāwī and jurists from various schools of Islamic law continue to adopt a cautionary stance. These jurists may differ on the level of accommodation for human needs, but they all agree that insects and all other animals have interests that need to be included in the equation. The two main factors in this equation are the facts that (1) humans, like any other creature, are justified to ward off harm and derive benefits for themselves, and (2) other creatures also have interests that must be respected at the risk of incurring divine punishment for failure to do so. How to balance the two factors is a matter of debate, but the fact that they must be balanced is not.

This ethic focuses on human and other creatures' needs rather than rights. The rights of every creature to life and welfare are treated as a given; however, it is also recognized that in a world shared by vulnerable creatures whose interests sometimes conflict, infringing on those rights may become necessary. It is still noteworthy, however, that even when al-Nafrāwī accepts the necessity of killing, this is not the path he promotes. He wrote that one should still feel free to spare the lives of insects even when they cause intolerable harm, and when their harm is tolerable, it is preferable not to kill them. While this ethic recognizes and seeks to meet humans' needs, it also expects or at least encourages humans to sacrifice some of their interests to accommodate the needs of other creatures.

The inclusion of all animals without exception in the circle of moral consideration, the focus on needs instead of rights, and the need to balance all creatures' interests are the hallmarks of this Islamic animal ethic. While the application of these overarching principles may lead some species, including humans, to forgo some of their rights, they offer a remedy to the problem of extensionism and provide a path for the inclusion of insects in moral consideration, something that ethicists should take more seriously if they are to abandon the prevalent yet increasingly untenable assumption that these animals lack consciousness and the ability to feel pain.

References

al-Dardīr, Abū l-Barakāt Aḥmad. 1986. *al-Sharḥ al-ṣaghīr ʿalā aqrab al-masālik ilā madhhab al-Imām Mālik* (including *Ḥāshiyat al-Ṣāwī*). Edited by Muṣṭafā Kamāl Waṣfī. Cairo: Dār al-Maʿārif.

Baracchi, David, and Luigi Baciadonna. 2020. "Insect Sentience and the Rise of a New Inclusive Ethics." *Animal Sentience* 5. https://doi.org/10.51291/2377-7478.1604.

Gjerris, Mickey, Christian Gamborg, and Helena Röcklinsberg. 2015. "Entomophagy—Why Should It Bug You? The Ethics of Insect Production for Food and Feed." In *Know Your Food: Food Ethics and Innovation*, edited by Diana Elena Dumitras, Lonel Mugurel Jitea, and Stef Aerts, 347–52. Wageningen: Wageningen Academic Publishers.

Hadley, John, and Elisa Aaltola. 2015. "Introduction: Questioning the Orthodoxy." In *Animal Ethics and Philosophy: Questioning the Orthodoxy*, edited by Elisa Aaltola and John Hadley, 1–12. London and New York: Rowman and Littlefield.

Horvath, Kelsey, Dario Angeletti, Giuseppe Nascetti, and Claudio Carere. 2013. "Invertebrate Welfare: An Overlooked Issue." *Annali dell'Istituto Superiore di Sanità* 49: 9–17.

Ibn Abī Zayd al-Qayrawānī. 1986. *al-Risāla al-fiqhiyya*. Beirut: Dār al-Gharb al-Islāmī.

Karp, R.D. 1996. "Inducible Humoral Immune Defense in Insects." In *Invertebrate Immunology*, edited by B. Rinkevich and W.E.G. Müller, 67–87. Berlin: Springer.

Klein, Colin, and Andrew B. Barron. 2016. "Insects Have the Capacity for Subjective Experience." *Animal Sentience* 9: 1–52. https://doi.org/10.51291/2377-7478.1113.

Matthews, Robert W., and Janice R. Matthews. 2010. *Insect Behavior*. 2nd ed. New York: Springer.

Mikhalevich, Irina, and Russell Powell. 2020. "Minds without Spines: Evolutionarily Inclusive Animal Ethics." *Animal Sentience* 29 (1). https://doi.org/10.51291/2377-7478.1527.

Monsó, Susana, and Antonio J. Osuna-Mascaró. 2020. "Problems with Basing Insect Ethics on Individuals' Welfare." *Animal Sentience* 29 (8). https://doi.org/10.51291/2377-7478.1589.

Other Recommended Resources

Attenborough, David. 2018. "Attenborough and the Empire of the Ants," DVD video. www.dailymotion.com/video/x717gjf.

Carere, Claudio, and Jennifer Mather, eds. 2019. *The Welfare of Invertebrate Animals*. New York: Springer.

Chittka, Lars. 2022. *The Mind of a Bee*. Princeton, N.J.: Princeton University Press.

Drouin, Jean-Marc. 2019. *A Philosophy of the Insect*. Translated by Anne Trager. New York: Columbia University Press.

Tlili, Sarra. 2012. *Animals in the Qur'an*. New York: Cambridge University Press.

10 Animal Theology

Allison Covey

In 1967, historian Lynn White, Jr. published a short article identifying Christianity as one of the principal roots of the ecological crisis. White made the provocative and enduring argument that "[e]specially in its Western form, Christianity is the most anthropocentric religion the world has seen" (White 1967, 1205). Since then, eco- and animal theologians have grappled with White's assertion that the ecological crisis will continue to worsen until Christianity rejects anthropocentric theologies that assign only instrumental value to other than human Creation (1207). What Christians believe about humanity's role within Creation and God's intended purpose for other animals is not merely a matter of theological interest but a question with significant implications for the lives of real animals today.

Imago Dei

To understand how Christian theologies impact believers' treatment of other than human animals, one must first consider a few of the competing ideologies present within Christian theological and moral traditions. White's concern about Christian anthropocentrism was echoed by Pope Francis in his 2015 encyclical *Laudato Si'*. Francis writes, "Clearly, the Bible has no place for a tyrannical anthropocentrism unconcerned for other creatures" (LS #68). *Anthropocentrism*, used in this sense, refers to the belief that all value is human-centered. The interests and perspectives of humanity are privileged, and the value of other species is determined primarily by their utility to human beings.

Christian theological anthropocentrism is often traced back to anthropocentric *cosmologies*. Religious cosmologies are stories about the origin and purpose (or *telos*) of the world. They explain how the universe came into being, but they also offer insight into the *telos* of each part of the created order. In other words, these stories shape the way Christians think about animals and about how God intends for humans to interact with them.

The Hebrew Bible, which some Christians refer to as the "Old Testament," contains two creation stories in the book of Genesis. The first of these stories describes God's creation of the world, beginning with the separation of light from darkness and ending with the creation of the first humans, Adam and Eve (Gen. 1:1-27). Having finished creating the animals of the sea, the air, and the land, God says,

> Let us make humankind in our image, according to our likeness; and let them have dominion over the fish of the sea, and over the birds of the air, and over the cattle, and over all of the wild animals of the earth, and over every creeping thing that creeps upon the earth.
>
> (Gen. 1:26)

DOI: 10.4324/9781003324157-14

The idea that humanity alone was created in the image and likeness of God is a concept theologians call the *imago Dei*. But the text does not explicitly explain what it *means* to "have dominion" or to be the *imago Dei*. This is where debate arises. Particularly in the early modern period, natural philosophers such as Francis Bacon, inspired by the developments of the Scientific Revolution, embraced the idea that, through scientific inquiry, humanity could regain control of the natural world. They came to believe that, through sin, Adam and Eve had lost control of Creation and that God intends for humanity to work its way back to dominating and subduing the planet in a rather imposing way (Harrison 1999, 98).

Modern eco- and animal theologians argue instead that humanity's dominion is intended by God as a special responsibility to *care for* Creation in a benevolent way. As the only creatures made in God's own image, human beings have been set apart and equipped for the important role of tending to all that God has made and ensuring its flourishing. Support for this understanding of the *imago Dei* comes especially from the second creation story of Genesis. In this version, the author notes that God creates the heavens and the earth but does not yet create any plant life since there is "no one to till the ground" (Gen. 2:5). God then creates Adam, the first human being, before creating any other life on earth. Having next created plants, "[t]he Lord God took the man and put him in the Garden of Eden to till it and keep it" (Gen. 2:15). Only after Adam is given this role of caring for the garden does God create animals, not as resources but as potential helpers and partners for Adam so that he is not alone (Gen. 2:18–19). This cosmology presents humanity's dominion in a custodial way, suggesting that the *imago Dei* is not intended to make Adam and Eve into despotic rulers but rather into caretakers of Creation.

The Value of Animals and the Role of Humans

These questions of how humanity ought to interact with other animals involve questions of value. On the one hand is the belief that animals have only or at least primarily *instrumental value*. On the other hand is the belief that animals also have *intrinsic value*. Instrumental value is value that comes from what something or someone can do. A gifted surgeon has much greater instrumental value in the operating theater, for example, than does a firefighter, while a firefighter is much more instrumentally valuable in a burning building. Nevertheless, most would argue that both the surgeon and the firefighter have value that transcends their particular skills or utility. They are both valued not merely for what they can do but also for who and what they are; they have intrinsic value. For human beings, this intrinsic value is often assumed to arise from their humanity itself—humans are valuable simply by virtue of being human. Within Christianity, the intrinsic value of humanity is also linked to humanity's special status as the *imago Dei*.

Other animals, not being human, are said to have only instrumental value. They are valued for their usefulness alone. Cows are valuable, for example, because they can be used to produce milk, meat, and leather. Dogs are valuable because they can be used to provide companionship or labor, to act as medical test subjects, or to be bred for profit. With few exceptions, other animals are not valued for who they are but for how they can be used to enhance the lives of human beings. They are valued as instruments of human flourishing.

Animal theologians such as Andrew Linzey, David Clough, and Christopher Steck argue that Christian scripture and theology do not support this anthropocentric, instrumental valuing of other animals. Instead, they advocate for a theocentric theology of *relationality* in which the value of each creature arises from their relationship with God, the Creator. *Theocentricity*, in contrast with anthropocentricity, holds that God, not humanity, is the center of all goodness. God's interests and relationship with Creation imbue all creatures with intrinsic value. In the first Creation story of Genesis, the author finishes the description of each day of creation with the refrain, "And God saw that it was good." Adam and Eve had not yet been created, and yet God notes the goodness of the birds and the fish and the cattle. They are not good *for* anyone, in an instrumental way; they are simply good in themselves, in an intrinsic way. They are good because God values them.

Theological attempts to challenge anthropocentricity and restore theocentricity have involved rethinking the *imago Dei*. Ecotheologians have proposed that it is best understood as *stewardship*. In the same way that Adam is entrusted by God with tilling and keeping the Garden of Eden, humanity is entrusted with caring for the rest of Creation as a steward. Stewards in antiquity were servants of great households, trusted by their masters to take care of the property, particularly in the master's absence. Human beings have been given unique capabilities, beyond those of other species, so that humanity is fully equipped to carry out this role of stewardship in Creation. Just as God rules over humanity with benevolence and love, so too is humanity, as steward, called to oversee other than human beings with this same compassion and care, reflecting God's image and kindness to the rest of Creation.

Animal theologians such as Andrew Linzey and some ecotheologians such as John Zizioulas and H. Paul Santmire, however, argue that the concept of stewardship falls short of encompassing the responsibilities of the *imago Dei*. Though a steward has great responsibility, they contend, it is a rather broad and anthropocentric responsibility to maintain the finances and flourishing of the household (Santmire 2006, 270). Ecotheological concepts of stewardship, critics point out, also imply the master's absence—humanity is tasked with caring for the master's household while the master is away. Mainstream Christian theology maintains, however, the existence of a present, personal God, not one who has completed the task of Creation and disappeared, leaving an employee to hold down the fort alone. Linzey and Zizioulas suggest instead that the *imago Dei* is best understood as *priesthood* (Linzey 1995, 45; Zizioulas 2006). Unlike stewards, priests are tasked not only with maintaining their flocks as-is but also with fostering and improving the relationship between the faithful and God. Like stewards, priests are often described as "servants," but their servanthood goes well beyond what is expected of a secular steward.

Consequences for Real Animals

The meaning of the *imago Dei* and the *telos* (ultimate purpose or meaning) of other than human animals might seem like questions that only matter to theologians, but they have real-world implications for the way Christians—and various societies shaped by contact with Christian ideas—treat other species. Whether a culture considers animals edible, which animals it chooses to eat, and how it goes about raising them for slaughter is influenced in large part by the religious beliefs that have shaped that culture. This is so whether or not individuals involved in animal agriculture and consumption themselves subscribe to those beliefs explicitly. The United States, for example, is a country with a history of colonization by Christian settlers and a population that, to this day, identifies as majority Christian. It is also one of the world's largest contributors to industrial animal agriculture. These facts are not unrelated. Christian beliefs about the primacy of human flourishing and about the instrumental value of other creatures are invoked to justify American use of other animals as mere resources (Copan 2019, 1). Despite this connection between Christian theology and the instrumental use of animals, animal theologians reject White's suggestion that only a departure from orthodox Christian doctrine can begin to right the wrongs brought about by anthropocentrism.

Animal theologians argue that embracing an understanding of human uniqueness that views humanity as priests rather than dominators of Creation is not a departure from Christian tradition but a return to it. Theologians call this a *retrieval*—a going back to earlier texts and ideas, attempting to recover their original meaning while clearing away later misconceptions or distortions of them. Returning to Genesis, for example, rereading its depiction of humanity's role and reconsidering the way it describes the other animals, has led animal theologians to conclude that the text does not support the idea that humans are meant to use other creatures as mere resources to further human goals. If the text has been interpreted incorrectly over time, then theological concern for other than human animals is not a new idea but a very old one, retrieved and in the process of being revived by modern theologians.

If religious ideologies have the power to shape the way individuals behave—how they vote, how they spend their money—then a shift in Christian theologies of Creation has the potential to bring about significant change for other than human animals. Christian rejection of anthropocentric theologies that view the value of other animals only instrumentally would necessarily involve a rethinking of Christian participation in systems of animal use and abuse. To take seriously the idea that God intends humanity to act as priests of Creation, nurturing the other than human world and strengthening its relationship to God, would require that Christians eschew industrial animal agriculture (and perhaps animal products altogether) because of the pain and suffering they inflict on living creatures, act to protect wildlife and restore ecosystems, and find alternatives to animal testing, animal-derived textiles, and the use of animals in entertainment. The cultivating of a peaceful relationship between humans and other animals would be a return to the original peace described in Eden, a return to God's original plan for Creation.

References

Copan, Paul. 2019. "Preface." In *What Would Jesus REALLY Eat? The Biblical Case for Eating Meat*, edited by Wes Jamison and Paul Copan. Burlington: Castle Quay Books. Kindle.

Harrison, Peter. 1999. "Subduing the Earth: Genesis 1, Early Modern Science, and the Exploitation of Nature." *Journal of Religion* 79 (1): 86–109.

Linzey, Andrew. 1995. *Animal Theology*. Urbana: University of Illinois Press.

Pope Francis. 2015. *Laudato Si'* [On Care for Our Common Home]. Accessed June 1, 2022. www.vatican.va/content/francesco/en/encyclicals/documents/papa-francesco_20150524_enciclica-laudato-si.html.

Santmire, H. Paul. 2006. "Partnership with Nature According to the Scriptures: Beyond the Theology of Stewardship." In *Environmental Stewardship*, edited by R.J. Berry, 253–72. London: T&T Clark International.

White, Lynn, Jr. 1967. "The Historical Roots of Our Ecologic Crisis." *Science* 155 (3767): 1203–07.

Zizioulas, John D. 2006. "Priest of Creation." In *Environmental Stewardship*, edited by R.J. Berry, 273–90. London: T&T Clark International.

Other Recommended Resources

Bauckham, Richard. 2011. *Living with Other Creatures: Green Exegesis and Theology*. Waco, Texas: Baylor University Press.

Camosy, Charles. 2013. *For the Love of Animals: Christian Ethics, Consistent Action*. Cincinnati: Franciscan Media.

Clough, David. 2012. *On Animals: Volume 1: Systematic Theology*. London: T&T Clark International.

_____. 2019. *On Animals: Volume 2: Theological Ethics*. London: T&T Clark International.

Deane-Drummond, Celia. 2019. *Theological Ethics Through a Multispecies Lens: The Evolution of Wisdom, Volume I*. Oxford: Oxford University Press.

Steck, Christopher. 2019. *All God's Animals: A Catholic Theological Framework for Animal Ethics*. Washington: Georgetown University Press.

Webster, Emily, producer. 2008. *Eating Mercifully*, Video. Washington, D.C.: Humane Society of the United States. www.youtube.com/watch?v=L-Va6F3iQFc.

11 Blue Theology and Water Torah
People of Faith Caring for Marine Wildlife

Dave Aftandilian

Introduction

When humans think of "animals," we most often think of the ones who share land habitats with us, from deer to dogs to downy woodpeckers. Yet biologists estimate there are more than 171,000 different species of animals who live in the ocean (which is a vast underestimate of the true total, since 91% of marine species have not yet been described; Mora et al. 2011). Indeed, if one counts up the total weight of different living organisms from various environments (biomass) and compares them, one finds that "for animals, most biomass is concentrated in the marine environment" (Bar-On, Phillips, and Milo 2018, 6508). And from Jewish and Christian perspectives, the oceans matter to God because God filled them with a wondrous diversity of animals. Psalm 104:25–26 tells us that God made not just the creatures of the earth, but also of "the sea, great and wide; creeping things innumerable are there, living things both small and great. There go the ships and Leviathan that [God] formed to sport in it."

Unfortunately, these marine animals whom God made are suffering greatly today due to the pollution that we humans dump into the ocean. According to the U.S. National Oceanic and Atmospheric Administration (NOAA), 80% of marine pollution comes from the land, and one of the biggest sources is nonpoint source pollution (pollution that cannot be linked to one specific location like a factory), especially untreated runoff from roads and farm fields that drains into storm sewers and eventually the ocean after rainstorms (https://oceanservice.noaa.gov/facts/pollution.html, accessed June 19, 2023). Pollutants dumped into the ocean directly or indirectly through runoff include raw sewage, pet waste, and other nutrients like nitrogen and phosphorous from fertilizers; pesticides and herbicides from homes and farms as well as industrial chemical wastes; oil (about half from land sources such as runoff from roads); thermal pollution (waste heat from industrial and power generation activities); noise; and plastics (Elenwo and Ankali 2015; U.S. EPA 2022). According to UNESCO, "Plastic waste makes up 80% of all marine pollution and around 8 to 10 million metric tons of plastic end up in the ocean each year. . . . Research states that, by 2050, plastic will likely outweigh all the fish in the sea" (Fava 2022).

All these ocean pollutants can have devastating impacts on marine animals. Nutrient pollution can lead to algal blooms that use up all the oxygen in the water nearby, suffocating fish who live there (Elenwo and Ankali 2015, 213; NOAA 2018). Oil pollution can also suffocate seabirds and marine life (Vikas and Dwarakish 2015, 385). Plastics can harm wildlife either through directly entangling them, which can cause suffocation or drowning, or through ingesting them as either macroplastics or microplastics (pieces

DOI: 10.4324/9781003324157-15

less than 5mm wide), which can damage an animal's digestive tract and/or ability to feed; this damage, in turn, can lead to starvation or poisoning with toxic chemicals that often become attached to microplastics (U.S. EPA 2022; Fava 2022; Gall and Thompson 2015).

In this chapter, I will discuss two different projects that people of faith have created to help care for these marine animals who are suffering due to human-caused pollution. One project, the Blue Theology Mission Station, is based in Christian theology, while the other, Tikkun HaYam (Repair the Sea) and its Water Torah, draws on Jewish traditions. Both projects pair firsthand personal experience with religious reflection to both educate participants about the problems ocean animals face and share what people of faith and others can do to help.

Blue Theology Mission Station

The Blue Theology Mission Station is sponsored by the Christian Church of Pacific Grove, which is located along California's central coast. In 2017 it was certified as the first "Aquamarine Chalice" congregation by the Christian Church's (Disciples of Christ's) Green Chalice Creation Care Ministry (see Chapter 29: Urban Wildlife in this volume for more information about Green Chalice).

Founded in 2008 and led since then by the congregation's minister, Rev. Dan Paul, Blue Theology hosts youth and others for weeklong summer programs "where current science in marine biology meets a theology of creation justice. . . . We believe that ocean conservation is a spiritual practice" (website home page, www.bluetheology.com, accessed June 3, 2023). Since 2008 Blue Theology has hosted more than 50 church groups and more than 500 individuals in Pacific Grove. In 2022, thanks to a grant-funded partnership with Creation Justice Ministries (which is part of the National Council of Churches in Washington, D.C.), the mission expanded to three new sites: Harbor Christian Church in Newport Beach, California; First Christian Church of Texas City in Texas; and a partnership between Ann Street United Methodist Church and the Duke Marine Lab in Beaufort, North Carolina.

Blue Theology pairs experiential, hands-on learning with theological reflection. During their visit to Pacific Grove participants learn about Christians' stewardship responsibility to care for creation (Gen. 1:28), go on what is described as a "pilgrimage" to the world-famous Monterey Bay Aquarium, learn about plastics pollution and then do a beach cleanup, and assist marine biologists with collecting data about sand crabs for an ongoing long-term project that studies the crabs to monitor the health of the Bay.

Rev. Paul told me that Blue Theology was inspired by his church's small congregation refocusing on their place of mission: the Monterey Bay, which lies less than a block from their church (telephone interview, June 7, 2022). As Rev. Paul explained,

> the story of Monterey Bay is really compelling. We nearly wiped out the abalone, elephant seals, sea otters, and whales, but we responded as a community to save these animals and create a marine sanctuary, and all these animals came back.

Blue Theology shares that story with their guests, helping them build what Rev. Paul describes as "a *heart* relationship with the animals." For example, during the pilgrimage to the aquarium, participants pick their favorite animal and spend 20 minutes watching them, then reflect in writing on what they noticed about the animal and why those features stood out to them. Later in their mission week, the visitors go whale watching and kayak with wild sea otters in Elkhorn Slough. Through activities like these visitors overcome their land bias: as ground-based creatures, humans tend to see land animals and ecosystems as more important, even though, as Rev. Paul explained, most of the world's oxygen comes from the oceans, and marine ecosystems are highly diverse and profoundly interconnected with those on land.

Rev. Talitha Amadea Aho vividly describes the powerful heart impact that engaging in the Blue Theology Mission had on her and the youth from her church when they visited in summer 2019:

> I was afraid my heart might break open with compassion for the plight of some struggling sea creatures and it might be too painful to bear. . . . [For example, sea otters] are super endangered and problematically cute. You would think God had designed them to emotionally manipulate us into caring for them, with their adorable little faces. They even play with toys! I did not want to start caring about them.
>
> (Aho 2022, 17)

I have also visited the Monterey Bay many times with my family over the years, and I share Rev. Aho's loving compassion for the sea otters there, and her desire to help them in spite of a fear of being hurt herself. So I was delighted to read what Rev. Aho learned from her theological reflections on the sea creatures she met during her visit to the Blue Theology Mission Station:

> Vulnerability is part of love.
> This pain, then, that I feel, is God's spirit of love in me.
> God aches for and loves the creatures in their peril.
> It is our holy work to care for the fragile creatures and ecosystems that God so loves.
> It is a holy thing to love what death can touch.
>
> (Aho 2022, 20)

Water Torah and Tikkun HaYam (Repair the Sea)

Christians are not the only people of faith who care about marine animals. Jewish groups interested in helping protect and preserve marine ecosystems and the creatures who inhabit them can draw on the expertise of Tikkun HaYam, or Repair the Sea, a nonprofit organization founded by Rabbi Ed Rosenthal (www.repairthesea.org). Among many other projects, Tikkun HaYam sponsors international Reverse Tashlich beach cleanups every year as a new High Holiday tradition for Jews. The program draws on the tradition of Jews ritually disposing of their sins into the water on the first day of Rosh Hashana. But instead of casting sins into the sea, during Reverse Tashlich, Jews and their community partners instead remove the human sins of plastic waste and other trash that had been thrown onto the beaches and into the ocean. As Rabbi Rosenthal explained, Reverse Tashlich "changed the concept from 'Let's go clean some beaches' to 'Let's clean the beach as a religious experience'" (Luby 2021).

Tikkun HaYam grew out of Rabbi Rosenthal's work as executive director of the Suncoast Hillels in Tampa Bay, Florida, including Eckerd College's Hillel program, which he founded. To engage Jewish and other students who would not otherwise come to Hillel, Rabbi Rosenthal started a program called Scubi Jew, which has now expanded to Hillels throughout Florida and nationwide through Tikkun HaYam.

> Based on the [Jewish] Tenet of Tikkun Olam (Repairing the World), and focusing on the marine environment, Scubi Jew is dedicated to educating students about the intersection of Judaism and the Sea. Our programs are intended to help repair the damage done to the oceans, rivers and lakes of the world and the creatures that live in them. We call it Tikkun HaYam (Repairing the Sea).
> (www.eckerdhillel.org/scubi-jew, accessed June 10, 2023)

Through Scubi Jew students learn about the threats faced by marine animals like sharks and manatees, and then dive with these animals to see them firsthand; as Rabbi Rosenthal explained, "When you get up close to something that is threatened with extinction and touch it and look it in the eye, your awareness changes and you will do whatever you can to save it from extinction" (Rubin 2018). But Scubi Jew members do more than just look at threatened marine animals; they also do hands-on work to care for them and their habitats, ranging from helping restore coral reefs in Key Largo to participating in biweekly "Dive Against Debris" programs to remove plastic waste and other trash from the St. Petersburg Downtown Reef in Tampa Bay.

What makes Tikkun HaYam unique among marine conservation organizations is the way it connects Jewish religious, ethical, and legal principles with caring for the ocean and the creatures who live there. Rabbi Rosenthal has developed what he calls the Water Torah to share these principles with Jews and others. Here are a few highlights that Rabbi Rosenthal shared with me in a conversation via Zoom (June 7, 2022):

- from the Psalms we learn that "the sea is God's" (Psalm 95) and "the dry land was given to humans" (Psalm 115); if this is true, how wrong is it to pollute the seas, which belong to God? If the ocean is the manifestation of the divine in creation, how can we justify pumping 200 million tons of raw sewage into the ocean every year in the U.S. alone?
- in the Kaballah, or spiritual teachings of Judaism, everything in this world is seen as a metaphysical reflection of its true spiritual essence; from this perspective the ocean of this world reflects the primordial substance of water in the heavens (*hashamayim*) from which it was created.
- all living beings are made, physically, of primarily water (for example, humans are 70% water); in a Kabbalistic sense so, too, spiritually, all living beings are made from the same primordial substance of water; this leads Rabbi Rosenthal to ask, "If we understood that we are all connected through this primordial substance of water, whether we walk on two legs or four, are fish or amphibian or mammal, how differently would we view every other creature and our responsibility towards them?"

Rabbi Rosenthal uses his understanding of the Water Torah and other Jewish principles to provide a religious reasoning for Jews living in coastal communities (or anywhere) of why they should act to protect marine animals. For example, he describes plastic pollution as a violation of the Jewish legal and ethical principle of *tsa'ar ba'alei chayim*, the duty of Jews to avoid causing unnecessary harm to living beings (also sometimes described as the duty to show kindness to animals; see Cohn-Sherbok 2006, 83–86). He explains that the plastics humans throw away eventually break down into microplastics; marine animals eat both the macro- and microplastics, which get absorbed into their bloodstreams, and accumulate as chemical toxins in their bodies. Hence, plastic pollution causes serious harm to marine animals, and Jews, therefore, have a duty to avoid wasting plastic themselves and should act to clean it up from the coasts and the ocean to show kindness to marine animals. (To help all religious communities reduce their use of plastics, not just Jewish communities, Tikkun HaYam sponsors a BlueGreen Initiative that allows them to purchase biodegradable silverware and dishes made from fallen palm leaves and scrap wood rather than plasticware at a much-reduced rate; see www. repairthesea.org/blue-green-initiative.) Similarly, when members of a Scubi Jew chapter dive to remove debris from underwater reefs:

> The students do it through a Jewish lens. It's not like, "We're doing this because we love the environment and we like to dive," they do it because they've learned about the values of *bal tashchit*, the prohibition against needless waste and destruction.
> (Rabbi Rosenthal, quoted in Malcom 2021)

Like the Blue Theology Mission Station, Tikkun HaYam also works to reach religious participants in their programs through their hearts and spirits as well as their minds. Rabbi Rosenthal has developed a program in underwater meditation that draws on his Water Torah; he has learned from surveys of Scubi Jew participants that they find these meditations to be some of the most impactful activities they perform (Zoom interview, June 7, 2022). The Sh'ma (Shema), a prayer which is recited in daily morning and evening prayer services, is one of the foundational practices of Judaism. A central part of this prayer can be translated into English as "the Lord is our God; the Lord is one" (see, e.g., Kimelman 2022). Rabbi Rosenthal asks Scubi Jew participants to recite the Sh'ma prayer for 20 minutes while they are immersed in the ocean during a dive, closing their eyes to better feel the motion of the waves, becoming one with everything. He argues that doing underwater meditations like this can help Jewish students (or anyone) remove the barriers that separate humans from other living beings, helping us to feel closer to them and more willing to act on their behalf.

Acknowledgments

Thanks a million to Rev. Dan Paul of Blue Theology Mission Station and Rabbi Ed Rosenthal of Tikkun HaYam for taking the time to speak with me. Thanks also to Adrienne Krone, one of my fellow contributors to this volume, for pointing me toward Tikkun HaYam's Scubi Jew initiative.

References

Aho, Talitha Amadea. 2022. *In Deep Waters: Spiritual Care for Young People in a Climate Crisis.* Minneapolis, Minn.: Fortress Press.

Bar-On, Yinon M., Rob Phillips, and Ron Milo. 2018. "The Biomass Distribution on Earth." *Proceedings of the National Academy of Sciences (PNAS)* 115 (25): 6506–11.

Cohn-Sherbok, Dan. 2006. "Hope for the Animal Kingdom: A Jewish Vision." In *A Communion of Subjects: Animals in Religion, Science, and Ethics*, edited by Paul Waldau and Kimberley Patton, 81–90. New York: Columbia University Press.

Elenwo, E.I., and J.A. Akankali. 2015. "The Effects of Marine Pollution on Nigerian Coastal Resources." *Journal of Sustainable Development Studies* 8 (1): 209–24.

Fava, Marta. 2022. "Ocean Plastic Pollution: An Overview, Data and Statistics." *UNESCO.* Accessed June 19, 2023. https://oceanliteracy.unesco.org/plastic-pollution-ocean/.

Gall, S.C. and R.C. Thompson. 2015. "The Impact of Debris on Marine Life." *Marine Pollution Bulletin* 92: 170–79.

Kimelman, Reuven. 2022. "The Opening of the Shema Prayer Explained." *The Jewish Experience, Brandeis University.* Accessed June 11, 2023. www.brandeis.edu/jewish-experience/holidays-religious-traditions/2022/may/shema-explained-kimelman.html.

Luby, Christine. 2021. "Scuba Diving Rabbi Adopts the Ocean as His Part of the World to Repair." *Religion News Service*, April 20. https://religionnews.com/2021/04/20/scubi-jews/.

Malcom, Rudy. 2021. "Scubi Jew Blends the Scientific with the Spiritual." *Hillel International*, June 1. www.hillel.org/scubi-jew-blends-the-scientific-with-the-spiritual/.

Mora, Camilo, Derek P. Tittensor, Sina Adl, Alastair G.B. Simpson, and Boris Worm. 2011. "How Many Species Are There on Earth and in the Ocean?" *PLoS Biology* 9 (8): e1001127.

Rubin, Debra. 2018. "Scubi Jew Dives for Jewish Values." *New Jersey Jewish News*, January 22. https://njjewishnews.timesofisrael.com/scubi-jew-dives-for-jewish-values/.

U.S. Environmental Protection Agency (EPA). 2022. "Learn About Aquatic Trash." Accessed June 19, 2023. www.epa.gov/trash-free-waters/learn-about-aquatic-trash.

U.S. National Oceanic and Atmospheric Administration (NOAA). 2018. "Land-Based Sources of Marine Pollution." www.noaa.gov/gc-international-section/land-based-sources-of-marine-pollution.

Vikas, M., and G.S. Dwarakish. 2015. "Coastal Pollution: A Review." *Aquatic Procedia* 4: 381–88.

Other Recommended Resources

Blue Theology Mission Station. www.bluetheology.com.

McAnally, Elizabeth. 2019. *Loving Water Across Religions: Contributions to an Integral Water Ethic.* Maryknoll, N.Y.: Orbis Books.

Morning MeditOceans: Guided Meditations with the Ocean. www.youtube.com/playlist?list=PLq_DVMr7CmlJ3DJothjCJNylwgyrB72V6.
- a series of six guided ocean meditations hosted by the Monterey Bay Aquarium

Shaw, Sylvia, and Andrew Francis, eds. 2014. *Deep Blue: Critical Reflections on Nature, Religion and Water.* London and Oakville, Conn.: Equinox Publishing.

Tikkun Hayam/Repair the Sea. www.repairthesea.org.

12 Animal Families in the Biblical Tradition

Beth A. Berkowitz

Encountering Animal Families

> All afternoon, young Jonah had seemed alone. But Jonah had been tracking her mother, Sophocles, from the surface, and reuniting with her for part of every hour.
>
> And so here's the thing: in the ocean vastness, maintaining family cohesion requires constant effort. It is *intentional*.
>
> For being a sperm whale there's no instruction manual, no rule book. There are only demands and generalities, rhythms and patterns. Mostly there is this: the wide, deep ocean and family bonds.
>
> (Safina 2020, 64–65)

That is ecologist Carl Safina's description of the sperm whales he got to know while aboard a ship off the coast of Dominica. For sperm whales, Safina reports, "family is everything" (Safina 2020, 15). Safina's account forms part of a longstanding tradition of curiosity about the intimate lives of animals. In the early Christian writing *Physiologus*, elephant parents are a model of sexual propriety from whom humans have much to learn (Curley 2009, 30). In a version of the Qur'an's story of Thamud, a tribe is destroyed for assaulting a mother camel and her little calf, who climbs a hill and plaintively asks, "God, where is my mother?" (Tlili 2012, 153). Studies of animals and religion tend to look at kinship *between* humans and animals more than kinship *among* animals, however. Both types are important, but this contribution is about religion's abiding concern for the families that animals themselves make, with a focus on the Hebrew Bible, and how that concern might speak to us today.

First, what exactly is an animal family? What is a family? The definition depends on dominant social norms. Anthropologist George Murdock understood the central elements of the family to be common residence, economic cooperation, and reproduction (Murdock 1965), but this definition excludes many families as we know them, such as families whose children have left home, parents who maintain independent finances, and non-reproductive families. The problem of definition is compounded for animal families, among whom the variety of configurations is even greater. A fluid definition is required, one that considers family less as a static entity or state of being than a process, with relationships thickening and thinning over time (Bamford 2019, 15, 19). A working definition might include any set of intimate relationships with significant material and affective dimensions that forms the framework for activities necessary for survival that give life

DOI: 10.4324/9781003324157-16

value and texture: loving, fighting, playing, sleeping, relaxing, feeding and eating, teaching and learning, bearing and raising children, getting sick and dying. The individuals who perform these activities together may or may not be thought to form a family and may or may not be biologically related.

Do all animals have families? In short, yes, though those families will look very different within and across species. The influence of kinship on behavior has been found in animals from single-celled organisms, insects, reptiles, and fish to highly social animals such as mammals (Hepper 2005). Individual animals sometimes recognize not just their parents and children but also siblings, half-siblings, cousins, grandparents, aunts, and uncles. Many mysteries remain about animal families: which relations animals recognize and how, and what behaviors they display toward those relations and why (Chapais and Berman 2004). One of the major debates in kinship studies of recent decades has been "nature" versus "culture": Is family biologically determined or culturally produced (Riggs and Peel 2016, 1–21)? Now that many scientists believe that animals, too, have cultures, this debate applies to animal families as well (Whitehead and Rendell 2014, 10–44).

Should animal families be called families? Is that language anthropomorphizing? Primatologist Frans de Waal has argued that anthropomorphism is bad only when it distorts animal experience by viewing it through a strictly human lens. "Animal-centric" anthropomorphism, by contrast, tries to see things from the animal's perspective (Waal 2001, 77). The question, then, is whether speaking of animal families can qualify as animal-centric. It must, argue psychologists Damien Riggs and Elizabeth Peel, if contemporary understandings of kinship are to move beyond an anthropocentric (human-centered) approach (Riggs and Peel 2016, 1–21). Whether to speak of animal families is ultimately best approached as an ethical rather than ontological question. Will it help animals, and us, to build better worlds? I will argue that it does by enhancing our curiosity about animals and our empathy with them.

The Paradox of Animal Families in the Bible

Notions of family in the Abrahamic traditions and modern anthropology are deeply influenced by the Bible's representation of family in the stories of Adam and Eve, Abraham and Sarah, and David and Bathsheba, and in many biblical laws such as incest prohibitions, inheritance, and impurity after childbirth (Delaney 2017). Yet little attention has been given to the presence in the Bible of the *animal* family. Four laws in the Bible address animal families: Do not cook a kid in his mother's milk (Exodus 23:19, 34:26; Deuteronomy 14:21); a newborn animal must remain together with their mother for the first week of life (Exodus 22:29, Leviticus 22:27); do not slaughter an animal and their child on the same day (Leviticus 22:28); and shoo away the mother bird before taking her eggs or chicks from the nest (Deuteronomy 22:6–7).

These four laws are scattered through the Pentateuch (the five books of Moses) but have been recognized since antiquity as related. The 1st-century C.E. Jewish philosopher Philo understood their purpose to be fostering compassion for animals (Gross 2017, 517–519). "By practicing on creatures of dissimilar kind," says Philo, "we may show humanity in a far fuller measure to beings of like kind to ourselves" (Philo, of Alexandria 1939, 8:249). Medieval commentators and modern scholars have followed suit in attributing to these laws a humanitarian rationale.

But this approach presents a paradox. Does cooking a young goat in oil or water make the end of the animal's life any less untimely than when he is cooked in milk? Does the lamb cry for the ewe any less when she is removed on Day Eight? The medieval Jewish thinker Maimonides quipped that had God wanted us to show compassion for animals, he would not have permitted us to slaughter them (Mishneh Torah Laws of Prayer 9:7; commentary on Mishnah Berakhot 5:3). In Genesis 9:2–4, God explicitly grants to humans the license to kill animals for food even though, initially in Eden, God intended humans to be vegan.

The rabbis of late antiquity largely rejected the humanitarian rationale. The Mishnah, the canonical Hebrew language collection of rabbinic teachings from the second and third centuries C.E., censors a prayer formula that seems to associate the mother bird commandment with compassion: "One who says 'May Your mercy reach the nest of a bird' . . . they silence him" (Mishnah Berakhot 5:3, Megillah 4:9). Rabbis cited in the two Talmuds speculate that the prayer formula insults God's compassion by implying that it is issued only toward the bird and not toward others, or it pits God's creatures against each other (Palestinian Talmud Berakhot 5:3 [9c]; Babylonian Talmud Megillah 25a, Berakhot 33b). One rabbi warns against guessing at the reasons for God's commandments altogether.

Compassion may seem morally compelling, a quality we might expect to appeal to ancient rabbis, but modern studies, in fact, confirm its potential shortcomings. Compassion and other humanitarian stances have been tied up with imperialist ventures that reproduce rather than reduce power asymmetries (Barnett 2013). As anthropologist Ilana Feldman observes, there is a "humanitarian politics of life" that determines not only who among the vulnerable will live but also how they will live and what sort of life they are due (Feldman 2018, 4). The humanitarian politics of animal life tends to take for granted, as the Bible's laws do, that human interests supersede animal interests and that our moral obligation extends only to avoiding *unnecessary* suffering (Radford 1999). But necessity is determined by us humans in the first place. In the next section, I give an example from the Mishnah of an alternative approach to the animal family laws that bypasses the compassion rationale.

Animal Families in Mishnah Tractate Hullin

Mishnah Tractate Hullin 5:3 fleshes out the prohibition against same-day slaughter found in Leviticus 22:28:

> One who slaughters a cow and [afterward] her two children, he incurs eighty [lashes]. One slaughtered her two children and afterward slaughtered her, he incurs forty. One slaughtered her, her daughter, and her daughter's daughter, he incurs eighty. One slaughtered her and her daughter's daughter, and afterward he slaughtered her daughter, he incurs forty. Somkhos said in the name of Rabbi Meir: He incurs eighty.

This Mishnah's four scenarios read almost like a detective story. Three cows end up dead in all four scenarios, and one person has killed them. The variables are the relationship of the cows to each other, the order in which the person slaughters them, and the severity of the punishment for the slaughterer (forty lashes is the standard rabbinic punishment for violating a negative commandment). The scenarios come two-by-two. Within the first two, the same cows die, a mother and two children. Within the last two scenarios, the same cows die, this time a mother, a daughter, and a granddaughter.

I will leave to my readers to puzzle out why the punishment in the first and third scenarios is eighty lashes, in the second scenario is forty lashes, and in the fourth scenario is the subject of dispute, whether forty or eighty. Important for my purposes is that this legal exercise brings animal family trees to the fore. Mothers, daughters, maternal grand-daughters, and siblings are all featured. The Mishnah uses the same kinship language for these animal relations that it does elsewhere for people, suggesting at least at the rhetorical level that animal families are conceptualized as being similar to human ones.

The significance of animal family ties is apparent in this Mishnah's continuation:

> At four times of the year, one who sells an animal to his fellow must announce: "I sold her mother for slaughter," "I sold her daughter for slaughter." And these [times] are: (1) The eve of the final festival day of the Festival [of Sukkot, or Booths]; (2) the eve of the first festival day of Passover; (3) the eve of Atseret (Shavuot); (4) and the eve of Rosh Ha-Shanah (the New Year); And, according to Rabbi Yosi the Galilean: Also on the eve of Yom Ha-Kippurim (the Day of Atonement) in Galilee.

If a person selling an animal has already sold that animal's parent or child, the seller must divulge that information four times a year. Because these four festivals are times of grand feasting, the chance that Buyer 1 and Buyer 2 would slaughter their animals on the same day is high. My interest is, once again, in the language of this Mishnah and its impact. The Mishnah presents a first-person script for the seller: "I sold her mother for slaughter; I sold her daughter for slaughter." There is a certain drama in the announcement. The animal is property for purchase, but her family relations must be accounted for, in a dramatic and public fashion, on a specially marked day. To buy and sell an animal for slaughter, one must know them first within their kinship webs.

Why Animal Families Matter

The English language often uses different terms for animal families than it uses for human ones. *Breeding Dogs for Dummies* tells the reader to "start with the bitches" and features chapters on the "brood bitch" and "stud dog" (Beauchamp 2011). The babies that result are the litter. The Mishnah's language of animal family and its requirement for public recognition of animal kin, by contrast, reminds the audience of animal personhood in a way that the English language resists. That reminder is issued, paradoxically, at precisely the moment when the animal is commodified as killable property. The humanitarian rationale asks human beings to show compassion for the animals whom they otherwise exploit, while the Mishnah requires a public reckoning with the parallels between human and animal families. Even if rhetorical parallels are just that—rhetorical, in language only, and not reflective of anything like real equity—they still point to pathways of thinking similarly about human and animal families that go back to the Bible.

What does it mean for us to read these laws today and to translate their concerns into modern-day practice? The first step is to recognize the impact on the animal family and especially on animal maternity of contemporary agriculture and development. The abuses of the animal agriculture industry are well-known. Even at its kindest, however, dairy farming relies upon forced reproduction and lactation along with the separation of baby from mother and herd. As legal scholar Maneesha Deckha writes, "So-called 'humane' farming also entails this separation (of mother from child) as well as forced insemination, pregnancy, birth, and other bodily interventions" (Deckha 2020, 252). Still, ethical farming, such as that advocated by the policy guide of the U.K.'s Christian Ethics of Farmed Animal Welfare, can work toward supporting maternal care among animals and life in family groups (Clough et al. 2020, 53). Animal science here complements religious traditions' concern with animal families by assessing the need for nurture within different species so that each animal family might flourish in their own way.

The end goal is to consider the obligations and opportunities the animal family presents. Let me suggest four areas of inquiry: 1) animal emotions, 2) animal agency, 3) family diversity, and 4) human response. The first line of inquiry pays attention not only to animal suffering but also to animal love, attachment, and other positive affective experiences. As legal scholar Taimie Bryant writes, "unless we can conceptualize animals as having other capacities in addition to sentience, such as parent-child relationships, there is little hope for increased legal protection and reform other than improved means of killing them more kindly" (Bryant 2010, 62). The second line of inquiry turns from the question of "How can we save animal families?" to a more holistic "How can human and animal families coexist peaceably on a habitable planet?" The third line of inquiry uses our developing knowledge of animal families to better appreciate the diversity among both animal and human families. The fourth line of inquiry throws the spotlight back on us. Most people find animal families adorable; the challenge is to consider how best to respect the intimate animal relationships that charm us so. While we may never be able to support every family, especially in the context of global market forces, a vegan utopianism inspired by strains within the world's religious traditions lets us dream of a world—a truly peaceable kingdom—in which all families, human and animal alike, survive and thrive (Quinn and Westwood 2018).

References

Bamford, Sandra C. 2019. "Introduction." In *The Cambridge Handbook of Kinship* (Cambridge Handbooks in Anthropology), edited by Sandra C. Bamford, 1–34. Cambridge and New York: Cambridge University Press.

Barnett, Michael N. 2013. *Empire of Humanity: A History of Humanitarianism.* Ithaca, N.Y.: Cornell University Press.

Beauchamp, Richard G. 2011. *Breeding Dogs for Dummies.* Hoboken, N.J.: John Wiley & Sons.

Bryant, Taimie L. 2010. "Denying Animals Childhood and Its Implications for Animal-Protective Law Reform." *Law, Culture and the Humanities* 6 (1): 56–74.

Chapais, Bernard, and Carol M. Berman. 2004. "Introduction: The Kinship Black Box." In *Kinship and Behavior in Primates*, edited by Bernard Chapais and Carol M. Berman, 3–11. Oxford and New York: Oxford University Press.

Clough, David L., Margaret B. Adam, David Grumett, and Siobhan Mullan. 2020. "The Christian Ethics of Farmed Animal Welfare: A Policy Framework for Churches and Christian Organizations." www.abdn.ac.uk/sdhp/divinity-religious-studies/cefaw/cefaw-policy-framework-2138.php.

Curley, Michael J., trans. 2009. *Physiologus.* Chicago, Ill. and London: University of Chicago Press.

Deckha, Maneesha. 2020. "Veganism, Dairy, and Decolonization." *Journal of Human Rights and the Environment* 11 (2): 244–67.

Delaney, Carol. 2017. "The Seeds of Kinship Theory in the Abrahamic Religions." In *New Directions in Spiritual Kinship: Sacred Ties across the Abrahamic Religions*, edited by Todne Thomas, Asiya Malik, and Rose Wellman, 245–61. Cham: Palgrave Macmillan.

Feldman, Ilana. 2018. *Life Lived in Relief: Humanitarian Predicaments and Palestinian Refugee Politics.* Oakland: University of California Press.

Gross, Aaron S. 2017. "Animals, Empathy, and Raḥamim in the Study of Religion: A Case Study of Jewish Opposition to Hunting." *Studies in Religion/Sciences Religieuses* 46 (4): 511–35.

Hepper, Peter G., ed. 2005. *Kin Recognition.* Cambridge: Cambridge University Press.

Murdock, George Peter. 1965. *Social Structure*. New York: Macmillan.

Philo, of Alexandria. 1939. *On the Virtues*. Translated by Francis Henry Colson. Vol. 8. Loeb Classical Library 341. Cambridge, Mass.: Harvard University Press.

Quinn, Emelia, and Benjamin Westwood. 2018. "Introduction: Thinking Through Veganism." In *Thinking Veganism in Literature and Culture: Towards a Vegan Theory*, edited by Emelia Quinn and Benjamin Westwood, 1–24. New York: Palgrave Macmillan Springer.

Radford, Mike. 1999. "'Unnecessary Suffering': The Cornerstone of Animal Protection Legislation Considered." *Criminal Law Review*, 702–13.

Riggs, Damien W., and Elizabeth Peel. 2016. *Critical Kinship Studies: An Introduction to the Field*. London: Palgrave Macmillan.

Safina, Carl. 2020. *Becoming Wild: How Animal Cultures Raise Families, Create Beauty, and Achieve Peace*. New York: Picador.

Tlili, Sarra. 2012. *Animals in the Qur'an*. New York: Cambridge University Press.

Waal, Frans B.M. de. 2001. *The Ape and the Sushi Master: Cultural Reflections by a Primatologist*. New York: Basic Books.

Whitehead, Hal, and Luke Rendell. 2014. *The Cultural Lives of Whales and Dolphins*. Chicago, Ill.: University of Chicago Press.

Other Recommended Resources

Adams, Carol J. 2015. *The Sexual Politics of Meat: A Feminist-Vegetarian Critical Theory*. New York: Bloomsbury USA.

Arnold, Andrea, director. 2021. *Cow*. IFC Films. www.ifcfilms.com/films/cow.

Berkowitz, Beth A. 2022a. "Birds as Dads, Babysitters, and Hats: An 'Indistinction' Approach to the Modern Bird Mitzvah in Deuteronomy 22:6–7." *Worldviews: Global Religions, Culture, and Ecology* 26: 79–105.

_____. 2022b. "Interpretation in the Anthropocene: Reading the Animal Family Laws of the Pentateuch." In *Studies in the History of Exegesis*, edited by Mark Elliott, Raleigh C. Heth, and Angela Zautcke, 39–52. Tübingen: Mohr Siebeck.

Berthelot, Katell. 2002. "Philo and Kindness Towards Animals (De Virtutibus 125–147)." *The Studia Philonica Annual* 14: 48–65.

Forbes, Scott. 2005. *A Natural History of Families*. Princeton, N.J.: Princeton University Press.

Gaard, Greta. 2013. "Toward a Feminist Postcolonial Milk Studies." *American Quarterly* 65 (3): 595–618.

Haran, Menahem. 1979. "Seething a Kid in Its Mother's Milk." *Journal of Jewish Studies* 30 (1): 23–35.

13 The Cat Mitzvah
Jewish Literary Animals

Andrea Dara Cooper

Can a cat become Jewish? I explore this question using a graphic novel as a point of focus, illuminating the complexity of Jewish identity and challenging the link between religion and spoken language. Along the way, I reflect on the relationship between animals and literature. Fictional narratives allow us to imagine a world in which animals, both human and nonhuman, can claim religious personhood. Through this literary case study, we can examine how human and other than human animal identities have been historically constructed alongside one another, particularly in colonial contexts.

Joann Sfar's graphic novel *The Rabbi's Cat* (*Le Chat du rabbin*) offers a compelling example of an animal portrayed as a religious subject. Set in 1930s Algeria, the novel features an animal protagonist who challenges the exclusively human coming-of-age/becoming-man ritual of Bar Mitzvah.[1] The titular cat obtains the ability to speak after swallowing his human's parrot.[2] Once the cat speaks, the rabbi begins treating him like a human. Language—particularly human speech—becomes identified with Jewish ethics and law (*halakha*).

The rabbi teaches selections from the Jewish textual tradition to the cat, lest the feline poison the mind of the rabbi's beloved daughter Zlabya. The cat worships Zlabya, with whom he has been scandalously reading Stendahl's decidedly secular novel *Le Rouge et Le Noir* (*The Red and the Black*). To make matters worse, the cat lies about the murderous act through which he gained speech; he insists that he does not know what happened to the parrot. The cat tells the reader,

> [The Rabbi] wants me to study the Torah and the Talmud—the Mishnah, the Gemara. He wants to put me back on the straight and narrow. He tells me that I have to be a good Jew, and that a good Jew does not lie. I answer that I am only a cat. I add that I don't know if I am a Jewish cat or not. The rabbi tells me that of course I'm Jewish, since my masters are Jews. . . . I tell him that if I am a Jewish cat, I want to be bar-mitzvahed.
>
> (Sfar 2005, 9–10)[3]

In a meta-textual wink to the reader, the author shows how the act of reading will allow the cat to become Jewish, despite the doubts of certain characters who are shown to have overly narrow and anthropocentric worldviews. Community and literature—ritual and reading—draw the cat to Judaism and lead him to build a richly textured Jewish identity that further enriches his rabbi/human's own Jewishness.

What is the place of the cat in the Jewish textual tradition? More broadly, we find in the Talmud (the central text of rabbinic Judaism) a concern for animal welfare and

DOI: 10.4324/9781003324157-17

the prohibition against the suffering of living creatures, *tsa'ar ba'alei chayim*, in which humans are forbidden to enact unnecessary cruelty against animals.[4] The Talmud exhibits more ambivalence about the roles of companion animals in particular. While some Talmudic sources suggest that raising cats serves no purpose or that keeping a cat is prohibited, in one notable source, domestic animals are permitted because of the function they serve in keeping homes free from pests: "One may raise village dogs, cats, monkeys, and genets, because they serve to clean the house of mice and other vermin" (Bava Kamma 80a). The implication here is that companion animals are allowed insofar as they are useful and perform a necessary service (Schwartz 2001, 223–224).[5]

In the graphic novel, the cat aspires to become Bar Mitzvah primarily so that he can be seen as responsible enough to be permitted companionship with the rabbi's daughter. But the cat is initially denied his wish by both the rabbi and the rabbi's own rabbi. The latter insists on enforcing animal/human distinctions. The author clearly favors the perspective of the theologically sophisticated feline, illustrating the problem with imposing binary categorizations such as animal/human, Jew/non-Jew, or Arabic/French. The narrative also highlights other dualisms: the inherent hybridity of Mizrahi Jewry in North Africa and of Algeria in relation to colonial France.[6] The cat protagonist asks how to live life as a Jew in these intertwined contexts. The novel represents the multiplicity of Jewish identities and practices, and Sfar deliberately alters his characters visually from panel to panel to illustrate how their identities are never fixed (Harris 2008, 192).

Language is implicated in political and social hierarchies in Algiers. The rabbi soon learns that to retain his position in his community, he must be proficient in French, not Arabic or Hebrew. In order to become the official rabbi of the community, he must pass a dictation test to be approved by the colonial authorities. His daughter responds, "Why is it any business of the French who gets to be rabbi here?" (Sfar 2005, 57). The cat agrees, indignant: "You've been the rabbi here for thirty years and these guys who've never set foot here want to decide who should be rabbi or not. And to lead prayer in Hebrew for Jews who speak Arabic, they want you to write in French" (Sfar 2005, 60).[7]

The rabbi's plight demonstrates how Ashkenazi (European) religious practices are privileged over Sephardic and Mizrahi practices. Just as the cat must seek admission to a Jewish community that would exclude him for not being human, "the rabbi faces the possibility of losing his position for not having mastered the language of the civilizing mission" (Kandiyoti 2017, 66). It is not enough that the rabbi and the cat are both multilingual (in human and animal languages, in the case of the cat). Sfar illustrates what is at stake politically in not having access to the correct language, which is enforced by French colonial notions of literacy. For both human and feline, lacking access to the proper language can become grounds for communal and religious exclusion. In this way, the humanimal tale illustrates the dangers of assigning moral and religious status according to so-called "civilizing" values.

The cat begins to tutor the Rabbi in French and suggests helping him during the exam. In another meta-textual nod to the reader, the rabbi studies by reading aloud from his daughter's book of French animal fables.[8] At the entrance to the exam, the cat is turned away by the administrators: "They won't let me in. They say animals aren't allowed in the school" (Sfar 2005, 61). Watching the difficult dictation from a window, the cat decides that the rabbi requires divine intervention in order to pass the test. "Among Jews, you only speak the Lord's name during actual prayers. . . . I don't care if it's forbidden, I invoke the name of God. 'Adonai, Adonai. Adonai. Adonai. Adonai. Adonai. Adonai. Meow'" (Sfar 2005, 63–66). The cat loses human speech as a direct result of this utterance, reverting to his previous status as a non-speaking housecat.[9] Ultimately, he gives up his ability to speak when he utters the ineffable name of God in order to aid his human.

When the rabbi initially asks the cat how long he has been able to read, the cat responds, "I always have. I learned at the same time as your daughter, but you didn't know before because I was mute" (Sfar 2005, 22). But does the cat ever really gain or lose speech? After all, for the reader, the cat's voice is consistently present throughout the novel. As literature scholar Marla Harris points out, "the cat's loss of voice is belied, as far as the reader is concerned, by his continued narration" (Harris 2008, 193).[10] In this way, the narrative pushes back on the widespread notion that speech is necessarily connected to ethics or religion, which are usually considered exclusively human domains because of their perceived connection to spoken language. Religious studies scholar Aaron S. Gross notes that for influential twentieth-century theorists in the study of religion, pre-speech humans (such as children) and humans who lost the capacity for speech and language were not considered properly human (Gross 2015, 68). For these thinkers in the domi-nant Western intellectual tradition, the emergence of religion was linked to the separation of the speaking human from the non-speaking animal.

When the presumed link between language and religion is dismantled, animals them-selves can be considered religious subjects. For example, drawing on observations of animal spirituality by primatologist Jane Goodall, religious studies scholar Donovan O. Schaefer argues that religion need not be predicated on language since religion is neither exclusively cognitive nor exclusively human.[11] In the graphic novel the rabbi undertakes to teach the cat about Judaism, but not the parrot, so there is clearly something beyond the ability to speak that makes the cat educatable in Jewish law and textual tradition. Similarly, losing the ability to speak does not make the cat any less Jewish or worthy of interspecies relationship and (non-spoken) dialogue. The story teaches us that animals should not be included or excluded from religious or ethical consideration (both in how they are treated and in how they are figured as subjects in their own rights) based on their access to spoken language.

In a parallel manner, the narrative demonstrates the absurdity of "civilizing" processes that grant religious or civil status to humans based on colonial definitions of linguistic belonging. The perils of enforcing the binaries of human/animal and civilized/primitive, which are often interrelated, are effectively mirrored in the author's chosen medium. Despite more recent cultural elevation in North America and Europe the form of the graphic novel is still largely associated with children (despite the decidedly adult and racy nature of some of *The Rabbi's Cat*'s illustrations), and the child-animal link has histori-cally served to legitimize damaging imperial impulses.[12]

Scholars of animals and religion have rightfully pointed out that representations of ani-mals, whether literary or artistic, should include reflection on real animals; otherwise they risk overlooking vital issues of animal ethics. Animal representations in literature, far from being isolated from the concerns of real-life animals, can offer alternatives for mul-tispecies engagement. The cat and his rabbi both face challenges in their quests to become socially and religiously legible. The narrative identifies a Jewish identity crisis that crosses species lines, implicitly and organically granting religious subjectivity to animal others.

Notes

1 A bar mitzvah is a coming of age ceremony in Judaism traditionally held for 13-year-old boys, which involves reading from the Torah, the first five books of the Hebrew Bible. The ritual confers legal adult status. Bar Mitzvah literally translates to "son of the commandment,"

and marks the time of obligation to Jewish law. In the twentieth and twenty-first centuries, the ceremony has expanded in liberal denominations of Judaism to include the Bat Mitzvah (literally, "daughter of the commandment") and B'nei Mitvah (the gender-inclusive "children of the commandment"). For more information, see www.myjewishlearning.com/article/bar-and-bat-mitzvah-101/.

2 I refer to the rabbi as the cat's human, and not "owner," intentionally—both because this is the language I prefer with my own animal companions, and because the cat of the story would surely find the notion of ownership by anyone to be laughable, save for his "mistress" Zlabya, the rabbi's daughter.

3 As Paul Eisenstein notes (2008, 165), "the cat seeks to concretize his (masculine) Jewish identity in the rituals and rites meant to ratify meaningfully one's Jewishness. . . . But can a cat be called to the Torah?"

4 See Cohn-Sherbok 2006, 83–84.

5 While *The Rabbi's Cat* opens with a statement about the Jewish aversion to dogs because "Jews have been bitten, chased, and barked at for so long that, in the end, they prefer cats" (Sfar 2005, 1), the Talmud displays ambivalence toward the role of the dog; see Menache 2013. In the twentieth century, the Jewish philosopher Martin Buber was famously inspired by the feline gaze. In his influential work *I and Thou*, a cat provides a model of dialogical encounter: "Sometimes I look into a cat's eyes. . . . The beginning of this cat's glance, lighting up under the touch of my glance, indisputably questioned me: 'Is it possible that you think of me?'" (Buber 1958, 97).

6 Mizrahi, literally "Eastern" in Hebrew, refers to Jews from Middle Eastern and North African countries, and Sephardi refers to Jews of Spanish or Portuguese descent. According to Marla Harris, Sfar's work is informed by "borders and border crossings—between Jews and Muslims, Jews and Christians, humans and animals, Africa and Europe, author and reader," illustrating, in turn, the complex relationship between national identity and Jewish identity (Harris 2008, 182).

7 The cat's reply shows "the ridiculous way colonial authority is naturalized and maintained in and through a privileged language, French," as the rabbi becomes "a victim of French supremacist thinking" (Eisenstein 2008, 169–70).

8 Dalia Kandiyoti notes that this instructional text, *Les fables de La Fontaine*, serves as a winking "mise-en-abyme of our own reading of a story about talking animals" (Kandiyoti 2017, 66). The graphic novel itself "oozes a fable-like charm, with its appealing animal and human characters" (54).

9 Following this act, "the cat can explain neither what he has done nor what has occurred as a result of it; the rabbi assumes the cat has made a conscious choice not to speak" (Hochman 2018, 51).

10 "Though the action in the novel is propelled by the cat's acquisition of speech, the novel's narration remains independent of it. The cat's thoughts drive the story" (Hochman 2018, 47).

11 By emphasizing the links between human and other than human animal bodies, including physicality and emotion (what scholars call "affect"), we can access "better understandings of the shared worlds spiraling around, through, and between us, as well as new modes of interspecies community" (Schaefer 2015, 18). See also Gross 2015.

12 This can be seen in the colonial categorization of religion, in which religious traditions viewed as closely aligned with nature, particularly animals, have been categorically dismissed as childish, primitive, and uncivilized. As Kimberley Patton observes, "[t]he equation of childhood with 'primitive' religions through the link of an ingrained affinity for animals" leads to a logic that supplements violent displacement, exclusion, and elimination (Patton 2006, 32). Also, as Dalia Kandiyoti notes (2017, 67–69), at the climactic moment of the story, the rabbi is reduced to taking the dictation test like a child in a schoolroom.

References

Buber, Martin. 1958. *I and Thou*. Translated by R.G. Smith. New York: Scribner Classics.

Cohn-Sherbok, Dan. 2006. "Hope for the Animal Kingdom: A Jewish Vision." In *A Communion of Subjects: Animals in Religion, Science, and Ethics*, edited by Paul Waldau and Kimberly Patton, 81–90. New York: Columbia University Press.

Eisenstein, Paul. 2008. "Imperfect Masters: Rabbinic Authority in Joann Sfar's *The Rabbi's Cat*." In *The Jewish Graphic Novel: Critical Approaches*, edited by Samantha Baskind and Ranen Omer-Sherman, 163–80. New Brunswick, N.J.: Rutgers University Press.

Gross, Aaron S. 2015. *The Question of the Animal and Religion: Theoretical Stakes, Practical Implications*. New York: Columbia University Press.

Harris, Marla. 2008. "Borderlands: Places, Spaces, and Jewish Identity in Joann Sfar's *The Rabbi's Cat* and *Klezmer*." In *The Jewish Graphic Novel: Critical Approaches*, edited by Samantha Baskind and Ranen Omer-Sherman, 181–97. New Brunswick, N.J.: Rutgers University Press.

Hochman, Leah. 2018. "The Ineffability of Form: Speaking and Seeing the Sacred in *Tina's Mouth* and *The Rabbi's Cat*." In *Comics and Sacred Texts: Reimagining Religion and Graphic Narratives*, edited by Assaf Gamzou and Ken Koltun-Fromm, 43–55. Jackson: University Press of Mississippi.

Kandiyoti, Dalia. 2017. "Imagining Cosmopolitanism, Conviviality, and Coexistence in World Literature: Jews, Muslims, Language, and Enchantment in Joann Sfar's *The Rabbi's Cat*." *Prooftexts* 36 (1–2): 53–82.

Menache, Sophia. 2013. "From Unclean Species to Man's Best Friend: Dogs in the Biblical, Mishnaic, and Talmud Periods." In *A Jew's Best Friend? The Image of the Dog Throughout Jewish History*, edited by Rakefet Zalashik and Phillip Ackerman-Lieberman, 36–51. Brighton: Sussex Academic Press.

Patton, Kimberley. 2006. " 'Caught with Ourselves in the Net of Life and Time': Traditional Views of Animals in Religion." In *A Communion of Subjects: Animals in Religion, Science, and Ethics*, edited by Paul Waldau and Kimberly Patton, 27–39. New York: Columbia University Press.

Schaefer, Donovan O. 2015. *Religious Affects: Animality, Evolution, and Power*. Durham, N.C.: Duke University Press.

Schwartz, Joshua. 2001. "Cats in Ancient Jewish Society." *Journal of Jewish Studies* 52: 211–34.

Sfar, Joann. 2005. *The Rabbi's Cat* [Le Chat du rabbin]. Translated by Alexis Siegel and Anjali Singh. New York: Pantheon.

Other Recommended Resources

Boggs, Colleen Glenney. 2013. *Animalia Americana: Animal Representations and Biopolitical Subjectivity*. New York: Columbia University Press.

Cooper, Andrea Dara. 2019. "Writing Humanimals: Critical Animal Studies and Jewish Studies." *Religion Compass* 13 (12): 1–11. https://doi.org/10.1111/rec3.12341.

Goldfeder, Mark. 2016. "Not All Dogs Go to Heaven: Judaism's Lessons in Beastly Morality." In *Beastly Morality: Animals as Ethical Agents*, edited by Jonathan K. Crane, 63–77. New York: Columbia University Press.

Harris, Marla. 2016. "Liminality, Language, and Longing for Home in Abdellatif Kechiche's *La graine et le mulet* [*The Secret of the Grain*] and Joann Sfar's *Le chat du rabbin* [*The Rabbi's Cat*]." *South Atlantic Review* 81 (1): 120–35.

Kalechofsky, Roberta. "Hierarchy, Kinship, and Responsibility: The Jewish Relationship to the Animal World." In *A Communion of Subjects: Animals in Religion, Science, and Ethics*, edited by Paul Waldau and Kimberly Patton, 91–99. New York: Columbia University Press.

Leroy, Fabrice. 2014. "Sfar Conjures Marc Chagall (Again): The Politics of Visual Representation in *Le Chat du Rabbin*." In *Sfar So Far: Identity, History, Fantasy, and Mimesis in Joann Sfar's Graphic Novels*, 142–61. Leuven: Leuven University Press.

McKinney, Mark. 2013. *Redrawing French Empire in Comics*. Columbus: Ohio State University Press.

14 Blessings of Pets in Jewish and Christian Traditions

Laura Hobgood

On a designated autumn morning in New York City, an unlikely gathering occurs annu-ally. Scores of dogs, cats, birds, hamsters, goldfish, turtles, and other pets come together for the Blessing of the Animals at the Cathedral of Saint John the Divine. This event has taken place on the first Sunday in October since 1985, and thousands of people from the city and beyond join in with their pets in tow. Officially titled the "Feast of St. Francis" that includes the "Holy Eucharist and Procession of Animals," it is one of the best-known blessings in the United States. The final ritual of the formal liturgy is the opening of the "great bronze doors" for the procession, which could include, in any given year, eagles, camels, llamas, hedgehogs, bees, and more (almost all from local sanctuaries or rescue groups). As the dean of the cathedral points out, these doors are only opened three times a year: Christmas, Easter, and the Procession of Animals. Thus, this ritual is designated as a high holy moment in the life of the congregation. Following the formal service, which takes place inside the huge Gothic cathedral, individual pets are blessed by an assembly of priests in the adjoining park space.

Some people bring their pets every year and attribute longevity and health to the annual blessing; others visit for the first time just to witness the impressive spectacle. While there are some problematic aspects to this entire event, overall, it offers an impor-tant recognition of the centrality of other animals in general, and pets specifically, to the lives of numerous human beings (Hobgood-Oster 2008, 113–118). Some scholars sug-gest that the establishment of this Feast of St. Francis celebration at St. John the Divine was the precipitating event for the growth of blessings of animals, at least in contempo-rary U.S. culture (Applebaum 2015).

When, where, and how did the blessings of animals and pets begin in the history of Judaism and Christianity? Who is included—all livestock, pets, or all animals? These questions are difficult to answer definitively, but some clues can be uncovered in texts, images, oral traditions, and changing cultural practices. Regardless of the history, in contemporary practice, the rituals of animal blessings are growing rapidly, particularly in some Jewish communities in the United States and in Christian communities globally.

One important piece of the trajectory of blessings is to consider just who is a pet and why that shifting category and practice is so impactful on blessings. Before the nine-teenth century and the rise of an economic "middle class" in some parts of the world, other animals who lived with or around humans were necessarily useful. In other words, they contributed to the economy of the household as a producer of food, clothing, or other resources, or as a worker, for example, by pulling a plow or assisting with hunt-ing. Some members of the upper class and royalty kept animals as purely companions, but it was not a widespread practice (Ritvo 1989). Then with the rise of the middle class

DOI: 10.4324/9781003324157-18

in Western contexts and similar economic shifts in other global settings, the propensity to keep pets often accompanied these changes in culture. Animals, particularly but not exclusively dogs, cats, and birds, were sometimes now part of a household just for the sake of companionship. One telling statistic is that 70% of households in the United States include at least one pet (Bedford 2022). Their station changed, and this transformation has impacted blessings in significant ways, as will be seen later.

Numerous texts in the Hebrew Bible lift up the significance of animals. One need only recall the story of Noah's Ark in the book of Genesis to recognize the centrality of animals, though the biblical story is also complicated since other animals are interpreted as inferior to humans in the overall hierarchy of creation. Still, some forms of blessings of animals exist in the history of the Jewish tradition, and some are being added into Judaism in contemporary practice. Also, if one considers sacrifice to include a blessing, then as part of ancient Jewish practice, scores of animals were blessed as part of the sacrificial rituals at the Temple in Jerusalem. But scant evidence exists of other forms of blessings of animals in the history of Judaism.

In contemporary practice, however, these recognitions are entering into the cycle of the Jewish year, with the first documented blessing taking place in 1997 (Aiello 2021). Blessings of pets are generally happening on one of three holidays in Jewish communities. Some congregations celebrate a blessing of pets on the seventh day of Passover (in the spring) as a part of the recognition of the Hebrews' and their animals' liberation from slavery in Egypt (Sweeney 2011). Other congregations observe blessings as part of the Torah reading cycle that includes Noah and the Ark. "Parashat No'ach" (the Noah portion) usually lands in late October or early November and is an obvious choice for the timing of animal blessings (Kent 2019). Finally, some congregations are choosing to connect this blessing with Tu B'Shvat, which is more specifically a recognition of trees but also connects with creation and earth's bounty. There are some concerns about several of these selections for pet blessings; for example, the transportation of animals on Shabbat could be problematic, and the ending of the Noah story establishes a relationship of fear between humans and animals. Because of those issues, another suggestion is to select a *hillula* (annual rejoicing on the anniversary of the death of an important rabbi) of a rabbi who is connected to animals as the day for blessings.

Regardless of which day is selected, hosting a blessing of the pets is a growing trend, especially in the United States and particularly in Reform Judaism. Most of these blessings are attended by congregants with their dogs and cats. Also, a number of rabbis are sharing their ideas for rituals, including prayers that are appropriate within their tradition.

There is slightly more evidence for historical traditions of animal blessing within Christianity. A lovely miniature image, likely from an illuminated manuscript by the Master of St. Veronica from around 1400 C.E., shows a gentle Saint Anthony Abbot (251–357 C.E.) blessing the poor, the sick, and the animals. The saint stands on a pedestal with his hand raised, looking down at those gathered. While the human poor and sick are off to the sides, the animals are front and center: a goose, sheep, a pig, a mule, a rooster, doves, and a buck are among those who stare gratefully up at him, seemingly listening to his words. Anthony, often portrayed with a pig by his side in his iconography, is the official patron saint of animals in the Roman Catholic tradition. His feast day, January 17, is frequently referenced as a day when blessings of animals occurred in Italy, probably for centuries, and then in other places globally where the Catholic Church has influence. This fifteenth-century image depicting a fourth-century saint helps uncover at least a small part of the mystery when searching for evidence of the blessing of animals in the Christian tradition.

Not only in Italy but also in places as distant as Mexico City and Madrid, one will still find animal blessings that take place in January. For example, a visitor to Rome in the 1930s describes a St. Anthony's Day blessing in front of the church of St. Eusebius. She states that "all the animals of Rome" congregated at this ritual gathering (McMurrough 1939, 83–86). In contemporary practice, the Italian Association of Livestock Farmers builds a temporary barn in the main square of the Vatican to house horses, chickens, cows, dogs, and other animals for their blessing on Anthony's feast day. Similar blessings happen nationwide.

Another longstanding animal blessing happens on a different day altogether, the Olvera Street (Los Angeles, California) Blessing, which occurs on the Saturday before Easter. This is particularly interesting since the history of that blessing extends back at least ninety years and likely longer. The location is the oldest surviving street in the city, dating from the time of Mexican rule. A cow decked with flowers leads this procession, and people bring a myriad of pets, many adorned in costumes. In the 1970s, a significant outdoor mural was added as a piece of public art commemorating the long history of the event.

A few changes have taken place that mark a contemporary turn for these rituals. First, the popularity of St. Francis (1181/2–1226 C.E.) moved some of the blessings to his feast day in early October, such as the one at the Cathedral of St. John the Divine mentioned earlier. In many ways, the connection of blessings of animals with Francis is quite appropriate since, as his story is told, Francis was the first friar to bring into the sanctuary a live nativity. In other words, he returned animals to the sanctuary in the thirteenth century and thus is a particularly good model for doing the same in the contemporary church. Second, the blessings have, in many cases, shifted from focusing on all animals or on agricultural animals to pets. However, other animals are still frequently included, at least by reference, if not in physical presence.

Most of the consideration here is on the blessings of animals in the United States, where their growth in popularity seems to be mirroring the increasing number of households with pets. But it is important to note that by the twenty-first century, blessings occurred in many countries with substantial Christian populations, including Italy, Kenya, the Philippines, Mexico, Peru, and more. Animal blessings are indeed becoming a more global phenomenon in the Christian tradition.

Two additional considerations are important in terms of the cultural impact of blessings in Jewish and Christian communities. First, the blessings of pets attract people who are not necessarily members of the congregation offering the event. Frequently, pet rescue groups or animal activist organizations participate in the blessing itself and/or in a larger event connected with it. Congregations might advertise fairly widely, inviting the larger community to join them. Also, as environmental concerns become linked more closely to religious concerns in many Jewish and Christian communities, the blessing of pets indicates a way to connect with creation overall. On a different note, some evangelical churches frame the blessings as a way to attract young people to the church. Myriad reasons emerge for offering blessings of pets.

Some of those cultural factors might be what has led to the second impact, which is an extension to interfaith, faith-secular, or largely secular blessings. One of the largest of these interfaith blessings takes place in Long Beach, California, and was initiated in 2002. In the nearly two decades since, leaders from Catholic, Baha'i, Unitarian

Universalist, Jewish, Lutheran, Wiccan, Buddhist, Islamic, and more religious traditions have participated. Other blessings might be sponsored by a local chapter of the ASPCA or even a municipal shelter. Often these blessings raise awareness about the status of pets, including overpopulation and homelessness, in particular communities.

While their exact history remains obscure, clearly blessings of pets and other animals became a growing phenomenon starting in the late twentieth century and extending into the twenty-first century. Various reasons and motivations contribute to the expanding practice of pet blessings, but these rituals do offer a direct connection between animals and religion in contemporary culture.

References

Aiello, Barbara. 2021. "Tu B'Shevat Blessing for Those Who Care for Animals." *Rabbi Barbara Blog*, January 28. Accessed June 1, 2022. www.rabbibarbara.com/tu-bshevat-blessing-for-those-who-care-for-animals/.

Applebaum, Patricia. 2015. "Why Blessing Animals Has Become So Popular in Recent Decades." *The Christian Century*, October 27. www.christiancentury.org/blogs/archive/2015-10/why-blessings-animals-have-become-popular-recent-decades.

Bedford, Emma. 2022. "Pet Ownership in the U.S.—Statistics and Facts." *Statista*, March 3. Accessed June 2, 2022. www.statista.com/topics/1258/pets/.

Hobgood-Oster, Laura. 2008. *Holy Dogs and Asses: Animals in the Christian Tradition*. Urbana: University of Illinois Press.

Kent, Evan. 2019. "How Blessing Our Pets Brought Holiness to Our Community." *ReformJudaism.org*, October 30. Accessed June 1, 2022. https://reformjudaism.org/blog/how-blessing-our-pets-brought-holiness-our-community.

McMurrough, Carola. 1939. "Blessings of Animals: Roman Rite" *Orate Fraters* 14 (2): 83–86.

Ritvo, Harriet. 1989. *The Animal Estate: The English and Other Cultures in Victorian England*. Cambridge, Mass.: Harvard University Press.

Sweeney, Jon. 2011. "Blessing Our Pets: In the Spirit of St. Francis and Judaism." *HuffPost: The Blog*, December 2. Accessed June 2, 2022. www.huffpost.com/entry/blessing-our-pets-st-francis-judaism_b_951906#:~:text=In%20both%20the%20Christian%20ceremony,they%20are%20gifts%20from%20God.

Other Recommended Resources

"Blessing of the Pets: Tifereth Israel." 2021. FaceBook Video, October 8. www.facebook.com/watch/live/?ref=watch_permalink&v=427196635783050.

"The Feast of St. Francis & the Blessing of Animals." 2020. Cathedral of St. John Divine, Video. www.youtube.com/watch?v=UFGdeXfoNIk.

Hobgood-Oster, Laura. 2010. "Ideas for Communities and Congregations." In *The Friends We Keep: Unleashing Christianity's Compassion for Animals* by Laura Hobgood-Oster, 181–91. Waco, Texas: Baylor University Press.

Wilmer, Amelie. 2019. "In the Sanctuary of Animals: Honoring God's Creatures Through Ritual and Relationship." *Interpretation: A Journal of Bible and Theology* 73 (3): 272–87.

15 Becoming Priceless Through Sacrifice

A Goat for San Lázaro-Babalú Ayé

Todd Ramón Ochoa

Animal sacrifice is a stunning and confounding activity for those unfamiliar with it, although people have practiced it throughout the world and across time. To appreciate the role of animal sacrifice in religious life, it is important to explore the specific history, culture, and communities surrounding any particular case. Theories to explain sacrifice are myriad, and no one theory can explain it in every case. Sacrifice is best understood as a convergent cultural practice with multiple social sources and, therefore, no unified explanation. In this chapter, I explore how animals become godlike in sacrifice, their costliness to the people who offer them, and the "becoming priceless" that the offering of animals makes possible.

Along Cuba's north-central coast, a string of towns celebrates a calendar of annual feasts for a pantheon of gods and goddesses called *orisás* (Ochoa 2020, xiii–xiv). The orisás are understood as sovereigns who preside over specific domains of human affairs, such as movement, money, struggle, and health. People in these towns are proudly descended from enslaved and emancipated African ancestors, and the feasts they host are replete with African-inspired resources: songs in several African languages, drum rhythms that can be traced to specific West African and Central African communities, as well as spirit possession and animal sacrifice. Their feasts are called *bembés*, which means "parties," and each orisá has her or his bembé celebrated on a date that aligns with a saint's feast day in Cuba's Catholic calendar. Folks in Havana, Cuba's capital, might call this *Santería* or *Lucumí*, these being terms for orisá praise in the city, but locals call their praise *bembé*, after the parties where the orisás are celebrated.

An example is the December 17 feast for *San Lázaro-Babalú Ayé*, a divinity compounded from the figures of *San Lázaro*—Lazarus the Beggar to Catholic Cubans—and *Babalú Ayé*, a West African god who presides over health and healing (and also commands pestilence and pandemics). The two figures are commingled such that folks in the towns use their names interchangeably or refer to a single entity—*San Lázaro-Babalú Ayé*. His favor is prized, for illness is just around the corner for each of us and our loved ones, as COVID-19 taught us.

An orisá like San Lázaro-Babalú Ayé is the guest of honor at his bembé. A bembé can only be successful if it is graced by his attendance. But he would be disappointed if other orisás did not also attend. In fact, a good feast will have every one of the orisás in the pantheon make an appearance, thus bestowing a full complement of divine grace on the attendees, who can number in the hundreds.

To ensure the orisás will come, the bembé must be carefully prepared. A bembé host will incite a crowd—family, neighbors, friends, and others—to sing and dance the feast away. Musicians will be arranged—several knowledgeable singers and several drummers

DOI: 10.4324/9781003324157-19

to rotate on each of three drums—their participation guaranteed by family ties and gift repayment. The musicians beckon the orisás with songs from repertoires specific to each divinity, in all hundreds of call and response songs devised by beloved ancestors and improvised upon in the present. Bembé hosts will vie for dancers, for it is through dance that orisás make their appearance. Orisás are said to arrive "mounted atop" human steeds, their "horses." Spirit possession in these towns is talked about in equestrian terms with medieval allusions—the orisás referred to as lords and ladies, the dancers who assume their likenesses referred to as their horses. Horse imagery is widespread in Black Atlantic praise—Haiti, Brazil, and Cuba all play with equestrian vocabulary to talk about spirit possession (Hurston 1990, 219–226; Deren 2004, 95; Strongman 2019, 199; Ochoa 2020, 15).

Hosts prepare for a bembé like the December 17 feast for San Lázaro-Babalú Ayé by assembling an altar where a Catholic likeness of the orisá and many African-inspired attributes, such as seashells and bouquets of wild herbs and flowers, will be gathered. These altars will be decorated with strings of lights and many little gifts, such as candles and homemade sweets. Hosts will have acquired the animals to be served at the feast by calling in debts incurred since the last feast, many for healing intercessions by the hosts before the noble San Lázaro-Babalú Ayé.

Animal sacrifice in Black Atlantic praise—in this case, rural Cuban bembé praise—must be understood in a context like this: a generations-old celebration where the living invite their neighbors and kin, the ancestral dead, and the sovereign orisás for exuberant conviviality. Bembés are held for the orisás to celebrate life with them through eating, singing, and dancing together.

The meal is central—the feast can't proceed without it. San Lázaro-Babalú Ayé is invited, before anything else, to eat. Hosts know his tastes by heart—each orisá has a menu that pleases them, just as each has a repertoire of songs in their honor. San Lázaro-Babalú Ayé is the first to eat when his preferred animals are killed and his avatar—a small wash basin holding collections of shells, stones, and corals—is brought forth to catch the animals' blood. His avatar soaks in the blood, "eating" it. The killing happens behind closed doors or amidst the invited crowd. This depends on the hosts and their concerns at a given feast. The space is usually a living room or a bedroom. The animal is made ready for the sacrifice by the the hosts and their guests, who sing the animal into elevated status by identifying it with San Lázaro-Babalú Ayé. Usually a man will wield the knife, though a woman may also kill. The act can stain clothes and shoes, so women prefer to handle the animals after they have been killed and skinned. The older women of the family then prepare the meat into stews for their guests. These are served with rice, beans, and plantains. Amidst the grueling hardships of life in the Cuban countryside, it is an honor to serve guests these sacrificial stews.

San Lázaro-Babalú Ayé has a taste for buck goat, and the longer the goat's beard, the better. This reflects the Spanish Catholic image of Lazarus the Beggar with his clothes ragged, his body diseased, and his beard long and straggly. His avatar varies from house to house but often includes a statuette of the bearded Catholic beggar saint supported on crutches.

The offering of animals at bembés "makes sacred"—it consecrates by exaltation (Hubert and Mauss 1964, 9–13). San Lázaro-Babalú Ayé would not grace a feast, and there would be no festivities, were a bearded buck not offered to his liking. The sacrifice brings his avatar into exalted exception, just as it ennobles those who share in the eating of the offered animal. To share in the orisás' meal places bembé guests in intimate company with them, inspiring confidence in attendees. A satisfied singer is more likely to recall near-forgotten Babalú Ayé songs and call them poetically to the chorus during the celebration to follow. A chorus that has eaten will be enthusiastic in response to the singer's calls, and dancers nourished by the orisá's goat will give their all to be chosen as steeds by San Lázaro-Babalú Ayé. The bembé is bound together by people having eaten food prepared from sacrificed animals. Animal sacrifice at orisá feasts—in Cuba and throughout the Black Atlantic—is not the culmination of a religious ritual but rather the auspicious beginning of an extended, open-ended praise scene in which orisás mount their dancer steeds and dispense healing grace.

A bearded goat is to San Lázaro-Babalú Ayé's liking, and it is in his likeness. He likes it, and it is like him. The beard is foremost. A buck will have a serene, if sometimes exhausted, expression communicated by his beard. The beard attunes devotees to the weathering of the goat—his horns curl back gnarled and cracked, his back is bowed, and his knees are knobby—like the weathering of San Lázaro-Babalú Ayé himself. The long beard points to his aging and suffering. The orisá of healing is depicted as a sick beggar on crutches, dogs lapping at his wounds. The toll of his illness is sought in the sagging stance of a mature animal.

Play on likeness is common in animal sacrifice. In Black Atlantic praise, the play brings the animal offerings into likeness with the orisá and the orisá into likeness with the hosts making the offering. Human hosts are in the middle, so it is no surprise that significant anthropomorphism is involved in each movement. Animals become human-like as their killing nears, and divinities become human-like the more people call to them. In the course of setting aside a goat for San Lázaro-Babalú Ayé, the animal accrues a persona, and stories cling to it. In the goat, people see San Lázaro-Babalú Ayé himself and refer to him in the same terms of pitying endearment they use to express their love for the diseased orisá and sovereign of healing. For his part, San Lázaro-Babalú Ayé approximates vulnerable humanity in his anguished suffering.

These movements work in tandem, and the trio—animal, human, and divinity—come into dizzying proximity as the offering culminates. As the animal is prepared to be killed, those present, sometimes an entire chorus, will sing the goat songs addressed to San Lázaro-Babalú Ayé, songs that later in the evening will be sung to "call the orisá" to mount his dancer steeds. A poetic likeness is produced here, which is that over the course of his keeping and preparation, the goat has come to resemble first his keepers, then his hosts, and finally the divinity being celebrated, such that in the moment of his killing the distinction between animal and god is reduced to a minimum (Hubert and Mauss 1964, 31–33). As the animal dies, he becomes godlike; paradoxically, his death is also the death of the god. Goat and god die together so that the San Lázaro-Babalú Ayé may return upon the backs of his steeds to be celebrated in his living greatness.

God-likeness and costliness are versions of one another. In the north coast towns, animal offerings are costly, and when the animals are closest to god-likeness, they become priceless. The goat for San Lázaro-Babalú Ayé becomes priceless as he dies. A failure to respect his godlike status would be a grave infraction against the hosts, their ancestors, and their guests—not to mention the orisás themselves. An auspicious goat could have taken years of care and keeping. In the near-subsistence reality of the Cuban countryside, the economic margins between life and death for domestic animals are extremely thin. A goat for San Lázaro-Babalú Ayé will have been spared many times, his status as future offering overcoming the economic logic of selling him or killing him for food. The importance of the sacrificial gesture is proportionate to its costliness for the giver, and every animal set aside for an orisá implies risks and costs (Bataille 1989, 45–50). This more than anything else is what that the orisás value in the animals' blood. A small town that annually celebrates a pantheon of ten orisás will have collectively set aside hundreds of animals in this way. A town's domestic herds and flocks are a vast reservoir of risks and costs, made real in the animals' sacrificial deaths (Evans-Pritchard 1956, 248–249).

There is sentimental costliness, too. Goats for San Lázaro-Babalú Ayé see much of the life of those who raise them. Their offering begins the moment they are set aside, sometimes months or years before a feast. Each day after the goat has been set aside, as his beard grows, his personality grows. As a praise animal, his quirks and needs become part of his charm. A family will care for an aging goat like they care for elders—taking into account his food, mobility, and need for company. The persona attached to him reflects an attached family, and when he is offered so are his many attachments—stories, tales of extended and costly care, family members who love him, and, at a remove, ties of debt and reciprocity, which his attachments address.

In the course of the goat's life, those who offer him and those who host his offering draw close to him and one another. Obligations are met, and trust is built. They also draw close to San Lázaro-Babalú Ayé. In the course of his offering, the animal makes possible a "becoming intimate," a becoming godlike, and, ultimately, a becoming priceless. "Becoming priceless"—this term denotes the connections that bind the community for a short while as they praise the animal and the orisá together.

The community for which all strive is comprised of both humans and domestic animals. Bembé praise would be inconceivable without one or the other. Were the animals to comment on this relationship, it is important to keep in mind that their reflection would be consistent with the terms and values of the community they help form. Intimate connection with an orisá would likely be the highest priority for the goat as it is for the goat's human companions. In that case, the goat might understand his place in bembé praise in surprising terms. He would know that orisás cannot or will not grace a community without eating first, and that it is his flesh that most pleases the orisá. This is because it is the goat who is most like the orisá. The goat would understand that a great number of his kin die to feed the community, and that strengthened by goat vitality the community brings about more goats. It would understand that not all goats become godlike, and that such becoming is a kind of fortune—a treasuring of goat life to make manifest in orisá praise the bonds that tie humans and animals together. The goat to be sacrificed might say to a younger goat,

> Each day I grow more godlike, more alike to San Lázaro-Babalú Ayé. The orisá and I are of the same stuff, as you can see by the esteem our people hold us in. They call me Babalú Ayé, don't you hear? They will sing to me on my day, which is the orisá's day. That day I will become divine, if I am not already. My life is destined to nourish our collective body, and to nourish our collective praise, too. We all must die, don't you know? On my day I will die priceless, an orisá in the flesh. If you are lucky, human or goat, you will die amidst praise, your divinity on the lips of our community.

References

Bataille, Georges. 1989. *Theory of Religion*. New York: Zone Books.
Deren, Maya. 2004. *Divine Horsemen: The Living Gods of Haiti*. New York: McPherson & Company.

Evans-Pritchard, E.E. 1956. *Nuer Religion*. Oxford: Oxford University Press.

Hubert, Henri, and Marcel Mauss. 1964. *Sacrifice: Its Nature and Function*. Translated by W.D. Halls. Chicago, Ill.: University of Chicago Press.

Hurston, Zora Neale. 1990. *Tell My Horse: Voodoo and Life in Haiti and Jamaica*. New York: Harper and Row.

Ochoa, Todd Ramón. 2020. *A Party for Lazarus: Six Generations of Ancestral Devotion in a Cuban Town*. Oakland: University of California Press.

Strongman, Roberto. 2019. *Queering Black Atlantic Religions: Transcorporeality in Candomblé, Santería, and Vodou*. Durham, N.C.: Duke University Press.

Other Recommended Resources

Bataille, Georges. 1988. *The Accursed Share: An Essay on General Economy*. New York: Zone Books.

Govindrajan, Radhika. 2018. "The Goat Who Died for Family: Sacrificial Ethics and Kinship." In *Animal Intimacies: Interspecies Relatedness in India's Central Himalayas*, edited by Radhika Govindrajan, 31–61. Chicago, Ill. and London: University of Chicago Press.

Patton, Kimberley. 2006. "Animal Sacrifice: Metaphysics of the Sublimated Victim." In *A Communion of Subjects: Animals in Religion, Science, and Ethics*, edited by Paul Waldau and Kimberley Patton, 391–405. New York: Columbia University Press.

Pérez, Elizabeth. 2016. *Religion in the Kitchen: Cooking, Talking, and the Making of Black Atlantic Traditions*. New York and London: New York University Press.

Robbins, Jill. 1998. "Sacrifice." In *Critical Terms for Religious Studies*, edited by Mark C. Taylor, 285–97. Chicago, Ill.: University of Chicago Press.

Taussig, Michael. 1998. "Transgression." In *Critical Terms for Religious Studies*, edited by Mark C. Taylor, 349–64. Chicago, Ill.: University of Chicago Press.

16 Refraining from Killing and Releasing Life? The Ethical Dilemmas of Animal Release Rituals in East Asia

Barbara R. Ambros

Mid-morning on June 5, 2016, the gray heron headed from the Kamo River to the Tat-sumi Shrine on the bank of the Shirakawa River, where she waited in eager anticipation. On this day, about two thousand sweetfish fry, a native freshwater species and local summer delicacy, were to be ceremonially released into the Shirakawa river in Kyoto. A placard explained the origins of the ritual in China about one-and-a-half millennia ago and the scriptural grounding of the practice, which is intended to cultivate compassion. At the same time, the release was advertised as an expression of gratitude toward the many animals who ended up as food for humans. The organizers had procured the sweetfish from a fish farm in neighboring Shiga Prefecture and placed them in a large glass tank filled with a mix of river water and pond water to allow them to acclimate. A canopy and a rattan blind sheltered the fry from the glaring sunlight while local dignitaries gave speeches and musicians performed a live concert.

After a highly ranked mountain ascetic from nearby Mt. Hiei performed the release liturgy, the liberation into the river began. Accompanied by rhythmic chanting, devotees scooped the sweetfish into buckets, which they then emptied into the river from a nearby bridge. The fish darted around and gathered in undulating schools in the shallow water. This drew the attention of the heron, who knew what the annual commotion near the river meant: a delicious feast downstream. After gorging herself during the two-hour ritual, the heron flew off, even though some of the sweetfish lingered near the bridge. The remainder were swept into the Kamo River, where a hungry murder of crows and the heron had alighted in the shallow river mouth.

Developed in fifth century C.E. China alongside the practice of vegetarianism as a nonviolent Buddhist alternative to sacrificial practices and carnivorous foodways, ritual life releases have long served to cultivate compassion and benevolence toward living beings and generate merit (karmic rewards) for the human sponsors and the animals. Nonetheless, the rituals have often faced criticism for being wasteful, disregarding animal welfare, and negatively impacting the environment. This chapter traces this ritual from its scriptural foundations and emergence in China to the early modern and contemporary periods while also probing its inherent ethical dilemmas and the practical limitations of compassion.

In the ideal case, life releases were intended to rescue and release animals on the brink of an untimely death. They typically involved small animals such as fish, turtles, and birds but could also include insects, snakes, game animals, and livestock. Domestic animals were cared for in sanctuaries for the remainder of their lives. Since the release extended the animals' lifespan, the karmic rewards were said to include longevity, health, good fortune, and even the prevention of natural disasters.

DOI: 10.4324/9781003324157-20

Such benefits were illustrated by karmic tales. For instance, one famous story from the *Sutra of the Storehouse of Sundry Valuables* (translated into Chinese in the late fifth century) frequently cited in karmic tale collections is that of a young novice who served an arhat:

> Once there was a man of the path, an arhat, who was bringing up a *śrāmaṇera* (novice). He knew that this *śrāmaṇera*'s life was sure to end after seven days. He gave him a leave of absence and let him return home. He told him to come back on the seventh day. The *śrāmaṇera* took leave of his master and went home.
>
> On his way he saw many ants floating about on the water. Their life was about to come to an end, and he had compassionate thoughts. He took off his *kaṣāya* [monastic robe], filled it with earth, made a dam in the water, and rescued the ants. He put them up in a high and dry place, so that they all could live. When he returned to his master on the seventh day, his master was very astonished. The master subsequently entered into concentration. Contemplating with his heavenly eye, he knew that (the *śrāmaṇera*) had no longer had any remainder of merit, but that he had obtained (merit) by saving the ants. He did not die on the seventh day but prolonged his life.
>
> (Willemen 1994, 107)

This story conveys the ideal conditions of a life release: the rescue is a spontaneous response to the life-threatening circumstances of the helpless animals. The rescuer generates compassion and saves the animals from certain death. In return, his own life is extended as a karmic reward. Both the rescued animals and the rescuer benefit from the release.

The two most important Buddhist texts for the development of the practice were the *Brahma's Net Sutra*, a Chinese Buddhist scripture from the mid-fifth century C.E., and the *Golden Light Sutra*, which was first translated into Chinese around the same time. The *Brahma's Net Sutra* promotes kindness and pity toward living beings as the first two nourishing mental states. The first major precept in this scripture admonishes against killing living beings, while the twentieth minor precept promotes the release of animals for two reasons related to the kinship between humans and other animals. According to the text, all animals were once our fathers and mothers in a former life; thus, killing and eating them is cannibalistic patricide and matricide. Second, all living beings are constituted from the same material substances; thus, killing animals means we are killing ourselves. Because of these familial and corporeal entanglements, we should release captive animals on the brink of death and cultivate compassion (Muller and Tanaka 2017, 13–14, 44, 55).

Highlighting the helplessness and suffering of beings in the animal realm (an existence considered unfortunate compared to the realms of humans and divinities), the *Golden Light Sutra* tells the story of the Elder Jalavāhana, the Buddha in a former life, who rescued tens of thousands of dying fish and ensured their fortunate rebirth in their next life. Jalavāhana noticed that many carnivorous animals were headed to a forest pond. Following these animals, he saw tens of thousands of fish on the brink of death because of the low water level in the pond. Worried, he cut branches to shelter the fish from the scorching sunlight and then borrowed the king's elephants to carry water to refill the pond. He also had his sons bring food from his own house to feed the famished fish. Concerned not only with the physical well-being but also the future rebirth of the fish, he then preached the Buddhist teaching of dependent origination (the idea that all phenomena, including suffering, arise dependently on one another and that it is possible to reverse this causal chain to attain liberation from the cycle of rebirth) to them and recited the name of the Buddha Ratnabhava so that they would be reborn into the Heaven of the Thirty-Three Gods, thanks to the vow of this Buddha. Having died and been reborn in this heaven soon after, the fish appeared to Jalavāhana in a dream to thank him by giving him precious pearls, showering him with flowers, and performing divine music before returning to the pleasures of the heavenly realm (Losang 2006, 81–86). While the *Brahma's Net Sutra* was often cited as the justification for ritual releases, the story of Jalavāhana became the basis for life release liturgies that developed in China.

From the fifth century C.E., life releases gained popularity, first in China, then in other parts of East Asia, and eventually also in Southeast Asia and Tibet. In the sixth century, sanctuaries for released animals became common at Buddhist temples. Often, these took the form of life release ponds, the first of which was said to have been established by the Tiantai patriarch Zhiyi (538–597) after he convinced local fishers to release their catch in such a pond and thus saved people in the region from disasters and illness (Pu 2014, 130–131). Early on, large-scale life releases were often sponsored by the state to pacify a war-torn country, allay natural disasters and famine, or counteract pandemics because such calamities were understood as divine and karmic retribution for harmful actions such as killing living beings. In some instances, releasing animals was even thought to preserve natural resources (Eschenbach 2020). However, they also could have deadly consequences for the released animals. In medieval Japan, for instance, the state procured thousands of fish—three times as many as needed for the release—because two-thirds of the fish would die before the ritual at the Iwashimizu Hachiman Shrine (Williams 1997).

From the fifteenth through the nineteenth centuries, devotional life releases conducted by individuals or charitable associations flourished in East Asia as public expressions of compassion and piety. While detractors of the ritual criticized releases as wasteful, ineffective because they saved only a few animals without systemic change, and potentially harmful to the liberated animals, proponents argued that they were saving animals from certain death. As the Buddhist monk Zhuhong (1535–1615) is said to have put it, life release ponds were like walled cities that might be crowded and filthy but protected people from brigands. Early modern proponents of life releases also strove to ensure the well-being of the animals by not procuring animals always from the same vendors, refraining from preordering animals for the ritual, and keeping releases secret so as not to encourage vendors to capture animals for the release, as well as abbreviating ceremonies to protect delicate species from harm, not releasing carnivorous species into the same ponds as other aquatic species, avoiding contaminating ponds with harmful substances, and refraining from feeding the animals unsuitable foods. They spent much effort and many resources to build and dredge life release ponds and establish and maintain terrestrial sanctuaries for domestic animals (Handlin Smith 2009; Eichman 2016; Ambros 2019, 2021; Darshani 2021).

Devotional animal releases are now more popular than ever among the Buddhist laity in many parts of East Asia and East Asian communities overseas. On the one hand, they are an accessible and affordable devotional practice whose emotional impact is unmatched by meditation or vegetarianism since participants buy live animals to save them from hellish pain and certain death in a market or slaughterhouse and then release them into a paradisical setting in a temple garden or the wild (Yang 2015). But on the other hand, the ethical complications of life releases have become amplified in an increasingly global marketplace. Many such rituals are questionable because they may turn a blind eye to animal welfare, encourage the capture of endangered native species, and unwittingly result in high animal mortality rates. They have also led to the introduction of invasive species that stress fragile ecosystems. Therefore, life releases have faced intense criticism from Buddhist leaders, scientists, and the news media.

This has spurred reform efforts ranging from recommendations to release animals responsibly and integrating conservation efforts with release activities to discouraging life releases altogether in favor of practicing vegetarianism (Shiu and Stokes 2008; Darshani 2021). For example, Miidera, a Tendai temple in Ōtsu City, Japan, has established a native pond turtle breeding program because the number of pond turtles in the wild has declined steadily due to habitat loss. These turtles are then released into a dedicated pond on the temple grounds during the annual life release in mid-May. However, since the turtles are not released into the wild, there is little to no impact on wild turtle populations except for the odd turtle that escapes from the pond.

The Gion Life Release in 2016 that was described previously also showcases these dilemmas. Careful management ensured that the fry were not harmed before the release, but their purchase sustained the fish farm where they were raised to become food, and the majority did not survive long in the Shirakawa because birds of prey consumed them. Nonetheless, sweetfish are a native species with a chance of survival in the wild while being kept in check by native predators and sport fishing. Assuming they are healthy, the sweetfish do not cause unintended environmental harm even if they are released in large numbers. Did the release give the fish destined for the dining table a chance at living out their lives in the wild, or did it inflict suffering and hasten their death? Debates continue on how and whether it is possible to conduct life releases in a manner that is ecologically sustainable and mindful of the released species' needs.

The ethical quandaries of life releases compel us to reflect on whether it is possible for humans to truly help animals for their own sake and without discrimination and on what our own deeply rooted assumptions about animal lives are. Is their corporeal existence all that other than human animals have and know? Should we help the frog being swallowed by a snake at the cost of making the snake starve? If killing leads to adverse karmic outcomes, should we prevent animals from killing each other, or should only humans avoid killing while letting animals follow their nature? Are good intentions and compassion enough to better the lives of animals and humans, or does inadvertent harm negate the benefits of such efforts? Such questions have been raised by both the detractors and proponents of life releases for centuries, and they remain relevant today.

References

Ambros, Barbara R. 2019. "Cultivating Compassion and Accruing Merit: Animal Releases During the Edo Period." In *The Life of Animals in Japanese Art*, edited by Robert T. Singer and Kawai Masatomo, 16–27. Princeton, N.J.: Princeton University Press.

_____. 2021. "Tracing the Influence of Ming-Qing Buddhism in Early Modern Japan: Yunqi Zhuhong's *Tract on Refraining from Killing and on Releasing Life* and Ritual Animal Releases." *Religions* 12 (10): 889. https://doi.org/10.3390/rel12100889.

Darshani, Avi. 2021. "Releasing Life or Releasing Death: The Practice of and Discourse on Buddhist Animal Liberation Rituals in Contemporary Xiamen." *Journal of Chinese Religions* 49 (1): 109–43.

Eichman, Jennifer. 2016. *A Late Sixteenth-Century Chinese Buddhist Fellowship: Spiritual Ambitions, Intellectual Debates and Epistolary Connections.* Leiden: Brill.

Eschenbach, Silvia Freiin Ebner von. 2020. "The Dilemma of Ecological and Nutritional Policies in View of Buddhist Campaigning." *Monumenta Serica: Journal of Oriental Studies* 68 (1): 69–106.

Handlin Smith, Joanna. 2009. *The Art of Doing Good: Charity in Late Ming China*. Berkeley: University of California Press.

Losang, Dawa, trans. 2006. *The King of Glorious Sutras Called the Exalted Sublime Golden Light*. Dunedin: Foundation for the Preservation of the Mahayana Tradition. Accessed June 27, 2022. https://fpmt.org/wp-content/uploads/teachers/zopa/advice/pdf/sutragoldenlight0207lttr.pdf.

Muller, A. Charles, and Kenneth K. Tanaka, trans. 2017. *The Brahma's Net Sutra*. Berkeley: Numata Center. Accessed June 27, 2022. https://bdkamerica.org/download/1959.

Pu, Chengzhong. 2014. *Ethical Treatment of Animals in Early Chinese Buddhism: Beliefs and Practices*. Newcastle upon Tyne: Cambridge Scholars Publishing.

Shiu, Henry, and Leah Stokes. 2008. "Buddhist Animal Release Practices: Historic, Environmental, Public Health and Economic Concerns." *Contemporary Buddhism* 9: 181–96.

Willemen, Charles, trans. 1994. *The Storehouse of Sundry Valuables*. Berkeley, Calif.: Numata Center. Accessed June 27, 2022. https://bdkamerica.org/download/1858.

Williams, Duncan R. 1997. "Animal Liberation, Death, and the State: Rites to Release Animals in Medieval Japan." In *Buddhism and Ecology*, edited by Mary Evelyn Tucker and Duncan R. Williams, 149–62. Cambridge, Mass.: Harvard University Press.

Yang Der-Ruey. 2015. "Animal Release: The Dharma Being Staged Between Marketplace and Park." *Cultural Diversity in China* 1 (2): 141–63.

Other Recommended Resources

Stevenson, Daniel, trans. 2004. "Freeing Birds and Fish from Bondage" and "Against Animal Sacrifice." In *Buddhist Scriptures*, edited by Donald Lopez, 394–415. New York: Penguin.

Verchery, Lina, director. 2007. *The Trap*. Montreal: National Film Board of Canada. Accessed July 10, 2022. www.nfb.ca/film/trap/.

Yemoto, Linda. 2020. *Chinese New Year's Bullfrogs—Linda Yemoto—Regional Gems 2020*, Video. Storytelling Association of California. Accessed June 27, 2022. www.youtube.com/watch?v=7lZiWUDtU1I.

Yen, Master Sheng. 2012. "Freeing Captive Animals—Its Meaning and Methods (GDD-131, Master Sheng Yen)." *Great Dharma Drum*, September 27. Accessed June 27, 2022. www.youtube.com/watch?v=otz_kHS20hI.

———. 2015. "Setting Animals Free to Save Their Lives (GDD-25) DVD." *Great Dharma Drum*, September 7. Accessed June 27, 2022. www.youtube.com/watch?v=exclomnsIVo.

17 Vegetarianism, Prohibited Meats, and Caring for Animals in Chinese Religious History

Vincent Goossaert

Introduction

Vegetarianism developed in China from several sources. An indigenous tradition linked to Daoism considered slaughtering animals and eating meat impure. It also encouraged renouncing pleasurable foods and promoted ideas about nonviolence to animals imported by Buddhists from the Indian world. Not all Buddhists are vegetarian, but early on (between the third and fifth centuries), it became the norm in China that Buddhist clerics (monks and nuns) and the most devoted lay practitioners should permanently observe a vegetarian diet (Greene 2016). More generally, during the mid-first millennium, vegetarianism became a widely shared ideal in China, and strict, permanent vegetarians were often described with admiration, while it was also widely admitted that this was a very difficult choice, cutting one off from communal banquets and sacrifices.

Moreover, several religious movements (usually termed "sectarian" by scholars) that developed from the fifteenth century onward advocated permanent vegetarianism for all their members. These groups were millenarian (expecting a cataclysmic end of this word, from which only the elect would be saved), which led the imperial state to ban them, and sometimes brutally repress them. As a result, during most of the second millennium, being identified as a vegetarian could also land one in trouble. In other words, there was a tension between a vegetarian ideal and the many problems created by adopting a permanent vegetarian diet. This tension could be managed in different ways, notably first, temporary vegetarianism—that is, alternating vegetarian periods with meat eating ones—and, second, specific taboos on certain kinds of meat.

Temporary Vegetarianism

Chinese common religion is fundamentally sacrificial, grounding the alliance with the spiritual entities (gods, ancestors, saints) in a communion centered around offering and sharing meat with them. Buddhism and Daoism both tried to ban animal sacrifices but never managed to impose such a ban on the cults of local gods that form the bedrock of Chinese religion. The slaughter of sacrificial victims is a sacred act; as such, it cannot be accomplished lightly. Killing is justified by legitimate sacrifice, whereas both the slaughter of animals and the consumption of meat are proscribed in certain other circumstances (Kleeman 1994).

In the first place, ancient religion held that at certain times of the natural cycle (spring, the period of reproduction and birth, as well as times of natural disasters, when life must be sustained), the fact of killing living beings (humans and animals) goes against the

DOI: 10.4324/9781003324157-21

natural course of the world and, therefore, constitutes an offense against heaven. Hunting, fishing, butchering, and the execution of convicts were, therefore, prohibited during these periods. The motivations were linked to the management of natural resources and to religious belief, specifically the fear of going against the moral order of the universe and thereby triggering catastrophes. These notions were adopted by Confucians so that, until the end of the empire in 1911, an official proclamation was issued prohibiting butchers from slaughtering any animal whatsoever during the emperors' birthdays or the official prayers in times of natural disaster.

In addition, both killing animals and eating meat were prohibited during purifications and penances. One of the corollaries of sacrifice, and therefore one of the foundations of Chinese religion, was the preparation period of one or more days (the duration varying according to the importance of the ritual and each participant's status). This preparation according to the code of ritual purity (*zhaijie*) allowed the officiant to spiritually unite with the recipient deities of the sacrifice. This code entailed three essential elements: meat, alcohol, and sex. Thus, when someone is under a period of purification, they cannot consume meat or alcohol and must sleep alone. Moreover, the prohibition of meat was ever since antiquity associated with a ban on the use of the five pungent plants of the Alliaceae family (e.g., garlic and onions): there are several native as well as scholarly explanations for this, an important one being that these condiments give one bad breath and thus disqualify one to speak to the gods.

In addition to purification before individual, familial, and community rituals, periods of mourning, and state-mandated times of abstinence, individuals can also choose to observe these rules according to a ritual calendar focused on the birthdays of the various gods. There are many templates of such calendars, but people pick and choose, according to their particular connections to specific gods, when to be pure by abstaining from eating meat (and alcohol) and killing any living being. This periodical vegetarianism was likely much more common than permanent vegetarianism before the contemporary period.

Specific Taboos

Along with periodical abstinence, people could limit the sins accrued from slaughtering animals to eat by permanently abstaining from the meat of certain animals considered especially valuable and close to humans. In China, as in many other cultures, interdictions or taboos on various specific meats coexist, sometimes based on different rationales. The most commonly observed is that on beef, or more precisely, the flesh of bovines, including oxen and water buffalos, which are two distinct species but are classified by the Chinese under one larger category (Goossaert forthcoming).

The beef taboo gradually formed around the tenth to the twelfth century and quickly became a major element of the moral discourse that only partially disappeared during the twentieth century. The origins of this taboo are multifaceted, including changes in the ecology and pastoral economy (the disappearance of great estates with herds of bovines during the first millennium, replaced with many small landowners, each sharing one or a few draft animals raised for that labor purpose only); changes in sacrificial practices; and the roles of new deities that imposed specific taboos. As a result, the vast majority of Chinese stopped offering beef to gods and ancestors and eating it themselves; this was called being "half-vegetarian" (Goossaert 2005). There were many different justifications provided for this interdiction, including the fact that bovines are sentient and can plead for mercy (many ballads, poems, and even theatrical plays stage their emotional pleas);

that they are reincarnated humans; and that they are gods who incarnated as draft animals to help humans plow the fields. Bovines are very closely associated with plowing the lands and thus with the cereal-based Chinese civilization. Equines (horses, donkeys, and mules) are similarly protected as draft animals working for human welfare.

The dog taboo also developed in parallel, based on a similar rationale: because dogs guard the house and are thus in close cooperation with humans, they are working companions who should enjoy reciprocal bonds of gratitude with their owners and, as such, cannot be slaughtered and even less eaten. To the present day, dog eating exists but is relatively marginal in China, concentrated in specific regions, and considered by many to be a transgressive practice of the underclass and ruffians (Poon 2014). Beef consumption was considered the same way for centuries (and beef butchering was mainly in the hand of Muslim communities); it is less so now, but it remains a distinct meat, sometimes sold separately, quite like horsemeat is in much of Europe (Zhang 2021).

Animals in Morality Books

Much of Chinese discourse on morality in general, and respect for animal life in particular, is found in a genre called "morality books" (*shanshu*) that combines revelations from various gods, essays, tracts, edifying stories written by humans, and illustrations. These texts have been extremely common since the twelfth century. In them, one can find innumerable stories of people being showered with blessings from the gods for showing mercy to suffering animals or vowing to abstain from beef, dog meat, or even all meats.

Respect for life has been a major teaching of morality books from the earliest days of this genre. It encompasses all forms of life, from tiny insects all the way to humans, in a graduated way: all lives are precious, but not to the same degree. Some morality books propose a quantified scale of value for the animal realm, with a human life valued as, say, that of ten bovines, a hundred small mammals, etc. (Goossaert 2019). I have identified six themes related to animals in the tradition of morality books over the long-term. These themes, of course, overlap and combine in all sorts of ways in actual texts. Many elements in these discourses derive from the different moral teachings, but in the context of morality books, they are recycled in a universal moral discourse encompassing the Three Teachings—Confucianism, Buddhism, and Daoism. I will discuss each of these themes in turn.

1) Respect for the natural cycles of life and the environment. This includes injunctions against killing young animals, disturbing hibernating animals, polluting rivers, or starting fires in mountainous areas. They derive from a very ancient tradition, documented in texts from late antiquity (fourth to third centuries B.C.E.) such as the seasonal calendars (*Yueling*), and also in the earliest Daoist precepts, such as the "Hundred eighty precepts of the Lord on High" (probably second century C.E.). Some contemporary scholars claim that these texts document early ecological ideas in Chinese culture in general and Daoism in particular (Miller, Yü, and van der Veer 2014), but such claims tend to neglect serious contextualization. In fact, these ancient rules are linked to ideas of a natural cosmic order and the management of resources, including wild and domesticated animals.

2) Injunctions against killing animals (*jiesha*), whether for food or other reasons. While contemporary scholars tend to associate this precept with Buddhism, morality books

have consistently supported it with Confucian and Daoist, as well as Buddhist, references. Permanent vegetarianism was often described as very difficult to achieve, but readers of morality books were enjoined to refrain from killing animals themselves or ordering their servants to do so (i.e., buying a chunk of pork at the market was a lesser sin than having the animal slaughtered at home). Beyond the question of domesticated animals raised for meat, these injunctions also included attention to insects while walking or farming, the protection of natural habitats, and the denunciation of cruel games (animal fights).

3) Exhortations to release live animals (*fangsheng*), that is, buying animals destined for slaughtering and releasing them either in the wild (e.g., fishes in rivers) or at protected places (ponds, farms), often maintained by temples or charities for that purpose. This practice is already attested at the beginning of the first millennium but became very common around the twelfth century and has remained so (Smith 1999). Again, morality books referred to all Three Teachings to justify this meritorious practice, which can, to some extent, offset the sin incurred by eating meat.

4) Taboos against killing/eating bovines and dogs, as mentioned earlier.

5) Other specific taboos against serpents, turtles, eels, wild geese, frogs, etc. Some of these taboos existed earlier than the all-important ones on bovines and dogs, while others developed as the discourse on "useful" (thus tabooed) vs. edible animals further developed. By the late imperial period, lists of tabooed meats could run to dozens of items, with acceptable meat being increasingly limited to pork, poultry, and fish (the modern "three sacrificial victims" commonly offered to gods and ancestors).

6) Injunctions to love and care for living animals, especially draft and other domestic animals.

Care for Animals

While the previous first five types of moral injunctions focused on killing animals and consuming their meat, the question of animal welfare is also present in the morality books tradition, with numerous accounts of the divine punishments incurred by those who mistreat their animals. One of the genre's early classics, the "Ledger of merits and demerits revealed by Immortal Lord Taiwei" (revealed in 1171), lists divine punishments for those who treat their animals cruelly and rewards for those who take care of sick or wounded animals (*Taiwei xianjun gongguoge*, translated into French in Goossaert 2012). This text also enjoins people to bury dead animals as they would humans. Some texts (again, following rules found in early Daoist texts) even enjoin readers not to keep animals, whether as pets or for other purposes.

Naturally, there is always a disjunction between what moral tracts advocate and what people actually do. Throughout Chinese history, we see evidence of a lack of care or even downright cruelty toward animals. Yet it remains true that there existed a massively diffused religious discourse expounding that all forms of life are precious, even though not equally so, and that humans who mistreated animals would be punished by the gods. Many people acted on these principles and treated domesticated animals with kindness, even burying them after they died. Many sanctuaries for animals existed in temples or other venues. When Western-inspired movements such as the Society for the Prevention of Cruelty to Animals (SPCA) took root in China in the early twentieth century, the two traditions converged to a certain extent, even though their religious roots were very different (Poon 2019). Since the twentieth century, we have seen activists involved in both kinds of advocacy movements, just as many Buddhist, Daoist, and other Chinese religious activists are also involved in environmental protection groups.

References

Goossaert, Vincent. 2005. "The Beef Taboo and the Sacrificial Structure of Late Imperial Chinese Society." In *Of Tripod and Palate: Food, Politics, and Religion in Traditional China*, edited by Roel Sterckx, 237–48. New York: Palgrave.

_____, trans. 2012. *Livres de morale révélés par les dieux*. Paris: Les Belles Lettres.

_____. 2019. "Animals and Eschatology in the Nineteenth-Century Discourse." In *Animals Through Chinese History: Earliest Times to 1911*, edited by Roel Sterckx, Martina Siebert, and Dagmar Schäfer, 181–98. Cambridge: Cambridge University Press.

_____. Forthcoming. *The Beef Taboo in China: Agriculture, Ethics, and Sacrifice*. Translated by Barbara R. Ambros. Honolulu: University of Hawai'i Press.

Greene, Eric. 2016. "A Reassessment of the Early History of Vegetarianism in Chinese Buddhism." *Asia Major* 29 (1): 1–43.

Kleeman, Terry F. 1994. "Licentious Cults and Bloody Victuals: Sacrifice, Reciprocity, and Violence in Traditional China." *Asia Major*, third series 7 (1): 185–211.

Miller, James, Dan Smyer Yü, and Peter van der Veer, eds. 2014. *Religion and Ecological Sustainability in China*. London: Routledge.

Poon, Shuk-Wah. 2014. "Dogs and British Colonialism: The Contested Ban on Eating Dogs in Colonial Hong Kong." *Journal of Imperial and Commonwealth History* 42 (2): 308–28.

_____. 2019. "Buddhist Activism and Animal Protection in Republican China." In *Concepts and Methods for the Study of Chinese Religions, Volume III: Key Concepts in Practice*, edited by Paul R. Katz and Stefania Travagnin, 91–112. Berlin and Boston, Mass.: De Gruyter.

Smith, Joanna F. Handlin. 1999. "Liberating Animals in Ming-Qing China: Buddhist Inspiration and Elite Imagination." *Journal of Asian Studies* 58 (1): 51–84.

Zhang, Shaodan. 2021. "Cattle Slaughter Industry in Qing China: State Ban, Muslim Dominance, and the Western Diet." *Frontiers of History in China* 16 (1): 4–38.

Other Recommended Resources (English language only)

Broy, Nikolas. 2019. "Moral Integration or Social Segregation? Vegetarianism and Vegetarian Religious Communities in Chinese Religious Life." *Concepts and Methods for the Study of Chinese Religions, Volume III: Key Concepts in Practice*, edited by Paul R. Katz and Stefania Travagnin, 37–64. Berlin and Boston, Mass.: De Gruyter.

Shahar, Meir. 2019. "Newly-Discovered Manuscripts of a Northern-Chinese Horse King Temple Association." *T'oung Pao* 105 (1–2): 183–228.

18 The Difficult Virtue of Vegetarianism in Tibetan Buddhism

Geoffrey Barstow

Introduction

Tibetan Buddhist texts and teachers often emphasize the need to practice compassion and nonviolence toward all other beings, a category that explicitly includes animals. Unlike in Chinese Buddhism, however, neither veganism nor vegetarianism ever became the norm in Tibet. There were plenty of vegetarians in premodern Tibet, and there is a movement favoring vegetarianism (and sometimes even veganism) in Tibetan communities today. But many religious leaders have held that being a good Buddhist does not require avoiding all meat, and as a result, the question of meat eating has remained an unsettled issue in Tibet, with vocal advocates for and against. This chapter surveys the contours of that debate, asking why some Tibetan religious leaders have felt that eating meat was acceptable while others have argued—sometimes vociferously—against it. In the end, I argue that vegetarianism has been seen as a virtuous but not required practice that is fraught with difficulty. Most Tibetans have admired those who adopted it while simultaneously feeling that it is beyond their own abilities.

On Human and Other Than Human Animals

Before getting into the practice of vegetarianism, however, it is helpful to step back and look at an important assumption that Buddhism makes about animals and human-animal interactions. In a nutshell, Buddhists in general (and Tibetan Buddhists in particular) assume that animal experience, and particularly animal suffering, matters. Unlike members of some other religious traditions, Buddhists assume that animals have minds, experience sensations like pain, and have emotional lives, including feelings of fear and love. In fact, Buddhists often present a certain fluidity between the human and animal realms: someone currently enjoying a human life might be reborn as an animal and vice versa. This is possible because both "humans" and "animals" are subcategories of the broader category of "sentient beings," that is, beings who have minds. The fundamental difference, therefore, is not between humans and animals but between sentient beings and insentient objects like rocks.

This does not mean that Buddhists have seen humans and other than human animals as morally equivalent. Humans, they tend to assume, are more developed mentally and therefore matter more, morally speaking (Ohnuma 2017). However, despite this elevation of human needs over animal needs, most Buddhist thinkers still acknowledge that animal pain and suffering matter and that, therefore, what we humans do to other animals also matters. Just as we need to consider the impact of our actions on other humans, Buddhism makes clear that we also need to consider the impact of our actions on animals.

DOI: 10.4324/9781003324157-22

The Rule of Threefold Purity

Despite this acknowledgment that what we do to animals matters and that killing them is a particularly grievous act, a strong majority of Tibetans in both the premodern and contemporary eras continued to eat meat. There are many reasons for this, of course, including economic needs, environmental constraints, and, perhaps most importantly, the simple fact that meat eating has been a Tibetan cultural norm since long before the introduction of Buddhism. Justifications for eating meat by devout Buddhists, however, largely hinge on something known as "the rule of threefold purity."[1] This rule is found in the *Vinaya*, the canonical texts that contain the rules that Tibetan Buddhist monks and nuns are expected to follow, and explains that meat is allowed as long as the monk or nun eating it did not personally request the animal's slaughter. Khenpo Shenga, an early twentieth-century Tibetan commentator, explained it simply: "Meat is not allowed if one sees, hears, or suspects that the meat was prepared by the donor specifically for the eater" (Barstow 2018, 48). Monks and nuns are allowed to eat meat as long as they have no reason to believe that the animal was killed specifically for them.

In effect, the rule of threefold purity insulates monastics from the charge that they are responsible for killing animals. The act of slaughter is clearly a negative act and is recognized as such by all concerned. But adhering to the rule of threefold purity means that the monk or nun is not directly responsible for the animal's death. The butcher (or whoever killed the animal) bears that responsibility, while the eater only comes along after the animal is dead.

In Tibet, this rule has often been extended to meat purchased from butchers: even if an animal is killed for sale, many Tibetans have felt, its meat still meets the requirements of threefold purity as long as the specific monk or nun buying it did not ask the butcher to kill that specific animal. The seminal Geluk master Khedrup Jé is perhaps the most prominent proponent of this view of threefold purity. In his fifteenth-century *Polishing the Jewel of the Sage's Teachings*, Khedrup Jé points to the need for a monk or nun to specifically request the slaughtering of an animal in order to make the meat unacceptable. He then invokes a prominent Indian author to emphatically deride the idea that *all* slaughtered meat violates the rule: "Some fools say that meat that has been killed is necessarily meat that does not have threefold purity. This is complete nonsense stated by those who have not seen the words of Dharmamitra's commentary" (Johnson 2019, 132). Khedrup Jé's position—that it is OK to eat meat purchased in the market as long as you do not request the slaughter of a specific animal in advance—has been widespread in Tibet, with the result that most monastics and other devout Buddhists have felt that eating meat purchased from a butcher does not violate the rule of threefold purity.

Health Concerns

Among Tibetan Buddhists the permission to eat meat found in the rule of threefold purity dovetails with a strong sense that meat is necessary for a healthy diet. Tibetan medicine teaches that the body contains three humors: phlegm, wind, and bile.[2] If these humors are in balance, the person will be healthy and vital. But if they fall out of balance, the person will become ill (Kilty 2010, 17). Eating meat has long been held to be an essential part of maintaining that balance. Specifically, eating meat is said to balance out the wind humor. Without it, a person's wind humor would likely become too strong, leading to a decrease in physical strength and increased susceptibility to illness.

This sense that meat is medically necessary is based in the Tibetan medical tradition but has also been widespread among Tibetans without medical training. We see this in some of the biographical accounts of those Tibetan religious leaders who did choose to practice vegetarianism. The author of the fifteenth-century *Biography of Ngorchen Künga Zangpo*, for instance, notes that Ngorchen was a strict vegetarian and that this impacted his health: "Because he chose to hold firm to vegetarianism, his body was very weak" (Barstow 2018, 128). Meat, in this medical perspective, helps support bodily health, and giving it up can lead to weakness and other health concerns.

But What About Compassion?

Most Tibetans, including most Tibetan monastics, have understood meat eating to be both allowed by the rule of threefold purity and medically necessary. While this permissive view was widespread, however, it has not been universal. A significant and persistent minority of Tibetan religious practitioners have personally adopted a vegetarian diet and encouraged others to do so as well. This push for vegetarianism has been, almost universally, based on an ideal enshrined at the heart of Tibetan religiosity: compassion. Tibetan Buddhism self-consciously adheres to the Mahāyāna, a Buddhist movement that originated in India around the start of the Common Era and which prioritizes the practice of compassion for others. This compassion takes different forms in different contexts, and the emphasis is often on practicing compassion by helping others achieve enlightenment. But even when the practice of compassion focuses on such abstract concerns, Mahāyāna Buddhism also emphasizes reducing the immediate suffering of others. And animals are unambiguously included among appropriate recipients of human compassion.

For some Tibetan religious leaders, this call to have compassion has meant that humans should not eat slaughtered meat. For them, meat eating is unambiguously connected to the act of slaughter, even if the technicalities of the rule of threefold purity might suggest otherwise. As Shabkar puts it in his mid-nineteenth century *Nectar of Immortality*:

> So it is that, thanks to buyers and killers, working hand in glove, hundreds and thousands of goats and sheep are slaughtered. Now if this entails no fault and if meat of this kind is pure in the three ways, it can only mean that, for such people, everything has become infinite purity!
>
> (Shabkar 2004, 115)

For Shabkar, those who eat meat are responsible for the death of animals, even if they did not specifically ask a butcher to kill a particular animal. A similar point is made even more directly by the early twentieth-century master Shardza Tashi Gyeltsen, who opens his *Faults of Meat* by noting, "Compassion is the essence of all the Buddha's teachings." As for those who eat meat, Shardza is unsparing in his criticism: "Those who eat meat have not even a trace of compassion or kindness" (Barstow 2019, 239; 242). For Tibetan Buddhists like Shabkar and Shardza, meat eating was simply incompatible with the compassion expected of them as Mahāyāna practitioners.

But how did these vegetarians reconcile this belief with the canonical passages advocating the rule of threefold purity? Most argued that the rule of threefold purity was provisional and applied only to those at the initial stages of the Buddhist path. Mahāyāna values, in this view, effectively supersede the monastic rules found in the Vinaya. Sakya Paṇḍita makes this point clearly in his *Distinguishing the Three Vows*, written in 1232:

"Disciples [i.e., those who adhere only to non-Mahāyāna Buddhism] may partake of meat that is pure in three ways. . . . In the Mahāyāna, meat is forbidden" (Sakya Paṇḍita Künga Gyaltsen 2002, 66). In this perspective, eating meat—even meat that technically adhered to the rule of threefold purity—is incompatible with Mahāyāna Buddhism's call for compassion and must be abandoned.

Only a minority of Tibetan Buddhists have ever adopted a vegetarian diet. But while few Tibetans have actually adopted vegetarianism, the association of vegetarianism with compassion has been widely acknowledged. The diet is usually portrayed in a positive light and as a virtuous practice. When a biography mentions that someone is vegetarian, it almost always implies that they were admirably virtuous. This is seen, for instance, in the mid-twentieth century *Biography of Ngawang Lekpa*: "Since the time he requested monk's vows," the author claims, "he [Ngawang Lekpa] abandoned eating meat, drinking alcohol, and eating after noon" (Barstow 2018, 6). Ngawang Lekpa's vegetarianism, teetotaling, and avoidance of the evening meal are all held up as markers of his exemplary virtue.

Tibetans have admired vegetarianism not just because of its connection to compassion but also because of the widespread assumption that it harms one's health. In some cases, vegetarianism was even believed to be a contributing factor in a religious leader's early death. This was the case for the twelfth-century master Jikten Sumgön, whose vegetarianism was so strict that he refused life-saving medicine because it was made from powdered yak lungs, which resulted in his premature death (Barstow 2018, 127). Jikten Sumgön was not criticized for refusing the medicine but was instead praised for his commitment to virtue. In this, his life and death are a good example of Tibetan attitudes toward vegetarianism generally: they have admired vegetarianism, but see it as difficult and dangerous, and therefore do not expect it of most people.

In this, Tibetan Buddhism contrasts with other Mahāyāna forms of Buddhism, particularly those found in China. There, monastics and other devout Buddhists have long been expected to practice vegetarianism, and while the prohibition on meat eating is not universally observed, it is generally the norm (Kieschnick 2005, 187). The rule of threefold purity has long been acknowledged in China, but most Chinese Buddhists felt that it was superseded by Mahāyāna commitments to compassion (Kieschnick 2005, 190). This position is reminiscent of the arguments made by Shabkar, Shardza, and others in Tibet. In China, however, such a view has been normative for most Buddhists, while in Tibet it has only been defended by a minority.

Conclusions

In Tibet, vegetarianism has been viewed as both virtuous and somewhat perilous. This has placed it beyond the reach of many people. But it has also meant that when someone did adopt it, they were respected and admired for their choice. Vegetarianism aligns clearly with Mahāyāna Buddhism's compassionate ideal and marks its practitioners as willing to undertake hardship in order to alleviate the suffering of (animal) others. Vegetarianism may never have become the norm in Tibet, but it has remained present, an admired practice taken up by a small but vocal subset of the religiously devout.

One interesting result of this is the prominence given to what we might call partial vegetarianism. Anti-meat authors rarely demand that their readers completely abandon all meat in all contexts. More often, they point to the moral problems inherent in meat eating, then suggest that readers reduce their consumption as much as possible. Sometimes this might mean adopting veganism or vegetarianism, but it might also simply mean avoiding meat during festivals or on holy days. Or it might mean avoiding slaughtered meat and eating only meat from animals who have died in accidents.[3] Or it might simply mean trying to reduce how much meat is consumed without necessarily giving it up entirely. As Terdak Lingpa puts it in his 1689 *Rules and Regulations of Mindrolling Monastery*: "While we do not absolutely implement a rule of vegetarianism, it is important that festivals and the like do not have lots of meat, and that meat is not the main basis of one's diet" (Barstow 2018, 170). The goal remains the same throughout this literature: reducing the number of animals killed for their meat. Full vegetarianism might have been the ideal, but any practice that reduced animal suffering was commendable.

Overall, then, we can conclude that for most Tibetans, vegetarianism has been seen as a difficult but admired practice. This meant that most individuals have felt full vegetarianism was beyond their abilities. Some of those who did not feel they were up to the task of full vegetarianism may have adopted some form of partial vegetarianism, but the majority continued to eat meat as they always had.

In many ways, this basic situation remains the same today. There is an active vegetarian movement among contemporary Tibetans, both inside Tibet and in exile. Some are even calling for the adoption of veganism, a diet never seen in premodern Tibet. Furthermore, shifting attitudes toward health have combined with the availability of new foods to make it easier to be meat-free than ever before. But vegetarianism and veganism largely remain the purview of devout Buddhists, and the arguments used to support these diets continue to rest on the Buddhist call to practice compassion. It is that compassion, so central to Tibetan Buddhism, that motivates these individuals to give up meat, whether for a meal or a lifetime.

Notes

1 Sanskrit: *tikoṭiparisuddha*. Tibetan: Usually *rnam gsum dag pa'i sha*, but also: *snang gsum dag pa'i sha*, or *brags pa rnam gsum*.
2 Tibetan: *bad kan, rlung, mkhris pa*.
3 Such "naturally dead" meat could come from accidents like lightning strikes or falls, but few Tibetans would be willing to eat meat from an animal who died of either old age or illness, out of concern that the meat might not be healthy.

References

Barstow, Geoffrey. 2018. *Food of Sinful Demons: Meat, Vegetarianism, and the Limits of Buddhism in Tibet*. New York: Columbia University Press.
_____, ed. 2019. *The Faults of Meat: Tibetan Buddhist Writings on Vegetarianism*. Boston, Mass.: Wisdom Publications.
Gyaltsen, Sakya Paṇḍita Künga. 2002. *A Clear Differentiation of the Three Codes: Essential Differentiations Among the Individual Liberation, Great Vehicle, and Tantric Systems*. Translated by Jared Douglas Rhoton. New York: SUNY Press.
Johnson, Anna. 2019. "Khedrup Jé on Meat in the Monastery." In *The Faults of Meat: Tibetan Buddhist Writings on Vegetarianism*, edited by Geoffrey Barstow, 119–58. Boston, Mass.: Wisdom.
Kieschnick, John. 2005. "Buddhist Vegetarianism in China." In *Of Tripod and Palate: Food, Politics, and Religion in Traditional China*, edited by Roel Sterckx, 186–212. New York: Palgrave Macmillan.
Kilty, Gavin. 2010. "Translator's Introduction." In *Mirror of Beryl: A Historical Introduction to Tibetan Medicine*, edited by Desi Sangyé Gyatso, 1–26. Boston, Mass.: Wisdom Publications.

Ohnuma, Reiko. 2017. *Unfortunate Destiny: Animals in the Indian Buddhist Imagination*. New York: Oxford University Press.

Rangdrol, Shabkar Tsogdruk. 2004. *Food of Bodhisattvas: Buddhist Teachings on Abstaining from Meat*. Translated by Padmakara Translation Group. Boston, Mass.: Shambhala.

Other Recommended Resources

Ambros, Barbara R. 2019. "*Partaking of Life*: Buddhism, Meat-Eating, and Sacrificial Discourses of Gratitude in Contemporary Japan." *Religions* 10: 279. https://doi.org/10.3390/rel10040279.

Buffetrille, Katia. 2014. "A Controversy on Vegetarianism." In *Trails of the Tibetan Tradition: Papers for Elliot Sperling*, edited by Roberto Vitali, 113–27. Dharamsala: Amye Machen Institute. http://himalaya.socanth.cam.ac.uk/collections/journals/ret/pdf/ret_31_09.pdf.

Finnigan, Bronwyn. 2017. "Buddhism and Animal Ethics." *Philosophy Compass* 12 (7): 1–12. https://doi.org/10.1111/phc3.12424.

Gayley, Holly. 2017. "The Compassionate Treatment of Animals." *Journal of Religious Ethics* 45 (1): 29–57. https://doi.org/10.1111/jore.12167.

Greene, Eric. 2016. "A Reassessment of the Early History of Vegetarianism in Chinese Buddhism." *Asia Major* 29 (1): 1–43.

Jaffe, Richard M. 2005. "The Debate Over Meat Eating in Japanese Buddhism." In *Going Forth: Visions of Buddhist Vinaya*, edited by William M. Bodiford, 255–75. Honolulu: University of Hawai'i Press.

19 Veganism as Spiritual Practice

Adrienne Krone

Introduction

In 2015, I spent a week at the Hallelujah Diet Health Retreat, where visitors are taught how to follow a vegan and mostly raw diet based on the diet of Adam and Eve in the Garden of Eden as described by the book of Genesis. I sat down with one of the retreat leaders, Anita, and she clarified her position on veganism, explaining that she's "not a PETA placard holder" and that she "wouldn't spray anybody with paint" (Koch 2015). Instead, Anita saw her veganism as part of her theology and spiritual practice as a Messianic Jew. She continued,

> my spiritual understanding now about how important animals are to the Lord and knowing how we treat them, which is terrible, and God does say in his word that he will hold man responsible for how he has treated the animals.
>
> (Koch 2015)

As she became a vegan, Anita's understanding of what God wanted her to do and the relationship she was meant to have with animals changed. And while her experience is not unique, it is also not definitive. For Anita, veganism is intertwined with her spiritual practice as a Messianic Jew, but for others, veganism *is* their spiritual practice.

Think about how you might define "religion" or "spiritual practice." When thinking about spiritual practice, people often mention conversion, rituals, and beliefs while definitions of religion often include references to theology, institutions, and deities. In this chapter, I'll focus on the first set of terms as I argue that many people in the contemporary United States engage in veganism as a spiritual practice. Veganism informs decision-making as vegans choose what to eat, what to wear, and how to spend their time. And as people settle into practicing veganism, it often shapes or reshapes their relationships with other humans, animals, and the divine. What I will focus on here is a relatively recent phenomenon of people practicing veganism as a spiritual practice itself, whether it is tied to their religious identity or not. Note that I'm not arguing that veganism is a religion. This is because it lacks deities, teachings about life and death, and the kinds of institutions that are generally indicative of religion. Instead, I'll focus on the many aspects of veganism that mirror the spiritual practices of religions.

Veganism as Spiritual Practice

A number of scholars have written about vegetarianism and veganism as spiritual practices. In an early article on this topic, Wesley Jamison, Caspar Wenk, and James Parker

DOI: 10.4324/9781003324157-23

described animal activism as a "functional religion" (2000, 307). They interviewed animal rights activists in the United States and Sweden and found five common practices among members of the animal rights movement that "function as religion": conversion, community, creed, code, and cult (Jamison, Wenk, and Parker 2000, 307). Jamison, Wenk, and Parker's informants described epiphanies that caused their conversion to animal rights activism and the communities they formed with others who shared their creed or belief that animals have rights (2000, 311–314). Informants also followed a code that was supported by their veganism: "Animals are not ours to eat, wear, experiment on, or use in any way!" and engaged in a cult, a shared set of symbols and rituals that included sharing meatless meals and attending meetings (Jamison, Wenk, and Parker 2000, 317–318).

The authors argue that the growth and intensity of the animal rights movement can be explained by the fact that it serves as a functional religion for those involved (2000, 320). This is a rather utilitarian understanding of the reasons people join and remain in the animal rights movement that does not account for primary driving factors such as the global expansion of factory farming and the suffering of animals who are raised in such conditions. The authors' argument is also specific to animal rights activism, which is different than veganism.

Identifying veganism as a spiritual practice separate from animal rights activism helps explain Anita's clarification in the opening example. She saw her veganism as a way to enact her understanding of how humans should interact with animals, but she explicitly distanced herself from activists who spray people wearing fur with paint. This practice may be spiritual for those who see animal rights as their central worldview, but it falls outside what Anita and many others consider to be the spiritual practice of veganism.

Moving toward veganism as spiritual practice, religious studies scholar Benjamin Zeller used the language of "quasi-religion" to describe another close relative of veganism— vegetarianism (2014). Zeller uses quasi-religion to refer to approaches to food that don't incorporate things like "Gods, supernatural forces, teachings about the soul or life after death, institutions or churches," which scholars often identify as central components of religion (2014, 294). But these approaches to food do involve "rituals, conversions, central texts, and ideas about saving the individual and the world," which scholars tend to think of as religious, as seen in the previous example (2014, 295). Zeller talks about two approaches to food—vegetarianism and locavorism—that exemplify this category of "quasi-religion" (2014). Zeller talks about some of his informants' conversions to vegetarianism and they are similar to stories I've heard during my research on religious food justice movements. Books like *Animal Liberation* ([1975] 2009) by Peter Singer, *Eating Animals* (2009) by Jonathan Safran Foer, and *Dominion* (2003) by Matthew Scully have come up multiple times as the source of vegan or vegetarian conversions. Thus, veganism seems to fit well into Zeller's framework for quasi-religions, even though his study focused on vegetarians and not vegans.

Vegan activists tend to describe veganism as an encompassing practice that is much more than a diet. In her introduction to the book *Veganism in an Oppressive World*, Julia Feliz Brueck notes that the term "vegan" was coined by Donald Watson and Dorothy Morgan of The Vegan Society in 1945 in the United Kingdom (2017, 2). The current definition of veganism used by the Vegan Society is "a philosophy and way of living which seeks to exclude—as far as is possible and practicable—all forms of exploitation of, and cruelty to, animals for food, clothing or any other purpose" (The Vegan Society Website 2022). The phrase "way of living" is common in vegan communities. It speaks to the understanding of many vegans that veganism is a spiritual practice—it is a practice that is informed by particular ideas about the appropriate relationship between humans and animals. It is enacted when vegans avoid exploiting animals through the food, clothes, and medicines they choose.

The Vegan Society encourages visitors to their website to take a pledge to try going vegan for 30 days (The Vegan Society Website 2022). They go on to say that this pledge helps "over a thousand people each month go vegan and stay vegan" so we might think of this as a vegan proselytization effort (The Vegan Society Website 2022). This carries forward the suggestion of scholars that conversion is a key element when we think about what counts as a spiritual practice and suggests that for many vegans, converting others is also part of how they practice their veganism.

Lisa Johnson, a scholar of law and business, used a survey of 163 adults conducted in the United States in 2013 to conclude that "ethical veganism meets the definition for religion under U.S. law" and should be recognized as such because of shared beliefs and practices like those described earlier (2015, 31, 34). Moreover, many of the people who were surveyed for this study themselves felt that their veganism had religious aspects, as these direct quotes show (Johnson 2015, 47, 49):

- "[Veganism] is a part of my life that is recognized each and every day, more than some people practice their religion."
- "My belief is as important as any organized religion."
- "The Bible teaches us that our bodies are temples for the Holy Spirit to dwell in and for God to communicate with us. A body that is muddled by a poor diet is like an untidy, filthy house, not fit for a king to be in."
- "It is a directive that was born in my heart without a set of rules to tell me whether it is right or wrong. It is comparable to a religious belief."
- "I would think that checking foods to make sure that animal products are not present is like a kosher person making sure the food item they are going to eat is kosher, so I'd say that is parallel with religion."

Therefore, veganism can stand alone as a spiritual practice, but in many cases, veganism is one aspect of a spiritual practice informed by other factors.

Varieties of Veganism as Spiritual Practice

Many contemporary forms of veganism as spiritual practice are intertwined with the other identities of vegans. Julia Feliz Brueck points out that "the practice of veganism will and does change depending on someone's lived experiences and cultural background." In this way, veganism is again similar to other spiritual practices subject to alteration and adaptation (2017, 3). In the examples that follow, we'll see veganism serving as a spiritual practice for Black vegans, Jewish vegans, and South Asian vegans.

Aph and Syl Ko, theorists and authors of the book *Aphro-ism*, are clear that when they talk about Black veganism, they are not just talking about being Black and being vegan (2017, 51). Instead, they write that Black veganism "encourages activists to think about and articulate the animal situation as they see fit *through* their lived situation" [emphasis in original] (Ko and Ko 2017, 53). They explain that peoples' identities affect how they see and think about the world, influencing how they "choose to act on what is going on" (Ko and Ko 2017, 52–53). So just as the spiritual practice of Christianity often looks different for Black Americans than white Americans, for those who practice it, Black veganism looks different than white veganism. Syl Ko later clarifies in a different essay in the same book that for many vegans, there is a struggle to make a connection between animal exploitation and human oppression. But she suggests that "black veganism is internal to the project of black liberation" (Ko and Ko 2017, 121). Syl Ko ends this essay by pointing out that Black veganism is primarily a "methodological tool" that should be used to "reactivate" imaginations. It is meant to reshape the practice of veganism for those concerned with dismantling racism, which she argues "will also require us to reconsider how we view and treat all life" (2017, 126). Thus, the spiritual practice of Black veganism incorporates practices aimed at ending the oppression of both humans and animals. Christopher Carter expands on these ideas about Black veganism in his book *The Spirit of Soul Food* as he argues that if soul food is going to continue to be a response to food injustice in the Black community, then it should be vegan (2021, 3).

Jacob Ari Labendz, a Jewish Studies scholar who coedited the book *Jewish Veganism and Vegetarianism*, wrote a chapter for the book about his veganism, which he called an "embodied practice" (2019, 289). He writes in the chapter that he is "culturally, intellectually, and politically Jewish" but also an atheist who does not consider himself a member of the Jewish religion. Labendz argues in the chapter that veganism can provide the framework for cultural Jews that Jewish religion lacks (2019, 290). He thinks that veganism could serve as a spiritual practice for cultural Jews partly because it resembles the Jewish food system, *kashrut*, in the ways that it establishes rules for eating and boundaries for social meals inside and outside the home (Labendz 2019, 298–300). Labendz similarly likened many values associated with veganism—justice, preventing the suffering of living creatures, and reducing waste—to values central to Judaism (2019, 300). Thus, for Labendz, veganism is his embodied practice, and it is not religiously Jewish but culturally Jewish.

In an essay titled "Exploring Vegan Spirituality," six South Asian vegan womxn discuss their approach to veganism as a spiritual practice (Kaur et al. 2017; "womxn" is an alternative spelling used by many intersectional feminists to avoid the perceived sexism and exclusivity of words that include "man" or "men"). They describe their veganism as a "food-centric spirituality that emphasizes the wholeness in nourishing the body as well as the mind without deliberate harm to other sentient beings" (Kaur et al. 2017, 123). The authors stress that "vegan spirituality should not be a privilege but an accessible, non-exploitative way for us to experience connections to ourselves and to nature" (Kaur et al. 2017, 124).

The authors had different experiences with vegan spirituality; in some cases, it drew them closer to religion, while in others, it distanced them from religion. For Winnie Kaur, veganism helped her embrace her Sikhism. She "started researching connections between diet and spirituality" and began going to the local Gurudwara, which is where Sikhs worship, in many cases bringing friends along with her (Kaur et al. 2017, 133). On the other hand, Bipasha Ahmed found that her veganism distanced her from her Bengali Muslim friends and family, but she also was "beginning to develop an understanding about spirituality and veganism" even though she does not consider herself to be spiritual (Kaur et al. 2017, 136). These examples again suggest that veganism is a spiritual practice separate from but related to the expression of other religious identities.

Conclusion

As a spiritual practice, veganism is a diverse practice informed by the identities of those practicing it. There are many common features, including a conversion experience; the adoption of an ideology that emphasizes that animals should not be exploited by humans and subsequent avoidance of foods, clothes, medicines, and other products that exploit animals; the practice of sharing meals and attending meetings with other vegans; and in some cases, efforts to convert others to veganism.

As a spiritual practice unto itself, veganism can complement or replace other religious practices and/or identities. To return to Anita, when she found veganism, she reshaped her life around it and began running retreats to help others adopt and maintain veganism in their own lives. Her religion is Messianic Judaism, but she engages veganism as a spiritual practice every day as she prepares raw vegan meals and juices for her guests and leads classes on why veganism is better for humans, animals, and the world.

References

Brueck, Julia Feliz, ed. 2017. *Veganism in an Oppressive World: A Vegans of Color Community Project*. Sanctuary Publishers.

Carter, Christopher. 2021. *The Spirit of Soul Food: Race, Faith, and Food Justice*. Urbana and Chicago, Ill.: University of Illinois Press.

Foer, Jonathan Safran. 2009. *Eating Animals*. New York: Little, Brown and Company.

Jamison, Wesley V., Caspar Wenk, and James V. Parker. 2000. "Every Sparrow That Falls: Understanding Animal Rights Activism as Functional Religion." *Society & Animals* 8 (3): 305–30.

Johnson, Lisa. 2015. "The Religion of Ethical Veganism." *Journal of Animal Ethics* 5 (1): 31–68.

Kaur, Vinamarata "Winnie," Bipasha Ahmed, Deepta Rao, Meenal Upadhyay, Ankita Yadav, and Laila Kassam. 2017. "Exploring Vegan Spirituality: An Interview with Six South Asian Vegan Womxn." In *Veganism in an Oppressive World: A Vegans of Color Community Project*, edited by Julia Feliz Brueck, 123–49. Sanctuary Publishers.

Ko, Aph, and Syl Ko. 2017. *Aphro-Ism: Essays on Pop Culture, Feminism, and Black Veganism from Two Sisters*. New York: Lantern Books.

Koch, Anita. 2015. "Interview with author, Hallelujah Diet Health Retreat Kitchen." June 25.

Labendz, Jacob Ari. 2019. "Jewish Veganism as an Embodied Practice: A Vegan Agenda for Cultural Jews." In *Jewish Veganism and Vegetarianism: Studies and New Directions*, edited by Jacob Ari Labendz and Shmuly Yanklowitz, 289–313. Albany: State University of New York Press.

Scully, Matthew. 2003. *Dominion: The Power of Man, the Suffering of Animals, and the Call to Mercy*. New York: St. Martin's Press.

Singer, Peter. (1975) 2009. *Animal Liberation: The Definitive Classic of the Animal Movement*. New York: HarperCollins Publishers.

The Vegan Society Website. 2022. "Definition of Veganism." Accessed June 4, 2022. www.vegansociety.com/go-vegan/definition-veganism.

Zeller, Benjamin E. 2014. "Quasi-Religious American Foodways: The Cases of Vegetarianism and Locavorism." In *Religion, Food, and Eating in North America*, edited by Benjamin E. Zeller, Marie W. Dallam, Reid L. Neilson, and Nora L. Rubel, 294–312. New York: Columbia University Press.

Other Recommended Resources

Jackson, Thomas Wade, director. 2019. *A Prayer for Compassion*, Film, 91 mins. The Compassion Project. http://aprayerforcompassion.com/.

Robinson, Margaret. 2013. "Veganism and Mi'kmaq Legends." *Canadian Journal of Native Studies* 33 (1): 189–96.

Tuttle, Will, ed. 2018. *Buddhism and Veganism: Essays Connecting Spiritual Awakening and Animal Liberation*. Danvers, Mass.: Vegan Publishers.

20 The Spiritual Practice of Providing Sanctuary for Animals[1]

Barbara Darling

Introduction

Reflections by students in my 2022 Religion and Animals class say it all. Tony Smith wrote:

> Winslow Farm Animal Sanctuary is a place where . . . animals can find a home, that aims to restore that relationship among . . . animals and people by providing them with . . . an abundance of love.

Karina Novais, referencing what she had learned that semester about the systematic abuse of animals, reflected:

> Despite their history of abuse or negligence, [the animals] still had so much love to give and the desire to get some in return . . . all the cats were eager . . . [to be petted]. It was so heartwarming to see these animals get a second chance and one that they fully get to take advantage of and enjoy.

Violet Windham summed it up this way:

> I'm so grateful that our class was able to go together and learn from each other, Ms. White [the sanctuary's founder], and the animals at [Winslow] Farm. I feel that our world is in great need of patience and understanding towards living creatures . . . different from ourselves, and Winslow Farm . . . encourages us to be the best version of ourselves by treating humans and non-human animals with respect and compassion.

Animal sanctuaries in the United States were created to protect animals from exploitation, abuse, cruelty, violence, and neglect—to give them a safe haven. They also provide education and advocacy.[2] Rescuing farm animals and caring for them as a spiritual (as distinct from religious) practice is the focus of this chapter, drawing on case studies of three farmed animal sanctuaries. I have visited Winslow Farm Animal Sanctuary (Norton, Massachusetts) many times with my classes, family, and friends, and interviewed Debra White, founder and president. I went in person to Indraloka Animal Sanctuary (Dalton, Pennsylvania) and had a lovely conversation with founder Indra Lahiri. Finally, I toured Pasado's Safe Haven virtually (Sultan, Washington) and spoke at length with Stephanie Perciful, their director.[3]

DOI: 10.4324/9781003324157-24

Figure 20.1 Zebulon and Isaiah, Finnsheep, both age 12, resided at Winslow Farm Sanctuary in Norton, Massachusetts after being rescued as part of a cruelty investigation. For the first eight months of their lives, they had been kept in a small cage. Both developed severe arthritis because of their early confinement

Source: Copyright Isa Leshko, from *Allowed to Grow Old: Portraits of Elderly Animals from Farm Sanctuaries* by Isa Leshko, published by the University of Chicago Press

All three directors believe farmed animals *matter*; they see the *sacred* in these animals. The honor and respect they show for each animal's individuality and subjectivity, and their wholehearted commitment to the animals' flourishing, are so striking and touching, especially in a country and a world where farmed animals are commodified, exploited, abused, and painfully, violently killed.

Animals in these sanctuaries are respected and treated compassionately. They have found a home, as Violet and Tony mentioned in their papers cited earlier. The profound difference made in the lives of sanctuary animals has been illustrated dramatically in photographs by award-winning photographer Isa Leshko. I am grateful to include in this chapter some images from her moving book *Allowed to Grow Old: Portraits of Elderly Animals from Farm Sanctuaries* (Leshko 2019). These photos record animals settling into

Figure 20.2 Violet, a potbellied pig, age 12, was born with her rear legs partially paralyzed. She was surrendered to Wildlife Rescue and Rehabilitation in Kendalia, Texas, because her guardian could not properly care for her special needs

Source: Copyright Isa Leshko, from *Allowed to Grow Old: Portraits of Elderly Animals from Farm Sanctuaries* by Isa Leshko, published by the University of Chicago Press

life in a sanctuary free from trauma and violence. Instead of having their lives cut short, they are nurtured and loved, and can reach old age with dignity and peace.[4]

Sanctuaries and Spirituality

The focus of this chapter is on rescuing farm animals as a spiritual, but not religious, practice. Some animal sanctuary founders speak explicitly about their own connection with a religion, such as Rooterville in Florida (Christian), and Luvin Arms in Colorado (Jain). Kenneth R. Valpey's chapter in this volume explores "Cow Care in Hindu Ethics," and Thomas Berendt's 2018 Temple University dissertation is entitled "Bovine Benefactories: An Examination of the Role of Religion in Cow Sanctuaries across the United States."

None of the sanctuary directors in my case studies, by contrast, mention affiliation with a religious community. Wesley Jamison and colleagues argue that even though animal rights activism is not allied with any religion as conventionally understood, it still fulfills a functional definition of religion. They carefully analyze key aspects of religion, such as creed, code, conversion, community, etc., and show how the animal rights movement exhibits each of these (Jamison, Parker, and Wenk 2000; see also Adrienne Krone's Chapter 19 in this volume on "Veganism as Spiritual Practice"). Bron Taylor's book *Dark Green Religion* also suggests a "malleable" definition of religion, which would give the label of religion to "affective connections to the earth and its living systems . . . wonder and awe at the beauty . . . in our universe, the kinship some people feel toward their fellow living travelers in this earthly odyssey" (Taylor 2010, 221). He notes that these experiences have been a part of human existence for a very long time.

Roger Gottlieb similarly highlights the deep links between the secular and the sacred in the environmental movement, finding them so melded together that "it becomes hard to tell [religion and environmentalism] apart" (Gottlieb 2009, 148). One striking similarity is the experience found in many traditional religions of "a sense of the dissolution of the ego, of the boundaries that sharply divide one's own self from others" (Gottlieb 2009, 153)—an experience also found among environmentalists and certainly among the sanctuary directors I spoke with.

These scholars make a persuasive case for a broader definition of religion, and in religious studies scholarship we sometimes define religion in a functional way. I will not, however, be characterizing the practices of the three directors I spoke with as "religious." The spirituality embedded in their worldviews and lived-out dedication to animals is deep and it powerfully influences their lives, just as religion can do. But they themselves rejected that term and referred to their calling to offer animals sanctuary as "spiritual" instead.

When I asked Indra Lahiri if she thought of her actions as religious, she told me she purposefully chooses the language of spirituality, rather than religion, to describe Indraloka. Because all the sanctuary's human and other than human community members represent multiple religious perspectives, Indra instead focuses on the general spiritual beliefs they hold in common. Similarly, Debra White of Winslow Farm isn't connected to any organized religion but her spirituality is deep and clearly observable; she has been drawn to Native American spiritual values since childhood. She called her spiritual approach "eclectic."

Stephanie Perciful of Pasado's affirmed: "The sanctuary is my church," and a higher power connects us. Even though she observed that she had not previously named as "spiritual" her choice to dedicate her life to working with animals, she is comfortable with that terminology because "it was and remains a decision that fulfills the soul and who I am as a person, and not any sort of material or physical gain."

Spirituality, due to its individualized nature, is a notoriously slippery term. For the purposes of this chapter, however, I take spirituality to include deep connection and oneness with others and with the universe, which provides meaning to life; being enveloped in love and its healing powers; and profound engagement with the mystery of death. My conversations with the three directors and direct observation of the sanctuary teams' interactions with the animals clearly showed these spiritual values in action—and also the monumental difference sanctuaries make in the lives of animals.

Oneness with the Animals and the Universe

When animals arrive at the sanctuary, said Stephanie of Pasado's, the humans tell them: "We are now part of each other's lives. For however long you need us, we are in this together."

Indra thinks about the specific reasons these animals, out of the billions that are suffering, came to her. She believes that powers we cannot see are protecting them since the odds are so stacked against them. Sunita, a little sheep, illustrates this protection. She escaped from a live market as a baby and survived on her own for *six months* before being rescued and coming to Indraloka. Furthermore, Indra finds that the needed funds come in; she doesn't believe in a universe that saves these animals, only to let them die for lack of money.

In Debra's similar philosophy, the universe responds and gives her what she needs for Winslow's work. She learned that if she stays 100% true to her cause, when she thinks about something, she sees it manifesting—for example, volunteers who help with fundraising and publicity. There were no volunteers in Winslow Farm's first eight years, and

Figure 20.3 Penny Power, a 30-year-old Hereford crossbreed, was rescued from slaughter after spending her youth as a "breeder" on a beef farm. She lived her remaining years at Indraloka Animal Sanctuary in Dalton, Pennsylvania

Source: Copyright Isa Leshko, from *Allowed to Grow Old: Portraits of Elderly Animals from Farm Sanctuaries* by Isa Leshko, published by the University of Chicago Press

Debra did all the caregiving for every animal, forming one-on-one relationships with each rescued being. She established a rhythm and learned to respond intuitively in the moment to the needs, desires, and preferences of each animal.

Debra feels that she becomes one with the animals. Even with, say, a hundred chickens, she observes them so carefully that she knows every single one as intimately as she would a beloved pet. She knows when they need her healing presence so that she can be there with them. If a horse's leg hurts, her leg hurts. She believes she would not be such a healing force for the animals if she couldn't feel their pain. She accepts the pain as the price of being able to feel one with the animals and works to "glide above" it.

Healing and Learning and Love

This oneness with the animals that Debra described is closely related to the healing that happens. When I asked Stephanie if she sees her sanctuary work as spiritual, she immediately responded: When animals come, a healing process begins that is not just medical; it is also emotional (Pasado's priority is cruelty cases). The sanctuary allows the animals space to be who they are meant to be and to come to trust humans again. But then human guests arrive and the animals help the humans to heal! "They are so forgiving. It's not just us healing them. Being with the animals is very healing, too." The love and healing flow in both directions. She told me that neurodiverse children practice reading to the animals, who listen without judgment, and the children's faces light up.

The animals also *teach* the humans, as my student Violet observed in her paper cited previously. One thing they teach, according to Stephanie of Pasado's, is "Stop being a complicated human and making things so difficult when it can be so simple and so lovely." For example, Stephanie remarked that Pasado's cares for a pair of best friends, a sheep and a chicken, who teach eloquently (if wordlessly) about diversity!

Debra of Winslow also learns from animals—they teach her how to live in the present. Similarly, Indra of Indraloka believes that animals live in the present. That doesn't mean that they don't suffer trauma, but they move through trauma more quickly than humans—because of their ability to live in the present and to not get overly caught up in their egos. As humans, she commented, our story about our past trauma keeps us in the pain and out of the present. Animals are wonderful teachers about how to move through trauma and can therefore help us heal ourselves.

For Debra, bringing an animal through an unhealthy condition is a blessing to her, and interacting with the animals makes her feel emotionally satisfied. What she does at Winslow Farm requires her to give love 24/7. She feels she pours her "laser beams" of loving energy into the animals. I asked if they responded by loving her. Certainly, she replied, but she doesn't usually think about getting anything back and that is *not* why she does what she does for the animals. She does it to share love with them. She is open to the healing energies of the universe. Debra showed me the healing room she built, fragrant with the scent of patchouli, where she brings animals who are sick; and where Petey, a one-footed chicken, sleeps every night.

Figure 20.4 Ash, a Broad Breasted White turkey, age 8, was a factory farm survivor who resided at Farm Sanctuary's shelter in Orland, California

Source: Copyright Isa Leshko, from *Allowed to Grow Old: Portraits of Elderly Animals from Farm Sanctuaries* by Isa Leshko, published by the University of Chicago Press

Engagement with Death

Sadly, however, sometimes the healing doesn't happen. All the directors have to deal with the loss of animals whom they love very much. Indra noted that rarely does anyone else on earth experience death as frequently and personally as human caregivers at a sanctuary. Many animals arrive sick, wounded, frail, and close to death, which takes an enormous emotional toll on her and the whole Indraloka team. She honors all their pain and provides space for everyone to grieve and mourn. She also finds an opportunity in all this death to come close to one of life's greatest mysteries and to grapple with her own mortality. These experiences remind her and her colleagues of how fragile life is and how quickly it passes, and these encounters with death teach that life is too short not to spend time with those we love.

Indra continues to open her heart to every single animal, despite knowing she may lose them. She explained why she doesn't allow herself to become closed-off, numb, or self-protective: she would miss the opportunity for a sacred friendship. And also—it's almost impossible not to love the animals that way! They come to Indraloka sick and needy, and they begin to blossom. It would be impossible for humans to close their hearts to them! She feels strongly that if someone is meant to do this work, they can't do anything else; otherwise it is too hard: too painful, too expensive, and too physically demanding. Going into this profession doesn't make any sense unless one has a profound reason—a calling—for doing it.

Stephanie of Pasado's responded very similarly when I asked if she was tempted to numb herself. She admitted that sometimes she asks herself how many times her heart can break. But numbing herself wouldn't work anyway; and why would she deprive herself of such true and beautiful relationships? Besides, "you couldn't do this work if it wasn't part of who you are. You do it because it is a passion. The animals are worth the pain and worth the heartbreak."[5]

Debra allows the other animals to see and realize when their friends have passed, so they, too, can grieve.[6] Then she buries the animals on her property. Frequently hawks circle above as animals are being buried; Debra remarked that they carry the animals' spirits away.

Stephanie described some ways Pasado's memorializes the passing of their beloved residents. They cremate the animals and scatter their ashes in a creek running through the sanctuary. Sometimes they hold a memorial service. A memorial garden contains a stone personally created for each animal.[7] Some are funny, while others are deeply moving:

Nora Pig (rescued from food production)
Lived her life
Full of sass
Knocked her vet on her a**

Everson Rooster (rescued from being dumped)
Our fierce warrior
Sunrise is not quite as
Bright without your voice.

Volunteers come weekly and distribute flowers throughout the garden as an additional memorial practice.[8]

It all comes back to love—an "abundance of love," as the opening quotation by Tony Smith makes clear. The love flows freely in all directions, as observed by Karina Novais in her statement, noted earlier, that the animals "still had so much love to give and the desire to get some in return."

According to Stephanie, with a sentiment that I am sure is shared by Indra and Debra,

The animals have known nothing but love all the time they are with us. In their time with humans their needs came first before ours, we respected them, and they finally got to be the individuals they deserve to be. When they leave, they know that they are loved.

And, in the mystery of love, they never truly leave us because they remain in our hearts.

Figure 20.5 Babs, a 24-year-old donkey who resided at Pasado's Safe Haven in Sultan, Washington, was a former rodeo animal used for roping practice prior to her rescue

Source: Copyright Isa Leshko, from *Allowed to Grow Old: Portraits of Elderly Animals from Farm Sanctuaries* by Isa Leshko, published by the University of Chicago Press

Notes

1 Many thanks to the editors, especially Dave Aftandilian; to Ted Goodfleisch, Nancy Stockford, JoDee Keller, Vicki Bartolini, Jonathan Brumberg-Kraus, Terry Darling, and Mary Albert Darling for helpful conversations about this chapter; and above all to Debra White, Indra Lahiri, Stephanie Perciful, and Isa Leshko.
2 Education, outreach, and advocacy are key to the sanctuaries' mission of building a kinder world—for the animals they are able to rescue directly **and also** for the billions of animals who are suffering from human cruelty in factory farming. By allowing visitors to experience the preferences and personalities of formerly farmed animals, sanctuary staff hope to inspire them to become more compassionate by reducing or eliminating animal products from their diets; and, in so doing, ignite a larger social movement that will reduce cruelty to animals on a large scale.
3 Animal sanctuaries face a number of ethical challenges (Abrell 2021; Donaldson and Kymlicka 2015; Jones 2014), such as the decisions sanctuaries make to limit resident animals' freedom to move around, mate, reproduce, etc. This chapter does not address those debates.

4 Isa Leshko's own compassion for the animals and respect for the individuality and flourishing of her photo subjects are patently obvious both in her pictures and in her written "Introduction" (Leshko 2019, 2–13, 19–87).

5 In *Compassion Fatigue in the Animal-Care Community*, Charles Figley and Robert Roop sensitively explore the pressing problem of compassion fatigue among animal care workers in sanctuaries, veterinary hospitals, etc. (Figley and Roop 2006). They note that the empathy and kindness that motivate shelter and sanctuary volunteers and professionals to devote themselves to animals can sometimes lead to exhaustion and stress. In addition to the remarks I've cited by Indra and Stephanie, Debra is also aware of the risks of compassion fatigue. She addresses it by trying to let go of negative thoughts so that she does not adversely affect the animals. She told me she is able to flush out bad ideas and open herself to goodness and love.

6 Many different species show mourning and grieving behaviors, as observed compassionately by Barbara J. King in her thoughtful exploration *How Animals Grieve* (King 2013).

7 Resident animals' memorials are considered part of Pasado's operating expense. "We commit to them," said director Stephanie, "until they are no longer with us, and this includes their stones."

8 pattrice jones and Lori Gruen argue that rituals of remembrance for departed sanctuary animals are vital to maintaining a healthy interspecies community (jones and Gruen 2016). They also see memorials as a way to fight the compassion fatigue mentioned earlier.

References

Abrell, Elan. 2021. *Saving Animals: Multispecies Ecologies of Rescue and Care*. Minneapolis and London: University of Minnesota Press.

Berendt, Thomas. 2018. "Bovine Benefactories: An Examination of the Role of Religion in Cow Sanctuaries across the United States." PhD thesis, Department of Religion, Temple University. https://scholarshare.temple.edu/handle/20.500.12613/778.

Donaldson, Sue, and Will Kymlicka. 2015. "Farmed Animal Sanctuaries." *Politics and Animals* 1 (1): 50–74. www.politicsandanimals.org.

Figley, Charles, and Robert Roop. 2006. *Compassion Fatigue in the Animal-Care Community*. Washington, D.C.: Humane Society Press. www.wellbeingintlstudiesrepository.org/ebooks/5/.

Gottlieb, Roger. 2009. *A Greener Faith: Religious Environmentalism and Our Planet's Future*. Oxford and New York: Oxford University Press.

Jamison, Wesley, James Parker, and Caspar Wenk. 2000. "Every Sparrow That Falls: Understanding Animal Rights Activism as Functional Religion." *Society and Animals* 8 (3): 305–30. https://doi.org/10.1163/156853000511140.

Jones, Miriam. 2014. "Captivity in the Context of a Sanctuary for Formerly Farmed Animals." In *The Ethics of Captivity*, edited by Lori Gruen, 90–101. Oxford: Oxford University Press.

jones, pattrice, and Lori Gruen. 2016. "Keeping Ghosts Close: Care and Grief at Sanctuaries." In *Mourning Animals: Rituals and Practices Surrounding Animal Death*, edited by Margo DeMello, 187–192. East Lansing: Michigan State University Press.

King, Barbara J. 2013. *How Animals Grieve*. Chicago, Ill. and London: University of Chicago Press.

Leshko, Isa. 2019. *Allowed to Grow Old: Portraits of Elderly Animals from Farm Sanctuaries*. Chicago, Ill. and London: University of Chicago Press.

Taylor, Bron. 2010. *Dark Green Religion: Nature Spirituality and the Planetary Future*. Berkeley: University of California Press.

Other Recommended Resources

Indraloka Animal Sanctuary. indraloka.org.
Isa Leshko Photography. www.isaleshko.com.
Pasado's Safe Haven. pasadosafehaven.org.
Winslow Farm Animal Sanctuary. winslowfarm.com.

21 Cow Care in Hindu Animal Ethics

Kenneth R. Valpey

Introduction

Widespread among people who identify as Hindus is a special regard or even reverence for cows. In this chapter, we look briefly at the relationship of cows with religion in India and beyond as an important living tradition of *go-rakṣa*—"cow protection"—that for many Hindus has become a critical locus of ethical issues concerning the treatment of animals by humans. As a religious practice, the maintenance of *gaushalas* (shelters or sanctuaries) for cows to live out their natural lifespan has become, in modern times, a practical way to uphold what are considered essential Hindu ethical values, encapsulated in the Sanskrit term *dharma*.

In the context of the pressures of modernization and globalization in India, the ideals and practices of what may be called "cow care" are being increasingly challenged, yet dedicated practitioners still see their work with cows as a calling. Here we view one *gaushala* in northern India and another in Great Britain to see how an ethics of care inspired by ancient Indian religious cultures sustains a vision of humanity thriving together with these large—and largely peaceful—bovines.

Cows Sacred; Cows Neglected

"Nandu was struck by a car in the winter and left by the side of the road. He was so weak and emaciated that he could not get up by himself. He was close to giving up the will to live." So begins a typical short account of a young bull rescue recorded in Care For Cows International's occasional newsletter (Kurma Rupa 2013). Care For Cows (www.careforcows.org) is a cow sanctuary on the outskirts of Vrindavan, a major pilgrimage destination three hours' drive south of New Delhi, India. The particular case of Nandu (so named by the sanctuary staff) has a happy ending, as the newsletter's before and after photos of the young bull clearly illustrate. But the example of Nandu points to a deeply conflicted general mentality in this land of the sacred cow. Like much of India today, where cows are understood to be uniquely sacred creatures, such regard here in Vrindavan is eclipsed by motor vehicles' speeding traffic as drivers show little or no caution amidst the numerous wandering street cows.

That such accidents happen nowadays in Vrindavan strikes me as ironic in that this area is particularly celebrated as the land of Krishna, the divine cowherd revered for his charming boyhood exploits. Krishna's devotees (*bhaktas*) will tell you that Krishna established the exalted status of cows by personally tending them when he was present here in ancient times. Whereas Krishna is the object of worship for millions of people, he would lovingly care for the cows of his father, Nanda Baba.

DOI: 10.4324/9781003324157-25

Like numerous Hindus, including activists for cow protection (*go-rakṣa*) in India today, the manager of Care For Cows, Keshi Das, draws inspiration from the sense that cows hold, by divine arrangement, a special place in relation to humans. By dedication to cows' welfare, Keshi says, one is directly connecting oneself to divinity. As he explained to me, "When you love the cows . . . the Lord [Krishna] is pleased. But you must give them sincere service. You must be able to sacrifice twenty-four hours per day and dirty your hands." Thus, one sure way to please Krishna—the essential aim of *bhakti-yoga* (the yoga of devotion, whereby the term *yoga* can mean "connection")—is to *serve* cows, with the understanding that the cows one serves are especially dear to Krishna.

Among the around 1800 registered *gaushalas* in India (Sharma, Schuetze, and Phillips 2020), Care For Cows is modest in size, with (at this writing) around five hundred cows, bulls, and oxen. For this and all *gaushalas*, maintaining and caring for these bovines is minimally meant to allow them to live out their natural lives in the best possible conditions for their well-being and flourishing. Typically, the cowherds and managers of such sanctuaries will tell you that their cows show awareness that their lives will not be cut short: they are peaceful, even friendly, responding to the calling of their names, and there is a strong sense of reciprocation that the cowherds say is a special reward for their labors. Moreover, enabling cows to live out their natural lives puts into practice a core principle of Hindu traditions, namely, *ahimsā* or nonviolence—the conscientious avoidance of all unnecessary violence toward other living beings. This is considered the first and fundamental step in the practice of *yoga*.

Tied to the *ahimsā* principle is a core understanding of life dynamics that relates particularly to cow care. For people who identify themselves as Hindu (and, more broadly, persons of other Indian religious traditions, including Jainism and Sikhism), sanctuary cows' peaceful behavior confirms not only their sentience but also their identity—like all living beings—as trans-temporal souls who, as such, have a core desire for continued life. "Transmigration of souls" from one to another bodily form, whether "upward" to human or higher forms or "downward" to animal species with lesser capacities of consciousness, is understood to be the mechanism by which an individual soul, *ātmā*, changes its "residence" from one temporal life-form to another. Integral to this mechanism is the complex cosmic regulatory function of *karma*, literally "action"—the aggregate of a soul's behavior in the course of multiple lives, particularly in the human form. All other life-forms (including plants) are understood to follow their ways of survival without karma's reactive implications through a gradual progression toward the human form.

Of all bodily forms, the cow's body, in particular, is, according to sacred Hindu texts, potentially a final step before subsequently receiving a human body. To have a human body is to finally—after countless lives in other species—be able to prepare oneself to permanently end the seemingly perpetual suffering of repeated death and rebirth (a cycle known as *samsara*) and to come to eternal life of ever-expanding awareness and blissfulness in relation to the supreme, eternal, all-knowing, and all-blissful being (identified as Krishna by many if not most Hindus).

Saying that a cow's body is "potentially a final step" toward transmigrating into a human body points to the danger of missing this opportunity for the cow, especially by being killed unnecessarily and prematurely. Much worse is the danger for one who kills a cow (or even for one who *approves* of the killing of a cow). According to sacred Hindu texts, this act could force the guilty human to be born several times over as a cow to be themselves slaughtered, lifetime after lifetime.

Globalized Cow Care

Such warnings about the dire invisible consequences of cow slaughter may not be foremost in Indians' minds as they speak about the value of keeping cows for life. Many Hindu cow care activists speak more about cows' tangible and intangible benefits to humans. Most prominent among tangible benefits from the female lactating cow is, of course, her milk. In Indian—especially orthodox brahmanical—communities, milk from peaceful cows maintained for life and allowed to suckle their young plentifully is regarded as "liquid religion." This means that such milk is seen to be the richly nourishing physical manifestation of a piously conducted life. In turn, a piously conducted life constitutes a constellation of values and practices that are thought to best facilitate human thriving, and these values and practices are, in turn, seen to revolve around the proper practice of cow care.

But one may wonder if this constellation of values and practices in which cow care is so highly valued is not just an ethnic—and archaic—Indian tradition that has no place in the wider world. Arguably not. One small but significant practical sign of change and expansion of these values that include care for cows is to be seen in Great Britain: many people who identify strongly with these values and practices and appreciate the many challenges of lifelong cow care are ready to pay for milk from such protected cows at a higher price that includes payment into a pension fund for retired cows and for bulls. Responding to this small but growing market, since 2011, the nonprofit Ahimsa Dairy Foundation, located near Leicester in Great Britain, supplies milk and other dairy products to regular customers on a membership basis (ahimsamilk.org). Significantly, this project has been inspired by a cow care program called New Gokul at Bhaktivedanta Manor, the headquarters of the "Hare Krishnas" (the International Society for Krishna Consciousness, ISKCON) in the U.K. To be sure, as part of a global mission promoting the practices of Krishna devotion (*bhakti-yoga*), ISKCON is very keen to showcase cow care as integral to Krishna worship, based particularly on Krishna's teachings in the Bhagavad-gītā, in which *go-rakṣa*—protection of bovines—is prescribed as integral to human thriving.

Yet along with this organization's missionary religious spirit, one sees a cosmopolitanism that encourages everyone to draw from the tradition whatever tangible benefits are seen to be useful in modern life. From this perspective, Ahimsa Dairy, Bhaktivedanta Manor, and similar communities are eager to show how, as one practitioner put it to me, "a live cow is worth more than a dead cow." In addition to rich and healthy milk from protected cows, the urine and manure from cows offer important regenerative properties for soil fertility, fuel, and even medicinal purposes. These benefits are seen to be affirmed in the ritual as well as agricultural use of five products of the cow in combination, known as *panchagavya*—milk, yogurt, clarified butter, manure, and urine (Bajaj et al. 2022; Gandhi 2018). Furthermore, when trained, bulls (or oxen) can provide traction (pulling power) for farming, transport, milling, and generating electricity. Most importantly, practitioners report that living in the proximity of lifelong protected cows yields a sense of peace and well-being that compensates well for the challenges of long-term cow care, which complements and enriches the practice of devotional yoga (*bhakti-yoga*). This sense of peace and well-being makes practitioners of cow care and *bhakti-yoga* acutely aware of how unnecessary and self-destructive the killing of cows for meat and leather is—a phenomenon that, worldwide, takes the lives of more than 900,000 bovines per day, or nearly 38,000 per hour (based on U.N. Food and Agriculture Organization statistics for 2021, which show that 331,952,032 cattle were slaughtered worldwide that year; see Ritchie, Rosado, and Roser 2021).

Conclusion

If Hindus have so much concern for cows, what about other animals? A comment by Mahatma Gandhi in this regard may be telling:

> We can realize our duty towards the animal world and discharge it by wisely pursuing our dharma [roughly: duty] of service to the cow. At the root of cow protection is the realization of our dharma towards the sub-human species.
> (Gandhi 1999, vol. 81, 139–140)

Since, as we noted earlier, all living beings are understood to be of the same supertemporal nature, transiting from life to life through various bodies, Hindus and other practitioners will say that it behooves human beings to live by this principle. To do so is a process of *realization*—a conscious practice leading to higher consciousness of one's own identity beyond the temporal body. And as many Hindus and others would agree with Gandhi, the best way to facilitate this realization, for the benefit of all beings, is for humans to care for cows throughout their natural lives.

References

Ahimsa Milk: Slaughter-Free Milk. www.ahimsamilk.org.

Bajaj, Komal K., Vishal Chavhan, Nishikant A. Raut, and Shailendra Gurav. 2022. "*Panchgavya: A Precious Gift to Humankind.*" *Journal of Ayurveda and Integrative Medicine* 13 (2): 100525. https://doi.org/10.1016/j.jaim.2021.09.003.

Dasa, Kurma Rupa, editor. 2013. "Care for Cows International." *Newsletter*, October 2013. https://newgokul.bhaktivedantamanor.co.uk.

Gandhi, Maneka Sanjay. 2018. "The Utility of Panchagavya," *New Delhi Times*, July 16. Accessed June 20, 2023. www.newdelhitimes.com/the-utility-of-panchgavya/.

Gandhi, Mohandas K. 1999. *The Collected Works of Mahatma Gandhi (CWMG)*, 98 volumes. Electronic Book. New Delhi: Publications Division, Government of India. www.gandhiashramsevagram.org/gandhi-literature/collected-works-of-mahatma-gandhi-volume-1-to-98.php.

Ritchie, Hannah, Pablo Rosado, and Max Roser. 2021. "Meat and Dairy Production." Accessed June 20, 2023. https://ourworldindata.org/meat-production.

Sharma, Arvind, Catherine Schuetze, and Clive J.C. Phillips. 2020. "The Management of Cow Shelters (Gaushalas) in India, Including the Attitudes of Shelter Managers to Cow Welfare." *Animals* 10 (2): 211. https://doi.org/10.3390/ani10020211.

Other Recommended Resources

Berendt, Thomas. 2018. "Bovine Benefactories: An Examination of the Role of Religion in Cow Sanctuaries across the United States." PhD thesis, Department of Religion, Temple University. https://scholarshare.temple.edu/handle/20.500.12613/778.

Govindarajan, Radhika. 2018. "The Cow Herself Has Changed: Hindu Nationalism, Cow Protection, and Bovine Materiality." In *Animal Intimacies: Interspecies Relatedness in India's Central Himalayas*, 62–89. Chicago, Ill.: University of Chicago Press.

Jain, Pankaj. 2011. *Dharma and Ecology of Hindu Communities: Sustenance and Sustainability*. Farnham: Ashgate.

Krishna, Nanditha. 2014. *Sacred Animals of India*. New Delhi: Penguin Books India.

Lodrick, Deryck O. 1981. *Sacred Cows, Sacred Places: Origins and Survivals of Animal Homes in India*. Berkeley: University of California Press.

Nagy, Kelsi. 2019. "The Sacred and Mundane Cow: The History of India's Cattle Protection Movement." In *The Routledge Handbook of Religion and Animal Ethics*, edited by Andrew Linzey and Clair Linzey, 245–63. London: Routledge.

Nelson, Lance. 2006. "Cows, Elephants, Dogs, and Other Lesser Embodiments of Atman: Reflections on Hindu Attitudes Toward Nonhuman Animals." In *A Communion of Subjects: Animals in Religion, Science, and Ethics*, edited by Paul Waldau and Kimberley Patton, 179–93. New York: Columbia University Press.

Valpey, Kenneth R. 2020. *Cow Care in Hindu Animal Ethics*. Cham: Palgrave Macmillan. https://rd.springer.com/book/10.1007%2F978-3-030-28408-4.

"Why Cow Is Sacred and Are Worshiped by Hindus?" [*sic*]. Brief Informal Video Documentary. Accessed June 20, 2023. www.youtube.com/watch?v=Sh5joha5X1I.

22 The Council of All Beings

A Deep Ecology Ritual Connecting People with Animals and the Natural World

Eric D. Mortensen

I think the Council allowed me to better understand where my peers stood in terms of their personal revolutions, and also provided me a lot of insight into the common issues plaguing a wide array of seemingly unrelated species. Speaking for a species is no easy task, and I think the amount of care and intentional effort we put into finding out what each species has to say helped with aligning the notion that we as humans are also nature. The issues our species face are not only theirs, but are shared amongst all beings on Earth.

—Jessica Kelliher, student in the Guilford College course
Deep Ecology & Revolution, Spring 2021

The Council of All Beings is a deep ecology ritual wherein participants initially open themselves to being communicated to by an archetype of the natural world: an animal, swamp, the sun, lichen, mountain, etc. Participants then create masks of the beings they represent and speak for the beings at a Council. It is a ritual of lament and healing, of "despair and empowerment," motivated by the ecological crises our world is facing (Seed 1988b, 6). Reorientating away from the anthropocentric (human-focused) and toward the biocentric (Earth-focused), it is a ritual performed by humans who represent beings of the world who are threatened by changes brought about by humans.

Conceived in the mid-1980s by John Seed and Joanna Macy, following in the steps of deep ecologist Arne Naess, the Council of All Beings is a translation of the philosophy of deep ecology into ritualized action. The Council of All Beings is explained in detail in their 1988 book *Thinking Like a Mountain: Towards a Council of All Beings*. Quoting Vietnamese Zen monk Thich Nhat Hanh, Seed explains: "It is a form of group work which prepares and allows people to 'hear within themselves the sounds of the earth crying' . . . and to let other life-forms speak through them" (Seed 1988b, 7). *Deep* ecology refers to delving deeply enough to engender radical and fundamental change in humanity's relationships with the natural world, "[in] contrast to reform environmentalism which attempts only to treat some of the symptoms of the environmental crisis" (Seed 1988b, 9).

The Council of All Beings is "intended to dispel the illusion of separation and alienation" (Nesker [1992] 2000, 290). Thus, for example, the *deep* ecology movement traditionally eschews superficially working within systems to effect *surface-level* change. Instead, deep ecologists advocate for more revolutionary, transformative, and urgent reorientation. For a deep ecologist this might mean using electric vehicles (or not driving at all) instead of cars with only better gas mileage, veganism instead of mere "meatless Mondays," and radical engaged political action instead of mere theorizing. On an even more profound level, deep ecology "questions the fundamental premise and values of contemporary civilization," including the premise of the value of "our technological

DOI: 10.4324/9781003324157-26

Figure 22.1 Mahogany Copeland as Dorcas Gazelle and Sasha Jones listening to other beings speaking during the Council of All Beings in the campus woods, Guilford College, Greensboro, North Carolina, Spring 2021

Source: Photo by the author

culture" and the very notion of anthropocentrism (Seed 1988b, 9). The deep ecology movement has profoundly influenced environmental action organizations and related groups, many members of which have participated in the Council of All Beings. Deep ecology argues that "nothing short of a total revolution in consciousness will be of lasting use in preserving the life-support systems of our planet" (Seed 1988b, 9).

The Council of All Beings ritual was developed and has primarily been practiced by white Euro-American people, yet it draws deeply from Buddhism and Indigenous religio-cultural traditions.[1] The ritual does run the risk of cultural appropriation and/or essentialization in that it suggests spirit-animal bonding and shamanic and spirit medium practices of animals speaking through people who are characterized as being "chosen by another life-form" while on a "Vision Quest" (Macy and Fleming 1988, 109). In 1985, the very "first Council of All Beings took place in a rural place outside Sydney, Australia with forty humans participating, to the haunting earthy sounds of the aboriginal *didgeridoo*" (Seed 1988b, 7).

Importantly, there is a strong current of white privilege that simultaneously undergirds *and is the target of critique of* the Council of All Beings. Seed, juxtaposing modern humans with an essentialized Indigenous people, opined, "All indigenous cultures have, at the very center of their spiritual life, similar kinds of ritual and ceremony that acknowledge and nurture interconnectedness in the larger family of life" (Nesker 2000, 290). This is what the deep ecology movement is getting at, that humans have become disconnected and alienated from the natural world and that a deeper connection to the natural world and the other than human beings therein is needed for an awakening toward radical healing. However, either the ritual risks assuming that all humans are similarly or equally alienated from the "natural" world (let alone define "natural" the same way), or the ritual, while flexible, is designed for a specific set of participants.

Participants typically represent archetypes—rarely individual animals or specific features of the natural world—and speak for "mountain," and not "Mt. Kailaś," for "horse," not *their* horse, for "whale" or even "humpback whale," not a specific individual humpback whale. Seed explains the role of the archetype in the ritual as decreasing the role of the ego and broadening our problematic "narrow ego selves."[2]

Masking is a central feature of the ritual. The time it takes to gather the materials and create a mask allows for contemplation and nurturing a sympathetic connection with the represented being/archetype. The process of creating a mask and figuring out how it will be employed and worn allows the participant to delve into issues of voice, movement, and transformation. The participant wears the mask at the council, which is a gathering, typically in a circle, ideally outdoors.

Councils of All Beings are quite different in style, flexible, and certainly not orthodox. Some do not involve masking. Others focus entirely on endangered animals. Others still are conducted with participants donning their masks only when it is their turn to speak, while some Councils see all participants wear their masks from the moment the beings arrive on the scene to the moment they depart. Some Councils emphasize the transformation engendered by donning a mask so that the person becomes the animal, while others focus on speaking *for* the animal and the interplay between the beings (species) present.

Given the transformative aspect of masking and the responsibility participants face in speaking either as or for the animal, the relationship with the mask becomes the most formative aspect of the larger ritual for many participants. As Maryn Leonard, a student participant in the council who was part of our 2021 course and spoke *for/as* the Blue Whale, put it:

> The finishing touch of the mask was the eyes and once they were glued on I didn't put the mask on until the moment in the woods, right before the counsel (*sic*).

When I asked permission to speak for the whale I felt so clearly that the answer was yes that it made me cry.

The following spring semester (2022), student Liliana Rojas explained:

I felt a big responsibility to make sure the animal could say what it needed to say and that I made sure that animal spoke through me. I wanted to make sure that I did it justice because the animal can't speak for itself to humans. I also wanted to make sure that I wasn't only speaking for the animal but listening to what it wanted me to say as well, I didn't want to blur that line . . . that I was the speaker and that's all.

Figure 22.2 Maryn Leonard speaking for Blue Whale during the Council of All Beings in the campus woods, Guilford College, Greensboro, North Carolina, Spring 2021

Source: Photo by the author

While some are highly improvisational and unstructured, other Councils are scripted. Indeed, some Councils are rehearsed and are highly theatrical. This new religious ritual was intentionally developed to expand Indigenous performative ceremonies to a wider set of participants in order to help people reconnect with the natural world.

I involve the Council of All Beings in my college teaching today, and the students find the ritual process of reconnecting with the natural and other than human animal world profound and heartening. In the summer of 1991, a traveling counterculture theater company performed the inestimable Martha Boesing's play *Standing on Fishes* to audiences in dozens of locations across Eastern North America. The ensemble play stemmed from a council in which the company participated, and the production itself culminated in a performed Council of All Beings with large papier-mâché animal masks. Inspired by that theatrical tour experience (for which I served as part of the ensemble cast), I teach a course titled *Deep Ecology & Revolution* at Guilford College in North Carolina. The centerpiece of the course is a Council of All Beings. We hold all class periods in the campus woods or by the beautiful lake regardless of the season or the weather. By the time we begin to engage in the initial steps of the Council of All Beings ritual, the students have become accustomed to, awakened to, and perhaps most importantly connected with the natural space where they attend college.

When we begin the process of the larger frame of the ritual, the students disperse into the forest and sit alone for over an hour, opening themselves to being communicated with by an animal. Students are encouraged to avoid fixating on their favorite animal or an animal they think is particularly cool, intriguing, or most like them in terms of imagined or aspirational personality or style. As Devon Burrell put it after our 2022 course, "being selected by a bobcat was an interesting experience." The students are assured that the animals need not be ones who live in the Guilford Woods (lest they all become squirrels, interesting as that might be); they might be a loggerhead turtle, a gazelle, a pangolin, or a moss spider.

We explicitly problematize potentially appropriative or ethically suspect aspects of the ritual process and refashion each stage of the council ritual until we are in consensus about how best to proceed. For example, we discuss the distinctions between teaching and preaching as we engage in a "ritual" in a college course.[3] We decide what we will do with the masks when the ritual is complete. We delve into what it really means to be "chosen" by an animal and wrestle with issues of suspension of disbelief, skepticism, imagination, different religious worldviews, and the *agency* of the *actual* animals with whom we engage and from whom we seek permissions and wisdoms.

For the purposes of our course, our Council of All Beings is about animals (broadly defined). Framed in the larger context of climate change, species decimation, and intersectional oppressive and liberative systems, the Council of All Beings resonates with passions for social and environmental justice. In the words of Jordan Keller, a Guilford College student in our Spring 2021 *Deep Ecology & Revolution* course:

> The council ended up being an exercise in this kind of empathy that I didn't know I needed. I think there's always been a small part of me that believed activism for non-human animals came at the expense of other movements for justice. I don't think it's something I would have articulated to anyone; it was just a crude feeling. My experience in the council forced me to confront this scarcity mindset and rendered my relationship to non-human animals wonderfully complicated. How could one go through that sort of process of embodiment and not feel a sense of consequential tenderness

towards the nonhuman world? I've spent the last two days thinking about the spruce-fir moss spider, the blue whale and the donkey, the crayfish and pangolin—do they, like the chimps, experience wonder? I would bet that the barn owls do.

Although it is difficult to discern reliable data, at least tens of thousands of people have participated in Councils of All Beings in locations worldwide. The influence of the Council of All Beings and deep ecology on ecological activism remains profound. It will be interesting and important to note the ways in which this new ritual will adjust to less appropriative and more inclusive and power-aware sensibilities as we approach the four-decade anniversary of its inception. Will the ritual evolve, be rethought, or supplanted, or re-envisioned vis-à-vis ongoing dynamics of oppression of Indigeneity? It is even more challenging to discern the effects these rituals have had on species or individual animals, but the Council of All Beings remains one of the most prominent and engaging exercises about the process of transforming human ecological consciousness toward the subjectivities of the nonhuman. The Council of All Beings can certainly also strengthen the human community of participants in beautiful ways:

> I have a lot of gratitude for everyone's willingness to step outside of their comfort to participate and engage and honor, to share this experience with each other. This is how healing happens. This is how we can move forward and hope for a better world. By honoring one another, by honoring the creatures that chose us. By being willing to "go there" with one another. By daring to dream and imagine a world that is willing to undergo the pain of healing and the beautiful transformation that results from that excursion.
>
> —Aylen Bernal, student in the Guilford College course
> *Deep Ecology & Revolution*, Spring 2022

Notes

1 The Council of All Beings is religious in that it is a ritual and in that its foundations are rooted in Animism and Buddhism (Kaza 2000). The deep ecology movement undergirding the Council of All Beings understands features of the landscape to be life-forms (Seed 1988b; Naess 1988). Naess, Seed, and Macy's writings and workshops are deeply influenced by or are explicitly Buddhist, although the New Age spirituality (including ingestion of psychedelics; see Nesker 2000) that also influences their work infuses The Council of All Beings with a decided animism. The concept of celestial bodies, the winds, plants, and the earth as animate, sentient, and living is not solely the purview of animistic religious traditions. It is also present in some (notably Japanese Zen) Buddhist perspectives, stretching the Indic concept of "sentient beings" to include such things as mountains, islands, trees, etc. (Dōgen 1986; LaFleur 1989; LaFleur 2000; Kaza and Kraft 2000; Shaner 1989; Tanabe 1995). It is worth noting that while Seed was aware of meditation teachers "embracing" deep ecology, he purported the axiom that, "Activists often don't have much time for meditation" (Seed 1988a, 37).

2 As he notes that the Council of All Beings is not intended to replace other forms of direct ecological action, Seed writes: "Ritual also helps us be more aware of the ritualized character of virtually all nonviolent direct action, and thus helps us make those actions more powerful. While at times we may be defending a particular stand of trees or mountain ridge or stream, our defense is also symbolic in that we are making our defense in the name of *all* trees, *all* mountain ridges, *all* streams which need defending, and we are asking all who understand these threats wherever they may be to stand with us. . . . When we hear the earth speak to us, we are transformed and come to understand our actions from a new perspective" (Seed 1988b, 15–16, emphasis in original).

3 On the one hand, the non-existence of objectivity in a postmodern sense dissolves any pretense that teaching is not subjective. But on the other hand, this does not, therefore, mean that the teacher/preacher dichotomy is so irrelevant that polemics or the coercive blending of opinion and power in the crucible of a ritual in a classroom space should go unscrutinized.

References

Dōgen, Kigen. 1986. *Shōbōgenzō: Zen Essays by Dōgen.* Translated by Thomas Cleary. Honolulu: University of Hawai'i Press.
Kaza, Stephanie. 2000. "To Save All Beings: Buddhist Environmental Activism." In *Engaged Buddhism in the West*, edited by Christopher S. Queen, 159–83. Boston, Mass.: Wisdom Publications.
_____, and Kenneth Kraft, eds. 2000. *Dharma Rain: Sources of Buddhist Environmentalism.* Boston, Mass.: Shambhala.
LaFleur, William R. 1989. "Saigyō and the Buddhist Value of Nature." In *Nature in Asian Traditions of Thought: Essays in Environmental Philosophy*, edited by J. Baird Callicott and Roger T. Ames, 183–209. Albany: State University of New York Press.
_____. 2000. "Enlightenment for Plants and Trees." In *Dharma Rain: Sources of Buddhist Environmentalism*, edited by Stephanie Kaza and Kenneth Kraft, 109–16. Boston, Mass.: Shambhala.
Macy, Joanna, and Pat Fleming. 1988. "Guidelines for a Council of All Beings." In *Thinking Like a Mountain: Towards a Council of All Beings*, edited by John Seed, Joanna Macy, Pat Fleming, and Arne Naess, 97–113. Gabriola Island, B.C.: New Society.
Naess, Arne. 1988. "*Self* Realization: An Ecological Approach to Being in the World." In *Thinking Like a Mountain: Towards a Council of All Beings*, edited by John Seed, Joanna Macy, Pat Fleming, and Arne Naess, 19–30. Gabriola Island, B.C.: New Society.
Nesker, Wes. (1992) 2000. "The Rainforest as Teacher: A Conversation with John Seed." In *Dharma Rain: Sources of Buddhist Environmentalism*, edited by Stephanie Kaza and Kenneth Kraft, 286–93. Boston, Mass.: Shambhala.
Seed, John. 1988a. "Beyond Anthropocentrism." In *Thinking Like a Mountain: Towards a Council of All Beings*, edited by John Seed, Joanna Macy, Pat Fleming, and Arne Naess, 35–40. Gabriola Island, B.C.: New Society.
_____. 1988b. "Introduction: 'To Hear Within Ourselves the Sound of the Earth Crying.'" In *Thinking Like a Mountain: Towards a Council of All Beings*, edited by John Seed, Joanna Macy, Pat Fleming, and Arne Naess, 5–17. Gabriola Island, B.C.: New Society.
Shaner, David Edward. 1989. "The Japanese Experience of Nature." In *Nature in Asian Traditions of Thought: Essays in Environmental Philosophy*, edited by J. Baird Callicott and Roger T. Ames, 163–82. Albany: State University of New York Press.
Tanabe, George J., Jr. 1995. "Myōe's Letter to the Island." In *Buddhism in Practice*, edited by Donald S. Lopez, Jr., 88–91. Princeton, N.J.: Princeton University Press.

Other Recommended Resources

Boesing, Martha. 1991. "Interview with Martha Boesing, Playwright of 'Standing on Fishes.'" Interviewed by Paula Schroeder for Minnesota Public Radio. Audio File. https://archive.mpr.org/stories/1991/04/20/martha-boesing-playwright-of-standing-on.
Devall, Bill, and George Sessions. 1985. *Deep Ecology.* Layton, Utah: Peregrine Smith.
Macy, Joanna, and Molly Brown. 2014. *Coming Back to Life.* Gabriola Island, B.C.: New Society.
Seed, John, Joanna Macy, Pat Fleming, and Arne Naess, eds. 1988. *Thinking Like a Mountain: Towards a Council of All Beings.* Gabriola Island, B.C.: New Society.

23 Commemorating Animals in Asia, Europe, and the U.S.

Celebrating Kinship or Manifesting Difference?

Barbara R. Ambros

Introduction

When Totoribe no Yorozu was overpowered and committed suicide during a rebellion in 587 C.E., his faithful white dog stayed with his corpse, howling. The dog then picked up Yorozu's head, placed it on an old tomb mound, lay down next to it, and starved himself to death. When the Japanese court heard about the dog's extraordinary conduct, they felt pity, rescinded the order to dismember and disperse Yorozu's body, and issued a decree that Yorozu's kin should build tombs for Yorozu and his dog. Yorozu's relatives then constructed tomb mounds in the village of Arimaka and buried Yorozu and his dog there (Aston 1972, II.115–117). To this day, the dog's tomb mound, measuring twenty meters in diameter and known as the "Tomb Mound of the Righteous Dog," stands next to Yorozu's thirty-meter mound. A tombstone inscribed "Dog Mound of the Yorozu Family" also marks the site. The Tsukamoto family, Yorozu's descendants, conduct an annual memorial service at the site in the autumn (Ukai 2018, 88–89).

When humans die, their death is typically marked with funeral and commemorative rituals that are often religious. When other than human animals die, such rituals may also take place, but they are often fraught with religious and social debates. In most cases, animal death goes unrecognized, raising questions about why humans commemorate animals, which animals are deemed worthy of commemoration, whether and how the commemoration of animals differs from that of humans, and what implications such commemoration has for living animals. This chapter explores these questions through examples from Asia, North America, and Europe. Such commemorative rituals demonstrate that some charismatic animals have been included as subjects in religious communities and provide the human participants with opportunities for emotional resolution. But due to persistent ritual and spatial differences from human mortuary practices, commemorative rites tend to reaffirm ontological distinctions between humans and other than human animals. In other words, such rituals reflect how the existence of humans and other living beings is conceptualized differently. Therefore, they have not brought about systemic changes that would prevent animal exploitation.

Why Do Humans Commemorate Animals?

There is no single definitive answer to this question. The concept that commemorative rituals for other than human animals are for the emotional benefit of humans—for example, to manage grief and assuage guilt—also applies to similar rituals for deceased humans. Rites of mourning may be crucial for animal sanctuary workers to help them cope with the many deaths they encounter in their challenging job (jones and Gruen 2016).

DOI: 10.4324/9781003324157-27

However, psychological reasons are not the only possible explanation. This is especially true for religious traditions that do not assume *a priori* that animals are merely material beings. In many religious traditions, including those of East Asia, animals are understood to have souls or spirits similar to those of humans. Thus, commemorative rites can serve not just to help humans find emotional closure but also to appease the animals' spirits, ensure their well-being in the beyond, or help them attain a better rebirth. For instance, Elizabeth Kenney notes that in the case of "the Japanese religious setting, with its relaxed mixture of possible afterlives for humans and animals (reincarnation, heaven, wraiths [ghosts]), the courteous treatment of animal corpses (and perhaps more importantly animal spirits) is 'common sense'" (Kenney 2004, 45).

In one example from Tang China (618–907 C.E.), Mr. Pei's parrot had learned to recite the name of the Buddha Amitabha from his pious human keeper. When the parrot was nearing the end of his life, Pei encouraged the bird to recite this Buddha's name to ensure the bird's rebirth in Amitabha's paradise, the Western Pure Land. In the moments before his death, the bird chanted the Buddha's name ten times while Pei struck a sounding stone for percussion. After the bird was given a ceremonial cremation, more than ten glistening jade-like relic beads were found among the bird's cremated remains, a sign that the parrot had attained the wisdom of a Buddha. A Buddhist monk later erected a porcelain stupa to house the relics on Mount Wutai, a famous pilgrimage site dedicated to Manjusri, the bodhisattva of wisdom, to commemorate the extraordinary event (Stevenson 1995, 600–602). This parrot was extraordinary since relic pearls, considered powerful material manifestations of Buddhahood, were usually only found in the cremated remains of the most spiritually advanced Buddhist practitioners.

In the Ming dynasty (1368–1644), morality books, drawing on Daoist, Buddhist, and Confucian teachings, encouraged the burial of ordinary animals as good deeds that earned humans merit, that is, karmic rewards. For instance, in the Buddhist cleric Zhuhong's *Record of Self-Knowledge* (1604), animal burials were integrated into a list of various good deeds to promote living animals' well-being and save them from death and slaughter. Burial and mortuary rites were thus an extension of good deeds for living beings and earned half as much merit as saving live animals from death:

> When domestic dogs, domesticated water buffalo, or draft horses die, bury them.
> For each large animal buried, count ten merits.
> For each small animal buried, count five merits.
> If one further helps animals through religious services for speedy deliverance, each animal counts five merits.
>
> (Yü 2020, 235–236)

Zhuhong (1535–1615) distinguished not only between good deeds for large and small animals but, following historical precedent, also assigned more merit to deeds benefiting working animals that were useful to humans: dogs, cattle, and horses. Cattle, in particular, were considered special because they helped humans plow the fields.

Cattle burials and funeral rites have been documented from the second century C.E. From the Song dynasty (960–1279) until the early twentieth century, it was widely considered immoral to slaughter cattle and consume beef. To avoid harsh karmic retribution and divine punishments, proponents of cattle protection thought it advisable to bury dead cattle—or if that was impossible, cast them in a river—rather than dismember them in slaughter and thus violate the integrity of the animals' bodies. Similar arguments were also made in the case of dogs because they guarded people's homes (Goossaert 2005, 136, 189–191; see also Goossaert's Chapter 17 in this volume). Since living beings received their bodies from their parents, dismemberment was considered a humiliation and a violation of filial obligations that was felt to be particularly egregious in the cases of humans, cattle, and dogs.

Charismatic Animals Worthy of Commemoration

These examples raise another crucial question: what kinds of animals tend to be considered worthy of commemoration? In the cases described previously, charismatic animals were singled out for ritualized commemoration: they displayed exceptional loyalty and heroism, demonstrated extraordinary piety, or provided essential services to humanity. The animals distinguished themselves by demonstrating ideal traits prized in humans or by proving themselves exceptionally useful to humans.

The case of contemporary Japan is particularly instructive in this regard. There we find a wide range of animals targeted for memorial rituals. Working animals such as service dogs; military horses, dogs, and pigeons; zoo animals; animals killed through hunting and fishing; beef cattle and poultry; and animals used for research in laboratories all are given annual memorial rituals and commemorated with material objects such as stone monuments, grave markers, and memorial tablets (Ambros 2012, 51–89).

A similar example in contemporary Europe and North America is the commemoration of military animals or police dogs, though these are typically civil rites and monuments rather than explicitly religious ones (Kean 2012, 2016). As in Japan, such memorialization may honor the animals' exemplary service and help foster human camaraderie and even nationalism.

Companion animals, who are often regarded as family members and whose death may lead to intense experiences of grief, have also been the focus of commemoration. In Japan, it is common for Buddhist temples to have pet cemeteries on temple grounds and to offer pet funeral and memorial services that are essentially identical to human mortuary rituals, if in abbreviated form. Such rituals for companion animals have been documented starting in the late eighteenth century but became widespread in the late twentieth century, with increasing pet ownership in urban areas. While pet memorial rites are frequently criticized as excessive in the news media, they have still become widely accepted because they are considered important for helping owners grieve for their animal companions. According to the Japanese Animal Funeral and Cemetery Association, there were 1035 pet funeral providers and cemeteries in 2019. Of these, 739 operated pet cemeteries or columbaria, and 170 pet mortuary businesses were located on the grounds of Buddhist temples. Moreover, pet cemeteries not affiliated with Buddhist temples will often engage Buddhist clerics for major memorial days such as the equinoxes, the Festival of the Dead in mid-summer, and monthly collective memorial services (Ambros 2020, 471–472). Similar commemorative practices are now found in other parts of Asia, such as Korea and Thailand (Veldkamp 2016; Ellis-Petersen 2018).

Beginning in the eighteenth century and increasingly from the twenty-first century, companion animals have been commemorated ceremonially in North America as well. While these rituals have typically been taking place outside institutional religious frameworks, Christian and Jewish communities in North America have also made accommodations over the past two decades to provide mortuary rites for other than human animals and establish memorial spaces. The Episcopal Church adopted a liturgy for commemorating pets at its General Convention in the U.S. in 2012, and as of 2020, at least 45 Episcopal churches in the U.S. had established pet memorial gardens on church grounds, often called St. Francis Memorial Gardens. Individual Jewish rabbis, particularly those belonging to Reform and Reconstructionist Judaism, have also begun to create liturgical resources, and a few synagogues have established pet remembrance boards or memorial gardens. However, unlike Episcopal churches, synagogues do not typically allow the interment of the pets' physical remains.

Moreover, even those who support some degree of memorialization of companion animals within religious spaces or with religious rituals tend to insist on separate spaces and rituals highlighting the conceptual distinctions between humans and other animals. For instance, Episcopal funeral liturgies for pets tend to stress the celebration of God's creation rather than the resurrection, which is the focus of human funerals. Meanwhile, Jewish leaders tend to oppose the recitation of the Kaddish, the mourners' prayer that extols the greatness of God, for companion animals (Ambros 2020, 464–470).

Manifesting Conceptual Differences Between Humans and Other Beings

Such debates raise the thorny question of how the commemoration of animals and humans differs or, rather, ought to differ. In Germany, several municipal and a few church cemeteries have begun to allow the cremated remains of companion animals to be interred with their owners even though opponents, including doctrinal authorities within the Protestant and Catholic churches, have argued that this violates human dignity. However, while such joint-species burials may at first appear to be inclusive gestures, they also signal a fundamental difference in how humans and other animals are viewed. Even when joint-species interment in a human cemetery is possible, cremation and interment are conducted separately, and the animals do not receive religious funerary rites. Joint burial is considered to be for the psychological benefit of the human subject and an act of pastoral care, whereas the animal's remains are regarded as a mere material grave good.

According to the German Catholic theologian Julia Enxing, this does not sufficiently acknowledge the creaturely dignity of animals, who are thus treated as inanimate objects. She also raises the question of why being buried next to an animal violates human dignity when many humans do not mind ingesting dead animal flesh in the form of meat. Moreover, she notes, cemeteries are already full of small animals and microbes that transform dead human bodies into soil and thus play crucial roles in the burial of humans. Enxing's position, however, is not widely shared by the Catholic or Protestant mainstream in Germany (Konersman 2016; Specks 2016; Röther 2019).

Despite the greater institutional acceptance of pet funeral and memorial services at Buddhist temples in Japan, joint-species burial and commemoration in home altars remain controversial even though some cemeteries operated by commercial funeral businesses and a few Buddhist temples have begun to offer joint-species interment in their cemeteries. In the absence of strong central doctrinal authorities, such decisions are made by individual Buddhist clerics who need to obtain the consensus of their parishioners, and only then can an existing cemetery begin to allow joint interment. By contrast, newly established cemeteries have the advantage that they can develop separate sections for joint-species burials, and interment in a new grave that does not house the remains of multiple generations removes the possibility that the inclusion of animal remains might offend the family's ancestors (Ambros 2012, 124–155).

Nonetheless, as in Germany, joint-species interment is legally possible in Japan precisely because dead animal bodies are considered material objects—in contrast to human remains that are subject to different laws that recognize their more than material status. This difference played an essential role in a legal case to determine whether pet funerals conducted by a Buddhist temple were a tax-exempt religious activity or whether they constituted an unrelated business activity subject to income taxes. One of the arguments that led to the court ruling that the Buddhist temple should pay income tax on pet funerals was that a pet cemetery was technically a waste-storage facility, a categorization that cannot be applied to a human cemetery (Ambros 2012, 94–104).

Conclusion

In conclusion, we can ask how, besides laying bare that humans value some animals over others and grant a unique status to humans, commemorative rituals for other than human animals affect the lives of animals. Memorial ceremonies may not be directly physically harmful or psychologically distressing to animal participants, who are dead, after all. Who can judge whether Yorozu's white dog or any other animal objected to their commemoration? If any harm occurs, it is systemic. Nakamaki Hirochika has argued that when commemoration occurs for animals whose lives were cut short by human agency, it typically validates the killing of animals by assuaging the psychological and spiritual burden of the humans implicated (Nakamaki 2005, 44–46, 55–56). In other words, commemorative rituals may express mourning for animal death, but they typically do not imply systemic changes that prevent the exploitation of animals or their untimely deaths. Nonetheless, in some cases, such as Zhuhong's in Ming China and the contemporary Episcopal Church in the U.S., the commemoration of animals may also be one element in a more extensive campaign to promote kindness toward animals, animal welfare, and environmental protection. Commemorative rites for animals convey that other than human lives can matter, but unfortunately, this does not include all animal lives.

References

Ambros, Barbara R. 2012. *Bones of Contention: Animals and Religion in Contemporary Japan.* Honolulu: University of Hawai'i Press.

———. 2020. "Celebrating Creation and Commemorating Life: Ritualizing Pet Death in the U.S. and Japan." In *The Routledge History of Death since 1800*, edited by Peter Stearns, 460–80. New York: Routledge.

Aston, William George. 1972. *Nihongi: Chronicles of Japan from the Earliest Times to A.D. 697.* Tokyo: Tuttle.

Ellis-Petersen, Hannah. 2018. "'A Ticket to the Next Life': The Lavish Buddhist Dog Funerals of Bangkok." *The Guardian*, May 24. Accessed August 2, 2022. www.theguardian.com/cities/2018/may/24/ticket-next-life-buddhist-dog-funerals-bangkok.

Goossaert, Vincent. 2005. *L'interdit du bœuf en Chine: Agriculture, éthique et sacrifice.* Paris: Collège de France Institut des Hautes Études Chinoises.

jones, pattrice, and Lori Gruen. 2016. "Keeping Ghosts Close: Care and Grief at Sanctuaries." In *Mourning Animals: Rituals and Practices Surrounding Animal Death*, edited by Margo DeMello, 187–92. East Lansing: Michigan State University Press.

Kean, Hilda. 2012. "Animals and War Memorials: Different Approaches to Commemorating the Human-Animal Relationship." In *Animals at War: Studies of Europe and North America*, edited by Ryan Hedinger, 237–62. Leiden: Brill.

_____. 2016. "Britain at War: Remembering and Forgetting the Animal Dead of the Second World War." In *Mourning Animals: Rituals and Practices Surrounding Animal Death*, edited by Margo DeMello, 115–22. East Lansing: Michigan State University Press.

Kenney, Elizabeth. 2004. "Pet Funerals and Animal Graves in Japan." *Mortality* 9 (1): 42–60.

Konersman, Paula. 2016. "Tierliebe bis ins Grab." *Domradio.de*, November 20. Accessed August 2, 2022. www.domradio.de/artikel/mehrere-deutsche-friedhoefe-erlauben-mensch-tier-bestattung.

Nakamaki, Hirochika. 2005. "Memorials of Interrupted Lives in Modern Japan: From Ex Post Facto Treatment to Intensification Devices." In *Perspectives on Social Memory in Japan*, edited by Tsu Yun Hui, Jan van Bremen, and Eyal Ben-Ari, 44–57. Folkestone: Global Oriental.

Röther, Christian. 2019. "Mensch und Tier im Grab vereint." *Deutschlandfunk*, December 30. Accessed August 2, 2022. www.deutschlandfunk.de/bestattung-mensch-und-tier-im-grab-vereint-100.html.

Specks, Tim. 2016. "Friedhof in Gefrath: Kirche erlaubt Bestattung mit Haustier." *RP.Online*, May 19. Accessed August 2, 2022. https://rp-online.de/nrw/staedte/kempen/grefrath-kirche-erlaubt-bestattung-mit-haustier_aid-18185859.

Stevenson, Daniel, trans. 1995. "Deathbed Testimonials." In *Buddhism in Practice*, edited by Donald Lopez, 592–602. Princeton, N.J.: Princeton University Press.

Ukai, Hidenori. 2018. *Petto to sōshiki: Nihonjin no kuyōshin o saguru*. Tokyo: Asahi Shinsho.

Veldkamp, Elmer. 2016. "To All That Fly or Crawl: A Recent History of Mourning for Animals in Korea." In *Mourning Animals: Rituals and Practices Surrounding Animal Death*, edited by Margo DeMello, 55–64. East Lansing: Michigan State University Press.

Yü, Chün-Fang. 2020. *The Renewal of Buddhism in China: Zhuhong and the Late Ming Synthesis*. New York: Columbia University Press.

Part III
Religious Responses to Animal Lives

24 Contemplative Practices for Connecting to Animals (and Ourselves)

Dave Aftandilian

Introduction

Animals can teach us many things if only we pay attention to them. Did you know that crows coo to each other like pigeons when they are courting a potential mate or asking for food from a parent? Or that cicadas need to take time to warm their bodies and dry their wings after molting their exoskeletons before they can fly off on their next adventure? Or that red foxes and many other city creatures use alleyways to travel unmolested through our cities?

I know all this about the animals with whom I share my neighborhood not because I read about them in a book or heard about them from a nature show on TV, but because I have practiced watching and listening to them for years so that I can learn from them directly. In applying contemplative practices like these, of attending closely to animals, I am following a model of mindfulness that Native North American peoples have perfected over thousands of years of living on these lands (see, e.g., Nelson 1986 and Linda Hogan's opening essay) and that Buddhists and followers of other religious traditions have honed through meditation.

In this chapter, I will offer a series of contemplative practices that I use myself and teach in my classes to help students utilize mindfulness of animals as a tool to deepen their understandings of themselves, of animals as living beings in the world (both as species and as individuals), and of the relationships between humans and other animals. After defining some key terms, I will focus on the benefits these practices can bring to animals and humans. I will then discuss several practices in detail, including a Three World Circle Breathing practice I have developed based on Native North American cosmologies, several practices for attending to wild animals and understanding their personhood, and finally loving-kindness (*mettā*) meditation adapted to focus on animals. I will briefly introduce a few other relevant contemplative practices related to animals and end by considering whether other animals themselves engage in such practices.

Mindfulness, Contemplative Practice, and Their Benefits for Animals and Humans

Mindfulness is a word that is often used but seldom clearly explained, especially in relationship to contemplative practice. Vietnamese Zen Buddhist master, teacher, and peace activist Thich Nhat Hanh offered this definition:

> Mindfulness is a non-judgmental awareness of all that is happening inside us and around us. It takes us back to the foundation of happiness, which is being present

DOI: 10.4324/9781003324157-29

in the here and now. Mindfulness is always mindfulness of something. We can be mindful of our breath, our footsteps, our thoughts and our actions. Mindfulness requires that we bring all our attention to whatever we're doing, whether walking or breathing, brushing our teeth or eating a snack.

(Nhat Hanh 2013, 34)

Contemplative practices such as meditation or prayer can teach us to focus our attention on the present moment, helping us learn to become more mindful of ourselves and others, including animal others. In his book *Introducing Contemplative Studies*, Daoist practitioner and scholar Louis Komjathy explains that these contemplative practices, whether done from the point of view of a religious tradition or in secular contexts, offer us a particular kind of knowing—one that is first-person, practical, and experiential (2018, 15). Moreover, he describes contemplative practice as a method or approach that can be applied to anything from art and dance to research and teaching to walking (14), including looking at animals with the goal of learning about and from them (see also Nhat Hanh 2004, 515; on gardening mindfully, see Murray 2012).

But why should we do contemplative practices in relationship with animals? Why should we engage with animals mindfully? How can they, and we, benefit? While there are a few examples of animals benefiting directly from contemplative practices done with the intention of helping them (see, e.g., Lesniak 2006), the strongest benefits for animals are likely to be more indirect. When humans mindfully focus our attention on other than human animals, we can come to know them at a deeper level, including as individuals. Through this closer knowing, we can develop a feeling of connection with them, which in turn can encourage us to have compassion for them, and work to care for them in species-appropriate ways. Picture a circle labeled with the following terms, with arrows pointing from each to the next: *attentiveness* is key to developing a deeper *understanding* of animals; deeper understanding is key to building strong *connections* with animals; connection is key to *compassion*; compassion is key to *care* (including species- and individual-appropriate action).

For example, as Lina Verchery explains in her chapter in this volume about Taiwanese Buddhist nuns and insects,

> it is not that we pay attention to those we care about, but that we care about those to whom we pay attention. By going out of their way to pay attention to insects, the nuns strengthen their capacity for compassionate care. Attention, in other words, is not an *expression* of compassion; it is a *method* of developing it.

And there is empirical evidence that contemplative practice can deepen humans' compassion for other animals (see Simonsson, Goldberg, and Osika 2022).

Finally, in terms of benefits for animals, contemplative practices done in relationship with other animals can help us come to see and respect them as our teachers. From a critical animal studies perspective, Lauren Corman and Tereza Vandrovcová argue that learning directly from animals "is vital for a more non-anthropocentric, anti-speciesist, and holistic pedagogy" (2014, 135).

Doing contemplative practices in relationship with animals also brings benefits to humans. First, engaging in such practices can help us learn different ways of resolving "the animal question"; of understanding what it means to be human, animal, and human-animal (Komjathy 2022). Moreover, because Native peoples have traditionally learned what they know about animals through first-person relationships with them (see chapters by Linda Hogan and Margaret Robinson in this volume), students who engage in experiential contemplative practices with animals will better understand Indigenous worldviews, traditional ecological knowledge (TEK), and the natural laws upon which they are based (see, e.g., Nelson 2008; Nelson and Shilling 2018).

But perhaps most importantly, by becoming more mindful of and attentive to animals, humans can start to heal "from our separation from all the other species that are our relatives," as Micah Mortali put it in his book on rewilding, a disconnection he argues has played a significant role in the spiraling rates of anxiety and depression that we have been seeing in the U.S. and other countries (Mortali 2019, 80). Similarly, Claire Thompson writes, "When we bring our awareness to nature, we soon understand that one of the essential natural laws is interconnectedness. Life is fundamentally one. We *are* life."; moreover, "if we *are* nature then a deeper connection to nature encourages a deeper connection with our true selves" (Thompson 2013, 59, 122).

One last note before we begin discussing specific contemplative practices for connecting with animals. When we use practices developed by other people, especially in religious contexts, we always need to do so respectfully and with an awareness of the possibility of appropriating cultural knowledge (in legal terms, intellectual property). Here our intentions become most important. If our intent is to learn to become more mindful of ourselves and other living beings so that we can become more compassionate toward them, then we are using the practices acceptably according to the purpose for which they were intended.

From a Native American point of view, Abenaki author Joseph Bruchac has explained that many Native storytellers like him have chosen to write down their stories because the ethical lessons they teach "have never been more needed by human beings than they are now"; "The stories . . . were for all human beings. Their purpose was to help people learn how to live in balance with each other and with the earth" (Bruchac 1996, 92, 204).

From a Buddhist perspective, the situation has been complicated by the intentional secularization of Buddhist mindfulness practices by Western teachers to make them more accessible and attractive to a range of American audiences (see Kabat-Zinn 2005, 110 for an example, and Wilson 2014 for a detailed analysis of this history). Yet we can also say that respected Buddhist teachers such as the Dalai Lama and Thich Nhat Hanh believe that mindful meditation can benefit all people, not just Buddhists—otherwise they would not have spent decades teaching and writing books that make these practices accessible to everyone (see, e.g., Ho 1975, xii and Nhat Hanh 2008). In fact, this makes it possible for such practices to be taught in secular spaces such as religious studies classrooms, where we are employing them to learn more about the source traditions and animals, not to achieve enlightenment or freedom from the cycle of death and rebirth (which would be the ultimate goal for Buddhists).

That said, we should always credit the sources of our practice, as I will do later.

Animal-Facing Contemplative Practices

Follow the Breath . . . to Animals

Let's start where I began this chapter: by focusing on our breath. Thich Nhat Hanh wrote,

> The foundation of all mindfulness practice is awareness of the breath. There is no mindfulness without awareness of our in-breath and out-breath. Mindful breathing

unites the body and mind and helps us to become aware of what is going on inside us and around us.

(Nhat Hanh 2013, 40; see also Nhat Hanh 2022, xiii)

I will add that because breathing is something crucial we share with other animals yet seldom think about, focusing on the breath can offer us an unexpected and powerful way to connect with them (see also Chapple 2008, 59 and Mortali 2019, 46).

We can use a wide variety of practices to become more mindful of our breath or to "follow the breath," as meditation teachers often describe it. Once you become familiar with them, you can do these practices for as long as you like; but I suggest to my students that they start small, doing each for no more than 5 or 10 minutes. The keyword here is *practice:* the benefits of mindfulness do not begin to accrue unless one practices meditation on a regular basis, and a 5-minute practice is a lot easier to do daily than a 30-minute or hour-long one.

In my classes we learn several simple breathing practices before we engage in more complex ones involving animals. One that I and many students enjoy employs this simple gatha (poem to guide meditation) by Thich Nhan Hanh, which can be abbreviated to just its first two lines for beginners (see Nhat Hanh 2022, 3–4 for a longer version):

I know I am breathing in;
I know I am breathing out.

I calm my body and mind;
I smile.

I dwell in the present moment;
I know this is a wonderful moment.

Practitioners quietly say the first line of each stanza to themselves as they breathe in and then the second as they breathe out.

Another commonly taught breath practice is called "box breathing." The basic concept is very simple and consists of just four equal steps:

1) Breathe in for a slow count of five
2) Hold your breath for a slow count of five
3) Breathe out for a slow count of five
4) Hold your breath again for another slow count of five before breathing in and returning to the start of the practice

I have developed a modified form of box breathing based on Native American cosmologies and animal dancing that I call Three World Circle Breathing (not to be confused with circular breathing techniques used by musicians!). By engaging in this practice, students can gain a deeper understanding both of this cosmology and of what it might feel like to be a waterbird.

Many Native American peoples share an understanding of the world as divided into three parts: this world of Earth, which is seen as a flat plain or island; an upper world above that is shaped like an inverted bowl filled with the heavens; and an under world below that is shaped like a bowl and filled to the brim with water (for Beaver Indian [*Dunneza*] three world cosmology see Ridington and Ridington 1970; for the Cherokee

[*Ani-Yunwiya* or *Tsalagi*], see Hudson 1976, 122–169 and Mooney [1900] 1995). An axis mundi (symbolic center pole of the world) connects all three of these realms, such as a tree whose branches touch the upper world, whose trunk is in this world, and whose roots stretch into the under world (for a European comparison, think of the world tree Yggdrasil from Norse mythology). This world rests somewhat precariously on the surface of the under world, which can be roiled by the movements of great serpents in the waters or the depths of the Earth; a key human role in Cherokee worldview is to maintain the delicate balance between the upper and under worlds.

Each of the three worlds of being is associated with specific traits and animals. For example, the upper world is a place of peace and order, epitomized by the soaring birds like hawks or eagles who dwell there. This world is symbolized by four-footed animals such as deer or buffalo. Finally, the under world is viewed as a place of chaos and disorder, yet also of life-giving water and fertility; the animals who epitomize it are the serpents, fish, and similar creatures. Animals who can cross between these worlds are known as liminal animals and are viewed as especially spiritually powerful; think of beavers who swim and live in their lodges in the under world yet feed on trees in this world, or ducks who dive for fish or dabble for vegetation in the under world yet fly through the upper world.

Here is a practice that I share with my students after we have discussed Native American three world cosmology:

Three World Circle Breathing
  For this practice, one follows the same four-step pattern of box breathing, but instead of a box, one imagines mentally traveling a circle or sphere. Moreover, for this exercise, one borrows the body of a waterbird who both flies and dives for fish, like a cormorant.

1) As you breathe in for a slow count of five, picture yourself ascending to the apex of the blue sky of the upper world, with the wind and the chill air pushing against your feathers.
2) Then, as you hold your breath for a slow count of five, imagine unfurling your wings and gently gliding down to the water's surface below.
3) As you exhale for a slow count of five, dive deeply beneath the waves, feeling the water rush past you as you go all the way to the very bottom of the watery depths of the under world.
4) Finally, as you hold your breath again for a slow count of five, picture yourself gently floating up to the water's surface—ready to fly up into the heavens on your next inhale.

With this practice I want to help my students better understand Native American three world cosmology by mentally mapping its contours with the aid of their breath. I also hope they will start to see and feel how each animal moves through the three worlds differently by imagining traversing them in the form of a cormorant—a powerful liminal animal.

Better Understanding Animal Being Through Noticing, Dancing, and Reflecting

As one becomes accustomed to becoming more mindful through breath practice, one can progress to more in-depth meditations. I assign students in my course on Animals, Religion, and Culture their first written meditation after we have read about animal personhood. The goal of this practice is to help students become more aware of other animals and what their ways of being in the world are like compared with ours:

Attending to Animals and Exploring Personhood

This meditation is intended to help you use mindfulness practices to explore the world through other than human eyes. First, choose a place outdoors where you can be free of distractions and in contact with nature. Take a moment to breathe slowly and center yourself in this place (closing your eyes may help). Then spend 15 to 20 minutes observing any nonhuman animals you see there (remember that many of these animals may not be immediately apparent; they might be flying in the sky or perched in a tree, swimming in the water, or crawling through the grass or soil at your feet).

1) Pick one animal in particular and observe what she or he looks like, how they move, how they interact with their surroundings, how they react to you (if they do), etc.; write down your observations.
2) Now, put down your pen or laptop, close your eyes, and imagine that you *are* the animal you have been studying. a) How would your experience of the world as that animal be similar to and different from your own experience of the world? b) Would you feel comfortable describing the animal you have been watching as a person? Why or why not?

The question about personhood is meant to help students think through the three main ways that we can come to understand animals in an ethical sense: as being similar to us, different from us, or sharing unexpected traits with us (see Matthew Calarco's Chapter 7 in this volume). By this point in class, we will have discussed the main ways that animals are said to differ from humans, many of which do not hold up to scientific or ethical scrutiny (e.g., supposed lack of rational mind, self-consciousness, emotion, etc.; see chapters in Part I of this book for detailed examples of how many animals actually do possess all of these traits). This meditation allows students some time to really look and listen closely to real animals and think about how their ways of being in the world relate to ours. (Speaking of listening, that is another excellent way to come to know animals and nature in general; see Aftandilian 2022 for a review and sample listening practices.)

At first, students in my class often struggle to see how animals are *like* us because many of the messages we receive in religious and secular contexts tell us how *different* they are from us and how these differences make them less-than-us and available for us to use as we see fit. The written meditation I just shared often helps students get over this hump (for a selection of written responses to this practice from students, see Aftandilian 2019). But as Matthew Calarco points out in his chapter in this book, we might perhaps get farther in terms of according proper respect to other animals if we focus on how they are different from us—but in ways that show them to have traits and abilities that we do not possess.

I will discuss two contemplative practices that can help us think through animal difference as a source of wonder and respect rather than denigration. The first is a set of audio contemplative practices available online at AnimalMeditations.com (or through

Soundcloud). The founder and curator of the project, Jon Leland, explains the goals of these difference-focused practices on their website ("About This Project"):

> *Animal Meditations* is a series of guided meditations designed to take listeners inside the experience of wild animals in their habitat. The subjective experience of these animals is impossible for us to truly comprehend. It is particularly difficult when their physical, sensory, or mental capacities differ greatly from our own. . . . But the sincere imaginative exercise of placing our consciousness within their experience can be illuminating. It is not only calming but creates a deeper appreciation for other beings.

There are four seasons' worth of meditations available, covering 27 animals as of this writing. Most meditations are less than 10 minutes long and can work well at the start of class. I especially like to have students listen to meditations from the point of view of animals we discuss at some length, such as elephants and whales, as well as ones who have very different ways of being in the world from us, such as sockeye salmon, cicadas, and tardigrades (tiny animals who are also known as water bears). Many of these animal meditations explore the concept of how moving through the world in a different sort of body, such as that of a snake, or using very different senses to navigate it, such as a bat, can shape how each animal experiences the world (see Donovan O. Schaefer's discussion of *Umwelt* in his chapter on emotion in this volume).

The second practice is one that I have developed to help students use their bodies in motion to better understand other animals and how they move in ways that are often quite different from ours. It draws on practices of "dancing your animal" that are widely performed as ways to show respect to and better understand other animals (for detailed examples of such dances in Cherokee practice, see Speck, Broom, and Long [1951] 1983). This exercise can give the practitioner an embodied, deeply felt sense of what it might be like to be living in the body of another animal, which helps both engage empathy and encourage positive reflection on difference. Here is the practice I assign:

Dancing Your Animal
    Return to the natural area you visited for your first meditation (or a different one if you wish) and select an individual other than human animal to watch for at least 15 to 20 minutes. Write down as detailed a description as you can about how the animal moves.
    Now return to a private indoor space and imitate the motions of that animal as best you can. This is sometimes referred to as "dancing" an animal. If you get stuck, you might try focusing on how the animal moved their eyes or head and/or moving just your hand in a way that reflects the pace, energy, rhythm, or weight of the animal's movements. You may also find it helpful to watch videos of the animal online to refresh your memory about how the animal moves.
    Reflect in writing about what, if anything, dancing your animal showed you about them that you did not know before. Feel free to express your reflections in a poem or visual artwork if you wish.

Like me, many of my students often feel awkward and a bit embarrassed as they try to move their bodies like that of another animal. But once that feeling passes, they usually have a lot of fun trying to waggle their tail feathers like a duck or leap and land gracefully like a squirrel (which is tough without a long tail for balance!). And many come away with a deep appreciation for movements that other animals make fluidly and rapidly, which humans can only achieve awkwardly and slowly, if at all.

Loving-Kindness (Mettā)

The last meditation I will discuss is loving-kindness (*mettā*). As Thich Nhat Hanh explains, *mettā* is an ancient practice that was already being shared by yogis in India at the time of the Buddha to help people generate love and compassion for themselves and others (2022, 124–125). It is one of the four foundational practices taught by the Buddha, along with compassion, sympathetic joy, and equanimity (Kabat-Zinn 2005, 287). Gil Fronsdal notes, "When describing mettā, the Buddha used the analogy of the care a mother gives her only child" (2008, 82).

Traditional *mettā* practice begins with oneself because to truly share a feeling of love and compassion for others, one must first experience those feelings for oneself. This can be difficult for various reasons, societal and personal, but it is crucial to the deep, embodied learning this practice makes available. You then extend that warm, heartfelt feeling of loving-kindness to someone beloved to you, then someone neutral, then someone whom, for whatever reason, you find difficult, perhaps someone who harmed you. A focusing phrase is repeated quietly to oneself at each stage of the practice. (For other *mettā* scripts, see Fronsdal 2008, 85–87; Kabat-Zinn 2005, 288–294; Nhat Hanh 2022, 123–124).

Although *mettā* is traditionally practiced with humans in mind, I ask my students instead to focus on extending loving-kindness to other animals, to help them develop and deepen their compassion for all beings (Jon Kabat-Zinn asks his students to include the entire planet in their *mettā* practice; see 2005, 292–293). Here is the *mettā* script that I use:

Loving-Kindness for Animals

1) Start with remembering or imagining the feeling of yourself being loved unconditionally and selflessly. Let this warm feeling surround you and cradle you in its gentle, loving embrace. Perhaps you might think of how it felt when you were a child and one of your parents held you so close you could feel their heartbeat and rocked you to sleep. Rest here with this feeling of total, unconditional love for a moment. [PAUSE]

2) As you keep this warm feeling of a loving embrace wrapped around you, say quietly to yourself:

   May I be happy
   May I be healthy
   May I be safe
   May I be at peace
   Let's say those words again. [REPEAT]

3) Now, think of another animal whom you love deeply. Perhaps they are a companion animal, one living with you now or one who has passed on. Maybe they are a beautiful bird whose brightly colored feathers and cheerful song brings joy

to your mornings. Extend your warm embrace to this other beloved living being and say to them:

May you be happy
May you be healthy
May you be safe
May you be at peace
[REPEAT]

4) Now bring to mind one or more wild animals you do not know well but see occasionally. Perhaps they are a small mob of crows you see in your neighborhood or a herd of deer you encounter on walks in a local park. Maybe they are a turtle or fish whom you have seen swimming in a nearby pond or stream. Think of these neighborhood animals who are fellow members of your community, wrap them in a loving mental embrace, and say to them:

[REPEAT phrases from step 3]
[REPEAT phrases from step 3]

5) Next, call to mind an animal you find difficult to deal with. Maybe they are a dog who barks loudly every time you walk by their yard. Or perhaps they are an animal you are afraid of, such as a bee, snake, or spider. Mentally extend your loving embrace to this difficult animal and say to them:

[REPEAT phrases from step 3]
[REPEAT phrases from step 3]

6) Now consider one or more animals who is/are facing difficulty and suffering in their lives. Maybe they are confined on a factory farm or in a scientific lab. Perhaps their home has been destroyed by one of the many wildfires that have been raging more widely and burning hotter in this time of human-caused climate change, or polluted runoff has poisoned the waters they live and breathe in. Hold this wounded creature tightly in your loving mental embrace and say to them:

[REPEAT phrases from step 3]
[REPEAT phrases from step 3]

7) Now, let's extend our field of loving-kindness and compassion to encompass all the animals living anywhere in the world: in the air, on land, and in the waters. Think of your favorite kinds of animals and also the animals you know nothing about. Hold all of them in your mind and heart and say to them:

[REPEAT phrases from step 3]
[REPEAT phrases from step 3]

8) Finally, let us return to ourselves. It can be hard to think of animals facing difficult situations, but try to keep in mind that even if you cannot help them in person, you can still extend compassion to them in your heart. But first, you need to hold yourself in loving-kindness so that you can then share that feeling with all living beings. Call to mind the feeling of being loved unconditionally once more, and rest here in that warm embrace for a while. [PAUSE]

Other Relevant Contemplative Practices for Connecting to Animals

Of course, one could perform a wide variety of other contemplative practices in relationship with animals. Walking meditation in nature, for example, lends itself well to observing other animals more closely, as well as the places one passes through, and can connect one more deeply with them (see Nhat Hanh 2013, 48–52). To focus my own walking meditations, I will often think of the Native American three world cosmology described previously and watch and listen for animals from each of the worlds.

One could also engage in an extended journaling practice focused on animals who live in a particular place. First, one selects an animal to observe closely for a week or even a whole semester. After engaging (respectfully, at a distance) with this animal in a sustained manner, one then reflects in writing and/or drawings on what one has learned from this unexpected sort of teacher/student relationship (see, e.g., Komjathy 2022, 15 and Lupinacci 2019, 95–96).

One might also try to engage in prayer or meditative practice directly with other animals. Myrian Monnet Pouso, for example, has explored the benefits for Christians of engaging in prayer alongside their companion animals, either indoors or outdoors (2012). And the interfaith Compassion Consortium that we describe in Chapter 29 on urban wildlife in this volume invites participants in their services to explore interspecies spirituality with other animals, recognizing these other animals' capacity and right to "have access to experiences of awe, peace, and divine connection" (Bowen 2022, 35). Such practices might involve chanting *Shalom* (Peace) with sheep living in a farm animal sanctuary, praying amidst the sound of frogs calling, or meditating with a pig or rooster "to change the socialized narrative about what these animals are for" (Bowen 2022, 34–35). However, when including other animals directly in one's contemplative practice, the practitioner needs to be mindful of respect, care, and reciprocity; if the animals show signs of being stressed by participating, one should end the practice, and one should always consider what one can give back to the animals in return for the mindfulness they share with us.

The idea of meditating with other animals also raises the question of whether such animals have the capacity and/or are known to engage in contemplative practice themselves, beyond the numerous accounts one often hears of companion animals participating in their humans' meditative practice. In terms of *capacity*, many animals seem to have the cognitive abilities and self-consciousness (see Chapter 2 by Robert W. Mitchell and Mark A. Krause in this volume; also Safina 2015, 16–35) that would make it possible for them to engage in contemplative practice. Moreover, consider the definitions of mindfulness and contemplative practice that we discussed at the start of this chapter, which explained that one can engage in even ordinary everyday activities in a mindful or contemplative manner. Could we consider the single-minded concentration of hunting animals like herons or big cats a kind of contemplative practice? Do birds focus their attention mindfully as they construct a nest, or spiders as they spin their webs? (Also see Komjathy 2022, 12 for a Daoist story of fighting roosters successfully being trained to meditate, and Stevenson 1995, 600–602 for the Pure Land Buddhist story of the Parrot of Hedong who acquired the wisdom of a Buddha through contemplative practice.) In terms of other animals being *known* to engage in contemplative practice outside of their ordinary daily activities, there are indeed intriguing examples for baboons, chimpanzees, and perhaps other species from field studies and personal observations (see Chapter 30 by Barbara Smuts et al. in this volume for an extended discussion of this topic).

Conclusion

In this chapter, I have argued that engaging in contemplative practice can bring us closer to animal others, connecting with them on a deeper level and learning about their lives and experiences in ways that are not accessible to us from reading about them or other third-person perspectives. By engaging in such first-person practices on a regular basis, we can become more mindful of and attentive to animals, which will help us better understand them, connect with them, and have compassion for them, which opens the possibility for us to come to respect and care for them. We can then bring this more mindful perspective on animal and human-animal being to all of our interactions with other animals, from the food choices we make to whom we include in our prayers to how we study other animals.

But can learning contemplative practices that more closely connect us with animals actually help living animal beings in the world? Of course, you will know from reading this chapter that my answer to this question is, "Yes!" And I am not the only one who feels this way. So let us end this chapter where we began it, with a quote from Zen Buddhist master and teacher Thich Nhat Hanh:

> To meditate is not to run away from life but to take the time to look deeply into ourselves or into a situation. . . . If we feel helpless or overwhelmed, if we have anger, fear, or despair, then no matter what we do to heal ourselves or our planet, it will not succeed. Meditating is the most basic, crucial thing we can do. To meditate is to give ourselves a chance to free ourselves from despair, to touch non-fear, and to nurture our compassion. With the insight and fearlessness born from meditation, we will be able to heal not only ourselves, but also other species, and our planet.
>
> (Nhat Hanh 2013, 43–44)

Acknowledgments

First and foremost, I offer deep gratitude to the crows, foxes, cicadas, and many other animals who have offered me the gifts of their knowledge, which I do my best to share, in return, with my students. Next, to the memory of Ray Fogelson—elder, anthropologist, teacher, trickster—who first introduced me to Native American three world cosmology (which he had learned directly from Cherokee teachers and also from Robin Ridington's studies with the Beaver Indians). Susan Douglas Roberts, a retired member of Texas Christian University's Dance faculty, suggested language I could use to help guide practitioners in how to mimic animal movements with their eyes, head, or hand. Thank you also to Lucy Berry for research assistance and to Rev. Sarah Bowen for recommending the article on intercessory prayer and wound healing in bush babies. Finally, many, many thanks to the faculty, alumni, and other community members who have participated in the group meditations sponsored since 2020 by Texas Christian University's program in Contemplative Awareness and Living Mindfully (CALM), codirected by Mark Dennis and Blake Hestir. You helped keep me sane during the COVID-19 pandemic and grounded thereafter.

References

Aftandilian, Dave. 2019. "Connecting Students (and Faculty) to Place and Animals through Contemplative Practices." In *Grounding Education in the Environmental Humanities: Exploring*

Place-Based Pedagogies in the South, edited by Lucas F. Johnston and Dave Aftandilian, 17–38. New York and London: Routledge.

———. 2022. "Listening Contemplatively to Nature and Ourselves." *CrossCurrents* 72 (2): 93–111.

Bowen, Sarah A. 2022. *Sacred Sendoffs: An Animal Chaplain's Advice for Surviving Animal Loss, Making Life Meaningful, and Healing the Planet.* Rhinebeck, N.Y.: Monkfish.

Bruchac, Joseph. 1996. *Roots of Survival: Native American Storytelling and the Sacred.* Golden, Colo.: Fulcrum Publishing.

Chapple, Christopher Key. 2008. "Imitation of Animals in Yoga Tradition." In *Yoga and the Luminous: Patanjali's Spiritual Path to Freedom*, 49–59. Albany: State University of New York Press.

Corman, Lauren, and Tereza Vandrovcová. 2014. "Radical Humility: Toward a More Holistic Critical Animal Studies Pedagogy." *Counterpoints* 448: 135–57.

Fronsdal, Gil. 2008. *The Issue at Hand: Essays on Buddhist Mindfulness Practice.* 4th ed. www.insightmeditationcenter.org/books-by-gil-fronsdal/.

Ho, Mobi. 1975. "Translator's Preface." In *The Miracle of Mindfulness: An Introduction to the Practice of Meditation*, edited by Thich Nhat Hanh, vii–xiii. Boston, Mass.: Beacon Press.

Hudson, Charles. 1976. *The Southeastern Indians.* Knoxville: University of Tennessee Press.

Kabat-Zinn, Jon. 2005. *Coming to Our Senses: Healing Ourselves and the World Through Mindfulness.* New York: Hachette Books.

Komjathy, Louis. 2018. *Introducing Contemplative Studies.* Hoboken, N.J. and Chichester: Wiley Blackwell.

———. 2022. "Religion, Animals, and Contemplation." *Religions* 13 (5): 457. https://doi.org/10.3390/rel13050457.

Lesniak, Karen T. 2006. "The Effects of Intercessory Prayer on Wound Healing in Nonhuman Primates." *Alternative Therapies in Health and Medicine* 12 (6): 42–48.

Lupinacci, John. 2019. "Teaching to End Human Supremacy: Learning to Recognize Equity in All Species." In *Education for Total Liberation: Critical Animal Pedagogy and Teaching Against Speciesism*, edited by Anthony J. Nocella II et al., 81–98. New York: Peter Lang.

Mooney, James. (1900) 1995. *Myths of the Cherokee.* New York: Dover.

Mortali, Micah. 2019. *Rewilding: Meditations, Practices, and Skills for Awakening in Nature.* Boulder, Colo.: Sounds True.

Murray, Zachiah. 2012. *Mindfulness in the Garden: Zen Tools for Digging in the Dirt.* Berkeley, Calif.: Parallax Press.

Nelson, Melissa K., ed. 2008. *Original Instructions: Indigenous Teachings for a Sustainable Future.* Rochester, Vt.: Bear & Co.

———, and Dan Shilling, eds. 2018. *Traditional Ecological Knowledge: Learning from Indigenous Practices for Environmental Sustainability.* Cambridge and New York: Cambridge University. Press.

Nelson, Richard K. 1986. *Make Prayers to the Raven: A Koyukon View of the Northern Forest.* Chicago, Ill. and London: University of Chicago Press.

Nhat Hanh, Thich. 2004. "Earth Gathas." In *This Sacred Earth: Religion, Nature, Environment*, edited by Roger Gottlieb, 515–16. 2nd ed. New York and London: Routledge.

———. 2008. *The World We Have: A Buddhist Approach to Peace and Ecology.* Berkeley, Calif.: Parallax Press.

———. 2013. *Love Letter to the Earth.* Berkeley, Calif.: Parallax Press.

———. 2022. *The Blooming of a Lotus: Essential Guided Meditations for Mindfulness, Healing, and Transformation*, rev. and expanded ed. Translated by Annabel Laity. Boston, Mass.: Beacon Press.

Pouso, Myrian Monnet. 2012. "Animal Spirituality: Integrating Animals into Contemplative Spiritual Practices." D.Min. thesis, Claremont School of Theology.

Ridington, Robin, and Tonia Ridington. 1970. "The Inner Eye of Shamanism and Totemism." *History of Religions* 10 (1): 49–61.

Safina, Carl. 2015. *Beyond Words: What Animals Think and Feel*. New York: Henry Holt.

Simonsson, Otto, Simon B. Goldberg, and Walter Osika. 2022. "Man's Best Friend(s): Effects of a Brief Befriending Meditation on Human-Animal Relations." *PLoS One*. https://doi.org/10.1371/journal.pone.0278704.

Speck, Frank G., Leonard Broom, and Will West Long. (1951) 1983. *Cherokee Dance and Drama*. Norman: University of Oklahoma Press.

Stevenson, Daniel B. 1995. "Death-Bed Testimonials of the Pure Land Faithful." In *Buddhism in Practice*, edited by Daniel S. Lopez, Jr., 592–602. Princeton, N.J.: Princeton University Press.

Thompson, Claire. 2013. *Mindfulness and the Natural World: Bringing Our Awareness Back to Nature*. New York: Metro Books.

Wilson, Jeff. 2014. *Mindful America: The Mutual Transformation of Buddhist Meditation and American Culture*. New York: Oxford University Press.

Other Recommended Resources

Coleman, Mark. 2022. *A Field Guide to Nature Meditation: 52 Mindfulness Practices for Joy, Wisdom and Wonder*. Awake in the Wild.

Komjathy, Louis, ed. 2015. *Contemplative Literature: A Comparative Sourcebook on Meditation and Contemplative Prayer*. Albany: State University of New York Press.

Magee, Rhonda V. 2019. *The Inner Work of Racial Justice: Healing Ourselves and Transforming Our Communities Through Mindfulness*. New York: TarcherPerigee.

Metta Meditation: A Complete Guide to Loving-Kindness. www.lionsroar.com/metta-meditation-guide/.

Morning MeditOceans: Guided Meditations with the Ocean. www.youtube.com/playlist?list=PLq_DVMr7CmlJ3DJothjCJNylwgyrB72V6.
- A series of six guided ocean meditations hosted by the Monterey Bay Aquarium, most of which involve captive animals housed in the aquarium

Rogers, Holly B. 2016. *The Mindful Twenty-Something: Life Skills to Handle Stress . . . and Everything Else*. Oakland, Calif.: New Harbinger Publications.
- Several free guided meditations related to this book are available online at https://student.korumindfulness.org/free-guided-meditations.html

Simmer-Brown, Judith, and Fran Grace, eds. 2011. *Meditation and the Classroom: Contemplative Pedagogy for Religious Studies*. Albany: State University of New York Press.

Watson, Gay. 2017. *Attention: Beyond Mindfulness*. London: Reaktion Books.

25 Companion Animals

Laura Hobgood

Introduction

Companion animals surround humans both within our bodies and around our bodies in everyday life. Arguably, humans live with companion species in our intestinal systems, on our skin, on our dinner plates, and on our sofas. Well-articulated arguments even suggest that our "animal connection"—an "intimate and reciprocal set of interactions between animals and humans"—significantly influenced and still influences human evolution (Shipman 2010, 519).

Yet, "companion animals" proves an inherently difficult and even elusive category to delineate, and might be too defined by humans. One possible definition is offered by Jay McDaniel: "an animal 'other' with whom were are in daily relationship" (McDaniel 2006, 134). As I write this piece I'm fostering tiny infant squirrels who were orphaned following a major storm. For sixteen weeks, they will be companion animals to a human (me). But obviously they do not play the same roles in my life as do the dogs in my family.

At its heart, this chapter examines lived examples of these definitions by focusing on three different "domesticated" companion animals. These three groups provide a sampling of the ways companion animals function in the religious lives of humans (and these animals): dogs, bovines (cows/bulls, oxen, buffalo), and cats (specifically "house cats," not the broader feline family that includes lions, jaguars, etc.). Through this process, I hope to reveal some of the interesting ways certain companion animals function in the religious sensibilities and systems of humans. In doing so, similar ideas can be employed to consider the many other companion animals with whom humans live globally (some fish, birds, rodents, horses, donkeys, other primates, and more).

While arguably the microscopic communities that make up human bodies also exist in a kind of companion relationship with us, the popularly conceived notion of a companion animal, and even the academic definition, focuses on those animals with whom humans live in intentional relationship and those animals who, in some cases, choose to live in intentional relationship with humans. Generally, humans initiate the relationship, though not always. As Paul Waldau states, "The category is, then, constructed by humans for human purposes" (Waldau 2013, 27). He continues by emphasizing that this construction does make the category "elastic," with new species, sometimes those called "pet," entering and later being "spoken of as a companion animal" (Waldau 2013, 27). Donna Haraway suggests that companion animals tell "a story of co-habitation, co-evolution, and embodied cross-species sociality" (Haraway 2003, 4). In other words, companion species intertwine with humans in a variety of ways, but the animals on both sides of this relationship directly impact each other's lives.

DOI: 10.4324/9781003324157-30

These impacts can make quite a difference in the ways that humans think about other animals. And, since it has been claimed that animals are "good to think" (Lévi-Strauss 1963, 89), what appears unique or helpful about thinking with or about companion animals? Or is there something more to companion animals? Haraway argues that companion animals "are not here just to think with. They are here to live with" (Haraway 2003, 5). Specifically, some animals are good to think, but they live in separate spheres or worlds within our world (imagine animals deep in the oceans or high in treetops). Companion animals exist in the ecological niche of humans, even if they have been forced to adapt to that niche or to live in it without choosing to do so. Waldau proposes,

> The beings we have slotted into the category "companion animals" can open minds and hearts, as evidenced by the extraordinary number of fact-based accounts and fiction-based works that use companion animal theme to increase awareness of the benefits of living in the presence of these animals. Companion animals, then, create opportunities.
>
> (Waldau 2013, 29)

In short, thinking about or with companion animals appears unique likely because of the close proximity of their lives to the lives of humans.

This closeness also leads to a unique bundle of religious expressions connected to companion animals. Their direct impact on human lives, be that in the form of intimate relationship or as a source of food or labor and more, seems to require that humans figure out how to incorporate them into religious practice and thinking. In other words, religious questions arise when pondering these companions: What happens when they die and how do we recognize that? How do we thank or condemn the divine for their very presence? Why are they here at all (which begs the question of why humans are here at all)? What is the value or purpose of companion animals?

Too many companion animals exist across time and cultures to think about all of them in a brief chapter. But through the lens of three kinds of companion animals, each with particular and different forms of relationship with humans, others can be pondered as well. Dogs exist in a very unique companion relationship with humans since they are generally accepted as our longest-term companion species, and in a form of relationship that likely initiated from both parties, not just from human selection, in more than one geographic location and at more than one time. Bovines (a broad group of animals, but thinking about cows/bulls, buffalo, and oxen here) function as sacred beings, kin, and commodity depending on when and where in the world one encounters them. Cats have also lived with humans for millennia and, similarly to dogs, likely entered into this companionship through some choice of their own. Mostly hailing from the ancient Mediterranean world, house cats first became close companions to humans in ancient Egypt, and probably spread from there throughout the world. Cats still have a somewhat complicated relationship with humans and live more independently than dogs, but more cats live in households with humans than any other companion animal. Hopefully these three groups of animals can serve as a window into thinking about myriad others.

Dogs

> To me it is a strangely appealing and even elevating thought that the age-old covenant between man [*sic*] and dog was "signed" voluntarily and without obligation by each of the contracting parties.
>
> (Lorenz 1997, 29)

Regardless of the exact definition of who qualifies as a companion animal, many would agree that the quintessential species in this category is *Canis familiaris*—the dog. Dogs and humans have lived with each other for at least 15,000 years and perhaps longer than that (Bergström et al. 2022; Hobgood-Oster 2014). It has proven difficult to determine the exact time frame when dogs became distinct from several subspecies of gray wolf (from whom all dogs descended) because "proto-dogs likely spent generations betwixt and between their eventual domesticated forms and wolves" (Hobgood-Oster 2014, 8). Expanding evidence suggests that the process of becoming companions initiated in different locations with instigation, or agency, on the part of both early dogs and humans. In other words, some gray wolves and pre-Ice Age humans, likely in areas of Eurasia, started to share a mostly human-impacted ecological niche. Both species hunted and scavenged, lived in groups with dominance hierarchies, were omnivorous (though early dogs were likely more carnivorous than humans), and migrated rather easily because of their ability to adapt to different climates.

As generations of both species lived together, dogs became almost irreplaceable in the cultural development of many humans. Dogs served as guardians, hunting companions, herders, haulers, an emergency food source, and possibly even healers (see Hobgood-Oster 2014, 59–78; for the Arikara, see Dorsey [1904] 2004, 17; for the Lakota, see Meyers and Weston 2020). Some suggest that without dogs, humans might not have domesticated sheep, goats, or cattle since humans required the speed and agility of dogs to trap these other animals in order to domesticate them. For example, 5,000-year old cave carvings in the mountains of what is now Armenia portray humans using dogs to herd goats. An archaeological site in Egypt includes rock art from approximately 5,200 years ago, about the time of the domestication of cows, which depicts a dog standing on top of a bull or cow (Hobgood-Oster 2014, 27).

While the exact beginning of the companionship of humans and dogs is somewhat uncertain since it likely started at different times in different places, by the Bronze Age (approximately 3,300 to 1,200 B.C.E.) humans took some control of breeding and multiple dog types, many with specialized abilities, started to emerge (Crockford 2008, 150). It took centuries to select for very large and very small dogs, but different body and muzzle sizes, along with different skills (such as hunting or herding) appear in the archaeological record from that early point. A new and somewhat human-controlled relationship began.

With all of this history of the pragmatic connections between humans and dogs, the question to pose at this juncture is how dogs became part of humanity's religious life. Interestingly, one of the earliest pieces of archaeological evidence jumps right into the world of religion. About 14,000 years ago, close to what is now Bonn, Germany, a burial took place that included a young woman, an old man, and the jawbone of a dog. The "Bonn-Oberkassel dog" held the position of the most ancient evidence of a domesticated dog for years (Crockford 2008, 12). This intentional presence of a dog in a grave with humans points to the significance of dogs in the spiritual practices of people that long ago. And this practice of dog internment continues through the present. In the upper Jordan Valley at the entrance of a 12,000-year-old home, a human skeleton was found curled on its right side in a fetal position (common for ritual burials). The person's left hand was stretched out to rest on the chest of a puppy. Scholars suggest that the puppy's presence indicates that the deceased human desired the dog's companionship in the afterlife (Davis and Valla 1978, 608–610). These are not the only examples, since evidence exists of prehistoric ritualized burials of dogs on every human-inhabited continent.

Ritual dog burials continued throughout history but have reemerged in the modern era with a new vigor as pet keeping became more common with the rise of the middle class in some cultures. These more contemporary practices connect to other companion animals in addition to dogs, but dogs play a prominent role. Pet cemeteries started to appear in Victorian England, then spread rapidly to other parts of Western Europe and the United States. From London to Paris to New York City, formal pet cemeteries established a location for households to grieve the loss of their beloved companions (see Chapter 23 on "Commemorating Animals" by Barbara R. Ambros in this volume). In many cases, those buried were dogs.

This practice shifted somewhat in the late twentieth century, with the growth of the idea of the "Rainbow Bridge," an "imaginary bridge connected to the Christian heaven where beloved pets go after death to await the arrival of their human companions" (Magliocco 2018, 39). The Rainbow Bridge concept quickly expanded beyond the boundaries of Christian belief and into global popular culture (see, e.g., Ambros 2010, 55–57). A number of people started memorializing their canines in the virtual world, while keeping their cremated remains at home.

However, burial rituals provide just one example of the roles dogs have played in religious ideas about the afterlife. In various cultures, dogs act as the intermediary between humans and the post-death experience. For example, Cerberus, the three-headed dog god of Greek mythology, bore the moniker "hound of Hades." While not a guide into or out of the underworld, Cerberus did guard the gates to this version of the afterlife, allowing people to enter but not allowing them to exit. Ancient Egyptian religious ideas included the central dog-headed god Anubis. As the protector of the dead, Anubis served as an ally in the afterlife, and his central place of worship was named Cynopolis (dog city). Interestingly part of the veneration of Anubis required the ritual sacrifice and mummification of puppies, most found in the catacombs of Saqqara (in northern Egypt). Here the dog catacombs contain the remains of an estimated eight million puppies mummified over the course of several hundred years. Though likely connected to a pilgrimage ritual, the purpose and meaning behind this practice remain unclear (Ikram and Nicholson 2018, 15–20).

The phenomenon of dogs as guides to the afterlife extends well beyond these Mediterranean belief systems. Classic Mayan culture, in this case from present-day Guatemala, includes the idea that "dogs should not be mistreated because the dead need the help of a dog to cross a river in the afterlife" (Burchell 2007, 10). According to one local shaman, the newly deceased "needs to grip the tail of the dog as it swims across the river in order to cross" (Burchell 2007, 10). Ancient Aztec culture held a similar belief regarding holding onto the tail of the god Xolotl, often depicted in a way that evokes contemporary Mexican hairless dog breeds. Such spiritual ideas extend into what is now the Southwest of the U.S. where researchers studied more than 700 dog burials from at least a 1700-year period (400 B.C.E. to 1300 C.E.) as well as rock art that shows dogs accompanying shamans (Fugate 2010, 35).

Not only can dogs be found in death rituals, but also as part of religious celebrations in life. Blessings of pets make up a rapidly expanding practice in myriad cultures globally, but particularly in North America. While the history of these blessings proves long and somewhat mysterious, starting in the last quarter of the twentieth century, their popularity grew significantly. A number of pets and other animals participate, via human companions, but dogs comprise the majority of those blessed. Most of these rituals take place either in early October in conjunction with the Feast of St. Francis or in mid-January in connection with the Feast of St. Anthony (the Catholic patron saint of animals). The blessings extend well beyond Catholic communities and are often conducted by Jewish, interfaith, or secular groups as well (for more see my Chapter 14 on "Blessings of Pets" in this volume).

Unsurprisingly because of the long history shared by humans and dogs, they emerge as, arguably, the most prominent animal represented in religious ideas and practices. Though the story is not monolithic, dogs also feature as condemned and pariahs in some institutional religions. The sacred texts of Judaism, Christianity, and Islam, while not necessarily completely clear on the topic, tend to frame dogs negatively. Myriad examples exist, but here are just a few:

- As a dog returns to its vomit, so fools repeat their folly (Proverbs 26:11, Hebrew Bible).
- Do not give what is holy to the dogs . . . (Matthew 7:6, Christian New Testament).
- Outside are the dogs, those who practice magic arts, the sexually immoral, the murderers, the idolators and everyone who loves and practices falsehood (Revelation 22:15).

In addition, the hadith (Muslim texts that report the sayings or actions of the Prophet Muhammad) suggest that "a dog prowling close to a believer in prayer invalidates the prayer and its presence prevents an angel from visiting the house" (Menache 1997, 35). As a matter of practice historically and even in contemporary culture, keeping dogs as pets features less prominently in most Muslim and Jewish cultures and communities. Indeed, often "the dog is a nonhuman animal who generally is regarded as 'dirty' in the Islamic religion" (Al-Fayez et al. 2003, 18). When so much contact between two species exists, certainly complications arise.

Thus, dogs appear, not surprisingly, throughout human religious traditions and practices because of their prominence in the shared history of our two species. From rock art to ancient burials to symbolic portrayals of deities to understandings of the afterlife, the liminal position of dogs as those betwixt and between humans and other animals, as well as humans and what is construed as "nature," fixes them as an almost perfect animal to think.

Oxen, Cattle, Buffalo

Buffalo peoples dream of their buffalo, their older brothers. They dream of them, and through those dreams, ceremony, and hard work, they are bringing back those herds, bringing back the buffalo.

(LaDuke 1999, 139)

The central plains that cover the middle of the North American continent provide the perfect landscape for buffalo. In the past, millions of them roamed these grasslands, literally enabling and creating the ecosystem. Along with the buffalo, complex human cultures emerged living in concert with them. This companion species, the buffalo, completely intertwines with the (human) buffalo people living in these great plains. As Birgil Kills Straight, an Oglala Lakota, states,

The four leggeds came before the two leggeds. They are our older brothers, we come from them. Before them, we were the root people. That is why we are spiritually related to them. We call them in our language *Tatanka*, which means "He Who Owns Us." We cannot say that we own the buffalo, because he owns us.

(LaDuke 1999, 136)

For generations, buffalo and humans made a life together on the plains, stretching from modern-day Canada through the United States into Mexico. Ceremonial attire, hunting rituals, and feasts of thanksgiving have linked the religious life of the (human) buffalo people to that of the buffalo. It is also important to note that ideas of kinship in Lakota culture have extended well beyond that with buffalo to encompass relations with all of the living beings. While this chapter cannot address that broader concept, it should be kept in mind when pondering the human-buffalo connection (Posthumus 2017).

In the nineteenth century, European invaders began to take over the land that buffalo and buffalo peoples had occupied for millennia. The invaders instituted policies and practices determined to destroy both the buffalo and the human inhabitants. Buffalo population dropped from over forty million to only twenty buffalo by 1894, all isolated to Yellowstone National Park. Simultaneously, white people relegated most of the human buffalo people to reservations. But this tragic moment did not stop the relationship, and by the end of the twentieth century, buffalo people had successfully reestablished the physical connection with the buffalo; the spiritual relationship never died (Zontek 2007, 75–98). Now, buffalo people are reestablishing herds on tribal reservations throughout the Northern Plains. These companion animals live on with the humans whose lives are intimately intertwined with theirs. (For more on settler ecocide of the buffalo peoples, see James Hatley's Chapter 28 on "Living with Ghosts" in this volume.)

Bovines fill symbolic and real roles in other cultures as well. In central Italy, where a combination of Catholic faith and pre-Catholic religious ideas meld, il Bui de San Zopito (the ox of Saint Zopito) looms large. As the religious legend goes, the bones of a saint (Zopito) moved in a procession from Rome to Loreto Aprutino (a small village in the central mountainous area of the country). Upon arrival, the bones would hold the sacred place as the holy relics for their small cathedral. Humans knelt in reverence along the route as the procession wound its way through the hills and valleys. As the procession approached one particular field, the farmer decided to ignore it in order to keep on working. An ox pulled his plow. The ox, however, recognized the saint, refused to move forward, and knelt in respect when he saw the holy in his midst (D'Angelo 2000; Hobgood-Oster 2008, 1–4).

Each year on the Monday after Pentecost, this miraculous event is reenacted in Loreto Aprutino. People come from miles around and a huge day-long festival ensues. Marching bands play, and a procession parades through the village streets carrying various religious and agricultural symbols. Finally, the most important part of the festival takes place: a large white ox, with a young girl on his back, kneels again before the bones of the saint as they process past him. This ox represents the sacred in this village and tells their story (Hobgood-Oster 2008). These connections to generations of farmers and agricultural life offer a different glimpse into the myriad roles of companion animals and can be found globally in many cultures (for a South Korean example, see the film *Old Partner* listed in Other Recommended Resources following).

In India, cattle fill yet another sacred role. Goddesses and gods incarnate in a variety of animal forms in Hinduism; thus many animals fill sacred categories. Monkeys, for example, inhabit numerous temples and represent Hanuman, the monkey god hero of the great epic *Ramayana*. Ganesh is the great elephant god and many sacred temples in India still keep captive elephants (Agoramoorthy and Hsu 2012, 6). But the cow seems to be the pinnacle of sacred animals in myriad and very pragmatic ways. Hindus frequently refer to the cow as "our mother" and she is associated with the goddess of fortune, Laksmi (Nelson 2006, 180). Mahatma Gandhi, social justice and nonviolence leader from India, once stated, "If someone asks me what the most important outward manifestation of Hinduism was, I would suggest that it was the idea of cow protection" (Agoramoorthy and Hsu 2012, 5; see also Kenneth R. Valpey's Chapter 21 on "Cow Care in Hindu Animal Ethics" in this volume).

Conflicts still do sometimes arise in India when considering the sacredness of cows. Ironically, in 2015, the same year that numerous anti-beef legislative initiatives were passed in India, the country was the largest exporter of beef in the world (Sarkar and Sarkar 2016, 329. 331). Simultaneously, in very crowded cities that include large numbers of cows living in the streets, the "divine cow" continues to hold the title of "giver of all desires" (Agoramoorthy and Hsu 2012, 7). In a way similar to dogs in some cultures, some Brahmins even believe the cow leads departed souls across the river into the world of the dead. One sacred ritual includes a worshipper holding tightly onto the tail of a cow to symbolize this guidance (Nelson 2006, 180). In addition, a number of rituals involve the use of cow milk, curd, butter, urine, and dung (which are known as the "five products" of the cow). Thus, in interesting and complex ways, cows exist as sacred companion animals in Hindu cultures.

But other stories of bovines as a type of companion animal, albeit maybe not in a positive way for cows, also abound. Indeed, cattle comprise one of the largest categories of industrial consumption in the world, mostly for their milk and meat, particularly in the United States, Brazil, Japan, India, and much of Europe. If one ponders that market capitalism functions as a religion, cattle are a central component of that religion. David Loy posits that "our present economic system should also be understood as our religion, because it has come to fulfill a religious function for us" (Loy 1997, 275). How, then, do cattle function as a central player in the religion of the market? Even in cultures that esteem cows as sacred, such as in South Asia with Hinduism as a dominant belief system, cows serve as a major component of an increasingly capitalistic economy. A cow finds herself to be both sacred and a commodity simultaneously (USDA 2022).

Looking at the statistics suggests that cattle play a central role in market capitalism by serving as a major commodity. In the twenty-first century, millions of cattle die in feed lots and factory farming facilities annually. For example, in the United States during the first two decades of the twenty-first century, at least 29 million cattle were slaughtered annually (Shahbandeh 2023), and in Brazil, slaughtered cattle numbered 27 to 29 million in 2021 (CEPEA 2022). According to the U.S. Department of Agriculture, the "beef" industry reported a gross income exceeding $63.5 billion in 2020 (USDA 2021, 11).

Yet, the statistics, while telling, reveal only part of the role of cattle in market capitalism. They feature centrally in marketing campaigns, often in feminized and alluring roles that endow them with human-like qualities while also making them appear more palatable (Adams 1990). And, in tragic ways, this feminizing functions not only in symbolic but also in real, physical ways. Cows provide the primary source of milk consumed by humans. This industry serves as a central aspect of the lives of cows not only in the U.S., but also in India and in Europe. As a matter of fact, India, with the traditional sacred cow, is the largest producer of milk in the world, over 200 million tons annually (Mashal and Kumar 2022).

While in market capitalism cattle fill a different companion role, nonetheless they point to an important symbolic shift with commodity as a marker of relationship. Cows, buffalo, and oxen might once have been, and in some ways still are, sacred companions; but in a world dominated by the religion of the market, their companionship role has emerged as a powerful and tragic commodity.

A stunning counter to this tragic situation for cows is found in the relationships developed between humans and rescued cattle at many farm sanctuaries. As pictured clearly in documentaries such as *Peaceable Kingdom: The Journey Home* (www.peaceablekingdomfilm.org), which also points to powerful spiritual connections, deep bonds grow in these compassionate companionship cultures. Such contrasts point to the intense complexity of this particular human-animal relationship and to the possibilities of considering cows as companion animals.

Cats

> I must make it clear from the start, the cat I am talking about is a real cat, truly, believe me, a *little* cat. It isn't the *figure* of a cat. It doesn't silently enter the room as an allegory for all the cats on earth, the felines that traverse myths and religions, literature and fables.
>
> (Derrida 2002, 374)

While dogs seem to clearly function as companion animals, and cows possibly less obviously so, what about the intriguing cat? It does seem necessary to consider the feline companion animal since the house cat holds the status of "most popular pet in the world" with nearly 600 million living among humans globally (Driscoll et al. 2009, 68). And as the previous quotation from the key philosopher Jacques Derrida suggests cats figure centrally in many myths and religions. Still, it seems that cats have filled various places on the spectrum in terms of human reception "from divine in ancient Egypt to evil during the Middle Ages in Europe, from enigmatic and exotic to sweet and friendly" (Nikolajeva 2009, 248).

As with dogs, early evidence for domesticated cats proves difficult to sort out, but genetic studies indicate that contemporary house cats descended from a Middle Eastern wild feline (Driscoll et al. 2009, 68). For decades the domestication of cats was dated to approximately four thousand years ago in Egypt based on artwork found there that pictured domesticated cats alongside humans. But in 2008 evidence was found suggesting an earlier date for domestication and also connecting house cats to religious belief systems. In a cemetery for elite Egyptians, dating from the fourth millennium B.C.E. (approximately six thousand years ago), skeletons of six buried cats were found—two pairs of kittens along with an older male and female. Researchers think that they were "born outside the breeding season for wild cats" possibly pointing to humans taking on a role in rearing them (Pappas 2014).

An earlier, additional archaeological find on the island of Cyprus in the Mediterranean stretches the potential domestication date even further back. Approximately 9,500 years ago, a human was placed in a shallow grave along with mortuary items, including "stone tools, a lump of iron oxide, a handful of seashells" and, most important for our purposes, "in its own tiny grave just 40 centimeters away, an eight-month-old cat, its body oriented in the same westward direction as the human's" (Driscoll et al. 2009, 69; also see Vigne et al. 2004, 259).

The domestication process for cats likely mirrored that for dogs in some ways with stutters and starts as wild cats morphed into proto-house cats. One significant difference is that cats are obligate carnivores, meaning that they really only eat meat (unlike dogs who evolved to be more omnivorous). As a matter of fact, even contemporary cats can "go feral" and fend for themselves much more easily than most other companion and domesticated animals (Nottingham et al. 2022).

Cats have worked their way, or humans have worked them into, religious belief systems as they became increasingly present in human habitations. This may well begin in Egypt, according to Jaromir Malek, author of *The Cat in Ancient Egypt*. Malek states that "The cat's strength lay in its humble origins and its apotropaic (protective) qualities, which first brought it widespread respect and a prominent place in the personal religion of ordinary people" (Malek 1997, 73). In turn, cats became representations of the goddess Bastet, and they were sacrificed and mummified in huge numbers at her temple in Bubastis (Driscoll et al. 2009, 71). Herodotus, a Greek historian who visited Egypt in the 5th century B.C.E., reported that cats indeed served as manifestations of the deity. So beloved and honored were they that when a house cat died, those living in the house went into deep mourning, even shaving their eyebrows (as it was customary to do when a human member of the family died; Eyck 2000, 21).

Though revered and almost worshipped in Egypt, cats did not fare as well in some other cultural and religious systems. In medieval Europe, for example, Christianity began to frame cats as symbolic of heretics. Some theological treatises posited that heretics took part in secret rites with cats, particularly cat kissing. Eventually cats became associated with witches and witchcraft, which led to their persecution even into the modern period (Kienzle 2006, 109). However, cats made something of a resurgence, even in these once hostile Christian circles, and in the late twentieth century, they gained several patron saints, including Gertrude of Nivelles and Julian of Norwich (Ostberg 2020; Bondy 2018).

Cats also find a mixed reception in Muslim cultures, where they are sometimes framed as evil and at other times lauded as the favorite animal of the Prophet Muhammad (see Katharine Mershon's Chapter 4 on "Gender and Sexuality" in this volume). This tension plays out in twenty-first century Muslim cultures in interesting ways. Research in Mali, for example, shows cats perceived as both companions of witches and of the Prophet. The shape-shifting sorcerer *subaga* (witch), is believed, by many Malians, to take the form of a cat in order to gather information and use it to "sinister ends" (Bell 2019, 458). Therefore, many people will chase cats away in order to get rid of the sorcerer. But in an interesting interaction between Islamic and Indigenous religious ideas, some Muslims in Mali accept cats willingly. They base this change in relationship on various sources from Muslim history, most importantly the teachings of the Prophet. For example, in sunna literature the Prophet "told a story of a prostitute in the desert who gave water to a cat and went to heaven, whereas a pious woman starved her cat and went to hell" (Bell 2019, 461). This cultural difference and syncretism displays well the difficulty of characterizing or absolutizing the roles that cats, as well as other companion animals, play in religious beliefs and practices.

In the twenty-first century in many European and North American settings, cats frequently are among the best represented pets at Christian and ecumenical blessings of animals. And, just as with dogs, cats sometimes emerge in ideas about the Rainbow Bridge (though with less frequency than dogs), so their deaths continue to be recognized and mourned by those millions of humans globally who love them.

Conclusion

Companion animals, those who live in very close proximity to humans and who elicit some sort of emotional connection from us, also impact our religious ideas and practices. Just three examples, among many possibilities, highlight these religious responses. Dogs, cats, and bovines function quite distinctly in different religions historically and globally. But from sacred burial practices, to representations of the divine, to those who become kin, to those who are blessed and mourned, companion animals change the ways humans think about their own religious lives through ritual and belief. They join humans in an inner circle of beings granted religious consideration.

References

Adams, Carol. 1990. *The Sexual Politics of Meat*. New York: Continuum.

Agoramoorthy, Govindasamy, and Minna J. Hsu. 2012. "The Significance of Cows in Indian Society Between Sacredness and Economy." *Anthropological Notebooks* 18 (3): 5–12.

Al-Fayez, Ghenaim, Hiroko Arikawa, Abdelwahid Awadalla, and Donald Templer. 2003. "Companion Animal Attitude and Its Family Pattern in Kuwait." *Society & Animals* 11 (1): 17–28.

Ambros, Barbara. 2010. "Vengeful Spirits or Loving Spiritual Companions? Changing Views of Animal Spirits in Contemporary Japan." *Asian Ethnology* 69 (1): 35–67.

Bell, Diana. 2019. "Companion Animal for a Prophet or a Witch? Changing Place of House Cats in Contemporary Mali." *Society and Animals* 27 (4): 452–63.

Bergström, Anders, David W. G. Stanton, Ulrike H. Taron, Laurent Frantz, Mikkel-Holger S. Sinding, Erik Ersmark, Saskia Pfrengle, et al. 2022. "Grey Wolf Genomic History Reveals a Dual Ancestry of Dogs." *Nature*, June 29. Accessed July 6, 2022. www.nature.com/articles/s41586-022-04824-9.

Bondy, Renee. 2018. "Pussy Power Unleashed." *Herizons* 32 (1): 10–11.

Burchell, Simon. 2007. *Phantom Dogs in Latin America*. Wiltshire: Heart of Albion Press.

Center for Advanced Studies on Applied Economics (CEPEA). 2022. Accessed July 25, 2022. www.cepea.esalq.usp.br/en/brazilian-agribusiness-news/cattle-slaughter-is-the-lowest-in-17-years-but-productivity-per-animal-is-a-record.aspx#:~:text=Between%20January%20and%20December%202021,the%20highest%20in%20five%20years).

Crockford, Susan. 2008. *Dogs Through Time: An Archaeological Perspective*. Oxford: Archaeopress.

D'Angelo, Orlando. 2000. "San Zopito non e Piu Leggenda." *Il Messagero*, December 27.

Davis, Simon, and Francois Valla. 1978. "Evidence for Domestication of the Dog 12,000 Years Ago in the Natufian of Israel." *Nature* 276: 608–10.

Derrida, Jacques. 2002. "The Animal That Therefore I Am (More to Follow)." Translated by David Wills. *Critical Inquiry* 28 (2): 369–418.

Dorsey, George A. (1904) 2004. *Traditions of the Arikara*. Reprint, Whitefish, Mont.: Kessinger Publishing.

Driscoll, Carlos A., Juliet Clutton-Brock, Andrew C. Kitchener, and Stephen J. O'Brien. 2009. "The Taming of the Cat." *Scientific American* 300 (6): 68–75.

Eyck, Laurie. 2000. "From Mouser to God." *Animals* 133 (3): 20–25.

Fugate, Dody. 2010. "Guardian of Souls." *Archaeology* 63 (5): 35.

Haraway, Donna. 2003. *The Companion Species Manifesto: Dogs, People, and Significant Otherness*. Chicago, Ill.: Prickly Paradigm Press.

Hobgood-Oster, Laura. 2008. *Holy Dogs and Asses: Animals in the Christian Tradition*. Urbana: University of Illinois Press.

———. 2014. *A Dog's History of the World: Canines and the Domestication of Humans*. Waco: Baylor University Press.

Ikram, Salima, and Paul Nicholson. 2018. "Sacred Animal Cults in Egypt: Excavating the Cata-combs of Anubis at Saqqara." *Expedition* 60 (3): 12–20.

Kienzle, Beverly. 2006. "The Bestiary of Heretics: Imaging Medieval Christian Heresy with Insects and Animals." In *A Communion of Subjects: Animals in Religion, Science, & Ethics*, edited by Paul Waldau and Kimberly Patton, 103–16. New York: Columbia University Press.

LaDuke, Winona. 1999. *All Our Relations: Native Struggles for Land and Life*. Cambridge, Mass.: South End Press.

Lévi-Strauss, Claude. 1963. *Totemism*. Translated by Rodney Needham. Boston, Mass.: Beacon.

Lorenz, Konrad. 1997. *King Solomon's Ring*. New York: Plume.

Loy, David. 1997. "The Religion of the Market." *Journal of the American Academy of Religion* 65 (2): 275–90.

Magliocco, Sabina. 2018. "Beyond the Rainbow Bridge: Vernacular Ontologies of Animal After-life." *Journal of Folklore Research* 55 (2): 39–67.

Malek, Jaromir. 1997. *The Cat in Ancient Egypt*. Philadelphia: University of Pennsylvania Press.

Mashal, Mujib, and Hari Kumar. 2022. "India, a Dairy Titan, Studies How to Keep Milk Flowing in a Hotter World." *New York Times*, August 24. Accessed October 10, 2023. www.nytimes.com/2022/08/24/world/asia/india-climate-change-milk-prices.html.

McDaniel, Jay. 2006. "Practicing the Presence of God: A Christian Approach to Animals." In *A Communion of Subjects: Animals in Religion, Science, and Ethics*, edited by Paul Waldau and Kimberly Patton, 132–45. New York: Columbia University Press.

Menache, Sophia. 1997. "Dogs: God's Worst Enemy." *Society and Animals* 5 (1): 23–44.

Meyers, Richard, and Ernest Weston, Jr. 2020. "What Rez Dogs Mean to the Lakota." *Sapiens.org*, December 2. Accessed May 14, 2023. www.sapiens.org/culture/rez-dogs/.

Nelson, Lance. 2006. "Cows, Elephants, Dogs, and Other Lesser Embodiments of *Atman*: Reflec-tions on Hindu Attitudes Toward Nonhuman Animals." In *A Communion of Subjects: Animals in Religion, Science, & Ethics*, edited by Paul Waldau and Kimberly Patton, 179–93. New York: Columbia University Press.

Nikolajeva, Maria. 2009. "Devils, Demons, Familiars, Friends: Toward a Semiotics of Literary Cats." *Marvels & Tales* 23 (2): 248–67.

Nottingham, Catherine M., Hannah L. Buckley, Bradley S. Case, Alistair S. Glen, and Margaret C. Stanley. 2022. "Factors Affecting Home Range Size of Feral Cats: A Meta-Analysis." *New Zealand Journal of Ecology* 46 (2): 1–11.

Ostberg, Rene. 2020. "Meet St. Gertrude: Cat Lady of the Catholic Church." *U.S. Catholic: Real Life*, March 16. https://uscatholic.org/articles/202003/how-st-gertrude-of-nivelles-became-the-cat-lady-of-the-catholic-church/.

Pappas, Stephanie. 2014. "Ancient Egyptian Kitten Skeletons Hint at Earlier Cat Domestication." *Scientific American*, March 18. Accessed February 5, 2023. www.scientificamerican.com/article/ancient-egyptian-kitten-skeletons-hint-at-earlier-cat-domestication/.

Posthumus, David. 2017. "Exploring Nineteenth-Century Lakota Ontology and Belief." *Ethnohistory* 64 (3): 379–400.

Sarkar, Radha, and Amar Sarkar. 2016. "Sacred Slaughter: An Analysis of Historical, Commu-nal, and Constitutional Aspects of Beef Bans in India." *Politics, Religion, and Ideology* 17 (4): 329–51.

Shahbandeh, M. 2023. "Total Slaughtered Cattle in the U.S. 2000–2021." *Statista*, April 17. Accessed May 14, 2023. www.statista.com/statistics/194357/total-cattle-slaughter-in-the-us-since-2000/.

Shipman, Pat. 2010. "The Animal Connection and Human Evolution." *Current Anthropology* 51 (4): 519–38.

U.S. Department of Agriculture. 2021. *Meat Animals Production, Disposition, and Income 2020 Summary*. Washington, D.C.: USDA National Agriculture Statistics Service.

———. 2022. *Livestock and Products Semi-Annual 2022*. Washington, D.C.: USDA National Agriculture Statistics Service. https://apps.fas.usda.gov/newgainapi/api/Report/DownloadReportByFileName?fileName=Livestock%20and%20Products%20Semi-annual_New%20Delhi_India_IN2022-0012.pdf.

Vigne, J.-D., J. Guilaine, K. Debue, L. Haye, and P. Gérard. 2004. "Early Taming of the Cat in Cyprus." *Science* 304 (5668): 259.

Waldau, Paul. 2013. *Animal Studies: An Introduction*. New York: Oxford University Press.

Zontek, Ken. 2007. *Buffalo Nation: American Indian Efforts to Restore the Bison*. Lincoln: University of Nebraska Press.

Other Recommended Resources

Adams, Carol J. 2018. *Burger*. New York: Bloomsbury Academic.

"Archaeology—Cats Tamed Early in Egypt." 2014. *Nature* 507 (7491): 142. www.nature.com/articles/507142d#:~:text=Ancient%20Egyptians%20might%20have%20domesticated,depicts%20domesticated%20cats%20alongside%20humans.

Franciscan Spirit Blog, Blessings of Animals. www.franciscanmedia.org/franciscan-spirit-blog/blessing-of-animals/#:~:text=The%20Blessing%20of%20Pets%20usually,them%20his%20brothers%20and%20sisters.

Harrod, Howard. 2000. *The Animals Came Dancing: Native American Sacred Ecology and Animal Kinship*. Tucson: University of Arizona Press.

Humane Society of the United States: Facts and Faith. www.humanesociety.org/resources/facts-and-faith.

Lee, Chung-Ryoul, director. 2010. *Old Partner*, DVD Video. San Bruno, Calif.: YA Entertainment Holdings.

Stein, Jenny, director. 2012. *Peaceable Kingdom: The Journey Home*, DVD Video. Ithaca, N.Y.: Tribe of Heart.

26 Domestication and Religion

Nerissa Russell

Introduction

The categories "wild" and "domestic" may seem very natural to us, and they structure our relations with other animals. However, these categories did not exist prior to domestication, which created the wild as well as the domestic (Russell 2002, 2022b; Hodder 1990). Domestication thus transformed human relations with both wild and domestic animals, including the religious role of animals in human life.

Foragers—people who subsist on wild plants and animals—tend to view other animal species as equals. Their religions are often described as animistic: where spirits (as a loose term for variously conceived non-corporeal essences) animate humans, animals, and often other beings such as trees, landmarks, or supernatural persons (Harvey 2005). These spirits may take different forms, with bodies often seen as clothing that can be taken on and off, although the bodily clothing shapes one's perspective and thus one's understanding of the world. This underlying spiritual similarity enables communication between humans and other species (Descola 2014; Guenther 2020a, 2020b; Willerslev 2007; Viveiros de Castro 1998). Foragers relate to other animals as persons if they behave like persons, by interacting as persons do (Nadasdy 2007; Descola 2009; Hill 2013; Kenrick 2002). Hunters owe their prey respectful treatment, without which future prey will withhold themselves (Brightman 1993; Ingold 1994). These ways of perceiving and relating to animals resemble and to a large extent inspired current multispecies approaches that seek to decenter humans and place them on the same plane as other beings (Kirksey and Helmreich 2010; Pilaar Birch 2018). These relationships change with domestication.

Domestication

Animal domestication is a complex phenomenon that is difficult to define and fuzzy around the edges, partly because the term is applied to a wide range of human-animal relations, and partly because domestication has both biological and social aspects (Russell 2002, 2007; O'Connor 1997). I will simplify this somewhat here by focusing on livestock domestication: herding animals for their products. It is useful to distinguish *taming*, a relationship between an individual human and an individual animal, from *domestication*, a relationship between populations of humans and animals that persists across generations (Clutton-Brock 1994; Harris 1996; Hesse 1984; Lainé 2018). Taming of individual animals occurs in most societies; while it is a necessary first step, most taming does not lead to domestication. A prolonged, multigenerational relationship produces reproductive isolation and alters selective forces such that domesticated animals change

DOI: 10.4324/9781003324157-31

morphologically, genetically, and behaviorally (Clutton-Brock 1992; Bökönyi 1989; Trut and Kharlamova 2020; Price 1984; Tchernov and Horwitz 1991; Zeder 2017). In these biological terms, domestication is not a state but a process; for livestock, it is an ongoing adaptation to the conditions of herding (Clutton-Brock 1992; Bökönyi 1969; Losey 2022).

However, domestication or herding is also a social relationship between sentient beings with profound consequences for both partners. I argue that domestication in this sense, while it may come about gradually and takes different forms, creates a starker divide. The point at which animals are converted into property marks a major change in both human-animal and human-human relations (Ducos 1978, 1989; Russell 2002). This transition is more important socially and religiously than the biological aspects of domestication. Animals owned by humans are treated not as equals but more as perpetual children or in the worst case as objects. Herders owe their livestock care and protection so that they will thrive and multiply, reversing the roles of human and animal in foraging relations (Armstrong Oma 2010; Ingold 1994). Danny Naveh and Nurit Bird-David (2014) document the appearance of this distinction among the Nayaka of southern India. Until the late twentieth century, the Nayaka were foragers with an animistic understanding of their world. They treated other animals as persons with whom they formed relationships. External forces have more recently pushed the Nayaka into farming, including keeping livestock. While they still generally treat wild animals as sentient, relational beings, they regard the livestock they own as purely utilitarian things.

On the other hand, domestic animals are the primary offerings in animal sacrifice cross-culturally, often for the reason that one can only offer what one owns (Ingold 1987; Smith 1987). Moreover, to the extent that sacrificial victims serve as a substitute or messenger for the sacrificer, they must be tightly linked by ownership and care (Abbink 2003). Domestic livestock play a major role in human-human relations as a store of wealth and medium of exchange. Humans create and maintain relationships through these exchanges, and the accumulation of concentrated wealth in herds may exacerbate inequality (Ingold 1980; Sherratt 1982; Schneider 1981; Orton 2010; Herskovits 1926).

Animal Domestication in the Southwest Asian Neolithic

The dog is the first domesticate, appearing in the late Pleistocene prior to plant agriculture in one or more parts of Eurasia (Germonpré et al. 2018; Perri 2016; Tchernov and Valla 1997). Livestock domestication follows plant cultivation and on present evidence occurred earliest in the Fertile Crescent region of Southwest Asia. While the process was extended and complex, there is good evidence for herding of sheep, goats, cattle, and pigs by ca. 10,500 calBP at least in the middle and upper Euphrates Valley region (Arbuckle 2018; Peters et al. 2013). Since this is about 5000 years before the first written records, we must study the process of domestication using the methods of archaeology, specifically zooarchaeology: the study of animal remains from archaeological sites (Reitz and Wing 2008; O'Connor 2000).

Morphological domestication, the physical results of adaptation to the conditions of herding, is visible in the skeleton as smaller size, reduced sexual dimorphism, smaller canines in pigs, and changes in horn shape and size (Helmer et al. 2005; Meadow 1989). When humans are providing protection from predators and controlling breeding, there is little benefit to greater size or larger tusks and horns for either mating competition or defense, while the denser flocks and more limited movement associated with herding advantage smaller animals that need less food (Tchernov and Horwitz 1991). However, these morphological changes will occur later than the beginning of herding; with the loose herding systems that likely characterized early husbandry, it might have been substantially later.

The main line of evidence for early herding is demographic analysis of the age and sex patterns in culling choices (which individuals are selected for slaughter). This analysis is not straightforward since there are many different hunting as well as herding strategies that generate differing and sometimes overlapping culling patterns. In general, however, hunters are more likely to kill adult males. In most wild herd animals, the males are larger, and often range further and take more risks than females with offspring, so that hunters are more likely to encounter them. In some cases, hunters may practice a form of wildlife management to preserve wild populations that targets males and spares females and immature animals to avoid reducing reproduction. Thus, hunted assemblages are usually dominated by adults and, among the adults, at least somewhat by males. (Generally, only adults can be sexed osteologically.)

Herders, on the other hand, need to preserve their breeding stock of mostly adult females and a few adult males; many males can be disruptive in a herd. Herders also need to tend and feed their animals, which makes adults and near-adults expensive to maintain since they eat more but add little weight. As a result, herders tend to cull younger animals, especially those that are approaching full size, and they differentially target juvenile males. Archaeological remains of herded animals, therefore, tend to have many young animals, and the adults are mostly female (Bökönyi 1969; Ducos 1993; Hesse 1982; Zeder and Hesse 2000).

Other lines of evidence can also be brought to bear. Stable isotope analysis of animal bones can give a rough idea of diet and may reveal foddering (the provision of stored food such as hay or grain) by humans, and dental microwear also provides dietary information (Hongo, Kikuchi, and Nasu 2021; Makarewicz and Tuross 2012; Mainland 1998). Herding tends to produce higher incidences of pathologies related to diet than are found in wild populations, which are more prone to traumatic injury; some of these conditions cause visible alterations in the bones (Davies 2005; Dobney et al. 2004; Zimmermann et al. 2018). Combining multiple lines of evidence builds a stronger case than any single analysis, especially when one can study changing patterns through time at one settlement or in a local area.

Domestication and Religion in Neolithic Southwest Asia

The period when herding was widely adopted in the Fertile Crescent, known in parts of the region as the Pre-Pottery Neolithic B (PPNB), was a time of substantial changes (Bar-Yosef and Meadow 1995; Verhoeven 2004). Plant agriculture and herding combined to form a mixed farming system that rapidly spread through the Fertile Crescent and soon surged beyond it to northern Africa, South Asia, and Europe (Baird et al. 2018; Bogaard 2005; Dunne et al. 2018; Meadow 1998). Human populations grew rapidly, reflected in both more and larger settlements, with for the first time a few very large mega-villages with thousands of inhabitants (Verhoeven 2006). In most places, round houses were replaced by rectangular ones, which could be more easily adjusted through additions or blocked rooms to match changing household sizes (Duru et al. 2021; Flannery 1972; Özdoğan 2010; Peltenburg 2004; Wilkins 2009).

Religions also seem to have changed, although not in the ways one might expect. The art of early farmers in Southwest Asia is bereft of scenes of plant agriculture or animal herding. Rather, especially in the northern Fertile Crescent, a region that increasingly appears to be a leader in this transition, images of wild animals become more prominent than before. The animals featured vary among local areas, although some, such as wild cattle (aurochsen), leopards, and vultures make widespread appearances. The media in which the animals are represented also vary geographically, from carvings on massive stone pillars to engravings on small plaques, designs on stone bowls, clay moldings, and paintings on interior walls. Most of these depictions appear to be associated with rituals and some appear in public buildings typically interpreted as shrines or temples. The newly-created category of "the Wild" was apparently of much greater religious interest in these contexts than the equally new herds (Hodder and Meskell 2011; Schmidt 2012; Benz and Bauer 2015; Stordeur 2010; Russell and Meece 2006).

Aurochsen held symbolic importance throughout the area. Larger than most present-day domestic cattle and with impressively long horns on the bulls, they would have been imposing and dangerous to hunt. They were often the centerpiece of feasts that could have fed hundreds or even thousands of people (Meier, Nigel Goring-Morris, and Munro 2017; Twiss 2008; Russell and Martin 2005). Especially in the northern Fertile Crescent and Central Anatolia, the remains of aurochsen, particularly the skulls and horns and scapulae (shoulder blades), held enduring religious power that was incorporated into houses and public buildings. Some of these bones were concealed in the walls or benches of buildings or buried beneath the floors (Russell, Martin, and Twiss 2009; Russell 2023; Stordeur 2010). Others, especially skulls with horns or frontlets (horns with connecting skull portion) were displayed mounted on walls or built into benches and pillars (Mellaart 1967; Russell and Meece 2006; Twiss and Russell 2009).

The special treatment of wild cattle skulls parallels that of human skulls in much of the region. Most spectacularly in the Southern Levant (western Fertile Crescent), where selected human skulls were plastered with life-like features and displayed before reburial, but also in the northern Fertile Crescent and Central Anatolia, human skulls were sometimes removed from the body and given special treatment (Bocquentin, Kodaş, and Ortiz 2016; Bonogofsky 2006; Croucher 2012, 2019; Haddow and Knüsel 2017; Santana Cabrera et al. 2012; Talalay 2004). The details of the treatment of these skulls varied regionally and locally, and their purpose may have as well. However, the special attention to skulls of both humans and cattle, and their display and burial, often in houses, do suggest a belief in some form of spiritual power that resides in the head and remains there after death. Often this power is associated with human ancestors (Bienert 1991; Croucher 2012; Cauvin 2000), and in Central Anatolia where such treatment of cattle skulls is most prominent, cattle may have been considered ancestors as well (Russell 2022a).

Special treatment of human skulls is most elaborate in the PPNB, when livestock herding was practiced throughout the region, but it is wild animal heads that receive similar treatment. The religious importance of wild cattle was so great in Central Anatolia that Neolithic inhabitants resisted adopting domestic cattle (although they did herd domestic sheep and goats) for about 500 years after domestic cattle skipped over this area and were herded to the west. When they were finally adopted at Çatalhöyük in Central Anatolia, this choice appears to have been contested, with a dramatic increase in displays of aurochs remains in some houses (Arbuckle 2013; Arbuckle et al. 2014; Russell 2022a).

Conclusion

This brief overview of animal domestication in Southwest Asia gives some sense of the variability of the process within one region, as well as the social upheaval and dramatic changes in religions that accompanied the conversion of animals into property. Livestock were domesticated independently in other parts of the world, notably China (Dodson and Dong 2016) and the Andean region (Capriles and Tripcevich 2016; Rosenfeld 2014), introducing further variation. Recent scholarship has defined multiple pathways to domestication in terms of human-animal relations, some more symbiotic/commensal, others more intentional (Zeder 2012). There are also common elements, however. In most if not all cases, livestock domestication follows plant agriculture. Domestic animals soon appear in ritual and sacrificial contexts. In all cases, ownership of animals and the creation of separate wild and domestic spheres have profound consequences for human relations with other animals, the natural world, and each other, and thus also for their religions.

References

Abbink, Jon. 2003. "Love and Death of Cattle: The Paradox in Suri Attitudes Toward Livestock." *Ethnos* 68 (3): 341–64. https://doi.org/10.1080/0014184032000134487.

Arbuckle, Benjamin S. 2013. "The Late Adoption of Cattle and Pig Husbandry in Neolithic Central Turkey." *Journal of Archaeological Science* 40 (4): 1805–15. https://doi.org/http://dx.doi.org/10.1016/j.jas.2012.12.008.

———. 2018. "Early History of Animal Domestication in Southwest Asia." In *Oxford Research Encyclopedia of Environmental Science*, edited by Hank H. Shugart, Jr. Oxford: Oxford University Press. https://doi.org/10.1093/acrefore/9780199389414.013.548.

———, Sarah W. Kansa, Eric C. Kansa, David C. Orton, Canan Çakırlar, Lionel Gourichon, A. Levent Atıcı, Alfred Galik, Arkadiusz Marciniak, Jacqueline A. Mulville, Hijlke Buitenhuis, Denise Carruthers, Béatrice De Cupere, G. Arzu Demirergi, Sheelagh Frame, Daniel Helmer, Louise Martin, Joris Peters, Nadja Pöllath, Kamilla Pawłowska, Nerissa Russell, Katheryn C. Twiss, and Doris Würtenberger. 2014. "Data Sharing Reveals Complexity in the Spread of Domestic Animals Westward Across Neolithic Turkey." *PLoS One* 9 (6): e99845. https://doi.org/doi:10.1371/journal.pone.0099845.

Armstrong Oma, Kristin. 2010. "Between Trust and Domination: Social Contracts Between Humans and Animals." *World Archaeology* 42 (2): 175–87. https://doi.org/https://doi.org/10.1080/00438241003672724.

Baird, Douglas, Andrew S. Fairbairn, Emma Jenkins, Louise Martin, Caroline Middleton, Jessica A. Pearson, Eleni Asouti, Yvonne H. Edwards, Ceren Kabukcu, Gökhan Mustafaoğlu, Nerissa Russell, Ofer Bar-Yosef, Geraldine Jacobsen, Xiaohong Wu, Ambroise G. Baker, and Sarah Elliott. 2018. "Agricultural Origins on the Anatolian Plateau." *Proceedings of the National Academy of Sciences* 115 (14): E3077–86. https://doi.org/10.1073/pnas.1800163115.

Bar-Yosef, Ofer, and Richard H. Meadow. 1995. "The Origins of Agriculture in the Near East." In *Last Hunters—First Farmers: New Perspectives on the Prehistoric Transition to Agriculture*, edited by T. Douglas Price and Anne Birgitte Gebauer, 39–94. Santa Fe, N.M.: School of American Research Press.

Benz, Marion, and Joachim Bauer. 2015. "On Scorpions, Birds, and Snakes—Evidence for Shamanism in Northern Mesopotamia During the Early Holocene." *Journal of Ritual Studies* 29 (2): 1–23. www.jstor.org/stable/44735499.

Bienert, Hans-Dieter. 1991. "Skull Cult in the Prehistoric Near East." *Journal of Prehistoric Religion* 5: 9–23.

Bocquentin, Fanny, Ergül Kodaş, and Anabel Ortiz. 2016. "Headless But Still Eloquent! Acephalous Skeletons as Witnesses of Pre-Pottery Neolithic North-South Levant Connections and Disconnections." *Paléorient* 42 (2): 33–52. www.jstor.org.proxy.library.cornell.edu/stable/44653800.

Bogaard, Amy. 2005. "'Garden Agriculture' and the Nature of Early Farming in Europe and the Near East." *World Archaeology* 37 (2): 177–96. https://doi.org/10.1080/00438240500094572.

Bökönyi, Sándor. 1969. "Archaeological Problems and Methods of Recognizing Animal Domestication." In *The Domestication and Exploitation of Plants and Animals*, edited by Peter J. Ucko and Geoffrey W. Dimbleby, 219–29. London: Duckworth.

———. 1989. "Definitions of Animal Domestication." In *The Walking Larder: Patterns of Domestication, Pastoralism, and Predation*, edited by Juliet Clutton-Brock, 22–27. London: Unwin Hyman.

Bonogofsky, Michelle. 2006. "Cultural and Ritual Evidence in the Archaeological Record: Modeled Skulls from the Ancient Near East." In *The Archaeology of Cult and Death*, edited by Mercourios Georgiadis and Chrysanthi Gallou, 45–70. Budapest: Archaeolingua.

Brightman, Robert A. 1993. *Grateful Prey: Rock Cree Human-Animal Relationships*. Berkeley: University of California Press.

Capriles, José M., and Nicholas Tripcevich, eds. 2016. *The Archaeology of Andean Pastoralism*. Albuquerque: University of New Mexico Press.

Cauvin, Jacques. 2000. *The Birth of the Gods and the Origins of Agriculture*. Cambridge: Cambridge University Press.

Clutton-Brock, Juliet. 1992. "The Process of Domestication." *Mammal Review* 22 (2): 79–85.

———. 1994. "The Unnatural World: Behavioural Aspects of Humans and Animals in the Process of Domestication." In *Animals and Human Society: Changing Perspectives*, edited by Aubrey Manning and James A. Serpell, 23–35. London: Routledge.

Croucher, Karina. 2012. *Death and Dying in the Neolithic Near East*. Oxford: Oxford University Press.

———. 2019. "Plastered Skulls: Evidence of Grief and Mourning?" In *Human Iconography and Symbolic Meaning in Near Eastern Prehistory*, edited by Jörg Becker, Claudia Beuger, and Bernd Müller-Neuhof, 85–96. Vienna: Austrian Academy of Sciences Press.

Davies, Jessica J. 2005. "Oral Pathology, Nutritional Deficiencies and Mineral Depletion in Domesticates—A Literature Review." In *Diet and Health in Past Animal Populations: Current Research and Future Directions*, edited by Jessica J. Davies, Marian Fabiš, Ingrid L. Mainland, Michael P. Richards, and Richard M. Thomas, 80–88. Oxford: Oxbow.

Descola, Philippe. 2009. "Human Natures." *Social Anthropology* 17 (2): 145–57. https://doi.org/10.1111/j.1469-8676.2009.00063.x.

———. 2014. "Modes of Being and Forms of Predication." *Hau* 4 (1): 271–80. https://doi.org/10.14318/hau4.1.012.

Dobney, Keith M., Anton Ervynck, Umberto Albarella, and Peter A. Rowley-Conwy. 2004. "The Chronology and Frequency of a Stress Marker (Linear Enamel Hypoplasia) in Recent and Archaeological Populations of *Sus scrofa* in North-West Europe, and the Effects of Early Domestication." *Journal of Zoology* 264 (2): 197–208.

Dodson, John R., and Guanghui Dong. 2016. "What Do We Know About Domestication in Eastern Asia?" *Quaternary International* 426: 2–9. https://doi.org/10.1016/j.quaint.2016.04.005.

Ducos, Pierre. 1978. "'Domestication' Defined and Methodological Approaches to Its Recognition in Faunal Assemblages." In *Approaches to Faunal Analysis in the Middle East*, edited by Richard H. Meadow and Melinda A. Zeder, 49–52. Cambridge: Peabody Museum, Harvard University.

———. 1989. "Defining Domestication: A Clarification." In *The Walking Larder: Patterns of Domestication, Pastoralism, and Predation*, edited by Juliet Clutton-Brock, 28–30. London: Unwin Hyman.

———. 1993. "Fawns, Kids and Lambs." In *Skeletons in Her Cupboard: Festschrift for Juliet Clutton-Brock*, edited by Anneke T. Clason, Sebastian Payne, and Hans-Peter Uerpmann, 85–90. Oxford: Oxbow.

Dunne, Julie, Savino di Lernia, Marek Chłodnicki, Farid Kherbouche, and Richard P. Evershed. 2018. "Timing and Pace of Dairying Inception and Animal Husbandry Practices Across Holocene North Africa." *Quaternary International* 471 (A): 147–59. https://doi.org/10.1016/j.quaint.2017.06.062.

Duru, Güneş, Mihriban Özbaşaran, Sera Yelözer, Melis Uzdurum, and Ian Kuijt. 2021. "Space Making and Home Making in the World's First Villages: Reconsidering the Circular to Rectangular Architectural Transition in the Central Anatolian Neolithic." *Journal of Anthropological Archaeology* 64: 101357. https://doi.org/10.1016/j.jaa.2021.101357.

Flannery, Kent V. 1972. "The Origins of the Village as a Settlement Type in Mesoamerica and the Near East: A Comparative Study." In *Man, Settlement and Urbanism*, edited by Peter J. Ucko, Ruth E. Tringham, and Geoffrey W. Dimbleby, 23–53. London: Duckworth.

Germonpré, Mietje, Martina Lázničková-Galetová, Mikhail V. Sablin, and Hervé Bocherens. 2018. "Self-Domestication or Human Control? The Upper Palaeolithic Domestication of the Wolf." In *Hybrid Communities: Biosocial Approaches to Domestication and Other Trans-species Relationships*, edited by Charles Stépanoff and Jean-Denis Vigne, 39–64. London: Routledge.

Guenther, Mathias J. 2020a. *Human-Animal Relationships in San and Hunter-Gatherer Cosmology, Vol. I: Therianthropes and Transformation.* Cham: Springer International Publishing.

———. 2020b. *Human-Animal Relationships in San and Hunter-Gatherer Cosmology, Vol. II: Imagining and Experiencing Ontological Mutability.* Cham: Springer International Publishing.

Haddow, Scott D., and Christopher J. Knüsel. 2017. "Skull Retrieval and Secondary Burial Practices in the Neolithic Near East: Recent Insights from Çatalhöyük, Turkey." *Bioarchaeology International* 1 (1–2): 52–71. https://doi.org/10.5744/bi.2017.1002.

Harris, David R. 1996. "Domesticatory Relationships of People, Plants and Animals." In *Redefining Nature: Ecology, Culture and Domestication*, edited by Roy F. Ellen and Katsuyoshi Fukui, 437–63. Oxford: Berg.

Harvey, Graham. 2005. *Animism: Respecting the Living World.* New York: Columbia University Press.

Helmer, Daniel, Lionel Gourichon, Hervé Monchot, Joris Peters, and Maria Saña Seguí. 2005. "Identifying Early Domestic Cattle from Pre-Pottery Neolithic Sites on the Middle Euphrates Using Sexual Dimorphism." In *The First Steps of Animal Domestication*, edited by Jean-Denis Vigne, Joris Peters, and Daniel Helmer, 86–95. Oxford: Oxbow.

Herskovits, Melville J. 1926. "The Cattle Complex in East Africa." *American Anthropologist* 28: 230–72, 361–80, 494–528, 633–64.

Hesse, Brian C. 1982. "Slaughter Patterns and Domestication: The Beginnings of Pastoralism in Western Iran." *Man* (n.s.) 17: 403–17.

———. 1984. "These Are Our Goats: The Origins of Herding in West Central Iran." In *Animals and Archaeology: 3. Early Herders and Their Flocks*, edited by Juliet Clutton-Brock and Caroline Grigson, 243–64. Oxford: British Archaeological Reports.

Hill, Erica. 2013. "Archaeology and Animal Persons: Toward a Prehistory of Human-Animal Relations." *Environment and Society: Advances in Research* 4 (1): 117–36.

Hodder, Ian. 1990. *The Domestication of Europe: Structure and Contingency in Neolithic Societies.* Oxford: Basil Blackwell.

———, and Lynn Meskell. 2011. "A 'Curious and Sometimes a Trifle Macabre Artistry.'" *Current Anthropology* 52 (2): 235–63. https://doi.org/10.1086/659250.

Hongo, Hitomi, Hiroki Kikuchi, and Hiroo Nasu. 2021. "Beginning of Pig Management in Neolithic China: Comparison of Domestication Processes between Northern and Southern Regions." *Animal Frontiers* 11 (3): 30–42. https://doi.org/10.1093/af/vfab021.

Ingold, Tim. 1980. *Hunters, Pastoralists, and Ranchers: Reindeer Economies and Their Transformations.* Cambridge: Cambridge University Press.

———. 1987. *The Appropriation of Nature: Essays on Human Ecology and Social Relations.* Iowa City: University of Iowa Press.

———. 1994. "From Trust to Domination: An Alternative History of Human-Animal Relations." In *Animals and Human Society: Changing Perspectives*, edited by Aubrey Manning and James A. Serpell, 1–22. London: Routledge.

Kenrick, Justin. 2002. "Anthropology and Anthropocentrism: Images of Hunter-Gatherers, Westerners and the Environment." In *Self- and Other-Images of Hunter-Gatherers*, edited by Henry Stewart, Alan Barnard, and Keiichi Omura, 191–214. Osaka: National Museum of Ethnology.

Kirksey, S. Eben, and Stefan Helmreich. 2010. "The Emergence of Multispecies Ethnography." *Cultural Anthropology* 25 (4): 545–76. https://doi.org/10.1111/j.1548-1360.2010.01069.x.

Lainé, Nicolas. 2018. "Why Did the Khamti Not Domesticate Their Elephants? Building a Hybrid Sociality with Tamed Elephants." In *Hybrid Communities: Biosocial Approaches to Domestication and Other Trans-Species Relationships*, edited by Charles Stépanoff and Jean-Denis Vigne, 221–34. London: Routledge.

Losey, Robert J. 2022. "Domestication Is Not an Ancient Moment of Selection for Prosociality: Insights from Dogs and Modern Humans." *Journal of Social Archaeology* 22 (2): 131–48. https://doi.org/10.1177/14696053211055475.

Mainland, Ingrid L. 1998. "Dental Microwear and Diet in Domestic Sheep (*Ovis aries*) and Goats (*Capra hircus*): Distinguishing Grazing and Fodder-Fed Ovicaprids Using a Quantitative Analytical Approach." *Journal of Archaeological Science* 25 (12): 1259–71.

Makarewicz, Cheryl A., and Noreen Tuross. 2012. "Finding Fodder and Tracking Transhumance: Isotopic Detection of Goat Domestication Processes in the Near East." *Current Anthropology* 53 (4): 495–505. https://doi.org/10.1086/665829.

Meadow, Richard H. 1989. "Osteological Evidence for the Process of Animal Domestication." In *The Walking Larder: Patterns of Domestication, Pastoralism, and Predation*, edited by Juliet Clutton-Brock, 80–90. London: Unwin Hyman.

———. 1998. "Pre- and Proto-Historic Agricultural and Pastoral Transformations in Northwestern South Asia." *The Review of Archaeology* 19 (2): 12–21.

Meier, Jacqueline S., A. Nigel Goring-Morris, and Natalie D. Munro. 2017. "Aurochs Bone Deposits at Kfar HaHoresh and the Southern Levant across the Agricultural Transition." *Antiquity* 91 (360): 1469–83. https://doi.org/10.15184/aqy.2017.179.

Mellaart, James. 1967. *Çatal Hüyük: A Neolithic Town in Anatolia*. London: Thames & Hudson.

Nadasdy, Paul. 2007. "The Gift in the Animal: The Ontology of Hunting and Human-Animal Sociality." *American Ethnologist* 34 (1): 25–43.

Naveh, Danny, and Nurit H. Bird-David. 2014. "How Persons Become Things: Economic and Epistemological Changes Among Nayaka Hunter-Gatherers." *Journal of the Royal Anthropological Institute* 20 (1): 74–92. https://doi.org/10.1111/1467-9655.12080.

O'Connor, Terence P. 1997. "Working at Relationships: Another Look at Animal Domestication." *Antiquity* 71 (271): 149–56.

———. 2000. *The Archaeology of Animal Bones*. College Station: Texas A&M University Press.

Orton, David C. 2010. "Both Subject and Object: Herding, Inalienability and Sentient Property in Prehistory." *World Archaeology* 42 (2): 188–200. https://doi.org/10.1080/00438241003672773.

Özdoğan, Mehmet. 2010. "Transition from the Round-Plan to Rectangular: Reconsidering the Evidence of Çayönü." In *Neolithic and Chalcolithic Architecture in Eurasia: Techniques and Spatial Organisation*, edited by Dragoş Gheorghiu, 29–34. Oxford: Archaeopress.

Peltenburg, Edgar J. 2004. "Social Space in Early Sedentary Communities of Southwest Asia and Cyprus." In *Neolithic Revolution: New Perspectives on Southwest Asia in Light of Recent Discoveries on Cyprus*, edited by Edgar J. Peltenburg and Alexander Wasse, 71–89. Oxford: Oxbow.

Perri, Angela R. 2016. "A Wolf in Dog's Clothing: Initial Dog Domestication and Pleistocene Wolf Variation." *Journal of Archaeological Science* 68: 1–4. https://doi.org/10.1016/j.jas.2016.02.003.

Peters, Joris, Hijlke Buitenhuis, Gisela Grupe, Klaus Schmidt, and Nadja Pöllath. 2013. "The Long and Winding Road: Ungulate Exploitation and Domestication in Early Neolithic Anatolia (10,000–7,000 cal BC)." In *The Origins and Spread of Domestic Animals in Southwest Asia and Europe*, edited by Susan M. Colledge, James Conolly, Keith M. Dobney, Kate Manning, and Stephen J. Shennan, 83–114. Walnut Creek, Calif.: Left Coast Press.

Pilaar Birch, Suzanne E., ed. 2018. *Multispecies Archaeology*. Abingdon: Routledge.

Price, Edward O. 1984. "Behavioral Aspects of Animal Domestication." *Quarterly Review of Biology* 59 (1): 1–32. https://doi.org/10.2307/2827868.

Reitz, Elizabeth J., and Elizabeth S. Wing. 2008. *Zooarchaeology*. 2nd ed. Cambridge: Cambridge University Press.

Rosenfeld, Silvana A. 2014. "Guinea Pig: Domestication." In *Encyclopedia of Global Archaeology*, edited by Claire Smith, 3172–75. New York: Springer.

Russell, Nerissa. 2002. "The Wild Side of Animal Domestication." *Society and Animals* 10 (3): 285–302.

_____. 2007. "The Domestication of Anthropology." In *Where the Wild Things Are Now: Domestication Reconsidered*, edited by Rebecca Cassidy and Molly H. Mullin, 27–48. Oxford: Berg.

_____. 2022a. "Cattle for the Ancestors at Neolithic Çatalhöyük, Turkey." In *Cattle and People: Interdisciplinary Approaches to an Ancient Relationship*, edited by Elizabeth Wright and Catarina Ginja, 225–40. Columbus, Ga.: Lockwood Press.

_____. 2022b. "Wild Meets Domestic in the Near Eastern Neolithic." *Animals* 12 (18): 2335. https://doi.org/10.3390/ani12182335.

_____. 2023. "Resting on Strong Shoulders: The Power of Animal Scapulae in the Near Eastern Neolithic." In *The Bloomsbury Handbook of Material Religion in the Ancient Near East and Egypt*, edited by Nicola Laneri and Sharon R. Steadman, 289–304. London: Bloomsbury.

_____, and Louise Martin. 2005. "The Çatalhöyük Mammal Remains." In *Inhabiting Çatalhöyük: Reports from the 1995–1999 Seasons*, edited by Ian Hodder, 33–98. Cambridge: McDonald Institute for Archaeological Research.

_____, and Stephanie Meece. 2006. "Animal Representations and Animal Remains at Çatalhöyük." In *Çatalhöyük Perspectives: Reports from the 1995–99 Seasons*, edited by Ian Hodder, 209–30. Cambridge: McDonald Institute for Archaeological Research.

_____, and Katheryn C. Twiss. 2009. "Building Memories: Commemorative Deposits at Çatalhöyük." In *Zooarchaeology and the Reconstruction of Cultural Systems: Case Studies from the Old World*, edited by Benjamin S. Arbuckle, Cheryl A. Makarewicz, and A. Levent Atici, 103–25. Paris: L'Homme et l'Animal, Société de Recherche Interdisciplinaire.

Santana Cabrera, Jonathan, Javier Velasco, Juan José Ibáñez Estevez, and Frank Braemer. 2012. "Crania with Mutilated Facial Skeletons: A New Ritual Treatment in an Early Pre-Pottery Neolithic B Cranial Cache at Tell Qarassa North (South Syria)." *American Journal of Physical Anthropology* 149 (2): 205–16. https://doi.org/10.1002/ajpa.22111.

Schmidt, Klaus. 2012. *Göbekli Tepe: A Stone Age Sanctuary in South-Eastern Anatolia*. Berlin: Ex Oriente.

Schneider, Harold K. 1981. "Livestock as Food and Money." In *The Future of Pastoral Peoples*, edited by John G. Galaty, D. Aronson, Philip C. Salzman, and A. Chouinard, 210–23. Ottawa: International Development Research Centre.

Sherratt, Andrew G. 1982. "Mobile Resources: Settlement and Exchange in Early Agricultural Europe." In *Ranking, Resource and Exchange: Aspects of the Archaeology of Early European Society*, edited by A. Colin Renfrew and Stephen J. Shennan, 13–26. Cambridge: Cambridge University Press.

Smith, Jonathan Z. 1987. "The Domestication of Sacrifice." In *Violent Origins: Ritual Killing and Cultural Formation*, edited by Robert G. Hamerton-Kelly, 191–235. Stanford, Calif.: Stanford University Press.

Stordeur, Danielle. 2010. "Domestication of Plants and Animals, Domestication of Symbols?" In *The Development of Pre-State Communities in the Ancient Near East: Studies in Honour of Edgar Peltenburg*, edited by Diane L. Bolger and Louise C. Maguire, 123–30. Oxford: Oxbow Books.

Talalay, Lauren E. 2004. "Heady Business: Skulls, Heads, and Decapitation in Neolithic Anatolia and Greece." *Journal of Mediterranean Archaeology* 17 (2): 139–63.

Tchernov, Eitan, and Liora R.K. Horwitz. 1991. "Body Size Diminution under Domestication: Unconscious Selection in Primeval Domesticates." *Journal of Anthropological Archaeology* 10 (1): 54–75.

Tchernov, Eitan, and François R. Valla. 1997. "Two New Dogs, and Other Natufian Dogs, from the Southern Levant." *Journal of Archaeological Science* 24 (1): 65–95.

Trut, Lyudmila N., and Anastasiya V. Kharlamova. 2020. "Domestication as a Process Generating Phenotypic Diversity." In *Phenotypic Switching*, edited by Herbert Levine, Mohit Kumar Jolly, Prakash Kulkarni, and Vidyanand Nanjundiah, 511–26. London: Academic Press.

Twiss, Katheryn C. 2008. "Transformations in an Early Agricultural Society: Feasting in the Southern Levantine Pre-Pottery Neolithic." *Journal of Anthropological Archaeology* 27 (4): 418–42.

_____, and Nerissa Russell. 2009. "Taking the Bull by the Horns: Ideology, Masculinity, and Cattle Horns at Çatalhöyük (Turkey)." *Paléorient* 35 (2): 19–32. www.persee.fr/doc/paleo_0153-9345_2009_num_35_2_5296.

Verhoeven, Marc. 2004. "Beyond Boundaries: Nature, Culture and a Holistic Approach to Domestication in the Levant." *Journal of World Prehistory* 18 (3): 179–282.

_____. 2006. "Megasites in the Jordanian Pre-Pottery Neolithic B: Evidence for 'Proto-urbanism'?" In *Domesticating Space: Construction, Community, and Cosmology in the Late Prehistoric Near East*, edited by Edward B. Banning and Michael Chazan, 75–79. Berlin: Ex Oriente.

Viveiros de Castro, Eduardo. 1998. "Cosmological Deixis and Amerindian Perspectivism." *Journal of the Royal Anthropological Institute* 4 (3): 469–88. www.jstor.org/stable/3034157.

Wilkins, Helen. 2009. "Transitional Change in Proto-Buildings: A Quantitative Study of Thermal Behaviour and Its Relationship with Social Functionality." *Journal of Archaeological Science* 36 (1): 150–56. https://doi.org/10.1016/j.jas.2008.07.017.

Willerslev, Rane. 2007. *Soul Hunters: Hunting, Animism, and Personhood Among the Siberian Yukaghirs*. Berkeley: University of California Press.

Zeder, Melinda A. 2012. "The Domestication of Animals." *Journal of Anthropological Research* 68 (2): 161–90.

_____. 2017. "Domestication as a Model System for the Extended Evolutionary Synthesis." *Interface Focus* 7 (5). http://rsfs.royalsocietypublishing.org/content/7/5/20160133.

_____, and Brian C. Hesse. 2000. "The Initial Domestication of Goats (*Capra hircus*) in the Zagros Mountains 10,000 Years Ago." *Science* 287 (5461): 2254–57.

Zimmermann, Michaela I., Nadja Pöllath, Mihriban Özbaşaran, and Joris Peters. 2018. "Joint Health in Free-Ranging and Confined Small Bovids—Implications for Early Stage Caprine Management." *Journal of Archaeological Science* 92: 13–27. https://doi.org/10.1016/j.jas.2018.02.004.

Other Recommended Resources

Barker, Graeme W.W. 2006. *The Agricultural Revolution in Prehistory: Why Did Foragers Become Farmers?* Oxford: Oxford University Press.

Descola, Philippe. 2013. *Beyond Nature and Culture*. Chicago, Ill.: University of Chicago Press.

Hodder, Ian. 2011. "The Role of Religion in the Neolithic of the Middle East and Anatolia with Particular Reference to Çatalhöyük." *Paléorient* 37 (1): 111–22.

Price, Edward O. 2002. *Animal Domestication and Behavior*. New York: CAB International.

Russell, Nerissa. 2012. *Social Zooarchaeology: Humans and Animals in Prehistory*. New York: Cambridge University Press.

Simmons, Alan H. 2007. *The Neolithic Revolution in the Near East: Transforming the Human Landscape*. Tucson: University of Arizona Press.

Sykes, Naomi J. 2014. *Beastly Questions: Animal Answers to Archaeological Issues*. New York: Bloomsbury Academic.

Vigne, Jean-Denis. 2015. "Early Domestication and Farming: What Should We Know or Do for a Better Understanding?" *Anthropozoologica* 50 (2): 123–50. http://dx.doi.org/10.5252/az2015n2a5.

27 The Ethics of Eating Animals
Jewish Responses

Aaron S. Gross

Eating Animals as Universally Fraught

A basic fact of human religious life is that killing and eating animals for food is not taken lightly. It is invariably the subject of intense regulations and often the subject of energetic disagreement (Ingold 1988). Cross-cultural anthropological studies have revealed that of all known human activities regarding food, none generate more taboos than the consumption of meat, especially the meat of larger animals (Fessler and Navarrete 2003). If you doubt the strength of these meat taboos today or think we have moved past such thinking, imagine inviting your neighbors over to barbeque a dog or cat and the reactions you might get.

Food in general is always bound to identity (Gross 2019), but not all foods are of equal importance. Meat consistently influences people's sense of identity more than other foods (Belasco 2008, 11–12). As we will see, Jewish traditions are no exception.

The fact that meat plays an outsized role in human identity is one of the most secure facts of food studies, but explaining why this is so is more complicated. Much of the answer lies in the fact that meat comes from beings who share important similarities with humans, especially the capacity to suffer in many of the same ways humans do. There is widespread evidence of a general human discomfort with killing animals (Burkert 1983, 12–22, 1996, 150; Frazer and Gaster 1959, 471–479; Ingold [2000] 2008, 69; Milgrom 1991, 712–13; Serpell 1996). Seeing animals in pain is difficult for most humans and one doesn't need to look far to see numerous examples of people moved to action by witnessing the plight of a suffering animal.[1] Humans may often choose to close off empathy with the animals we eat, but except for sociopaths, that empathy for the animal others is always there as a potentiality. It is simply a fact of human physiology that we have the brain structures and observational capacities to accurately identify some forms of animal suffering, to relate to them, and to care about them.

The spontaneous nature of human empathy for animals and the inevitable suffering bound to meat, even if it is minimized, makes meat *fraught* in culture generally and in religion in particular. Unsurprisingly, in all the so-called world religions[2]—Judaism, Christianity, Islam, Hinduism, Buddhism, Daoism, and so forth—passionate human disagreements and ethical debates continue to shape the practices that allow or restrict eating animals in the lives of particular communities today. These disagreements and ethical concerns show no sign of fading anytime soon, especially in the Jewish context (Labendz and Yanklowitz 2019).

The recent advent of factory farming has perhaps aggravated the tension between different human moral intuitions about the rightness or wrongness of eating animals.

DOI: 10.4324/9781003324157-32

The practices of factory farming pose serious challenges to traditional ideas about how animals should be treated that are only now being realized, let alone responded to, by religious institutions (Gross 2015). Factory farms are also a primary vector of zoonotic diseases—diseases carried into human populations by animals, as happened with the now infamous COVID-19 virus (which does not itself appear to come from factory farms). According to the CDC, "3 out of every 4 new or emerging infectious diseases in people come from animals" (CDC 2021; Wallace 2016). Sometimes new pathogens emerge directly on factory farms, especially in the poultry industry, but other times factory farms contribute to broader social and ecological conditions that indirectly support new pathogens (Upholt 2022; Wallace 2016).

This chapter will not further detail the nature of factory farming since good information on it is readily available (see "Other Recommended Resources" following). But as we turn to how Jews respond to this basic human predicament, it is worth noting that we do so in an era during which animals arguably suffer more acutely than ever before and in numbers that few conceived a generation ago (Foer 2009). As Yuval Noah Harari frames it, "If we accept a mere tenth of what animal rights activists are claiming, then modern industrial agriculture might well be the greatest crime in history" (Harari 2015). In the U.S. alone, we consume nearly nine billion chickens annually—more than one hundred times what Americans ate per capita roughly a century ago (Striffler 2005).

How do contemporary Jewish traditions respond to this universally common and fraught activity—eating animals—especially in an ethical register? Let us sketch a partial answer to this question by considering two stories: first, one told by contemporary Jewish novelist, Jonathan Safran Foer, in his 2009 nonfiction book critiquing the meat industry, *Eating Animals*—a book important enough to Foer that when he had a rare private audience with Pope Francis at the Vatican on October 5, 2023 in connection with his participation in the Vatican conference introducing the Pope's Apostolic Exhortation on the environment, *Laudate Deum*, he gave the Pope a copy of the book in Spanish (*Comer Animales*). Second, the biblical narrative about eating animals found in Genesis 1 and 9, what I will call the biblical story of meat. These two stories straddle an immense territory, from the popular appeal of contemporary nonfiction to the authoritative density of the Bible, and from the private sphere of one Jewish-American family's history to the communally held narratives of the Jewish textual tradition. Considering these stories can give us a feel for how Jews explore ethical questions, in this case about eating animals, through sharing and interpreting *stories*.

A Family Story: Foer's Opening to *Eating Animals*

Foer built his international reputation through his first novel, *Everything is Illuminated* (2002), which alternated between a fancifully imagined Eastern European Jewish past and a semi-autobiographical account of Foer's real-life confrontation with his past as the grandchild of a Holocaust survivor. The book was translated into more than thirty languages and won him the National Jewish Book Award. Foer's second novel, *Extremely Loud and Incredibly Close* (2005), also chose fictionalized autobiography as a vehicle and explored the psychological aftermath of the September 11 terrorist attack in New York City, where Foer still lives. Both books were published before Foer was thirty, leading *Newsweek* in 2006 to consider him one of a handful of young authors who serve as a "voice of this generation" (Grossman 2006). Both these books also contained sympathetic vegetarian characters, based in part on Foer himself, foreshadowing Foer's more serious turn to the issue of eating animals in his third book, also his first work of nonfiction, *Eating Animals*, in 2009.

Like his two previous novels, *Eating Animals* examined a form of distinctly modern, globally significant mass violence, in this case factory farming, which Foer defines as follows:

> Like pornography, factory farming is hard to define but easy to identify. In a narrow sense it is a system of industrialized and intensive agriculture in which animals—often housed by the tens or even hundreds of thousands—are genetically engineered, restricted in mobility, and fed unnatural diets (which almost always include various drugs, like antimicrobials). . . . Ninety-nine percent of all land animals eaten or used to produce milk and eggs in the United States are factory farmed. So although there are important exceptions, to speak about eating animals today is to speak about factory farming.
>
> (Foer 2009, 34)[3]

Eating Animals is part memoir, part exposé of the meat industry, and part philosophical reflection on the topic named in its title. Unlike most nonfiction authors addressing the situation in contemporary agriculture, however, Foer did not begin or end his book with an argument critiquing agriculture today (though he certainly gets to that in between). He opens and closes the book with chapters of the same title, "Storytelling," and it is stories, not the many important facts and arguments that Foer also relays, that dominate its opening.

Specifically, Foer opens with stories about his family life, especially his grandmother, a survivor of the Holocaust, and the tales she related to the family of her survival. "Then it all changed," his grandmother tells him, referring to the rise of Nazism:

> During the War it was hell on earth. . . . I was always running, day and night, because the Germans were always right behind me. If you stopped, you died. There was never enough food. I became sicker and sicker from not eating, and I'm not just talking about being skin and bones. I had sores all over my body. It became difficult to move.

These stories were the sacred stories of his family and by sharing them in this internationally bestselling book, they became sacred stories for many more. "Even at the worst times, there were good people, too," his grandmother continued.

> Someone taught me to tie the ends of my pants so I could fill the legs with any potatoes I was able to steal. I walked miles and miles like that, because you never knew when you would be lucky again. . . . You had to have luck and intuition.
>
> (Foer 2009, 16)

The story of his grandmother's survival in Nazi Europe reaches its crescendo at the end of the first chapter in the following exchange between Jonathan and his grandmother (Foer 2009, 16–17):

> The worst it got was near the end. A lot of people died right at the end, and I didn't know if I could make it another day. A farmer, a Russian, God bless him, he saw my condition, and he went into his house and came out with a piece of meat for me.

> "He saved your life."
> "I didn't eat it."

"You didn't eat it?"

"It was pork. I wouldn't eat pork."

"Why?"

"What do you mean why?"

"What, because it wasn't kosher?"

"Of course."

"But not even to save your life?"

"If nothing matters, there's nothing to save."

The point of this story as Foer wields it is not a return to traditional, ritually oriented kosher practice, in which Foer shows little interest. Rather, Foer utilizes the story to address the importance of drawing lines, drawing lines about the ultimate question of who we are, and drawing those lines not abstractly in our minds but with the concrete choices we make in the material world. What Foer learns from this story, as he then takes the reader on a tour of the dismal state of contemporary animal agriculture throughout the rest of the book, is that food matters. Food is one location where we draw the lines that determine who we are. In the Jewish context, as in so many others, food's importance is amplified through the transmission of food practices in families and communities and across generations. Foer's point in telling this story and mine in repeating it is, at minimum, to insist that food, ethics, and identity go together at the deepest conceivable level.

Eating Animals goes on to engage a tremendous volume of factual information about the state of contemporary animal agriculture and invites readers to follow Foer in trying to come to more firm ethical conclusions about the question of eating animals, a question which, for Foer, felt especially urgent after he had had his first child and started to make eating decisions for someone else. Foer passionately argues for the significance of eating animals as a moral issue, documenting the massive scale of human and animal suffering and ecological degradation that have been associated with factory farming. He ultimately concludes he and his children will be vegetarian but doesn't call on everyone to follow him, instead prioritizing an opposition to factory farming as the common ground that should unite public action.

Throughout *Eating Animals*, Foer makes multiple biblical allusions, and he disproportionately engages a number of Jewish thinkers over the course of his book, including Franz Kafka and Jacques Derrida. In addition to frequent personal stories that mention his Judaism, he discusses his own disappointment with the state of kosher slaughter. But *Eating Animals* is not an explicitly Jewish or religious book. Foer presents himself as just an ordinary American (who happens to be of Jewish descent) speaking about issues of universal concern. Despite the neutral presentation, I am indeed suggesting, for all the reasons listed at the opening of this paragraph, that his book *can* be read as distinctly Jewish, as one recent installment in a long line of *Jewish* reflection on the ethics of eating (among other things).

Let us now turn, however, to a more explicitly Jewish book: the biblical book of Genesis, specifically the (Priestly Source) narrative found in Genesis 1 and again in Genesis 9. According to the dominant contours of classical rabbinic commentary, Genesis 1 and 9 provide the core narrative about eating animals found in the Hebrew Bible.[4]

A Biblical Story: From Eden to Sacrifice

For most Americans, including Jewish Americans, the simple fact that God commands humans to be vegetarian in Genesis is often a surprising discovery, so let us start with this fact. In the first chapter of Genesis, we have the famous narrative of creation that is structured around the seven days of the week—six for the creation of the world and the seventh during which God rests, the archetype of the Sabbath that observant Jews celebrate every Friday to Saturday evening. On the sixth day of creation God creates both humans and land animals (birds and sea animals have already been created) and, according to this passage, God sets humans in relation to the rest of creation through two commands.

The first command is more well-known: human beings are granted dominion and told not only to be fruitful and multiply (which the animals are told to do as well), but also to *rule* creation. This verse, Genesis 1:28, is arguably the most famous verse in the whole of Genesis and most people who know little else about the Bible are aware that it articulates some kind of human rule over creation.

What is noteworthy for our purposes is that the immediately following verses, Genesis 1:29–30, as interpreted virtually unanimously by classical Jewish (and Christian) exegetes, declare that humans and animals must eat only plants. If you read closely, it appears that humans and animals are given slightly different vegan fare—humans are given plants "with seeds" but the animals receive only the leafy parts of plants, which perhaps points to the distinctly human aspects of seed-based agriculture. It is only after this command to eat only plants in Genesis 1:31 that God famously pronounces creation "very good" (*tov meod*), whereas each previous time creation was praised only as "good" (*tov*).

The biblical story of meat at first appears to end there, but as happens frequently throughout the Bible, it is picked up later in a process of intrabiblical exegesis. That is, later on in Genesis, the Bible returns to this story and interprets it further, commenting on the first telling much like the ancient rabbis, who founded Judaism as we know it, themselves interpreted biblical stories in the sacred texts they penned in the first six centuries of the common era, the Talmud and Midrash (Fishbane 1989).

In Genesis 9, Noah and his family have just emerged from the ark after surviving the punishing flood God had sent to destroy his corrupted creation, and at the moment of this re-founding of human civilization, God creates a new covenant with Noah, his family, and all of creation—and this covenant explicitly reverses the command to eat only plants given in Genesis 1:29–30. God now allows humans to eat animals, but not in a casual manner. As God declares meat to be permissible as food, God also insists that blood must be drained from animals first—the blood cannot be eaten. This is so, we are told, because the blood contains the life of the animals and, now interpreting the symbolism of the biblical text, the life of the animals is not given to humans but is the sole property of God (Goodfriend 2019). In other words, even when permission is given to eat meat, there is a qualification and restriction. Indeed, the blood prohibition is just the beginning of the massive complex of restrictions placed on consuming meat in the Bible, which ultimately constitute the core of the biblical system of animal sacrifice.

While the details of this biblical story are not frequently repeated in public today, virtually all Americans who eat meat—religious and secular—continue to follow the prohibition against consuming blood, which I mention here by way of suggesting that these stories continue to have real power in ways that are unexpected. So normal has the blood prohibition come to be seen that many seem to have assumed that blood is simply inedible (something I discovered when I started teaching the text in undergraduate courses). Blood, however, is a common food source cross-culturally and is known as quite tasty by those who consume it. Most Americans have a taboo on consuming blood not because there is any insurmountable pragmatic barrier to using it as food, but because it violates a symbolically charged biblical mandate. We have simply forgotten this.

So if the example of the persistence of the blood prohibition tells us that, often unconsciously, we are still in the grip of the biblical narrative, what has the narrative about eating animals I just reviewed meant to Jews historically, and what does it mean now? A truly detailed, historically rich answer is beyond the scope of this short chapter—one study of Genesis 1:28, a single verse, fills an entire book (Cohen 1989)—but there are at least two discernible streams of interpretation in the Jewish context. One stream of interpretation takes the fact that God originally planned a world without meat eating, along with other details, to mean that the "permission" given to eat meat in Genesis 9 is really a *concession*. Jews who have followed this stream of interpretation tend to view vegetarianism as a desirable ethical ideal. Vegetarianism here is a choice for lesser violence, a precursor to the messianic age that will reflect the perfect nonviolence of Eden. The first prestate, Ashkenazic rabbi of Israel, Rav Kook, is a notable recent representative of this view, and was famously known to eat almost exclusively vegetarian fare.

Another stream of interpretation simply does not dwell on the distance between Edenic life and life as we know it in this regard, and emphasizes instead the important role meat, often along with wine, can play in creating social cohesion and joy. In this second stream, the tradition can be read as greatly encouraging or even requiring the consumption of meat in celebration of the Sabbath and sometimes other holidays as a vital part of what makes these days special. Rav Kook famously honored this stream, even as the force of his teachings emphasized vegetarianism as an ultimate ideal, by consuming a small amount of meat on the Sabbath as an exception to his usually scrupulous vegetarianism.

In other words, far from telling Jews whether or not it is ethical to eat meat and how, the narratives of the Bible have instead given Jews (and others) a vocabulary with which to discuss the ultimate questions of meaning associated with meat. Working in community, specific answers have been given to these questions by Jews over the millennia, but the open-endedness of the Jewish textual interpretation is a counterweight to the creation of a final Jewish position on the question of eating animals. Most Jewish communities and individuals have decided, unlike Foer, that eating animals is ethically acceptable (or even desirable) and have gone on to articulate various anticruelty measures that are meant to address the moral dangers of meat.

This fits a broader pattern in which Jewish canonical texts evidence a "simultaneous insistence on both the value of animal lives and the greater value of human well-being," which is communicated "by juxtaposing countervailing principles of, on the one hand, kindness to animals (often coupled with an emphasis on human creatureliness), and, on the other hand, human ascendancy (often coupled with an emphasis on human distinctiveness)" (Gross 2013, 2). After all, meat may be acceptable in this dominant view, but cruelty to animals must be prevented. The classical rabbinic tradition reflected in the Talmud named this prohibition on "unnecessary suffering to animals" *tzaar ba'alei chayim* and the prohibition and its implications are detailed in every subsequent Jewish legal code.

Conclusion

Bringing these two stories together, we can note that, on the one hand, contemporary Jews like Foer who are concerned to raise the profile of attention to animal suffering and, on the other hand, Jews with opposite or different concerns about eating animals, not only have the earlier biblical narrative available to them as a starting point to discussions of the ethics of eating animals but also millennia of commentary on these narratives and, in addition, the various discussions of the principle of compassion for animals, *tzaar ba'alei chayim*, in the Talmud and beyond. However, Jews with concerns like Foer's will be frustrated by many (not all!) of the ways these ideas have developed. For example, at first glance *tzaar ba'alei chayim* would seem to provide a strong basis for opposing the cruelty of factory farming (say, for example, a basis to oppose breeding chickens to grow so fast that it hurts for them to move much of their lives, a ubiquitous practice Foer documents). However, in many cases, the ability of this principle to actually protect animals has been eviscerated by expansive interpretations of what counts as necessary suffering (recall that *tzaar ba'alei chayim* only prohibits *unnecessary* suffering). For some legal authorities in the Jewish tradition, any human interest whatsoever, no matter how trivial (such as earning one cent more), is sufficient justification for animal suffering (that is, any benefit whatsoever means the suffering was not arbitrary and in that sense was necessary).

Most of the American Jewish leaders who run today's kosher meat industry adopt in practice something like this latter view and therefore support raising animals in the same industrial settings that produce the rest of meat in America. A small minority of kosher businesses, most notably the kosher meat purveyor KOL Foods, has attempted to increase animal welfare standards in the kosher industry. This task, alongside efforts to promote meat reduction and/or vegan diets, are also being pursued by several nonprofit organizations including the Jewish Initiative for Animals (JIFA), a project of the anti-factory farming group Farm Forward; JewishVeg, the longest standing group, which under different names has operated since 1975; Shamayim: Jewish Animal Advocacy, affiliated with the orthodox social justice organization, Uri L'Tzedek; and Hazon: The Jewish Lab for Sustainability, the nation's largest Jewish environmental group.

Speaking from my own perspective as a Jew who cares about animal suffering, I find the limitations of this venerable ban on cruelty that dominate the conventional kosher industry today offensive to my Jewish sensibilities (and I'm not alone). It seems particularly egregious today to fail to critique the plight of animals on factory farms given what we know about the role they play in increasing pandemic risk, something Foer has recently emphasized (Foer and Gross 2020). However, as a scholar who has and is primarily attempting to give you a more neutral picture of the tradition in this chapter, I have attempted to bracket my own view *to the extent possible*. And just as I explicitly inserted my own view into this chapter in the preceding sentences, mingling it with the reflections of Jews past and present, so do all Jews who care to, insert their voices into the tradition and tell their own story.

Let's return to our question: How do contemporary Jewish traditions respond to this universally common and fraught activity—eating animals—especially in an ethical register? A pithy answer is now possible: They—we—tell stories. We pass them from grandparent to child, we tell them at home and sometimes in bestselling books, and we often have the audacious hope that these stories could change the actual world. Foer, after opening *Eating Animals* with the story of his grandmother, closes his book with an invitation: he invites his readers to tell a new story of eating animals at our own dinner tables. He suggests that storytelling might be a way to resist all the steel and concrete of the factory farm.

So to answer standing on one foot (i.e., to answer in brief), How do contemporary Jewish traditions respond to the question of eating animals? We listen to and tell stories of all kinds and we invite others to join. This is perhaps one of the most characteristic marks of what it means to respond "Jewishly" to any ethical question about food. Among other things, making food a *Jewish* ethical issue means to bring Jews in conversation with each other and with the inherited textual tradition. Everything else—from activism, to identity, to law—follows.

Acknowledgments

An earlier version of this chapter appeared in *Feasting and Fasting: The History and Ethics of Jewish Food*, which was published by New York University Press in 2019. It is reprinted here with their kind permission.

Notes

1 For an example in the Jewish case, see Jewish responses to an undercover video showing animal abuse at the AgriProcessors slaughterhouse (now AgriStar), a kosher abattoir in Postville, Iowa (Gross 2014, Chapter 6).
2 Although I use the category "world religions" because of its general familiarity, the category is problematic and bound to a colonialist legacy (Masuzawa 2005).
3 I have a special relationship with this book: I am mentioned in its prose, including a short monologue, and am thanked in the acknowledgments.
4 I will not here attempt the tedious but important task of explicitly tracing the historical continuities between the concerns of contemporary Jewish writers like Foer (sometimes producing deceivingly secular-looking texts) and more traditional Jewish content, but such would be worthwhile.

References

Belasco, Warren James. 2008. *Food: The Key Concepts*. Oxford and New York: Berg.

Burkert, Walter. 1983. *Homo Necans: The Anthropology of Ancient Greek Sacrificial Ritual and Myth*. Berkeley: University of California Press.

_____. 1996. *Creation of the Sacred: Tracks of Biology in Early Religions*. Cambridge: Harvard University Press.

CDC. 2021. "Zoonotic Diseases." *Centers for Disease Control*. Accessed October 6, 2023. www.cdc.gov/onehealth/basics/zoonotic-diseases.html.

Cohen, Jeremy. 1989. *Be Fertile and Increase, Fill the Earth and Master It: The Ancient and Medieval Career of a Biblical Text*. Ithaca, N.Y.: Cornell University Press.

Fessler, Daniel M.T., and Carlos David Navarrete. 2003. "Meat Is Good to Taboo." *Journal of Cognition and Culture* 3 (1): 1–40.

Fishbane, Michael. 1989. *Biblical Interpretation in Ancient Israel*. Oxford and New York: Oxford University Press.

Foer, Jonathan Safran. 2002. *Everything Is Illuminated: A Novel*. Boston, Mass. and New York: Houghton Mifflin Harcourt.

_____. 2005. *Extremely Loud and Incredibly Close: A Novel*. Boston, Mass. and New York: Houghton Mifflin.

_____. 2009. *Eating Animals*. New York: Little, Brown and Company.

_____, and Aaron S. Gross. 2020. "We Have to Wake Up: Factory Farms Are Breeding Grounds for Pandemics." *The Guardian*, April 20. www.theguardian.com/commentisfree/2020/apr/20/factory-farms-pandemic-risk-covid-animal-human-health.

Frazer, James George, and Theodor Gaster. 1959. *The New Golden Bough: A New Abridgment of the Classic Work*. New York: Criterion Books.

Goodfriend, Elaine Adler. 2019. "Food in the Biblical Era." In *Feasting and Fasting: The History and Ethics of Jewish Food*, edited by Aaron S. Gross, Jody Myers, and Jordan Rosenblum, 32–58. New York: New York University Press.

Gross, Aaron S. 2013. "Jewish Animal Ethics." In *The Oxford Handbook of Jewish Ethics and Morality*, edited by Elliot N. Dorff and Jonathan K. Crane, 419–32. Oxford and New York: Oxford University Press.

_____. 2014. *The Question of the Animal and Religion: Theoretical Stakes, Practical Implications*. New York: Columbia University Press.

_____. 2015. "Factory Farming (Confined Animal Feeding Operations)." In *The Sage Encyclopedia of Food Issues*, 3 volumes, edited by Ken Albala. Thousand Oaks, Calif.: SAGE.

_____. 2019. "Introduction." In *Feasting and Fasting: The History and Ethics of Jewish Food*, edited by Aaron S. Gross, Jody Myers, and Jordan Rosenblum, 1–28. New York: New York University Press.

Grossman, Lev. 2006. "Who's the Voice of This Generation?" *Time*, July 2. http://content.time.com/time/magazine/article/0,9171,1209947,00.html.

Harari, Yuval N. 2015. *Sapiens: A Brief History of Humankind*. New York: Harper.

Ingold, Tim, ed. 1988. *What Is an Animal?* London: Unwin Hyman.

_____. (2000) 2008. "From Trust to Domination: An Alternative History of Human-Animal Relations." In *The Perception of the Environment: Essays in Livelihood, Dwelling and Skill*, edited by Tim Ingold, 61–76. London: Routledge.

Labendz, Jacob, and Shmuly Yanklowitz, eds. 2019. *Jewish Vegetarianism and Veganism: Studies and New Directions*. Albany: State University of New York Press.

Masuzawa, Tomoko. 2005. *The Invention of World Religions, or, How European Universalism Was Preserved in the Language of Pluralism*. Chicago, Ill.: University of Chicago Press.

Milgrom, Jacob. 1991. *Leviticus 1–16. Anchor Bible Series*. New York: Doubleday Dell Publishing Group.

Serpell, James. 1996. *In the Company of Animals: A Study of Human-Animal Relationships*. Cambridge: Cambridge University Press.

Striffler, Steve. 2005. *Chicken: The Dangerous Transformation of America's Favorite Food*. New Haven, Conn. and London: Yale University Press.

Upholt, Boyce. 2022. "Will the Next Pandemic Start with Chickens?" *The New Republic*, September 19. https://newrepublic.com/article/167630/next-pandemic-chickens-bird-flu.

Wallace, Robert G. 2016. *Big Farms Make Big Flu: Dispatches on Infectious Disease, Agribusiness, and the Nature of Science*. New York: Monthly Review Press.

Other Recommended Resources

On Factory Farming

Eating Animals (2018), directed by Christopher Quinn.
FarmForward.com.
Sentientmedia.org/factory-farming.

On Judaism and Eating Animals

JewishInitiativeforAnimals.org.
JewishVeg.org.
Shamayim.us.
Wikipedia.com entry on "Jewish vegetarianism."

28 Meditations on Living with Ghosts

The Settlement Legacy of Buffalo Extinction

James Hatley

Where are you?

—Genesis 3.9

The destruction of the buffalo resulted from a campaign of biological terrorism unparalleled in the history of the Americas.

—Wade Davis[1]

i.

This truth begins in a dream, the dream of a two-headed, flesh-eating fish, spangled red on its sides. Mouth opened and with rows of teeth lined up like knife blades, each head is located at opposite ends of the fish's body. To make things even more complicated, this body doubles forward on itself as it emerges from shadowy depths so that the two mouths, each gaping open, position themselves side by side. All mouth, then, with only a hint of what lies behind.

This strange, awkward image lodged in my mind as I awakened a decade ago in a threadbare motel room at Prewett Creek campground in Montana, the first day I would spend volunteering down the road at the First Peoples Buffalo Jump State Park. An augury beyond anything I might have expected had been offered me. And this was so, even if dreams and their auguries have been repeatedly disqualified, at least in the ways of thinking informing the culture of American settlement,[2] as an appropriate place to begin (or end for that matter) one's search for truth. We live in the time of a great disenchantment, and we refer to it as the Enlightenment. And yet this surreal image, this icon of rapacious hunger and questionable greeting, has lingered, has guided me over the last decade of my ongoing residency on the killing grounds of Buffalo.[3]

I was born here, on the Great Falls of the Missouri, where the northern prairie rises up to greet the eastern front of the Rockies. After a life spent teaching on the East Coast, I have returned here. I hope to die here and, I hope this does not sound morbid, to be interred or at least have my ashes scattered here, too. Home, eventually, is where we come to be buried. Home is where we find ourselves invited, whether kindly or cruelly, to become a ghost. In such circumstances it behooves one to question with whom one will be sharing one's final resting place.

DOI: 10.4324/9781003324157-33

ii.

During the last decade, I have puzzled over that two-headed fish. I have wondered about whether its red-spangled sides suggested, perhaps, that it was a salmon. And just recently I have had the thought that like salmon who return after years of ocean-faring journeys to participate in a final, sacrificial act of engendering their next generation, I had returned to these home grounds to do something not unlike this. Dream imagery can work like that, moving sideways to have its say.

But the crucial insight that I have come to, the one that frames all the rest in regard to this dream, is that the creature fashioned by it is without an anus. At both its ends, this fish is toothed and rapacious, as if its sole vocation were to consume its surroundings without qualification, to swallow the world in its entirety without regard to aftermath.[4]

In this moment of reflection, please forgive the awkwardness of noting there is humility to be found in the acknowledgment of one's anus. And also there is a blessing to be had. Indeed in the *Asher Yatzar*, the Jewish prayer to be recited when one defecates or urinates, as well as each morning in one's daily prayers, one gives thanks for one's body having been created "with openings here and vessels there" (AJWS 2012). What goes in must stay a while and then come out. This is, as the prayer goes on to affirm, among "the wonders of creation" (AJWS 2012). This wonder, in turn, is one that humans share with all other earthly creatures.

Poet Roger Dunsmore points out that the very word in English used to refer to our own living kind, "human," stems from the same root in Latin as "humus" and "humble." This fact is something Dunsmore argues we should take much more seriously. "In my own language," he writes, "the word 'human' carried literally within itself the humus that we come from and return to" (Dunsmore 1997, 51). To claim that one is human, then, affirms for Dunsmore "connection to the land, and the implication that to realize *that* meaning of being human, being humus, carried with it a fundamental humility" (Dunsmore 1997, 51). If this is so, then our bodily functions are not only a wonder of creation but also deeply relevant to our very vocation as a living kind. Indeed, as Dunsmore notes, the Hebrew word for the first human, *Adam*, also can be translated as "earth" or "soil" or even "mud." In the Hebrew creation story, humans, along with all the rest of the animal living kinds, begin as mud into which the Creator breathes a spirit. A telling translation of "Adam," then, would be "Mudman."[5]

A strange topic indeed, and particularly so for the settlement culture to which I belong, the very same culture that has a lot to answer for in our treatment of the more-than-human living kinds, including Buffalo, with whom we humans have been called upon to share our place under the sun. Although many of my fellow citizens might be uncomfortable reciting a prayer in regard to one's daily functions, not to mention meditating upon them as a miracle of creation, the invitation to do so calls we who inhabit the earth to a more embodied and also more attentive engagement with a world that is not merely of our all-too-human making.

iii.

Yet in reciting this prayer within the ambit of Buffalo, its provocation becomes perhaps stranger still. For if a body with openings here and vessels there already proves to be remarkable, then Buffalo is arguably fourfold so. One of Buffalo's great achievements as a living kind involves the capacity to be nourished by the cellulose in grasses, a complex sugar that is tricky for most mammalian bodies to unlock. It takes four stomachs and specialized bacteria making their home in Buffalo's innards for this blessing, this particular wonder of creation, to occur.

Furthermore, given the large mass and prodigious appetite of Buffalo, their contribution through defecation to recycling the nutrients they ingest to the other living kinds who share their habitat is of critical importance. One of my favorite snapshots from time spent in the company of Buffalo at the American Prairie Reserve in central Montana shows mushrooms growing out of a thick Buffalo turd, as the blessings that accrue through it of nutrients and moisture form a small garden where the prairie is being given opportunity to renew herself. As every gardener knows, plants yearn for manure. This fact is no different when the garden turns out to be an ecosystem.

As this consideration of Buffalo in regard to the matter of defecation makes clear, from the perspective of the *Asher Yatzar*, the two-headed fish, then, would be a species of blasphemy, a creature that is hunger literally without an end, that consumes the world only to keep it within its own confines, as if the world were to be swallowed whole and subsumed solely to one's own shape and form. In such circumstances, one need not be called upon to meditate upon the wonders of creation because there is no humility, no anus, no giving back. As a fellow philosopher who would prefer to remain anonymous put it to me far more bluntly:

> we citizens of white settlement are more like that dream fish of yours and far less like Buffalo. We take twice as much as we need and give nothing back. And then we go on to praise this way of life as one that is efficient, when in fact, it is nothing more than depredation of the earth, depredation of creation.

One thing is for sure: if one were to listen carefully, Buffalo would have plenty to say on the matter of two-headed fishes.

iv.

There is then a truth, as the aforementioned opening lines affirm, that begins in a dream. But what indeed might this way of putting the matter indicate? For certainly my deliberations so far could be argued to be far afield from the intended topic, even disconcertingly so. Why not simply announce the matter straightforwardly, which is to say that one is opening up a discussion of the harrowing plight of Buffalo in a time characterized by the human-caused extinction of manifold species across the face of the earth? Why not begin simply and plainly with that way of putting the topic rather than engaging in dramas of indirection, in insisting in coming to the point by circling incessantly around it? And why all this talk of an anus?

v.

But being straightforward about such matters is no simple matter in the case of Buffalo, as well as in that of the innumerable other living kinds currently confronting human regimes of extinction and violence. In our time, questions are haunting one on every side in regards to how one can even raise the subject. For instance, where and when exactly can the extinction of any species in particular be located? Where and when does this sort of event even happen? Where and when, for instance, can it be claimed that Buffalo have ceased to exist as a living kind on the face of the earth?

The answer to that question turns out to be complicated and even paradoxical. For at the moment, around 360,000 are alive and kicking, 320,000 of whom are kept as livestock for the sake of human consumption (National Bison Association n.d.). Another 40,000 are still to one degree or another free-roaming, although none of these currently abide in the area of the First People's Buffalo Jump State Park near my childhood home of Great Falls, Montana.

So plenty of Buffalo abide today in other places but none here, precisely in this site along the eastern edge of the Rocky Mountains, where Buffalo once plentiful, once as numerous as stars in the sky,[6] sustained the lives and lifeways of a variety of Indigenous peoples. "Extirpation" is the special name used for that sort of extinction. We say that the Buffalo have been extirpated, ghosted from a region. But in the matter of Buffalo, the event, as it occurred, involved far more than all the Buffalo in a certain place suddenly not being there. As the interpretive center at the Jump makes clear, during the time of prairie settlement by American citizens, tens of millions of Buffalo were done away with across the entire expanse of North America with such abandon that Buffalo nearly ceased altogether to exist as a living kind. The entire center of the continent became one great killing field, as hunters and skinners roaming the land over several decades actively and efficiently scoured a living kind from its place under the sun. Of fifty million only a thousand or so were left in the end.[7]

vi.

To be extinct is not at all the same as to be dead. Indeed, it is debatable whether one can even speak of the death of a living kind.[8] Paradoxically, the ghosts of Buffalo that inhabit the Jump are specifically not the ones who were submitted to a regime of extinction but rather those who were participating in an ongoing, living relationship with First Peoples. Native hunters did not kill these Buffalo in order to do away with them, or even in a manner that would have inadvertently done so, but in order to participate in the great exchange of gifts that is creation. Land, as Aldo Leopold would put it, is that pyramid of energy welling up from the soil by which each living kind eats of others only in turn to become the food of yet other living kinds (Leopold [1949] 1989, 214–220). Consonant with this vision, the Jump was about humans being fed by Buffalo in a sustaining and reciprocal relationship of care and faithfulness.

It is important to reflect upon how profoundly we of settlement culture often miss the point of this relationship between First Peoples and Buffalo. One day, I shared my enthusiasm with an acquaintance, who will remain anonymous, about my plan to volunteer at the Jump. "Why would you do that," the interrogation went, "isn't that where Indians killed masses of Buffalo? What could be good about that?" I am not certain that for this speaker it was even clear that what happened at the Jump, when Buffalo died, was of another order entirely from what happened on the killing fields of settlement, where Buffalo were simply wiped off the face of the earth without remainder.

A technical point needs to be made here. One way a living kind can be understood as extinct is simply for enough of them to die (or be killed) that the next generation does not see the light of day. This is termed "numerical collapse" and has already happened to a long list of species across the face of the earth in the last two centuries or so, including Carolina Parakeets, Honshu Wolves, Chinese River Dolphins, Maryland Darters, Tasmanian

Tigers, Pyrenean Ibexes, Great Auks, and Stellers Sea Cows, among many others. Yearly the list is growing, although so far Buffalo has thankfully escaped being added to it.

But extinction can occur in other ways that so far have not been as conducive to our current mania for making lists of lost living kinds. In the case of ecological extinction, Buffalo might continue to exist as a boutique species but would no longer provide the important ecological services to the grassland ecosystems with which they coevolved and in which they were once at home. They would become a living kind that has lost the very context by which its distinguishing qualities were rendered meaningful.

In the case of genetic extinction, Buffalo would continue to exist but with a genotype that would be increasingly unrecognizable as the animals they once were—"hardy, efficient, disease-resistant, alert, agile, awe-inspiring" (Bailey 2013, 51). The buffalo of tomorrow might well be in the same relationship to the buffalo of yesteryear as present-day cattle are to the now-extinct aurochs of Eurasia. Buffalo's extirpation across a wide swath of their former habitat is arguably contributing to this process, as is the almost complete transformation of the great North American prairie grasslands into pasturage and cropland.

But the difficulty of asking a straightforward question about the extirpation of Buffalo does not end with a consideration of the exact nature of the affliction undergone in being wiped out by the hand of another. There is also a question of the state of mind, the state of being, indeed the state of soul, of those who authored this event, as well as those who have become its beneficiaries, the inheritors of a world sculpted, at the very least, by widespread Buffalo extirpation. And one cannot think of this "war upon the Buffalo," as it was termed by a firsthand observer (Hornaday 1889, 134), without also raising the question of how settlement culture treated those peoples already in possession of this land, already in an intimate and flourishing relationship with it and Buffalo. According to archeological data uncovered at the site of the First People's Buffalo Jump, for over a thousand years, human beings gathered here to harvest Buffalo (Montana Department of Fish, Wildlife & Parks 2005, 2). The traditional knowledge of the First Peoples speaks of how various tribal nations collaborated with one another over the years, as they came together to share in the work of maintaining drive lines channeling Buffalo toward the cliffs. From this great cooperative endeavor came a stunning list of gifts offered to them by the Buffalo. Buffalo died here for the sake of humans, and Native hunters were deeply grateful for this. In return, they offered meaningful gifts of their own, including respect, sustainable use, and performance of religious ceremonies to renew the world on behalf of the Buffalo and all living beings (see, e.g., Harrod 2000). These practices and the lifeways they supported were deliberately destroyed as an integral part of the establishment of settlement culture.

vii.

What happened? There are many answers to that question, some better and some worse. The state park located at the Jump has been set up in the hopes of eliciting the better. Early on in my time volunteering there, I became aware of the testimony of Crow Medicine Woman Pretty Shields concerning a moment when she confronted, in a horrifying scene played out in the Judith Basin, the ecocidal legacy of settlement eradication of the Buffalo. Inscribed at the entryway to the gallery of interpretive materials explaining the history and significance of the Jump, her words are best left to speak for themselves:

> My heart fell down when I began to see dead buffalo scattered all over our beautiful land, killed and skinned by white men. Many many hundreds of buffalo. The whole

country there smelled of rotting meat. Even the flowers could not put down the bad smell. Our hearts were like stones. We believed for a long time that the buffalo would come again to us but they did not.

Times have changed so fast that they have left me behind. I do not understand these times. Ours was a different world before the buffalo went away, and I belong to that world.[9]

On entering the gallery, visitors are invited, indeed, exhorted, to take these words to heart, words that ironically are meant to undermine the very capacity one has to feel in a manner that is heartfelt. Know in your heart, then, that another's heart became stone. The legacy of Buffalo extirpation is revealed by these words to be not only an attack upon Buffalo but also upon the very hearts of those who had lived through the generations in collaborative intimacy with this creature only to witness their wholesale demise during American settlement. The Buffalo's extirpation proves to be what today's settlement culture calls terrorism, violence that has the intent not only of direct material harm, but also radical demoralization, of the undoing of another's very soul and humanity.

As I read these words daily during my time volunteering at the Jump, the urgency of their message claimed and troubled me. Indeed their disturbance of my life continues, even now in this moment of writing these remarks. This provocation is one that I have come to think of as religious, which is to say, the testimony of Pretty Shields communicates an urgency that is not mine to master but rather one that binds and orients me.[10] Her appeal is undergone, suffered by me, before I could have ever intervened to decide on my own behalf how I should proceed. In this way the words of Pretty Shield function in a manner that I have come to understand as prophetic: they open up a future in which the suffering of others not only afflicts me but also alters the very sense of how the world in the first place emerges as meaningful and so as welcoming. In the prophetic, my very hold upon the world that I had been accustomed to assuming affirmed my residency within it is put into question.

viii.

One of the first tasks I was given in my time volunteering at the Jump was both relentlessly prosaic and deeply illuminating: the removal of the bottom strand of a barbed wire fence running along the boundary of the state park. Over several days I spent hours sweating under a blazing sun, incessant wind filling my ears, as I cut away with pliers long lengths of wire, ever on the alert for rattlesnakes hiding in the grass. The loosened wire was then looped into bundles to be returned at the end of the day to the maintenance shed.

At one level this contribution merely involved my doing some grunt work so that the maintenance officer for the park could get on with more important business. It also turned out he was not fond of rattlesnakes. But when I inquired as to why I was engaged in this odd task, the answer given was one that I found deeply heartening: to save the antelope roaming the area from tangling their horns in the barbed wire. It turned out that these graceful and swift running animals prefer to scooch under the fences rather than jump over them. The bottom strand was, at least for them, a death trap.

Repetitive work makes for curious trains of thought. For instance, I became fascinated with how my opened mouth would whistle if it was turned to just the right angle against the persistent wind. All about me, grasshoppers abounded, their antics always worth a quick look. My eyes fixed downward in my work, I began to notice the bones of small animals dotting the earth, mostly of field mice and other rodents, but also the entire skull of a meadowlark that sat serenely amidst a pile of desiccated feathers.

The creatures making their home upon this land, I began to reflect, die back into it. No matter where one turns, this place, as indeed, any earthly place under the sun, has been consecrated by these innumerable small deaths, as one generation—whether of Rattlesnake, Prairie Dog, Meadowlark, or Buffalo, and including we humans too—gives way to the next. Indeed the earthly lives only by renewing itself through its generations. As one Psalm puts it, "Thou withdrawest their breath, they perish and return to their dust. Thou sendest forth Thy spirit, they are created: And Thou renewest the face of the earth" (Psalm 104:29–30). This particular meadowlark's skull might no longer serve to sing its sweet song into the wind, but its progeny remain to fulfill this mission with grace and alacrity. This, the Psalm informs us, deserves our recognition and our reverence. The death of this meadowlark proves to be a blessing that fills the land around me with song even now.

Yet dark thoughts haunt these already mortal speculations. True, we are all creatures who are born into life from out of our forebears only then to die back into the land. But what of those Buffalo, left rotting in the sun, whose brutal demise was witnessed that summer day by Pretty Shield, those Buffalo whose fate was precisely not to die into the land so that that other Buffalo might take their place but instead were intentionally and methodically hunted to the very collapse of their generations?

ix.

As already noted previously, the remains of Buffalo still to be found at the base of the cliffs of the First People's Buffalo Jump State Park are of another sort altogether than of those slaughtered creatures once strewn across the Judith Basin as they were witnessed by Pretty Shield. One marks in her description of that terrible scene an attack upon the very meaning of Buffalo as a living kind, one that suggests a form of blasphemy. In working out the implications of this claim, the important insight is not only *that* Buffalo died and in great numbers then and there but also *how* this occurred. On the frontier, Buffalo were treated in such a manner that their very significance as a living kind was without meaning to those who were dispatching them into non-existence. The slaughter of these Buffalo occurred without any thought of their rebirth through the generations, of the renewal of Buffalo's life *as* Buffalo. To witness and meditate upon such a scene in its full scope, Pretty Shield insists, turns one's heart to stone. Yet even as this occurs, one is also led to ask, "Who would do such a thing?" Indeed, who would even think such a thing could be done, let alone ought to be?

The answering of that question—"who has done this?"—should take place in a manner that is engaged in vigilant and unending discernment. In those historical moments in which not only violence is inflicted upon others but also an entire world disappears, or is intended to disappear by means of that violence, loss reverberates across time in uncanny ways. This occurs not only in regard to those who suffer this loss but also to those who in one way or another bear responsibility for it. In her account of the scene at Judith Basin, Pretty Shield reflects directly on how a particular set of white hunters at a particular historical moment did a thing so terrible, so wrong, that not even the Crow People's worst enemies heretofore could have imagined, let alone contemplated doing. "Nobody believed," she says, "that the white man could kill all the buffalo. Since the beginning of things there had always been so many!" (Linderman 2021, 167).

But as I work over the fence a century later, making the land here and now more habitable for antelope, the irony is not lost upon me that the very existence of this fence, even with the shedding of its lowest strand, continues to contribute to that shattering event witnessed by Pretty Shield. The undoing of Buffalo as a living kind did not stop with the wiping out of nearly all Buffalo across the face of the North American continent. The very world in which Buffalo had made their home—the rich, open habitat of the North American prairie lands—was undone. Even as settlement finally abandoned the project of killing every last Buffalo, efforts were redoubled to undo the very home grounds by which Buffalo were sustained. In this process rambunctious ecosystems welling up into a startling diversity of living kinds were relentlessly transformed through agricultural industrialization into crop and grazing lands more narrowly suited to the settler's plants and animals. Along with the plow and eventually the tractor, barbed wire played a crucial role in this transformation.[11]

Given the breadth of this catastrophe, speaking of it as Prairie Ecocide—of which Buffalo extirpation was merely one element, although a crucial one—becomes helpful. The loss was not only of a world, of a life way that was Buffalo, but also of a world of worlds, of a vast entangling with one another of numerous living kinds and their lifeways. The legacy of this loss continues to impact the land in ways that are not only material, but also, just as importantly, spiritual.

All sorts of hints abound in the land around me speaking of this greater loss. For instance, one of the most common grasses populating the state park today is crested wheatgrass, a species brought into North America by agronomists in order to keep the Dustbowl—itself an unintended consequence of Prairie Ecocide—from being an even greater disaster than it turned out to be. I have heard crested wheatgrass referred to as the great savior of the American grasslands by government employees; quickly rooting and thriving in disturbed land, this living kind stabilized the desiccated land of the Great Plains, saving a good portion of its rich topsoil for practices of restorative conservation that eventually helped to end the Dustbowl. Yet, as a quick perusal of current literature makes clear, this species rapidly outlived its usefulness; today it has spread widely across the West, where it resists efforts to repopulate prairie lands with native grasses, including the First People's Buffalo Jump State Park.[12] An expert on grasses at the park bemoans how crested wheatgrass not only is less able than native grasses to nurture the creatures feeding on it, but also, even when it is eradicated from an area, leaves the soil there resistant to repopulation by other grasses. This resistance to renewal, which could be explained in strictly biochemical terms, resounds in my ears as an echo of what Pretty Shields might have meant when she said, "Even the flowers could not put down the bad smell."

x.

How wrong might it have gone, and might it still go? Linda Hogan, whose reflections open this volume, has observed how historically those who colonize "have a propensity for burning behind them what they cannot possess or control, as if their conflicts are not with themselves and their own way of being, but with the land itself" (Hogan 1995, 44). This is not to say that settlement does not find it is in conflict with itself, but rather that it does so precisely by its rejection, its throwing out of the inextricable entanglement of its inner life with the land, as well as with the other living kinds who make their home there. The regimes of colonization, Hogan charges, were and continue to be fueled by "a hatred of life itself, of fertility and generation," coupled with "a refusal to participate in a reciprocal and balanced exchange with life" (Hogan 1995, 44). We who inherit this way of being at odds with the earthly are in constant danger of becoming, according to Hogan, "far-hearted" in our thinking, capable only of seeing "other lives as containers for our own uses and not as containers in a greater, holier sense" (Hogan 1995, 45). This is the darkness witnessed by Pretty Shield, a darkness that not only is indifferent to the grace of other living kinds but also insistent on debilitating any possibility that the illumination of the world offered by this grace might even be acknowledged, let alone acted upon. In far-heartedness the entirety of one's life becomes a blasphemy against life itself.

Surprisingly, when Hogan speaks of the far-hearted, she does not excuse herself, in spite of her own Indigenous heritage, from this peril. This time itself, she suggests, is permeated with far-heartedness, with "our lives moving so quickly ahead" that they are continually in danger of becoming lost to themselves. The very language through which the things of our world are to be named turns out in these circumstances to be "limited, emotionally and spiritually," so that language itself, as Hogan puts the matter, fails to hear in its own ears "the songs of white egrets, the rain falling into stone bowls" (Hogan 1995, 46). To this list one might add, in the case of my sojourn along the barbed wire, "the teachings of Buffalo, the songs of Meadowlarks, the great thunderstorms rumbling across arid hills."

"Where are you?" This question asked of Adam by his Creator in the Garden of Eden is reminiscent of the one floating in the air, no matter which way I turn, as I labor at the park. In addressing the Jewish account of the human soul, Rabbi Adin Even-Israel Steinsaltz reflects upon how we humans, for all of our capacities, are ultimately creatures brought into being from a breath lying far beyond our own. We are nothing if we are not inspired, breathed into. Further, this in-breathing is not an event that occurs once and for all, but instead intervenes in innumerable moments of our lives, in the small epiphanies by which one's own soul not only comes to be revealed to oneself, but does so in a manner that teaches one anew about how one is to live one's life. Indeed, in fits and starts one learns in these moments about how it is that one even has a life to live or a death to die.

Among these epiphanies are those of *hirhurei teshuva*, "fleeting thoughts of repentance," which, as Steinsaltz puts it, "reveal the possibility of living differently" (Steinsaltz 2018, 19). Precisely the call to imagine how one might live one's life otherwise than one has heretofore has haunted me throughout my time at the Jump. The burden of violence that is Buffalo extirpation, not to mention the ongoing extirpation and extinction of innumerable other living kinds across the face of the earth, does not let me be, whether in my dreams, my thoughts, my relationships with others, or the innumerable habits composing my daily way of life. The very struggle to live differently, I am reminded, might culminate in action but begins in acknowledgment, in taking up with the depth of one's errors, errors that are capable, particularly when writ large across the lifeways of fellow humans, of undoing worlds. The evil that is named species extinction is permeated with a stubborn insistence on the part of settlement culture regarding its own preeminence, as if we humans, along with that two-headed fish of my dream, might become the sort of living thing that with impunity consumes world upon world, living kind upon living kind.

xi.

Yet Buffalo, in spite of the dire straits in which they have found themselves, have not yet succumbed to extinction, and rather are increasingly on a path of resurgence. This outcome is due in no small part to creative and persistent efforts by an array of Indigenous persons and their nations to reverse the demise of Buffalo over the entire time that settlement has been taking place—centuries of patient resistance.[13] Perhaps one of the most inspiring aspects of Buffalo's persistence in the face of the ecocidal forces deployed against it by settlement finds its expression in the Buffalo Treaty, originally proposed and signed in 2014 by a coalition of eight Indigenous nations (The Buffalo: A Treaty of Cooperation, Renewal, and Restoration n.d.).[14] In it, as Leroy Little Bear of the Kainai First Nation puts it, an "ethical space" is being opened up in which Indigenous peoples, as well as groups representing settlement culture, might come together to learn from and with one another how all might learn from Buffalo (Yellowstone to Yukon Conservation Initiative n.d.).[15]

According to one commentator, a telling feature of the treaty is that its signatories promise not only "to support the reintroduction of free-ranging buffalo but also to perpetuate the ceremonies, languages and harvest customs associated with Buffalo" (Schneider 2022, 5). In this latter set of responsibilities is codified the charge "that all parties have to learn from Buffalo and to participate in intergenerational knowledge transfer through ethical research and knowledge gathering" (Schneider 2022, 5). A crucial feature of this commitment is that the signatories take seriously "an interspecies kinship that includes Buffalo and other more-than-human relations" (Schneider 2022, 5). Being among our kin, Buffalo must be taken seriously as agents in the creation of our shared world.

Much thinking has been occurring regarding how going forward Indigenous peoples might recuperate ceremonies, languages, and customs that bring one into dialogical relation with the life and flourishing of Buffalo.[16] Envisioning how dominant settler culture might engage in this work, however, remains daunting.

On the one hand, settlement culture provided no less than religious justification for this ecocide, drawing especially on Christian (especially post-Reformation) biblical interpretation in ways that demeaned the value of human relationships with a more-than-human world. Adding to this religious diminishment has been widespread settler insistence on pursuing a political life that is not so much based on solidarity, even with other human beings, as on a robust notion of the autonomy of oneself and one's fellow citizens, each an individual acting in the first instance on their own behalf. In this way, a challenging reappraisal of often deeply held values seems required.

On the other hand, even when settlement culture views more positively its relationships with the numerous living kinds with whom our residency upon the face of the earth is shared, these others are still viewed in the main not as kin or as collaborators to be engaged with creatively and empathetically, but as entities to be managed scientifically and objectively for the sake of one's all-too-human ends, or, at best, with regard for their welfare as scientifically understood. As a result, even as settlement has endeavored to respond to Buffalo's plight, it remains fastened, politically, culturally, and spiritually, to a vision of Buffalo that fails to take them seriously as fellow subjects or to invite their unique participation in the practices of world making to which any living culture worthy of its name should be committed. Indeed, I suspect many readers will at this point find themselves bewildered about what it would mean to have a relationship with Buffalo. Such confusion is to be expected, but if those of us who are perplexed have the patience to stay with this challenge, new possibilities that could not previously be imagined may emerge.

All too often, responses to the quagmire in which settlement culture finds itself simply dismiss religion as incapable of providing orientation to how one might move beyond settlement's current plight in regard to Buffalo. Some even go so far as to insist religion is itself the main culprit in producing this quagmire.[17] But what I have learned in my time volunteering at the Jump suggests otherwise. What seems called for is not the abandonment of our traditions, in my case Jewish tradition, however complicit in the violence of ecocide they might be revealed to have been, but rather a reorienting and reimagining—or perhaps a rediscovery—of them that is in keeping with the penitential practice of *hirhurei teshuva*. Here one confronts how one has been engaged in the world in a manner that has undermined its very status as world. "Where art thou?" In such circumstances, no matter which way one turns, the call for what medieval and modern Jewish traditions have understood as *tikkun olam*, the healing of world, is to be heard, if only one will listen. This movement toward recognition and healing is initiated in a way of thinking that is not calculative, that is not obsessed with nailing down the truth, but rather that ponders, that is open to intimations of other ways of understanding the world that all along one has been resistant to hearing. In this way one engages in a thinking that is not intent on solving a predetermined problem, or clarifying an already acknowledged principle, but in provoking an upheaval.

As Leroy Little Bear and other Native Americans suggest, this upheaval might serve to put my own religious tradition into question in a manner that it might not have previously anticipated in its own right. Or perhaps this upheaval will call us to take up ancient questions buried in forgotten or disavowed traditions.[18]

What might Buffalo have to do with Judaism, and Judaism with Buffalo? In my time at the Jump, I have only begun to pose this curiously doubled question, let alone answer it. But along the way, two interrelated insights have emerged and deepened for me: Care for the soul as it is understood in the Jewish tradition is inextricably tied up with care for other humans and the worlds they inaugurate and sustain; further, this care, in turn, is deeply entwined in the land, which is to say, in a more-than-human creation in which all the living kinds have something to say about the subject of world making and world healing. Buffalo are not finished having their say about what Judaism itself, and what other traditions of diverse kind, will become.

Notes

1 Davis 2018, 23.
2 How one might characterize the worldview held by white American citizens who arrived in what only later was to be called "Montana," to displace the First Nations already inhabiting and caring for this land, is justifiably burdened by controversy. For purposes of the discussion here, "American settlement" names the culture into which I was born, a culture framed by European and colonial values, a culture whose aspiration for a home place was and remains entangled in histories of violence and usurpation targeting both other humans and the living kinds with whom those humans once lived in intimacy and reciprocity.
3 As related to me by a former director of the First People's Buffalo Jump State Park, the State of Montana's decision in naming the site to use "Buffalo" in lieu of "Bison" (the latter of which is the taxonomically correct scientific/settlement term for this animal) was motivated by the preference of Montana's First Peoples for the name in English they had incorporated over the centuries within their own local traditions of knowledge concerning Buffalo. Following this line of thought, "Buffalo" will be used throughout my discussion here instead of "Bison." See Schneider 2022, 4 for an analysis of this issue.
4 This condition contrasts provocatively to that of Ouroboros, the serpent who is content with swallowing its own tail perpetually.
5 Yet another translation would be "arable soil," suggesting how Adam is created to be the first farmer, a caretaker for the garden. See Hiebert 1996, 35.

6 One might well consider Genesis 26:4, in order meditate on how this iconic locution finds its sense in God's promise to Abraham versus how it comes to be formulated here: "I will make your heirs as numerous as the stars of the heavens, so that all the nations of the earth shall bless themselves by your heirs."

7 To complicate matters even further, a recent scientific study has determined that all bison descended from this genetic bottleneck, including the vaunted Yellowstone herd, show various degrees of hybridization with cattle. The authors conclude that no bison are left on the face of the earth whose genome has not been subjected to domestic cattle introgression. See Stroupe et al. 2022.

8 For a nuanced discussion of this issue, see Donahue 2021.

9 These words are excerpted from Linderman 2021, 167.

10 The reader should keep in mind here that "religion" comes from a Latin root meaning "to bind."

11 See Netz 2004, 232–33, where he suggests how the use of barbed wire by American settlement culture to enclose animals tellingly foreshadowed the application of this same technology by National Socialism in Germany to encage human populations in concentration camps.

12 See, for instance, Seidensticker 2012 and Falser and Mangold 2011.

13 For an introduction to the history since settlement of First People's interventions on behalf of Buffalo, see Zontek 2007. A more recent and condensed account is also to be found in Schneider 2022.

14 For the text of this treaty see: www.buffalotreaty.com/treaty.

15 For an extended discussion of this concept and the process by which the Buffalo Treaty came into being, see: www.youtube.com/watch?v=HK49kuWZcNA.

16 For an introduction to these efforts in which human kinship with the buffalo serves as the guiding principle, see Schneider 2022, 4–5.

17 See, for instance, White 1967 for an early and influential, but also often criticized, effort to make this argument.

18 Consider that in biblical thought all created beings are capable of praising God (for example, Psalm 148) and in Genesis 9 all creation is in a direct covenantal relationship with the Divine; these ideas remain commonplace in classical rabbinic traditions, however marginalized from contemporary Jewish practice they might have become. Of many excellent initiatives currently engaged in recuperating neglected Jewish wisdom in regard to a more-than-human world, one that stands out is Rabbi Ellen Bernstein's ongoing project over the last thirty years to elaborate a Torah of Creation. She is also a founder of Shomrei Adamah/Keepers of the Earth. Information is available about her thought, including a free downloadable version of her and Dan Fink's *Let the Earth Teach You Torah* (1992), at www.ellenbernstein.org/let-the-earth-teach-you-torah. See in particular the chapter titled "Ecology, Judaism and *Tikkun Olam*" (94–109), as well as Bernstein 2005. See also Gross 2013 and Seidenberg 2016 for other noteworthy approaches to the work of rediscovery and recuperation of ecological wisdom in Judaism.

References

American Jewish World Service (AJWS). 2012. "Bracha After Going to the Bathroom (Asher Yatzar)." *AJWS On1Foot*. Accessed January 10, 2023. www.on1foot.org/text/bracha-after-going-bathroom/.

Bailey, James A. 2013. *American Plains Bison: Rewilding an Icon*. Helena, Mont.: Farcountry Press.

Bernstein, Ellen. 2005. *The Splendor of Creation: A Biblical Ecology*. Cleveland, Ohio: Pilgrim Press.

———, and Dan Fink. 1992. *Let the Earth Teach You Torah*. Philadelphia, Pa.: Shomrei Adamah. https://www.ellenbernstein.org/let-the-earth-teach-you-torah.

"The Buffalo: A Treaty of Cooperation, Renewal, and Restoration." n.d. Accessed January 11, 2023. www.buffalotreaty.com/treaty.

Davis, Wade. 2018. "On Ecological Amnesia." In *Memory*, edited by Phillippe Tortell, Mark Turin, and Margot Young, 21–29. Vancouver, B.C.: Peter Wall Institute for Advanced Studies.

Donahue, Luke. 2021. "Survival and Extinction: Deconstruction, Extinction Studies, Paleontology." *Theory & Event* 24 (4): 922–50. https//doi.org//10.1353/tae.2021.0053.

Dunsmore, Roger. 1997. *Earth's Mind: Essays in Native Literature.* Albuquerque: University of New Mexico Press.

Falser, Valerie A., and Jane M. Mangold. 2011. "Restoring Native Plants to Crested Wheatgrass Stands." *Restoration Ecology* 19 (101): 16–23. http://doi.org/10.1111/j.1526-100X.2010.00678.x.

Gross, Aaron S. 2013. "Jewish Animal Ethics." In *The Oxford Handbook of Jewish Ethics and Morality*, edited by Elliot N. Dorff and Jonathan K. Crane, 419–32. Oxford: Oxford University Press. https://doi.org/10.1093/oxfordhb/9780199736065.013.0027.

Harrod, Howard L. 2000. *The Animals Came Dancing: Native American Sacred Ecology and Animal Kinship.* Tucson: University of Arizona Press.

Hiebert, Theodore. 1996. *The Yahwist's Landscape: Nature and Religion in Early Israel.* Oxford: Oxford University Press.

Hogan, Linda. 1995. "What Holds the Water, What Holds the Light." In *Dwellings: A Spiritual History of the Living World*, 42–46. New York: W. W. Norton & Company.

Hornaday, William Temple. 1889. *The Extermination of the American Bison.* Smithsonian: Washington Government Printing Office.

Leopold, Aldo. (1949) 1989. "The Land Ethic." In *A Sand County Almanac and Sketches Here and There*, 201–26. New York: Oxford University Press.

Linderman, Frank B. 2021. *Pretty Shield: Medicine Woman of the Crows.* New York: Harper Perennial.

Montana Department of Fish, Wildlife & Parks. 2005. *Ulm Pishkun State Park Management Plan.* Helena, MT: Montana Department of Fish, Wildlife & Parks.

National Bison Association. n.d. "Bison by the Numbers: Data and Statistics." Accessed January 7, 2023. https://bisoncentral.com/bison-by-the-numbers.

Netz, Reviel. 2004. *Barbed Wire: An Ecology of Modernity.* Middletown, Conn.: Wesleyan University Press.

Schneider, Lindsay. 2022. "Decolonizing Conservation? Indigenous Resurgence and Buffalo Restoration in the American West." *Environment and Planning E: Nature and Space.* http://doi.org/10.1177/25148486221119158.

Seidenberg, David Mervorach. 2016. *Kabbalah and Ecology: God's Image in the More-Than-Human-World.* Cambridge: Cambridge University Press.

Seidensticker, Rachel. 2012. "Fighting a Pervasive Invader: Crested Wheatgrass." *The Range Blog. University of Montana*, February 20. Accessed May 19, 2023. www.hcn.org/blogs/range/fighting-a-pervasive-invader-crested-wheatgrass.

Steinsaltz, Rabbi Adin Even-Israel. 2018. *The Soul.* New Milford, Conn: Maggie Books.

Stroupe, Sam, David Forgacs, Andrew Harris, James Derr, and Brian Davis. 2022. "Genomic Evaluation of Hybridization in Historic and Modern North American Bison" (*Bison bison*). *Scientific Reports* 12: 65397. https://doi.org/10.1038/s41598-022-09828-z.

White, Lynn. 1967. "The Historical Roots of Our Ecological Crisis." *Science* 144 (3767): 1203–07.

Yellowstone to Yukon Conservation Initiative. n.d. "Buffalo Treaty: Creating and Enacting an Ethical Space from the Mountains to the Plains." Accessed January 11, 2023. www.youtube.com/watch?v=HK49kuWZcNA.

Zontek, Ken. 2007. *Buffalo Nation: American Indian Efforts to Restore the Bison.* Lincoln: University of Nebraska Press.

Other Recommended Resources

Hubbard, Tasha. 2009. " 'The Buffalo Are Gone' or 'Return Buffalo'? The Relationship of Buffalo to Indigenous Creative Expression." *Canadian Journal of Native Studies* 29 (1–2): 65–85.

International Buffalo Relations Institute. n.d. Accessed January 11, 2023. https://buffalorelations.land.

Olson, Wes, and Johane Janelle. 2022. *The Ecological Buffalo: On the Trail of a Keystone Species*. Regina: University of Regina Press.

Wallwork, Deb, director. 2010. *Sacred Buffalo People: Bison in the Plains Indian Culture*. Red Eye Video. Video clip with Lakota Medicine Man Pete Catches telling the Buffalo's origin story. www.youtube.com/watch?v=33zB7JhKkpg.

Yale Forum on Religion and Ecology: Judaism. https://fore.yale.edu/World-Religions/Judaism.

29 Urban Wildlife

Threats, Opportunities, and Religious Responses

Seth B. Magle and Dave Aftandilian

Introduction

Every one of us resides on an urban Earth. There are a dizzying array of statistics to prove it—today, 55% of people live in urban areas, and this is expected to rise to 68% by 2050 (United Nations 2019). Over 10% of the Earth's surface is now characterized as urban (McGranahan et al. 2005). As the human population continues to add billions and billions of people, it is estimated that over 95% of this growth will occur in cities (Cohen 2003).

Cities function to house people and consolidate all the industries and activities we pursue, everything from commerce and industry to education, religion, and the arts. Another function of cities, probably important early on but more or less forgotten in modern times, was to exclude wildlife (Adams and Lindsey 2010). In prehistoric times, wildlife attacks on livestock or on people were presumably an ongoing concern, and a group of humans living together probably provided an effective deterrent to many such attacks. As the cities modified the landscape more and more intensely, through construction of roads, walls, and other attributes of city life, it resembled the natural habitat of most other species less and less, creating conceptual and actual barriers between urban dwellers and wildlife. *This is our space—we live in here; you live out there.*

Yet since at least as far back as ancient Egypt, and probably earlier, some animals have found a way to live in cities (Dixon 1989). Often they are in fact so common that we stop noticing them, as with pigeons (family *Columbidae*) or tree squirrels (family *Sciuridae*). Some, like rats and mice, try to get into our homes, filling us with revulsion, which is not entirely unwarranted, since they can carry dangerous diseases. Others, like raptors nesting in skyscrapers to swoop past our windows, can fill us with awe, while at the same time fulfilling an important ecological role such as controlling the populations of smaller creatures. Year after year it seems we see more species living in metropolitan areas, as if this filter we built is sprouting larger and larger holes. Here in Chicago we have seen coyotes in downtown sandwich shops and peregrine falcons hunting pigeons in the Loop (Van Horn and Aftandilian 2015). Perhaps wildlife are adapting to this urban landscape, or perhaps we are simply noticing animals who never really left (Zellmer et al. 2020).

Urban wildlife have been to most people an afterthought, a rounding error. They are the tiny fraction of living things that slid through the cracks in our carefully constructed world to live among us despite our best efforts; present, but invisible, or irrelevant. Most people still think of "nature" and "wildlife" as phenomena that exist far away, in a national park or protected area. Certainly urban dwellers live with a smaller suite of plants and animals around than would naturally have been present in their local environment. These reduced

DOI: 10.4324/9781003324157-34

chances to connect with our fellow species represent a lost opportunity, one with real costs for both us and other animals whom we will discuss in this chapter.

And yet urban wildlife live all around us, in every city across the globe. These species can be a nuisance, a threat, an opportunity to connect people to the more-than-human world, or a critical part of the Earth's biodiversity. It all depends on your point of view, on how we construct our cities, and on how we engage and interact with the other animals who share them with us.

Challenges to Wildlife

Cities are not safe places for wildlife. An organism living in an urban area, whether by choice or due to lack of other options, will face a huge number of hazards and stressors, including the presence of predators, encounters with people (including potentially animal control officers), lawnmowers and other habitat modifiers, and poisons such as rodenticides and herbicides (Ditchkoff, Saalfeld, and Gibson 2006). While a full review of every possible urban hazard is outside the range of this chapter, we will discuss some of the best understood.

The most obvious, and perhaps most important, threat is the simple loss of habitat (hospitable places for animals to inhabit). Where a city goes, something else once was, whether a forest, a prairie, a wetland, or other nature space, and doubtless creatures lived there. Not every species can adapt to city life, and unless habitat is set aside inside of urban regions—a rare practice only recently considered (Larson et al. 2018)—many species will either have to move elsewhere or die. This reduced diversity of wildlife in cities also, of course, means fewer wildlife species for people to interact with and connect to.

A related, but subtler, threat comes from *habitat fragmentation*. As cities consume habitat, the pockets of land they leave behind are small and separated from one another. Wildlife struggle to survive in these fragmented spaces, or to move between them. Large-bodied species that need a lot of room to roam and a lot of food to eat, such as, for example, wolves or mountain lions, are often excluded due to a lack of enough connected habitat (Crooks and Sanjayan 2006).

When discussing wildlife in urban areas, there is an important distinction to be made between *endemic species*, those that resided in an area before urban development, and *invasive species*, those that have expanded their range to new areas due to human activity. Rats are perhaps the classic example of an urban invasive species, naturally endemic to Asia but present worldwide due to their close association with humans. Pigeons are another. These invasive species certainly are examples of urban wildlife—but they also often outcompete and exclude native species from urban regions (Bailey et al. 2020; Blair 1996). For example, European starlings, which were introduced to New York City from Europe, may outcompete native North American species like sapsuckers for cavities used as nests (Koenig 2003).

The structure of the city itself can also be a challenge. For many terrestrial species, the most common way to die in the city is to be hit by a car (Forman et al. 2003; Gehrt, Riley, and Cypher 2010); this includes several rare species, such as the Florida panther (*Puma concolor coryi*, Foster and Humphrey 1995) and the Tasmanian devil (*Sarcophilus harrisii*, Jones 2000). For birds and bats, simple plate glass windows on buildings represent an enormous threat, with up to one billion birds killed annually in the U.S. alone by colliding with glass (Loss et al. 2014). Cities alter their surroundings in many other ways, including increasing light pollution (Longcore and Rich 2004), noise pollution (Francis,

Ortega, and Cruz 2009), warming temperatures (Kim 1992), and releasing various pollutants and toxins (Murray et al. 2019).

The most dominant species in any urban area is humans. Most urban wildlife species survive because they have learned to avoid humans—a classic example are coyotes, who despite reaching high populations in cities mostly remain out of sight and mind, howling infrequently and looking both ways before crossing streets (Gehrt, Riley, and Cypher 2010). Nonetheless, a problematic animal, whether a raccoon denning in an attic or a fox who has become aggressive toward neighborhood dogs, is likely to come to the attention of humans, and that attention is likely to lead to their removal and ultimately death. Human activity such as leaving out poison and traps for pests also causes direct mortality not just to those pests, but also to many species (Hindmarch and Elliott 2018). We can pose both a direct and an indirect threat to the wildlife living around us.

While beloved by their owners, and often a seemingly benign presence, pets also represent a real threat to many species of wildlife. Dogs are probably mostly a nuisance, though wild animals chased off by dogs may change their movement patterns, which may lead them away from the best resources (Lenth, Knight, and Brennan 2008). But outdoor cats have been shown to cause more serious impacts. Their hunting of birds, small mammals, and reptiles can have staggering consequences—one somewhat controversial study estimated that cats in the United States kill 1 to 4 billion birds annually, as well as 6 to 22 billion mammals (Loss, Will, and Marra 2013). In Australia, cats are estimated to kill approximately 272 million birds per year (Woinarski et al. 2017), and in Southern Canada, perhaps 2 to 7% of the total bird population is killed by cats each year (Blancher 2013). These studies are often disputed by cat advocates (Wolf 2016), but it does seem clear that cats left outdoors will hunt, and will often be successful in bringing down prey. Most urban cats will continue to hunt even rare prey, meaning that they can drive endangered species to extinction in urban areas (Medina et al. 2011)—a classic example is the extinct Stephens Island wren, the last few of which are believed to have been killed by a cat. There are interesting moral and ethical debates to consider on the relative merits of keeping cats enclosed indoors versus letting them roam free to hunt other species. Nonetheless, it is clear that people and their pets are an ongoing threat to other urban species.

Opportunities for Wildlife

For the most part urban areas do not closely resemble the habitats that wildlife evolved to use (but see Lundholm and Richardson 2010). Nonetheless, cities are full of resources, and some species have managed to not only survive but thrive by exploiting them. An obvious example is our discarded waste, which species like rats, raccoons, seagulls, and even hyenas are happy to find and consume (Adams and Lindsey 2010; Baynes-Rock 2013). In fact, one theory for why the canids who became dogs started hanging around with humans involves eating our trash, and this has been a key role played by semidomesticated village dogs around the world for thousands of years (Coppinger and Coppinger 2016; Dixon 1989).

But other examples abound—urban gardens and plantings are easy pickings for rabbits and other small herbivores. Many people actively feed birds (and usually inadvertently squirrels and other rodents at the same time) in their backyards. The abundance of these smaller organisms can be a boon to larger species like hawks (Boal and Dykstra 2018). There is no general shortage of food for wildlife in urban areas—the question is what sort of food, and what species can make use of it. Generalists like foxes who can eat a great many different things can usually find something, but specialists who eat only a few things, for example lynx who mostly eat snowshoe hare, may find urban life a struggle (Sorace and Gustin 2009).

When an urban area is embedded in a dry ecosystem, the city is often where the most free water is (Prudic et al. 2022). Urban dwellers make use of natural waterways, tap into aquifers, or divert water long-distance to water their yards, fill fountains, maintain landscaping, and sometimes fill bird baths. When water is limited, many species will seek it out, and as a result, these drier cities sometimes see much higher wildlife diversity than one would otherwise expect (Beninde, Veith, and Hochkirch 2015).

Of course, cities give other opportunities. There are many trees to nest in, and some enterprising bird species even nest in signs or on buildings (Indykiewicz 1991). The structure of the built environment provides all manner of places to den or hide. For example, one of us (S.B.M.) has often observed red foxes and raccoons using storm sewers to avoid humans. For species not at the top of their particular food web, the potential exclusion of predators due to a lack of sufficient habitat may also represent a significant perk. Some urban species even stop performing their anti-predator behaviors (Magle and Angeloni 2011).

Wildlife-Human Conflict

Based on surveys, conflicts between people and wildlife are very common in urban areas (Soulsbury and White 2015). The most common form of conflict is a minor nuisance event, such as an animal rummaging in a garbage can (Hadidian et al. 2010), followed closely by property damage (Bjerke and Østdahl 2004). It should be noted that many of these conflicts are in the eye of the beholder—what one person might consider an inconvenience, another would consider a fun chance to witness nature up close (Bjerke, Østdahl, and Kleiven 2003).

Property damage caused by urban wildlife can be significant—certainly in the hundreds of millions of dollars per year in the U.S. Much of this damage is to lawns, landscaping, or homes caused by animals digging or foraging (FitzGibbon and Jones 2006; Urbanek, Allen, and Nielsen 2011); common culprits in the United States include geese, raccoons, deer, coyotes, skunks, and beaver. Bird droppings are also an omnipresent nuisance in cities around the world (Clergeau et al. 2001; Fitzgibbon and Jones 2006).

Actual attacks by urban wildlife against people are much rarer, but receive much more attention (Poessel et al. 2013). When the animals in question are large—for example, bears or mountain lions—such attacks can even be fatal (White and Gehrt 2009), though these attacks happen so seldom in the developed world that they generate big news when they do. Usually attacks happen because animals have been hand-fed by humans or because they are defending their young or their territory (Soulsbury and White 2015). Even though these attacks are very rare, many people still report a high level of fear about wildlife (Harrison 1998), perhaps partly because the media sensationalizes these events (Cassidy and Mills 2012).

Much more common than attacks on people are attacks on pets (Grubbs and Krausman 2009; Poessel et al. 2013). Dogs left off-leash and cats left outside can be at risk from urban carnivores such as coyotes or foxes. Keeping animals inside can help, but maintaining healthy prey populations for these predators to hunt can also help reduce the risk of pet attacks (Magle et al. 2014). It is difficult to convey the deep pain felt by pet owners who lose their cherished pets to wildlife attacks, and often this experience can lead to a regrettable fear and hatred of all wildlife (Murray et al. 2023).

Collisions between vehicles and wildlife are also a serious concern. It has been estimated that one to two million animals are killed on U.S. highways every year (Huijser et al. 2008), and this number does not even include small animals that would cause insufficient damage to vehicles to be reported. Most attention is paid to collisions with large animals such as deer, which in the United States cause billions of dollars in property damage, tens of thousands of (human) injuries per year, and kill hundreds of people (Huijser et al. 2008; Romin and Bissonette 1996). We do not have good estimates for other countries and regions at this time, but they are likely to be similar, depending on human population and traffic patterns (Taylor and Goldingay 2010).

Disease is another realm of conflict worth taking very seriously. Many human diseases ultimately come from animals; these are called *zoonotic diseases* (Soulsbury and White 2015). The U.S. Centers for Disease Control and Prevention has concluded that "most new or emerging infectious diseases in humans are zoonotic" (Ghai and Behravesh 2023). Examples include rabies, West Nile virus, Lyme disease, Ebola, and Avian Influenza, as well as, most likely, COVID-19. Some, such as rabies, can be fatal to humans, while others, such as Lyme disease, cause an array of symptoms that can last for years and are hard to diagnose. Cities hold a high density of people, pets, and wildlife together in a relatively small space, creating situations of high risk for diseases to spread (Bradley and Altizer 2007; Deplazes et al. 2011). Efforts to improve nature and make a space for wildlife in the city, while admirable, unfortunately also have the potential to increase the prevalence of disease (Deplazes et al. 2004). Green planning and urban wildlife habitats are desperately needed, but should always draw on the latest research on wildlife biology and behavior to ensure that conflicts, including disease transmission, are minimized.

Wildlife-Human Opportunities

Much more research attention has been paid to conflicts between humans and wildlife than to the benefits people accrue from living with wildlife, which is unfortunate, since positive interactions are very common. A growing number of studies have shown that interacting with nature benefits people in numerous ways, including psychological, physiological, social, and spiritual (Keninger et al. 2013).

Perhaps the most obvious benefit of urban wildlife for humans is that we enjoy looking at them. The aesthetic value of wild places is also clear from human art and culture since prehistoric times (Parsons 2008), and is very obvious in our modern world in everything from the default images displayed on idle computer screens to the hundreds of millions of dollars people spend each year on outdoor recreation. In some cases we can directly measure the monetary value of aesthetics; for example, property values are always much higher if the home has a view of a forest, lake, or ocean (Nicholls and Crompton 2005).

Natural areas in cities provide wildlife with habitat, and people with a place to gather and bond socially. While traditionally green space in cities took the form of highly manicured lawns without much space for nonhuman animal life, increasingly natural areas are being planned and implemented that have spaces for both wildlife and people (Beatley 2011; Roelofs 1999). The value of outdoor recreation to urban residents is immense, almost impossible to quantify. One of the authors of this chapter (S.B.M.) lives in Chicago, Illinois, where the entirety of the shore of Lake Michigan has been conserved for recreation (Wille 1991). It is also (perhaps accidentally) a pathway for wildlife to move through the city across a connected ribbon of green. It is remarkable how often I have seen raccoons, coyotes, skunks, and a myriad of birds in the early morning as I jog, and these moments leave me with a sense of awe that lasts throughout the day.

Wildlife and nature provide other ecological benefits as well, usually lumped under the broad term *ecosystem services*. Pollinators such as bees and wasps help with flowers and urban gardens (Matteson and Langellotto 2009). Plants and trees help to purify water and improve the quality of the soil (Soulsbury and White 2015). Many species such as skunks and bats consume overabundant insect pests (Kunz et al. 2011; Rosatte et al. 2010), and others, such as terrestrial and aerial carnivores, may reduce the abundance of nuisance rodents (Whelan, Wenny, and Marquis 2008; Gehrt, Riley, and Cypher 2010). Scavengers can sometimes assist with waste disposal; hyenas are one example (Abay et al. 2011).

The relative costs and benefits of wildlife in urban areas are extremely difficult to quantify, even without taking into account the spiritual and psychological aspects. However, since removal of wildlife from cities would be impossible (not to mention highly unethical, if it could be done), the analysis seems somewhat moot. Given that wild animals are here to stay in our cities, the goal of architects, planners, and residents should be to minimize the negative interactions, and maximize (and celebrate) the good.

Religious Responses to Urban Wildlife

In addition to the aesthetic, social, psychological, and ecological benefits we just discussed, urban wildlife—and more specifically paying attention to and caring for urban animals within religious frameworks—can also bring spiritual benefits to humans. (By "caring for" urban animals we mean "including them in the community of others to whom we owe species-specific care," not something like hand feeding of wildlife, which should *never* be done, to keep both them and us safe.) These benefits can apply at the individual, community, and congregational levels, and can also help animals. In this section, we will first identify some of these benefits, and then discuss specific examples of the sorts of religious practices that can help people achieve them.

Why: Religiospiritual Benefits

It takes extra effort to pay attention to and care for animals in urban and suburban settings, such as by preserving or creating native plant habitats for them. So the first question we need to consider is: Why bother?

On an individual level, attending to animals more deeply, engaging them with our hearts as well as our minds, can connect us more closely to the places where we live, to the habitat-homes that we share with them (see Aftandilian 2019 and Chapter 24 on contemplative practices in this volume). For example, when we (D.A. & family) moved from Chicago, Illinois to Fort Worth, Texas, watching the animals I encountered on my walks along the Trinity River helped me feel more a part of our new home. This lesson is repeated for me every time the seasons change and new animals arrive, such as the cormorants who winter with us or the swallows who build their mud nests beneath highway overpasses in the spring. They remind me both of the place where I am, and the many other places to which this one is connected through flows of water and migratory animals. And as I have come to feel more a part of this place, I have come to care more deeply about it.

Caring for animals in cities can also connect us to other humans across the many differences that can divide us (class, ethnicity, gender, etc.). For example, when we lived in the Hyde Park neighborhood in Chicago, my wife and I (D.A.) experienced firsthand how a muskrat stranded in a sidewalk planter along a busy road brought together a small crowd of passersby to figure out how to get her or him back to the lakefront (Aftandilian and Van Horn 2015). And Mike Hogue has written persuasively about how learning to care for our dogs, including taking them to public dog parks where we encounter a wide variety of other people, "is great practice for the hard work of actively listening to and empathizing with" urban others (Hogue 2015, 99)—including wild animal others.

Paying attention to animals in the city as fellow members of our urban communities also offers us the chance to deepen our religious experience by learning to see the sacred in the everyday—learning to read the Book of (Urban) Nature alongside the Book of Scripture as a tool for coming closer to God and creation (Schweitz 2017, 18). Drawing on her experience as a practicing Lutheran and former director of the Zygon Institute for Religion and Science at the Lutheran School of Theology at Chicago, Lea Schweitz has explored a variety of ways in which we can learn to see the infinite in the finite and ordinary; to see that God "is in and through all creatures, in all their parts and places," as Martin Luther put it in one of his sermons (Schweitz 2020, 324). From this point of view, a prairie restoration project along the Chicago lakefront can become a metaphor for the beloved community, and the nightly visits of a ghostly opossum to the backyard can offer city dwellers a chance to experience what theologian Rudolph Otto described as the *Mysterium tremendens et fascinans*: religious mysteries that make people tremble in fear, yet also draw them in with the awe and wonder they inspire (Schweitz 2015).

Working to care for wild animals also offers a number of benefits to urban and suburban congregations and other religious communities. First and foremost, caring for animals helps people of faith fulfill their God-given role as stewards of creation, whether in the Judeo-Christian sense of "tilling and tending" the Garden of Eden (Gen. 2:15; see also Dickinson 2015, 168) or the Muslim sense of acting as Allah's trustees or vice-regents in caring for the world that Allah created (Sūrat al-An'ām, No 6, Āyat 165).

Focusing on the welfare of other animals in cities and suburbs can also help members of religious communities to expand their understanding of who counts among the neighbors to whom they should offer love and hospitality, and welcome into their beloved community. Brian Langlands argues that church-sponsored community gardens can help extend *koinonia* (fellowship with God and fellow Christians) and radical hospitality ("restorative exchanges of welcome that are rooted in a particular place") to others who live nearby but are different from us, shifting our views of these others "from that of *nearby resident* and *anonymous stranger* to that of *neighbor* (i.e., one who has a claim on my time, my concern and my talents)" (Langlands 2014, 12, 4).

We would simply add to Langlands's reflections that these "others" could well be other than human animals, if we consider pollinator gardens or other wildlife-focused native plant gardens built by members of religious communities. Naomi Edelson, Senior Director of Wildlife Partnerships for the National Wildlife Federation (NWF) and co-creator of their Sacred Grounds program that will be described in the next section, told D.A. that NWF focuses on the religious concepts of welcoming the stranger and offering hospitality as ways to engage congregations in planting gardens for wildlife (telephone interview, July 11, 2022).

Wilson Dickinson points out that if we are to encounter and learn to read God's Book of Nature in the city and suburbs, we may need to preserve and/or create natural areas in which to do this (Dickinson 2015, 171). In these garden spaces we can come to recognize that we are not so different from nonhuman others as we might think, and can start to build new, more caring relationships with them. As Dickinson puts it, "Gardens, today, are experimental and experiential places where urbanites and suburbanites are once again rediscovering their creatureliness and their call to care and attend. . . . In the garden, creatures meet and acknowledge not their separateness but their interdependence. . . . Working with the land will serve not only to meet some of their material needs, but it could also help repair our relationships" with each other and with other living beings (Dickinson 2019, 29–30).

Finally, at the community level, working to create gardens and sponsor religious practices to serve the needs of urban wildlife can be a great way for religious communities to deepen the level of engagement among their current members, and to attract more members. Naomi Edelson of NWF said that they have found strong interest among the congregations they have connected with through the Sacred Grounds program; "people like gardening, the caring for creation message resonates, and it's a great way for a congregation to get their members more engaged with the faith community" (telephone interview with D.A., July 11, 2022). And Laura Hobgood learned from her surveys of more than 30 U.S. churches that sponsor Blessings of the Animals that some of them sponsor these blessings specifically as "outreach to those who might not otherwise attend church" (Hobgood-Oster 2008, 122).

Finally, and from the point of view of this chapter perhaps most importantly, wild animals also benefit when city-dwelling people of faith work to pay closer attention to them as living subjects, not objects, and to provide for their needs (in an appropriately hands-off manner). In her study of megachurches and the environment, Susan Power Bratton explains that in contemporary green infrastructure planning, "hubs" such as larger nature reserves and parks work best when they are linked by corridors, and smaller "sites" can also offer important wildlife habitat. "As today's megachurches acquire natural habitats and have greater acreage than the typical municipal park, many have the potential to be 'sites' or even 'hubs.' Further, a surprising number of the largest U.S. churches share boundaries with greenways, riparian zones [lands that border bodies of water], public parks, or municipal nature reserves," thereby magnifying the impact of megachurches that act to preserve or create greenspaces (Bratton 2016, 256).

There can also be a significant snowball effect when religious communities create spaces that serve wildlife. Naomi Edelson of NWF explained that one of the overall goals of their Sacred Grounds program is to catalyze the creation of wildlife habitats on the grounds of faith communities so that they can serve as demonstration sites or models that can inspire individual members of those communities to create similar wildlife habitats in their own backyards (telephone interview with D.A., July 11, 2022).

How: Practices and Examples

For Congregations

Now that we have discussed a number of good reasons why people of faith can benefit from attending more closely to and acting to help urban wildlife, it's time to consider how best they might do this. What sort of specific practices or actions can people of faith in cities and suburbs engage in at community, congregational, and individual levels that can provide habitat, food, care, and other resources needed by animals, while also providing religious benefits for the humans involved?

At the congregational level, one of the simplest ritual practices that a faith community can adopt to help their members start to consider urban wildlife as part of their community of religious concern is to incorporate wild animals into a Blessing of the Animals. As Laura Hobgood has explained both in her chapter in this volume and in previous publications, Blessings of the Animals today are most often really Blessings of the Pets and are performed around the time of Saint Francis's feast day in October (whether the congregation is Catholic or not; see Hobgood-Oster 2008, 107–128). But there are a number of ways congregations could incorporate concern for wild animals into this service. For example, they could invite organizations that serve wildlife to participate in the informational fairs that are often part of Blessings of the Animals; at Texas Christian University (TCU) in Fort Worth, we invite student members of the TCU Rhino Initiative to educate visitors alongside the animal welfare and rescue groups we also invite to our Blessing. In 2022, we also asked the director of the Fort Worth Nature Center and Refuge, Rob Denkhaus, to speak about urban wildlife as important members of the Fort Worth community. And when I (D.A.) lead participants at our interfaith Blessing in a Buddhist loving-kindness meditation (*mettā*), I always name the wild animals who live near us as living beings to whom we should offer loving-kindness (for more on this meditation see D.A.'s Chapter 24 on contemplative practices in this volume).

People of faith who manage institutions with grounds can also work to create welcoming greenspaces for their wild neighbors—spaces that will also provide aesthetic, psychological, and religious benefits for human visitors. We have already mentioned the tremendous opportunities available to megachurches with large campuses to either preserve part of their grounds in a wild state, if these already exist, and/or to create gardens or trails with wildlife in mind. In her visits to over 200 U.S. megachurches, Susan Power Bratton found a number of examples of congregations that had gone the extra mile to show hospitality and provide care for their fellow creatures. While she found that such congregations were the exception rather than the rule (Bratton 2016, 276, 283), they still provide excellent models for others to follow. For example,

> Idlewild Baptist Church in Lutz, Florida [just north of Tampa], installed a cover of bald cypress [trees] and native grasses around the rim of a detention pond beside its entrance road. The constructed basin blends visually with the piney woods behind it, filters gasoline and coolant washing in from the road, and conveys respect for God's creation. The wild borders contribute to God's provision of habitat for the "stork in the cedars" and other creatures dependent on freshwater, as found in Psalm 104. . . . The wetland plants at the edge of the Idlewild Baptist roadside detention basins act as biofilters and reduce contaminant levels in the watershed [which in turn benefits fish and other animals living downstream]. At the same time, they provide a visual amenity and food for wildlife. The plantings are thus a form of service to the church's neighbors, both human and zoological.
>
> (Bratton 2016, 266)

But faith communities do not need to own a large tract of land to make meaningful contributions to the well-being of wild creatures. And a number of programs exist in the U.S. to provide technical advice and support to congregations that want to help urban wildlife, including the National Wildlife Federation's Sacred Grounds program and the Green Chalice creation care ministry of the Christian Church (Disciples of Christ).

Sacred Grounds is part of the National Wildlife Federation's (NWF) Garden for Wildlife Program, which was founded in 1973. It represents a step beyond their popular "Certified Wildlife Habitat" program, and focuses specifically on places of worship. The Sacred Grounds program was first suggested to Naomi Eldelson of NWF by her synagogue's rabbi, Rabbi Fred Scherlinder Dobb (who also serves on the board of Interfaith Power and Light), as a non-political way to engage people of faith in environmental conservation (telephone interview with Naomi Edelson, July 11, 2022). According to Patrick Fitzgerald, NWF's Senior Director of Community Habitat, 942 places of worship host Certified Wildlife Habitats, and more than 125 have implemented Sacred Grounds (email to D.A., August 4, 2022).

To participate in Sacred Grounds, a faith community first needs to plant gardens or other habitats that benefit native wildlife. They then need to engage their community or congregation in the project, and also reach out beyond the congregation to the wider community (see www.nwf.org/SacredGrounds/Take-Action). Examples of congregational engagement include using the wildlife habitat area as a sacred space (e.g., as a prayer garden or site for a worship service), hosting a workshop for members on how to create wildlife habitats at home, or recording and posting observations of wildlife using the habitat either as a congregation checklist or via a citizen science website such as iNaturalist (www.inaturalist.org). Congregations can reach out to the local community by hosting a public tour of their wildlife habitat or a volunteer workday to plant, sustain, and/or improve the habitat.

For instance, the Islamic Center of Greater Toledo created a prairie garden on their property that connects with a local trail system; they also planted it with milkweed, which is the only food that monarch butterfly caterpillars can eat. The People's Missionary Baptist Church in Toledo acquired a nearby abandoned property that used to be a drug house; they then renovated it into a safe and beautiful prayer park that is open to the community. And multiple houses of worship in Austin, Texas, have partnered through Sacred Grounds to create a Community Wildlife Habitat (including a Unitarian church, a Buddhist meditation center, a Jewish synagogue, and a Baptist church).

Although the Sacred Grounds program is open to any congregation from any faith tradition that fulfills the criteria listed earlier, the National Wildlife Federation has been focusing especially on engaging urban faith communities of color in the program. As NWF puts it on the program's website,

> The mission of the Sacred Grounds program is to promote the installation of native plant gardens that connect people to nature and provide access to nature for all. Particularly in urban communities, Black, Indigenous, and People of Color (BIPOC) have less access to nature and safe green spaces than white folks in the same cities. Native plants are not only a foundation for healthy ecosystems and wildlife, but also play an important role in mental, physical, and social health by providing opportunities for people to connect to nature in their neighborhoods and communities.
> (www.nwf.org/SacredGrounds/About; accessed June 9, 2023)

While Sacred Grounds offers guidance to congregations more on the practical end, such as which native plants to use to create gardens that support wildlife in a particular region, the Christian Church's (Disciples of Christ) Green Chalice ministry offers both practical and theological guidance to congregations of their denomination (see green-chalice.org). Green Chalice is also more wide-ranging, covering everything from steps congregations can take to reduce their energy consumption to providing lists of Bible verses from both the Hebrew Bible and Christian Scriptures that support creation care. A Disciples church can become a Green Chalice Congregation by forming a Creation Care Team, adopting and signing the Green Chalice covenant, inventorying their church's creation care practices, and then making three "greener choices." Congregations seeking a deeper level of engagement can choose to become formally certified, which can take a couple of years. There are currently 185 Green Chalice Congregations, only 20 of which have been formally certified by the Christian Church.

For example, Saint Andrew Christian Church in Olathe, Kansas (a suburb of Kansas City), is a Green Chalice Congregation that has created a certified wildlife habitat that attracts and serves birds, butterflies, and other wildlife. They also sponsor what they describe on their website as a "Birdseed ministry—Using donations from the congregation, volunteers fill multiple bird feeders in our natural habitat on the church grounds" (see https://sacchome.org/justice/practicing-justice-ecologically/; accessed June 9, 2023). The congregation also explicitly identifies their efforts to support urban wildlife as one of their three *justice* ministries (this one involves "practicing justice ecologically," while their other two justice ministries include providing school supplies to children of migrant farmworkers and helping welcome and mentor global refugees). In doing so the church makes it clear to their members that people of faith have a responsibility to care for and seek justice for not just our human neighbors, but also for the nonhuman ones. (See D.A.'s Chapter 11 on "Blue Theology and Water Torah" in this volume for another example of a Green Chalice Congregation that focuses on serving marine wildlife.)

For Individuals

While the religious responses to urban wildlife that we have discussed so far all involve communities or congregations, of course individuals can also choose to help wildlife for religious reasons. For example, homeowners can also draw on the resources of the National Wildlife Federation or other organizations to create wildlife habitats in their own backyards (see www.gardenforwildlife.com).

Another resource for Catholics, in particular, to draw on in creating home wildlife habitats with religious meaning is the Saint Kateri Habitats Program (www.kateri.org/saint-kateri-habitat-2/). The initiative is named after Kateri Tekakwitha, an Algonquin/Mohawk woman born in 1656 who converted to Catholicism as a teenager and in 2012 became the first Native American to be canonized (Buckley 2021). As the creators of the program explain on their website,

> With a focus on God and faith, our Saint Kateri Habitats Program offers living, sacred spaces for people to engage directly in the care of God's creation at home and in our local communities. By restoring habitats with reverence and gratitude for our Creator, the program draws people closer to God and his Church while protecting the integrity of creation . . . . Saint Kateri Habitats are more than healthful material habitats; they are inspirational spiritual habitats.

In terms of natural spaces for wildlife, Saint Kateri Habitats need to provide at least two elements such as food, water, and cover, while also avoiding the use of chemical fertilizers and pesticides. And they must also include some form of religious expression, ranging from religious symbols such as crosses or statues of Saint Kateri or Saint Francis to full-fledged prayer gardens or Mary gardens. Participants can choose to register their habitat on the program's website. They can also draw on expert guidance from the Kateri Center's professional ecologists (e.g., on what kinds of native plants might flourish best in their region). By December 2021, 190 Saint Kateri Habitats on five continents had been registered (Buckley 2021). A Story Map linked from the program's website provides both an interactive world map and descriptions of each habitat that participants submit. For example, a Kateri Habitat creator who lives in St. Vianney Parish in New Mexico wrote, "My garden is small but provides food for me and the birds, butterflies, bees, bunnies, and squirrels that frequent it. My soul is fed by feeding God's creations."

Another way for individuals to express spiritual care for urban wildlife takes place in a more public setting: along roads where animals have been killed by human motorists. Rev. Sarah Bowen describes this as a Roadkill Ministry, and it is one she has practiced since she was six years old, often for 10 to 15 animals a week; when people at seminary asked her, "What are you going to do? What is your mission?" her answer was to carry on the Roadkill Ministry (telephone interview with D.A., June 7, 2022). The need is great, since as we mentioned previously, in the U.S. alone, there are between one and two million collisions between vehicles and large animals every year, most of which are fatal for the animals (Huijser et al. 2008, 4). For some endangered animals like the Texas ocelot, collisions with vehicles are the number one threat to their survival (Wilkins, Kockelman, and Jiang 2019, 157–58).

Describing the Roadkill Ministry in her book *Sacred Sendoffs*, Rev. Bowen explains that she gently moves the dead animal off the road, abiding by the USDA's "Wildlife Carcass Disposal Guidelines." After burying or covering the animal with leaves, she says,

> Reverently, I offer a short apology on behalf of humanity for our encroachment on wildlands and our desire to drive at speeds that are hazardous to other life-forms, ending my words with, "May you have a most auspicious next lifetime."
>
> (Bowen 2022, 115)

She suggests that like-minded people of faith have a blessing, prayer, or mantra ready to recite when they encounter a dead animal; other folks like her husband prefer to make a personal gesture, such as placing a hand over one's heart and observing a moment of silence; still others might prefer to make a sketch of the animal and display the image for a time in a sacred space in their home.

Rev. Bowen concludes by explaining that "Reverently witnessing the losses of wild beings means recognizing each animal on this planet as an individual who was once filled with sacred life and connections to other beings who may now be grieving" (Bowen 2022, 125; for references on wild animals mourning, see Chapter 30 by Barbara Smuts et al. in this volume). Moreover, Buddhist friends have told her that the souls of recently killed animals are still in the Bardo (a liminal state between death and rebirth) and so can hear her prayer on their behalf, and Hindu friends say they think her prayer will help the animal's soul reach their next body more quickly (telephone interview with D.A., June 6, 2022). In addition to being an important spiritual practice for her, Rev. Bowen feels that the Roadkill Ministry can help others learn to see "invisible" animals, which will hopefully lead them to care more about and for wild animals in general. (For similar reasons Portland, Oregon-based artist Emma Kisiel has created a series of photographic memorials to animals killed on roads that she calls "At Rest"; see www.emmakisiel.com/work#/at-rest/, accessed June 10, 2023.)

Finally, individuals who have not been able to find a local congregation that shares their compassion for animals can participate in the Compassion Consortium (www.compassionconsortium.org), which Rev. Bowen cofounded with Rev. William Melton and his wife, vegan educator Victoria Moran, and clergy colleague Rev. Erika Allison (Bowen 2022, 31–35). The Consortium meets once a month by Zoom for a worship service at which "all kinds of animals [are] spoken about and their needs considered as important as human ones" (ibid., 32) and in which the voices and images of animals both wild and domestic are incorporated into the liturgy.

Rev. Bowen explained to D.A. (telephone interview, June 7, 2022) that each Compassion Consortium service begins with "a hymn from the natural world" that involves listening to other than human voices, such as sea lions barking. Rev. Bowen then offers a talk to the congregation, usually focusing on the concerns of free-living beings or wildlife. Participants also engage in interspecies spiritual practices from a variety of traditions, such as chanting "Shalom" ("Peace") with sheep, meditating with cows, or watching a video of a worm and reflecting on what it would be like to move in the world as they do, and what humans can learn from them about the (reckless?) speed with which we often act. Guest speakers then engage in a "spiritual conversation" about their work with animals, focusing on the spiritual side of their work and helping break down the binary of "science versus religion," as well as offering concrete suggestions for the congregation about how they can help animals like those the speaker cares for. Embodied movement practices inspired by other animals as well as joyful human dancing help participants engage with animals through lighthearted bodily motion as well as heartfelt spiritual reflection. As Rev. Bowen explained to D.A., the Compassion Consortium "can be your spiritual home or your spiritual R.V. add-on."

Urban Wildlife Design Examples

People of faith are not the only urban dwellers who are working to make cities and suburbs friendlier to wildlife, while also reducing the potential for conflict with humans. Clever and enterprising ecologists, architects, and city planners have explored many examples of *wildlife inclusive design*, and we will review some of the most promising.

One of the worst forms of human-wildlife conflict in urban areas is collisions between animals and vehicles. As such, several means have been devised to allow terrestrial wildlife to safely cross roads and highways. The most prominent are wildlife underpasses, which are small tunnels or other openings constructed under busy roads. When planned well, these are extremely effective in both reducing road mortalities and maintaining healthy wildlife populations (Forman et al. 2003). The more expensive, and much rarer, option is an overpass, a wildlife bridge spanning above a highway. Recently, a massive wildlife overpass was approved for construction over Highway 101 in California to benefit mountain lions and other carnivores (Love and Grigoryants 2022). There are other benefits to wildlife crossing structures, such as providing recreation opportunities for people (Forman et al. 2003).

Green spaces in cities have usually been represented by parks and other nature reserves. However, these days the buildings themselves can become a form of useful habitat. Green roofs—vegetated habitat maintained on top of buildings—are increasingly popular, and even required in some metropolitan regions for new construction.

These are created for many purposes, such as stormwater management and regulating temperatures, but have the potential to benefit wildlife species including birds, spiders, and insects (Oberndorfer et al. 2007). In addition, they can provide a space for people to interact with wildlife in a positive way, building an emotional bond with nature in the process (Benvenuti 2014).

There are clever engineering solutions that can help animals reside in cities. For flying animals such as birds and bats, windows are one of the biggest threats present in cities. As noted, at least one billion birds are killed annually in the U.S. alone by colliding with glass (Loss et al. 2014). However, some types of glass are easier for birds to detect and using them in buildings can reduce these deaths (Klem et al. 2009). Some cities such as San Francisco and Chicago have passed bird-friendly building ordinances requiring bird-safe glass when possible. Artificial light at night is another serious threat to wildlife (Schirmer et al. 2019), with animals altering their movement behavior and sometimes becoming lost due to bright downtown lights (Longcore and Rich 2004). Some cities have instituted "lights out" policies to encourage buildings to turn off their lights at night, especially during avian migration seasons, while others have mandated lights that are focused more tightly, use wavelengths that do not impact animals, or are angled toward the ground rather than up into the sky to avoid attracting bats and birds.

When we build, we can also build smarter. Clustered housing development is an approach that clumps houses together, creating connected open spaces where the yards would have been (Lenth, Knight, and Gilgert 2006). If yards are desired, backyard habitat programs like the ones described in the previous section recognize and certify residents who seek to replant some or all of their yard with native plants to attract wildlife (Widows and Drake 2014). These programs have been very successful in generating habitat for certain insects such as monarch butterflies who desperately need it (Baker and Potter 2019). Bird feeders and bird houses have long been used to attract birds to a property, but bat houses can work just as well in attracting bats, and are growing in popularity. Bats provide important services by eating insects and by pollinating plants, yet their populations are being ravaged by disease in some areas, and having places to roost—even in cities—can mean the difference between bat survival and local extinction (White 2004).

Unused urban spaces can also be converted into wildlife habitat. One good example is the transformation of unused elevated rail lines into nature spaces (Foster 2010). These former train lines tend to run straight through the heart of urban areas and as such can provide communities normally devoid of nature experiences with unique chances to interface with wildlife, and can also offer wildlife accessible corridors to use to safely traverse an urban world.

Conclusion

For centuries, our default idea of "wildlife" has usually been animals, probably large and fierce, living in undisturbed places far away from us. But the world has changed, and our conception of wildlife must change with it. A majority of humans now live in cities, and urban areas are spreading rapidly around the world. An increasing diversity of animals is finding a way to live in these cities, and if we choose to, we can shape this process— encouraging some species to flourish while discouraging others that create conflict with us. This great opportunity and responsibility will be necessary if we are to make a planet with space for wildlife in the future, and the benefits to us will be incalculable. Together we can build an Earth both urban and wild.

Acknowledgments

We thank the Lincoln Park Zoo and their support staff, as well as the scientists in the Urban Wildlife Institute and the Urban Wildlife Information Network. Funding for S.B.M. was provided by the Abra Prentice Foundation, the Davee Foundation, and the Grainger Foundation.

We would also like to thank everyone who took the time to help us learn more about religious responses to urban wildlife in the U.S. Deep bows, in particular, to the folks who generously shared their time and experience through in-depth interviews or emails with D.A., including Rev. Sarah Bowen of Compassion Consortium, Rev. Wilson Dickinson of Lexington Theological Seminary, Naomi Edelson of the National Wildlife Federation, and Lea Schweitz of Union Theological Seminary and Nature120. We are also very grateful for the contacts and ideas shared with us by Rev. Carol Devine of Green Chalice Ministry, Carrie Dohe of Bees for Peace, Liz Ferguson of Faith in Place, Patrick Fitzgerald of the National Wildlife Federation, Laurel Kearns of Drew Theological School and Green Seminary Initiative, Sarah Withrow King of CreatureKind, Abby Mohaupt of GreenFaith, Beth Norcross of the Center for Spirituality in Nature, Tim Robinson of Brite Divinity School, and others.

References

Abay, Gidey Yerga, Hans Bauer, Kindeya Gebrehiwot, and Jozef Deckers. 2011. "Peri-Urban Spotted Hyena (Crocutacrocuta) in Northern Ethiopia: Diet, Abundance and Economic Impact." *European Journal of Wildlife Research* 57: 759–65.

Adams, Clark E., and Kieran J. Lindsey. 2010. *Urban Wildlife Management*. 2nd ed. Boca Raton, Fla.: CRC Press.

Aftandilian, Dave. 2019. "Connecting Students (and Faculty) to Place and Animals Through Contemplative Practices." In *Grounding Education in the Environmental Humanities: Exploring Place-Based Pedagogies in the South,* edited by Lucas F. Johnston and Dave Aftandilian, 17–38. New York and London: Routledge.

_____, and Gavin Van Horn. 2015. "Introducing City Creatures." In *City Creatures: Animal Encounters in the Chicago Wilderness*, edited by Gavin Van Horn and Dave Aftandilian, 1–11. Chicago, Ill. and London: University of Chicago Press.

Bailey, Robyn L., Holly A. Faulkner-Grant, Victoria Y. Martin, Tina B. Phillips, and David N. Bonte. 2020. "Nest Usurpation by Non-Native Birds and the Role of People in Nest Box Management." *Conservation Science and Practice* 2 (5): e185.

Baker, Adam M., and Daniel A. Potter. 2019. "Configuration and Location of Small Urban Gardens Affect Colonization by Monarch Butterflies." *Frontiers in Ecology and Evolution* 7: 474. https://doi.org/10.3389/fevo.2019.00474.

Baynes-Rock, Marcus. 2013. "Life and Death in the Multispecies Commons." *Social Science Information* 52 (2): 210–27.

Beatley, Timothy. 2011. *Biophilic Cities: Integrating Nature into Urban Design and Planning*. Washington, D.C., Covelo, Calif., and London: Island Press.

Beninde, Joscha, Michael Veith, and Axel Hochkirch. 2015. "Biodiversity in Cities Needs Space: A Meta-Analysis of Factors Determining Intra-Urban Biodiversity Variation." *Ecology Letters* 18: 581–92.

Benvenuti, Stefano. 2014. "Wildflower Green Roofs for Urban Landscaping, Ecological Sustainability and Biodiversity." *Landscape and Urban Planning* 12: 151–61.

Bjerke, Tore, and Torbjørn Østdahl. 2004. "Animal-Related Attitudes and Activities in an Urban Population." *Anthrozoös* 17: 109–29.

_____, and Jo Kleiven. 2003. "Attitudes and Activities Related to Urban Wildlife: Pet Owners and Non-Owners." *Anthrozoös* 15: 262–72.

Blair, Robert B. 1996. "Land Use and Avian Species Diversity Along an Urban Gradient." *Ecological Applications* 6 (2): 506–19.

Blancher, Peter. 2013. "Estimated Number of Birds Killed by House Cats (*Felis catus*) in Canada." *Avian Conservation and Ecology* 8 (2): 3. http://dx.doi.org/10.5751/ACE-00557-080203.

Boal, Clint W., and Cheryl R. Dykstra, eds. 2018. *Urban Raptors: Ecology and Conservation of Birds of Prey in Cities*. Washington, D.C., Covelo, Calif., and London: Island Press.

Bowen, Sarah A. 2022. *Sacred Sendoffs: An Animal Chaplain's Advice for Surviving Animal Loss, Making Life Meaningful, and Healing the Planet*. Rhinebeck, N.Y.: Monkfish.

Bradley, Catherine A., and Sonia Altizer. 2007. "Urbanization and the Ecology of Wildlife Diseases." *Trends in Ecology and Evolution* 22 (2): 95–102.

Bratton, Susan Power. 2016. *ChurchScape: Megachurches and the Iconography of the Environment*. Waco, Texas: Baylor University Press.

Buckley, Cara. 2021. "Meet an Ecologist Who Works for God (and Against Lawns)." *New York Times*, December 3. www.nytimes.com/2021/12/03/climate/climate-change-biodiversity.html.

Cassidy, Angela, and Brett Mills. 2012. "'Fox Tots Attack Shock': Urban Foxes, Mass Media and Boundary-Breaching." *Environmental Communication* 6 (4): 494–511.

Clergeau, Philippe, Gwenaelle Mennechez, Andre Sauvage, and Agnes Lemoine. 2001. "Human Perception and Appreciation of Birds: A Motivation for Wildlife Conservation in Urban Environments of France." In *Avian Ecology and Conservation in an Urbanizing World*, edited by John M. Marzluff, Reed Bowman, and Roarke Donnelly, 69–88. New York: Springer Science.

Cohen, Joel E. 2003. "Human Population: The Next Half Century." *Science* 302 (5648): 1172–75.

Coppinger, Raymond, and Lorna Coppinger. 2016. *What Is a Dog?* Chicago, Ill. and London: University of Chicago Press.

Crooks, Kevin R., and M. Sanjayan, eds. 2006. *Connectivity Conservation*. Cambridge: Cambridge University Press.

Deplazes, Peter, Daniel Hegglin, Sandra Gloor, and Thomas Romig. 2004. "Wilderness in the City: The Urbanization of *Echinococcus multilocularis*." *Trends in Parasitology* 20 (2): 77–84.

Deplazes, Peter, Frans van Knapen, Alexander Schweiger, and Paul A.M. Overgaauw. 2011. "Role of Pet Dogs and Cats in the Transmission of Helminthic Zoonoses in Europe, with a Focus on Echinococcosis and Toxocarosis." *Veterinary Parasitology* 182 (1): 41–53.

Dickinson, T. Wilson. 2015. "Care of the Soil, Care of the Self: Creation and Creativity in the American Suburbs." In *Being-in-Creation: Human Responsibility in an Endangered World*, edited by Brian Treanor, Bruce Ellis Benson, and Norman Wirzba. New York: Fordham University Press.

———. 2019. *The Green Good News: Christ's Path to Sustainable and Joyful Life*. Eugene, Ore.: Cascade Books.

Ditchkoff, Stephen S., Sarah T. Saalfeld, and Charles J. Gibson. 2006. "Animal Behavior in Urban Ecosystems: Modifications due to Human-Induced Stress." *Urban Ecosystems* 9 (1): 5–12.

Dixon, D.M. 1989. "A Note on Some Scavengers of Ancient Egypt." *World Archaeology* 21 (2): 193–97.

FitzGibbon, Sean I., and Darryl N. Jones. 2006. "A Community-Based Wildlife Survey: The Knowledge and Attitudes of Residents of Suburban Brisbane, with a Focus on Bandicoots." *Wildlife Research* 33 (3): 233–41.

Forman, Richard T.T., Daniel Sperling, John A. Bissonette, Anthony P. Clevenger, Carol D. Cutshall, Virginia H. Dale, Lenore Fahrig, et al. 2003. *Road Ecology: Science and Solutions*. Washington, D.C.: Island Press.

Foster, Jennifer. 2010. "Off Track, in Nature: Construction Ecology on Old Rail Lines in Paris and New York." *Nature and Culture* 12: 316–37.

Foster, Melissa L., and Stephen R. Humphrey. 1995. "Use of Highway Underpasses by Florida Panthers and Other Wildlife." *Wildlife Society Bulletin* 23 (1): 95–100.

Francis, Clinton D., Catherine P. Ortega, and Alexander Cruz. 2009. "Noise Pollution Changes Avian Communities and Species Interactions." *Current Biology* 19 (16): 1415–19.

Gehrt, Stanley D., Seth P.D. Riley, and Brian L. Cypher, eds. 2010. *Urban Carnivores: Ecology, Conflict, and Conservation*. Baltimore, Md.: Johns Hopkins University Press.

Ghai, Ria, and Casey Barton Behravesh. 2023. "Zoonoses: The One Health Approach." Accessed June 26, 2023. https://wwwnc.cdc.gov/travel/yellowbook/2024/environmental-hazards-risks/zoonoses-one-health-approach-.

Grubbs, Shannon E., and Paul R. Krausman. 2009. "Observations of Coyote-Cat Interactions." *Journal of Wildlife Management* 73 (5): 683–85.

Hadidian, John, Suzanne Prange, Richard Rosatte, Seth P.D. Riley, and Stanley D. Gehrt, S. 2010. "Raccoons (*Procyon lotor*)." In *Urban Carnivores: Ecology Conflict, and Conservation*, edited by Stanley D. Gehrt, Seth P.D. Riley, and Brian L. Cypher, 35–48. Baltimore, Md.: Johns Hopkins University Press.

Harrison, Robert L. 1998. "Bobcats in Residential Areas: Distribution and Homeowner Attitudes." *Southwestern Naturalist* 43 (4): 469–75.

Hindmarch, Sofi, and John E. Elliott. 2018. "Ecological Factors Driving Uptake of Anticoagulant Rodenticides in Predators." In *Anticoagulant Rodenticides and Wildlife*, edited by Nico W. van den Brink, John E. Elliott, Richard F. Shore, and Barnett A. Rattner, 229–58. Cham: Springer.

Hobgood-Oster, Laura. 2008. *Holy Dogs and Asses: Animals in the Christian Tradition*. Urbana and Chicago, Ill.: University of Illinois Press.

Hogue, Michael S. 2015. "*Civitas Canis lupus familiaris*." In *City Creatures: Animal Encounters in the Chicago Wilderness*, edited by Gavin Van Horn and Dave Aftandilian, 95–101. Chicago, Ill. and London: University of Chicago Press.

Huijser, M.P., P. McGowen, J. Fuller, A. Hardy, A. Kociolek, A.P. Clevenger, D. Smith, and R. Ament. 2008. *Wildlife-Vehicle Collision Reduction Study: Report to Congress* (Report No. FHWA-HRT-08-034). McLean, Va.: Federal Highway Administration, U.S. Department of Transportation.

Indykiewicz, Piotr. 1991. "Nests and Nest-Sites of the House Sparrow *Passer domesticus* (Linnaeus, 1758) in Urban, Suburban and Rural Environments." *Acta Zoologica Cracoviensia* 34 (2): 475–95.

Jones, Menna E. 2000. "Road Upgrade, Road Mortality and Remedial Measures: Impacts on a Population of Eastern Quolls and Tasmanian Devils." *Wildlife Research* 27 (3): 289–96.

Keninger, Lucy E., Kevin J. Gaston, Katherine N. Irvine, and Richard A. Fuller. 2013. "What Are the Benefits of Interacting with Nature?" *International Journal of Environmental Research and Public Health* 10 (3): 913–35.

Kim, H.H. 1992. "Urban Heat Island." *International Journal of Remote Sensing* 13 (12): 2319–36.

Klem, Daniel Jr., Christopher J. Farmer, Nicole Delacretaz, Yigal Gelb, and Peter G. Saenger. 2009. "Architectural and Landscape Risk Factors Associated with Bird—Glass Collisions in an Urban Environment." *Wilson Journal of Ornithology* 121 (1): 126–34.

Koenig, Walter D. 2003. "European Starlings and Their Effect on Native Cavity-Nesting Birds." *Conservation Biology* 17 (4): 1134–40.

Kunz, Thomas H., Elizabeth Braun de Torrez, Dana Bauer, Tatyana Lobova, and Theodore H. Fleming. 2011. "Ecosystem Services Provided by Bats." *Annals of the New York Academy of Sciences* 1223 (1): 1–38.

Langlands, Brian K. 2014. *Cultivating Neighborhood: Identifying Best Practices for Launching a Christ-Centered Community Garden*. Eugene, Ore.: Resource Publications.

Larson, Courtney L., Sarah E. Reed, Adlina M. Merenlender, and Kevin R. Crooks. 2018. "Accessibility Drives Species Exposure to Recreation in a Fragmented Urban Reserve Network." *Landscape and Urban Planning* 175: 62–71.

Lenth, Benjamin E., Richard L. Knight, and Mark E. Brennan. 2008. "The Effects of Dogs on Wildlife Communities." *Natural Areas Journal* 28 (3): 218–27.

Lenth, Buffy A., Richard L. Knight, and Wendell C. Gilgert. 2006. "Conservation Value of Clustered Housing Developments." *Conservation Biology* 20 (5): 1445–56.

Longcore, Travis, and Catherine Rich. 2004. "Ecological Light Pollution." *Frontiers in Ecology and the Environment* 2 (4): 191–98.

Loss, Scott R., Tom Will, Sarah S. Loss, and Peter P. Marra. 2014. "Bird-Building Collisions in the United States: Estimates of Annual Mortality and Species Vulnerability." *The Condor* 116 (1): 8–23.

Loss, Scott R., Tom Will, and Peter P. Marra. 2013. "The Impact of Free-Ranging Domestic Cats on Wildlife of the United States." *Nature Communications* 4: 1396.

Love, Marianne, and Olga Grigoryants. 2022. "Ground Broken for $87 Million Wildlife Bridge over 101 Freeway to Save Mountain Lions and Other Creatures." *Los Angeles Daily News*, April 22. www.dailynews.com/2022/04/22/ground-broken-for-87-million-wildlife-bridge-over-101-freeway-to-save-mountain-lions-and-other-creatures-2/.

Lundholm, Jeremy T., and Paul J. Richardson. 2010. "Mini-Review: Habitat Analogues for Reconciliation Ecology in Urban and Industrial Environments." *Journal of Applied Ecology* 47 (5): 966–75.

Magle, Seth B., and Lisa M. Angeloni. 2011. "Effects of Urbanization on the Behaviour of a Keystone Species." *Behaviour* 148 (1): 31–54.

Magle, Seth B., Sharon A. Poessel, Kevin R. Crooks, and Stewart W. Breck. 2014. "More Dogs Less Bite: The Relationship Between Human–Coyote Conflict and Prairie Dog Colonies in an Urban Landscape." *Landscape and Urban Planning* 127: 146–53.

Matteson, Kevin C., and Gail A. Langellotto. 2009. "Bumblebee Abundance in New York City Community Gardens: Implications for Urban Agriculture." *Cities and the Environment* 2 (1): 5.

McGranahan, Gordon, Peter Marcotullio, Xuemei Bai, Deborah Balk, Tania Braga, Ian Douglas, Thomas Elmqvist, et al. 2005. "Urban Systems." In *Ecosystems and Human Well-Being: Current State and Trends*, edited by Rashid M. Hassan, R. J. Scholes, and Neville Ash, 795–825. Washington, D.C.: Island Press.

Medina, Félix M., Elsa Bonnaud, Eric Vidal, Bernie R. Tershy, Erika S. Zavaleta, C. Josh Donlan, Bradford S. Keitt, et al. 2011. "A Global Review of the Impacts of Invasive Cats on Island Endangered Vertebrates." *Global Change Biology* 17 (11): 3503–10.

Murray, Maureen H., Kaylee A. Byers, Jacquieline Buckley, Elizabeth W. Lehrer, Cria Kay, Mason Fidino, Seth B. Magle, and Danielle German. 2023. "Public Perception of Urban Wildlife During a COVID-19 Stay-at-Home Quarantine Order in Chicago." *Urban Ecosystems* 26 (1): 127–40.

Murray, Maureen H., Cecilia A. Sánchez, Daniel J. Becker, Kaylee A. Byers, Katherine E.L. Worsley-Tonks, and Meggan E. Craft. 2019. "City Sicker? A Meta-Analysis of Wildlife Health and Urbanization." *Frontiers in Ecology and the Environment* 17 (10): 575–83.

Nicholls, Sarah, and John L. Crompton. 2005. "The Impact of Greenways on Property Values: Evidence from Austin, Texas." *Journal of Leisure Research* 37 (3): 321–41.

Oberndorfer, Erica, Jeremy Lundholm, Brad Bass, Reid R. Coffman, Hitesh Doshi, Nigel Dunnett, Stuart Gaffin, Manfred Köhler, et al. 2007. "Green Roofs as Urban Ecosystems: Ecological Structures, Functions, and Services." *BioScience* 57 (10): 823–33.

Parsons, Glenn. 2008. *Aesthetics and Nature*. London and New York: Continuum.

Poessel, Sharon A., Stewart W. Breck, Tara L. Neel, Stephanie A. Shwiff, Kevin R. Crooks, and Lisa Angeloni. 2013. "Patterns of Human-Coyote Conflicts in the Denver Metropolitan Area." *Journal of Wildlife Management* 77 (2): 297–305.

Prudic, Kathleen L., Terese Maxine P. Cruz, Jazmin I.B. Winzer, Jeffrey C. Oliver, Natalie A. Melkonoff, Hank Verbais, and Andrew Hogan. 2022. "Botanical Gardens Are Local Hotspots for Urban Butterflies in Arid Environments." *Insects* 13 (10): 865.

Roelofs, Joan. 1999. "Building and Designing with Nature: Urban Design." In *The Earthscan Reader in Sustainable Cities*, edited by David Satterthwaite, 234–50. Abingdon and New York: Earthscan.

Romin, Laura A., and John A. Bissonette. 1996. "Deer-Vehicle Collisions: Status of State Monitoring Activities and Mitigation Efforts." *Journal of Wildlife Management* 24 (2): 276–83.

Rosatte, Richard, Kirk Sobey, Jerry W. Dragoo, and Stanley D. 2010. "Striped Skunks and Allies (Mephitis spp.)." In *Urban Carnivores: Ecology Conflict, and Conservation*, edited by Stanley D. Gehrt, Seth P.D. Riley, and Brian L. Cypher, 97–106. Baltimore, Md.: Johns Hopkins University Press.

Schirmer, Aaron E., Caleb Gallemore, Ting Liu, Seth Magle, Elisabeth DiNello, Humerah Ahmed, and Thomas Gilday. 2019. "Mapping Behaviorally Relevant Light Pollution Levels to Improve Urban Habitat Planning." *Scientific Reports* 9 (1): 1–13.

Schweitz, Lea F. 2015. "*Mysterium* Opossum." In *City Creatures: Animal Encounters in the Chicago Wilderness*, edited by Gavin Van Horn and Dave Aftandilian, 45–50. Chicago, Ill. and London: University of Chicago Press.

_____. 2017. "Reforming Our Visions of City Nature." *Intersections* 2017 (46): 17–22. https://digitalcommons.augustana.edu/intersections/vol2017/iss46/7/.

_____. 2020. "A Case Study for Lived Religion-and-Science: Theology of Urban Ecology." In *T&T Clark Handbook of Christian Theology and the Modern Sciences*, edited by John P. Slattery, 319–31. London and New York: T&T Clark.

Sorace, Alberto, and Marco Gustin. 2009. "Distribution of Generalist and Specialist Predators along Urban Gradients." *Landscape and Urban Planning* 90 (3–4): 111–18.

Soulsbury, Carl D., and Piran C.L. White. 2015. "Human-Wildlife Interactions in Urban Areas: A Review of Conflicts, Benefits, and Opportunities." *Wildlife Research* 42 (7): 541–53.

Taylor, Brendan D., and Ross L. Goldingay. 2010. "Roads and Wildlife: Impacts, Mitigation and Implications for Wildlife Management in Australia." *Wildlife Research* 37: 320–31.

United Nations. 2019. *World Urbanization Prospects 2018: Highlights*. New York: United Nations Department of Economic and Social Affairs, Population Division.

Urbanek, Rachael E., Kristin R. Allen, and Clayton K. Nielsen. 2011. "Urban and Suburban Deer Management by State Wildlife Conservation Agencies." *Wildlife Society Bulletin* 35 (3): 310–15.

Van Horn, Gavin, and Dave Aftandilian, eds. 2015. *City Creatures: Animal Encounters in the Chicago Wilderness*. Chicago, Ill. and London: University of Chicago Press.

Whelan, Christopher J., Daniel G. Wenny, and Robert J. Marquis. 2008. "Ecosystem Services Provided by Birds." *Annals of the New York Academy of Sciences* 1134: 25–60.

White, Ethan P. 2004. "Factors Affecting Bat House Occupancy in Colorado." *The Southwestern Naturalist* 49 (3): 344–49.

White, Lynsey A., and Stanley D. Gehrt. 2009. "Coyote Attacks on Humans in the United States and Canada." *Human Dimensions of Wildlife* 14: 419–32.

Widows, Steffenie A., and David Drake. 2014. "Evaluating the National Wildlife Federation's Certified Wildlife Habitat™ Program." *Landscape and Urban Planning* 129: 32–43.

Wilkins, Devin C., Kara M. Kockelman, and Nan Jiang. 2019. "Animal-Vehicle Collisions in Texas: How to Protect Travelers and Animals on Roadways." *Accident Analysis and Prevention* 131: 157–70.

Wille, Lois. 1991. *Forever Open, Clear, and Free: The Struggle for Chicago's Lakefront*. 2nd ed. Chicago, Ill. and London: University of Chicago Press.

Woinarski, J.C.Z., B.P. Murphy, S.M. Legge, S.T. Garnett, M.J. Lawes, S. Comer, C.R. Dickman, T.S. Doherty, et al. 2017. "How Many Birds Are Killed by Cats in Australia?" *Biological Conservation* 214: 76–87.

Wolf, Peter J. 2016. "What If Everything You Thought You Knew About 'Feral' Cats Was Wrong?" *Proceedings of the Vertebrate Pest Conference* 27 (27): 44–51. https://escholarship.org/uc/item/6ks593jz.

Zellmer, Amanda J., Eric M. Wood, Thilina Surasinghe, Breanna J. Putman, Gregory B. Pauly, Seth B. Magle, Jesse S. Lewis, et al. 2020. "What Can We Learn from Wildlife Sightings During the COVID-19 Global Shutdown?" *Ecosphere* 11 (8): e03215.

Other Recommended Resources

Chicago Wilderness Alliance. www.chicagowilderness.org.

Compassion Consortium. www.compassionconsortium.org.

Green Chalice Creation Care Ministry, Christian Church (Disciples of Christ). www.greenchalice.org.

Sacred Grounds Program, National Wildlife Federation. www.nwf.org/sacredgrounds.

Sacred Sendoffs. www.sacredsendoffs.com.

Saint Kateri Habitats Program. www.kateri.org/saint-kateri-habitat-2/.

Urban Wildlife Information Network. www.urbanwildlifeinfo.org.

Urban Wildlife Institute, Lincoln Park Zoo. www.lpzoo.org/conservation-science/science-centers/urban-wildlife-institute/.

Urban Wildlife Project, Elm Tree Theatre. www.urbanwildlifeproject.org.

Urban Wildlife Working Group. http://urbanwildlifegroup.org.

U.S. Fish & Wildlife Service's Urban Wildlife Conservation Program. www.fws.gov/program/urban-wildlife-conservation.

30 The Connection We Share

Animal Spirituality and the Science of Sacred Encounters

Barbara Smuts, Becca Franks, Monica Gagliano, and Christine Webb[1]

Introduction

I (B.S.) was driving across the southwestern U.S. when I stopped at a picnic site to stretch my legs and consider a difficult personal situation. Walking in scrubland, I encountered a kiva, a circular underground "bowl" structure built by Pueblo peoples for spiritual ceremonies. Partly hidden by vegetation and open to the sky, it was apparently deserted. I climbed down, knelt, placed my forehead on the ground, and prayed for help moving through pain to wisdom. After what felt like a long time, I lifted my head to see a half-dozen mule deer gathered around the edge of the kiva, peering down at me with huge ears and soft expressions. My deer companions did not startle or leave when I sat up but watched me a bit longer and then slowly moved away. Their lack of fear and deep stillness seemed inconsistent with mere curiosity, and I wondered if they sensed my emotional state. Although this happened over thirty years ago, I still remember how peaceful I felt in their presence.

Sometimes encounters like these with other than human animals seem magical, as in a storybook, where someone appears unexpectedly, and extraordinary events unfold. These same events, however, can also be understood as potentially everyday occurrences, but crucially, ones that tend to occur (or be noticed) only if we abandon the assumption that animals are inferior to humans. Under this assumption, humans are the pinnacle of life, somehow superior to and separate from all other beings (see Matthew Calarco's Chapter 7 on animals as "same, other, indistinct" in this volume). The linked ideologies of anthropocentrism and human supremacy are so deeply engrained in Western society that, without conscious effort, almost everyone, including scientists, accepts their basic premises (Jensen 2016; Tobias and Morrison 2017; Franks et al. 2023).

Abandoning, or at least reconsidering, these premises means rejecting relentless skepticism about the capabilities of other beings. However, such a profound shift in worldview cannot simply be willed. Instead, it requires practices like mindfulness (see section on "How Can Science Change?" later) that help transform who we are and how we see the world. Even seemingly simple mental shifts such as maintaining moment-to-moment awareness of the animals around us—both seen and unseen—can radically alter what we notice, and, therefore, who we understand animals to be.

In this chapter, we consider what mental shifts are necessary to open us to potential spiritual qualities in the ordinary lives of animals, and the scientific values and practices that might facilitate this opening, or at least not foreclose it. The possibility of animal spiritualities can inspire awe, wonder, and profound respect for the multitude of beings

DOI: 10.4324/9781003324157-35

with whom we share this planet, and it can bring us closer to the deep mysteries of existence that inspire religion.

Religious Naturalism

At first glance, it might seem that viewing animals as sacred or spiritual beings and studying them as scientists are antithetical. However, both religion and science are changing in ways that can bring them closer together. For some, scientific knowledge can intensify the experience of nature's magic. This view was powerfully expressed by Brian Swimme and Thomas Berry (1992), an astrophysicist and a theologian, who together articulated the Universe Story—a mythic retelling grounded in both scientific and spiritual understandings of the origins of the cosmos, galaxies, planetary systems, and life on earth. They urged readers to recognize that, "The natural world itself is the primary economic reality, the primary educator, the primary governance . . . the primary healer, the primary presence of the sacred, and the primary moral value" (Swimme and Berry 1992, 255).

A deep understanding of the Universe Story has inspired a number of scholars and others to identify as *religious naturalists* (Goodenough 2023; Rue 2011; Swimme and Tucker 2011; Tucker 2011). Ursula Goodenough and Paul Woodruff (2004) articulate two components of religious naturalism: mindfulness and reverence. Mindfulness is familiar to those who practice meditation. It involves non-egoistic apprehensions of reality based on direct experience, freed as much as possible from preconceptions about what something— one's own mind, a star, a flower, a fish—is or what that something means. It requires minimizing distraction, immersion in the moment, an open mind, and a soft heart.

Reverence involves feelings of awe, respect, and humility, associated with the realization that we exist in a "context that is vastly larger and more important than our selves" (Goodenough and Woodruff 2004, 592). We feel reverence for phenomena, actions, ideals, or material realities that inspire feelings of transcendence, wonder, and a deep sense of mystery.

For religious naturalists, the natural world is a source of mindful reverence (Goodenough and Woodruff 2004, 592). This represents a novel perspective for most Western worldviews for two reasons. First, as mentioned earlier, it encompasses not only our experiences of nature but also our scientific understanding. For religious naturalists, such understanding deepens their sense of what it means to be human, to be animal, to be alive, and to exist at such a perilous time for the earth.

Second, religious naturalists expand our notions of religious experience. Although Goodenough's worldview is nontheistic, she has a "profoundly religious relationship with the cosmos rooted in her detailed understanding of phenomena such as . . . the complex workings of a cell, and the astonishing evolutionary emergence of a mind capable of inquiring into its own nature" (Smuts 1999b, 100).[2] Sources of reverence among religious naturalists are myriad and varied. For us, encounters with other animals like those described here are religious experiences. For others, such experiences can be inspired by learning about the Big Bang or discovering that a plant can learn (e.g., Gagliano 2018).

When we revere something, it acquires profound meaning, and we are inspired to honor and protect it, whether it be a rainforest, a mountain gorilla, a human elder, the microscopic inhabitants of a puddle, or the entire planet. Caring deeply entails vulnerability because what we hold sacred may disappear or be harmed or defiled. Goodenough and Woodruff describe the religious naturalist community as a source of "relief from this vulnerability" where "we can suffer and celebrate with kindred spirits, sharing our reverence for all that we hold in awe, toward all that we find in our common search, to be transcendent" (Goodenough and Woodruff 2004, 594).

Although religious naturalism suggests ways to experience our own place in the cosmos, conventional scientific values and practices are too often inimical to efforts to identify and understand spirituality in *other* animals. Here we briefly describe some changes that might better unite science with these efforts, with a focus on different ways of doing science, including new ways scientists can relate to other animals.

How Can Science Change?

Different Ways of Doing Science

Studying animal spirituality scientifically would mean abandoning all notions of human supremacy that *predetermine who animals are and how we should treat them* (see Matthew Calarco's chapter in this volume). For example, many scientists start with the assumption that their animal subjects lack sentience (see Chapter 2 on "Animal Consciousness and Cognition" by Robert W. Mitchell and Mark A. Krause in this volume). How might we do science differently if we assumed, instead, that our subjects are sentient, so that our task is to discover how and what they think and feel (Webb et al. 2023)? For one, scientists could change their language, describing animals as decision-making creatures, not mechanistic automatons (Crist 1999); we could refer to them as "who," not "which"; and when their gender is known, as "she" or "he" or "they," not "it" (Goodall et al. 2021).[3] Also, when appropriate, our scientific writing could include anecdotes and qualitative data, since quantitative data, although a critical piece of the puzzle, leave gaps in our understanding of animals.

Scientists also need to reconsider exactly what they mean when they assert that science must be "objective." Objectivity supposedly avoids biases that might distort scientific findings, but conflating objectivity with the doubt and denial of animal sentience or adhering to the conviction that animals lack consciousness can introduce biases of its own—it is difficult, if not impossible, to observe what you do not believe exists. Since everyone brings preconceived attitudes and biases to their research, true objectivity is a myth. Conversely, sometimes, the opposite of detachment can produce scientific breakthroughs (see Rosner 1994 on Barbara McClintock's "feeling for the organism"). When we reject rigid and outdated notions of what constitutes objectivity, we can open new avenues of inquiry by studying animals with tools such as intuition and empathy, mental abilities that evolved precisely to enable humans to understand other beings (Webb et al. 2023; Wels 2013).

The values that guide science must also change. All too often, animals in research are treated as tools for exclusively human purposes (such as to develop new drugs for human diseases or to maximize agricultural profit) rather than beings whose lives and futures matter. "To meet the modern crises of climate change, radical declines in biodiversity, and mass species extinctions, animal interests (including the interests of the particular animals involved in the research) must be given priority" (Franks et al. 2020, 3).

Different Ways to Research and Relate to Other Animals

We believe that animal research should begin as a contemplative practice designed to release the scientist, as much as possible, from ideas and expectations about what the animals are like. Mindfulness and other meditative practices are invaluable for these purposes (see Chapter 24 on "Contemplative Practices" by Dave Aftandilian in this volume). Simone Weil (2002) and Hanne De Jaegher (2021) describe how approaches grounded in attention or love, respectively, can work profound changes in what is and can be known.

> In a state of attention, we let go of all efforts to decode the animal's behavior and instead allow the animal's own way of being to surface. What results is a diminishing of the self, helping to avoid self-serving and self-focused conceptualizations of who animals are.
>
> (Webb et al. 2023, 228)

Attentive love (see also Donovan 2007; Aaltola 2013) allows the scientist to determine the most appropriate ways to relate to the animals, partly in terms of how to facilitate observations but most importantly in terms of the animals' own interests.[4] Depending on a variety of factors, scientists can sometimes follow animals closely, but only after careful and often prolonged periods of mutual accommodation where the animals set the rules. In such situations, maintaining some distance may be necessary, but sometimes animals end up completely ignoring scientists in their midst, and in some instances, the animals come to regard scientists as sentient beings like themselves, with whom they can communicate. Remaining entirely neutral in the face of such invitations can confuse animals, foreclose any kind of relationship with them, inhibit their behavioral repertoire, and even render them fearful. Mutual engagement with the animals can, in contrast, offer insights impossible to attain any other way (see Smuts 2001b on wild baboons). Finally, bringing deep awareness to the study of other beings will likely enhance the scientist's compassion for them, which is necessary if we are to represent animals' interests not just as entities like populations or species but also at the level of individuals (Ramp and Bekoff 2015; Treves, Santiago-Ávila, and Lynn 2019; Rizzolo and Bradshaw 2021).

These ideas merely hint at myriad ways in which science can and must change for the sake of our fellow animals. For further discussion, see the section "Other Recommended Resources" at the end of this chapter.

Animals as Sacred and Spiritual Beings

Are other animals *sacred*? We consider this question to be about how humans perceive the beingness of other animals, so responses are subjective. It's a bit like asking, are snakes beautiful? Some people think so, and others don't. The authors of this chapter consider all life to be sacred. This belief has a lot to do with how much time we have spent with the more-than-human world and how much we love the beings we have encountered there—from the beings we live with, such as dogs, to the inhabitants of our gardens, to individual animals residing in less human-dominated spaces.

Are other animals *spiritual*? This is a different question; it is about who the animals actually are. At this stage, we do not think anyone can assert definitively that other animals are *not* spiritual creatures, but we likewise do not wish to assert that they definitely *are*. To resolve the question, we would first need to define what we mean by "spiritual" and then ask, If an animal were spiritual, how would we know? As scientists, we will not propose formalized answers to either of these questions.

However, we are not just scientists but also humans who have engaged intimately with many different creatures who made us feel that we were meeting spiritual beings.

Like the famous Buddhist analogy of the finger pointing at the moon, we gesture toward what we understand "spiritual" to mean by sharing some of our encounters with other animals. To us, these encounters suggest a capacity among animals to experience and act upon transcendent emotions—for example, expressing delight in and empathy for others, sometimes beyond one's own species, without necessarily expecting anything in return. They also resonate with participatory, embodied theories in which spirituality is construed not as an experience *of* something but *with* something (see Cunningham 2022a, 2022b; Schaefer 2015; Ferrer and Sherman 2008). As we share these episodes, we will reflect back on the aforementioned ideas about how science might change to accommodate experiences like ours in the hope that other researchers may feel similarly inspired.

Animal Encounters

For three summers, B.S. studied wild bottlenose dolphins in Shark Bay, Western Australia. Several student researchers had already identified dozens of individual dolphins by the shape and state of their fins (e.g., numbers and locations of nicks and holes). After a relatively short time, I came to regard fins as faces because they told me who was who. We studied the dolphins from small motorboats that helped us to keep up with their speedy movements (Smolker, Mann, and Smuts 1993; Connor et al. 2011; McCue et al. 2019). But I felt closest to the dolphins when I was the only human present, sitting on a small surfboard-like platform that I paddled like a kayak.

At dusk, when our studies were completed, I ventured out into the calm sea, envisioning which familiar dolphin I most wanted to encounter. A small group of dolphins always showed up. More often than not, the familiar animals included the dolphin I had hoped to see—an unlikely event, given the many dozens of dolphins we recognized individually.

The dolphins greeted me as they greeted our research boats, swimming alongside and lifting their heads to view me out of one eye. When we were in the boats, the dolphins would speed away after a short greeting, but when I was practically sitting in the water on the board, they would stay with me and play. First, two of them would repeatedly jump over me in synchrony, from opposite sides, so that they passed in the air.[5] (They leaped only over the board, not our research boats.) After a while, they rode the bow (front) of the board as a group, looking back at me to see if I got the joke. When dolphins ride the bow of a speeding boat, their movements gain an extra thrust, which they enjoy. However, my tiny vessel's movement was minimal compared to the speed with which dolphins can swim, so riding its bow had no effect. Thus, the joke.

After these antics, the small group would swim along with me for a while, diving and resurfacing in synchrony with each other, the only sound the soft pop of expressed air from their blowholes. We seemed to be alone in the vast sea, these few dolphins and I, and the fact that we knew one another as individuals made our gathering especially intimate. It seemed we had co-created a dolphin-human bubble of pure joy.

Dusk seems like a special time. For B.S. with dolphins, and for both B.S. and C.W. with baboons, during the day, both the animals and we maintained our separate spheres of activity. However, at dusk and afterward, normal rules of engagement mysteriously relaxed, allowing us to just *be*—together. For instance, young baboons would bounce off our bodies during high-speed chases, and dolphins would leap over the vessel, activities they did not do during the day. These are good examples of how scientists and their subjects can negotiate different ways of relating that afford new glimpses of one another.[6]

The dolphin habitat, Shark Bay, was on the edge of a vast inland desert, with no human inhabitants for miles around except a few like us who lived on the beach. On days when it was too windy to go out to sea, B.S. would walk in the bush. It was the start of Australia's winter, the rainy season, and the desert was in bloom with a profusion of pink and yellow flowers. I rarely saw anything but birds and footprints, but I knew kangaroos, emus, and other fantastic creatures were all around. We seemed to be in a magical play, where everyone shared the same stage but remained unseen. The invisibility spell broke only once when a male red kangaroo entered stage left, bounded over twenty feet in one leap, and exited stage right. I felt especially blessed once I discovered how rare red kangaroo sightings are; none of my students had ever seen one, despite frequent walks in the bush. I thought with great sadness about the dangers to red kangaroos and other animals during the dry season when normal seasonal outback fires are being greatly exacerbated by human-induced climate change.

Some encounters seem grounded in mutual empathy, as each becomes oriented to the embodied minds of the others. B.S.'s encounter with a female gorilla provides a good example. After wandering away from my fellow scientists at a colleague's field site, I came across a small circle of females and young gorillas resting in the shade. I settled a few yards away and sat quietly. An adolescent female glanced my way. I maintained eye contact and, with all my heart, beamed her the message: "I love you!" That's when she got up, left the circle, stood so close that her breath fogged up my glasses, and wrapped her arms around me. Her hug felt like a profound blessing. (Curious, I asked the field site director if female gorillas tended to hug humans; she said, "No.")

Many others have described moving encounters with wild animals. To us, one of the most astonishing involves a female diver who removes hooks from the mouths of large Caribbean reef sharks—who do not attack her during this painful process (BBC 2019).

As many people know firsthand, deeply moving and even awe-inspiring interactions with other animals are not limited to wild creatures. With domestic animals, and especially when they are in relation to us as companions, we often try to read their minds just as they seem always to be reading ours. But mutual, loving mind reading can be even more profound than many of us believe possible.

For example, during a distressing time in B.S.'s life, she and her dog, Safi, visited a nearby river. I was throwing sticks in the water, Safi's favorite game, but instead of retrieving them, she swam to a small island in the middle of the river and lay down about fifteen feet away, facing me. Safi stared at me, perfectly still, until I, too, finally sat quietly, meeting her gaze. She maintained eye contact for at least ten minutes. I lost all awareness of everything but Safi's eyes and felt completely at peace. That day Safi taught me to meditate (see also Smuts 1999a, 2001b).

Similarly, Picasso, M.G.'s dog, has participated in meditation circles during which he sat quietly and still on his cushion next to me (M.G.) until someone in the group encountered emotional pain—an internal state hidden to the human meditators. On several occasions, I witnessed Picasso getting up from his cushion and quietly approaching a person to place one of his front paws on the person's heart. Picasso stayed in that position for a time, which often resulted in the person bursting into tears. Picasso waited for the person to settle into a calmer state before returning to his cushion as quietly as he had left. Later, the person would describe Picasso's touch as a "healing intervention"—a touch full of love that facilitated an emotional release.

These stories suggest that animals can relate to us as spiritual beings, in the sense that they are profoundly sensitive and capable of behaving in loving ways toward humans, even strangers, perhaps especially if we are in a receptive frame of mind. In such encounters, they can watch over us (mule deer), offer love (gorilla, Safi, Picasso), bring us great joy (dolphins, baboons, ducks; see further down), astound us (ducks, red kangaroos), and offer (Safi, Picasso) or request (wild sharks) help.

However, we do not need to interact directly with animals to experience their presence as a spiritual gift. Many of the wild animals we know best often seem content. Perhaps this is because they do not dwell unduly on the past or future, tend to approach difficult tasks with enthusiasm, love socializing, and experience chances to goof off with great pleasure. Knowing how to live in the moment, being enthusiastic, caring for others, and relaxing into happiness—these are positive ways of being that are often associated with spiritual experiences. Even when we observe animals from afar, we can feel these and other positive emotions vicariously.

Similarly, we may be graced by transcendent moments of wonder or awe just by being in natural places where animals roam freely:

> My awareness shifted from the thoughts that filled my head to moment-to-moment reality. With each step, I could feel how I was designed to flourish in the wild. My eyes . . . are made to scan for bright-colored fruit. . . . My ears are made to notice a rustle in the grass [and] my feet are made to feel the texture of the ground . . . my heart to beat fast or slow in response to the matrix of sounds, sights and scents in which I am enveloped . . . my whole being is made to stay open every moment to every sensory nuance.
>
> (Smuts 2001a, 28)

Many animals, of course, live like this all the time. Being mentally alert with a relaxed body—the goal of many meditative practices—is usually the safest and most efficient way for a wild animal to be. Mirroring such states can, in many instances, bring us into greater harmony with the animals we study. We remember these ways of being as among our deepest spiritual experiences, and we believe others can feel like this, too, simply by spending quiet time in the natural world.

Of course, transformative moments can also occur in the everyday. During graduate school in New York City, B.F. regularly commuted by bicycle regardless of the weather. One dark winter evening, heading home with my head down against the snow and wind, a realization gradually took hold. I heard ducks, many ducks, vocalizing. But the commotion was coming from the left, where there was an embankment, not from the river on the right. Eventually, grudgingly (it was cold, and home was far), I braked to investigate. By then, the flock was mostly behind me, but one duck zipped close by, sliding across the bike path at speed. Stupefied, I pulled out my phone, took a short video of the scene, and mechanically resumed my route.

In reality, the ducks were sledding—tottering up the hill, turning at the top, taking a few quick steps downhill, tucking webbed feet beneath feathered bellies, and hurtling themselves down the snowy slope. What magic! Almost not to be believed. And indeed, I almost didn't believe it. And because I almost didn't believe it, I almost couldn't process it, and thus almost didn't see it, and even so, I almost didn't remember it (if not for that video; see Franks 2013).

We know the world is overflowing with information—more information than any single human mind can ever hope to process. So events get missed, sometimes systematically. When we decide that nonhuman beings are inferior, predictable, spiritless contraptions, it is easy to ignore evidence to the contrary. In this state of denial, it may take something as "outrageous" as a flock of quacking, sledding ducks to shake us from our non-attentive states.

Animals as Spiritual Beings

All of these examples have to do with how other animals behaved when interacting with us or how we perceived them when observing them. But do animals show behaviors that might indicate they have spiritual lives or spiritual experiences themselves, completely apart from how they relate to us?

Many years ago, Jane Goodall described male chimpanzees' rhythmic swaying, leaping, and rock-throwing displays at waterfalls and during intense storms. She suggested that these behaviors reflected feelings of awe similar, perhaps, to those that inspired "the first animistic religions, the worship of the elements and the mysteries of nature over which there was no control" (Goodall 2006, 653). These displays and similar activity during earthquakes (Fujimoto and Hanamura 2008) occur only in specific populations and thus appear to be socially learned traditions, an aspect of group culture.[7]

Ritualized behavior upon the death of a group member is the other main context in which animals' potential spiritual inclinations have been reported. A variety of animal species show behaviors around death that were previously thought to be limited to humans. These include postmortem transport of dead infants by marine mammals and nonhuman primates; complex behaviors toward dead or dying individuals in great apes and elephants, such as gathering as witnesses; as well as evidence of distress and attempts to help (e.g., Anderson 2020; Watts 2020). Elephants sometimes repeatedly investigate and handle conspecific bones and corpses and sometimes try to cover dead conspecific bodies with vegetation (Goldenberg and Wittemyer 2020). Such behaviors indicate both an awareness of death and, perhaps, rudimentary attempts to protect or even honor corpses.

Whereas these examples stem from repeated similar observations by different scientists, we include one more instance of possible animal spirituality witnessed (as far as we know) by only one person (Smuts 2001b). At Gombe, B.S. often followed baboons on forest paths they had worn alongside mountain streams. After being with them for months, I saw something new. The animals spread out along a stream, with many sitting on smooth rocks that lined the water. Everyone became completely silent, sat very still, and gazed into pools, without touching the water. Even the ordinarily rowdy juveniles became still and quiet. The animals sat this way for about thirty minutes and then slowly moved to their sleeping trees in what felt to me like a spiritual procession. Had I witnessed this only once, I think I would have doubted my perceptions, but I saw it twice, just a few days apart. I came to think of these times as the coming together of a baboon spiritual community.

While witnessing these events, I felt as if a normally opaque barrier thinned, like a veil, allowing me to see something that would otherwise remain hidden. If animals do have spiritual practices, we wonder if, in some instances, they are kept private. If we were wild animals, we would hide such practices from humans, who so often bring disruption or violence. Humans often share religious or spiritual practices only within trusted communities. Why should other animals be any different? However, B.S.'s baboon experience and others described here indicate that if we view animals with reverence and humility, believing, in our hearts, that their lives, loves, and even spiritual practices are as important as our own, perhaps we might glimpse worlds beyond the veil more often.

Conclusion

The encounters with animal spirituality described here harmonize with Swimme and Berry's assertion that "the universe is a communion of subjects rather than a collection of objects" (Swimme and Berry 1992, 243). They also resonate deeply with Indigenous ways of knowing and doing science, in which understanding and experiencing the natural world does not occur through the lens of objectification (Cajete 2000). These stories also suggest that perhaps the animals in our lives are potential spiritual partners, who are only waiting to be seen, both beautiful and brave (to paraphrase Rainer Maria Rilke).[8]

In this vein, we end where we began—with wild mule deer. In one of the most intimate studies of wild animals ever conducted, Joe Hutto spent every day for seven years living among a herd of these ordinarily shy animals (Hutto 2014). He began observing deer from within a mountain cabin, but they invited him into the herd, and he came to know every individual, developing profoundly tender relationships with these highly sensitive beings. Over time, he witnessed ever-increasing human-imposed threats to the herd's (and the species') very existence. Eventually, the human-caused deaths of individuals he loved caused him so much grief that he had to end this remarkable study.[9]

What if, like Hutto, more of us recognized how much we share rather than what supposedly separates us from other animals?[10] So often, we place human intelligence, consciousness, and the capacity for religion and spirituality on one side of a divide, with the supposed absence of these capacities in other animals on the other side. Because these assumptions have blinded scientists and non-scientists for so long, we are only beginning to understand (or remember) who animals really are. For the four of us, as scientists who know other animals well, they are utterly deserving of our respect, wonder, and reverence.

Notes

1 Barbara Smuts is lead author; the coauthors are listed in alphabetical order.
2 Religious naturalism is not a religion *per se*; it is a religious perspective. It is compatible with many aspects of traditional religions, and it may or may not involve belief in a deity (Goodenough 2023).
3 The next time you watch an animal documentary or read about them, notice how often even those that seem to respect the animals refer to them as "it."
4 When entering the animals' space would disrupt or endanger their lives, scientists must observe from a distance and/or consider using motion-activated cameras (a technology that in itself raises ethical questions). In such instances, scientists can nevertheless develop a deep sense of intimacy with their subjects.
5 Male bottlenose dolphins synchronize displays in this way when they jointly court females (McCue et al. 2019).
6 Similarly, religions specify times of day or days of the week to be held apart from the daily grind, times when everyone can relax and be with family and friends.
7 Barbara Smuts observed a silverback mountain gorilla displaying, while his groupmates held unnaturally still, about ten seconds before the humans present detected a nearby volcanic eruption.
8 "Perhaps all the dragons of our lives are princesses who are only waiting to see us once beautiful and brave" (Rilke 1934, 69).
9 However, Hutto continues to work for the protection of mule deer and the habitats they rely on.
10 See Matthew Calarco's (2018) relevant notion of the "three ethologies." Calarco uses Hutto's work as a lens through which to explore other ways of doing and thinking about science with other animals, intersecting with many of the themes explored in this chapter.

References

Aaltola, Elise. 2013. "Skepticism, Empathy, and Animal Suffering." *Journal of Bioethical Inquiry* 10 (4): 457–67.

Anderson, James R. 2020. "Responses to Death and Dying: Primates and Other Mammals." *Primates* 61 (1): 1–7.

BBC. 2019. "The Woman Who Swims with Sharks." Video. April 15. https://www.youtube.com/watch?v=uGzzQX0jNYY.

Cajete, Gregory A. 2000. *Native Science: Natural Laws of Interdependence.* Santa Fe, N.M.: Clear Light Publishers.

Calarco, Matthew. 2018. "The Three Ethologies." In *Exploring Animal Encounters: Philosophical, Cultural, and Historical Perspectives*, edited by Dominik Ohrem and Matthew Calarco, 45–62. Cham: Palgrave Macmillan.

Connor, Richard C., Jana J. Watson-Capps, William B. Sherwin, and Michael Krützen. 2011. "A New Level of Complexity in the Male Alliance Networks of Indian Ocean Bottlenose Dolphins (*Tursiops sp.*)." *Biology Letters* 7 (4): 623–26.

Crist, Eileen. 1999. *Images of Animals: Anthropomorphism and Animal Mind.* Philadelphia, Pa.: Temple University Press.

Cunningham, Paul. 2022a. "The Case for Animal Spirituality—Part 1: Conceptual Challenges, Methodological Considerations, and the Question of Animal Consciousness." *Journal for the Study of Religion, Nature and Culture* 16 (2): 186–224.

_____. 2022b. "The Case for Animal Spirituality—Part 2: Logical Arguments, Empirical Evidence, and Practical Consequences for Human Society." *Journal for the Study of Religion, Nature and Culture* 16 (2): 225–63.

De Jaegher, Hanne. 2021. "Loving and Knowing: Reflections for an Engaged Epistemology." *Phenomenology and the Cognitive Sciences* 20: 847–70.

Donovan, Josephine. 2007. "Attention to Suffering: Sympathy as a Basis for Ethical Treatment of Animals." In *The Feminist Care Tradition in Animal Ethics: A Reader*, edited by Josephine Donovan and Carol J. Adams, 174–97. New York: Columbia University Press.

Ferrer, Jorge, and Jacob Sherman. 2008. "Introduction: The Participatory Turn in Spirituality, Mysticism, and Religious Studies." In *The Participatory Turn*, edited by Jorge Ferrer and Jacob Sherman, 1–78. Albany: State University of New York Press.

Franks, Becca. 2013. "Duck Sledding." Video. https://vimeo.com/82227890.

_____, Monica Gagliano, Barbara Smuts, and Christine Webb. 2023. "Looking Up to Animals and Other Beings: What the Fishes Taught Us." In *Animal Dignity: Philosophical Reflections on Non-Human Existence*, edited by Melanie Challenger. London: Bloomsbury.

_____, Christine Webb, Monica Gagliano, and Barbara Smuts. 2020. "Conventional Science Will Not Do Justice to Nonhuman Interests." *Animal Sentience* 27 (17): 1–5.

Fujimoto, Mariko, and Shunkichi Hanamura. 2008. "Responses of Wild Chimpanzees (*Pan troglodytes schweinfurthii*) Toward Seismic Aftershocks in the Mahale Mountains National Park, Tanzania." *Primates* 49 (1): 73–76.

Gagliano, Monica. 2018. *Thus Spoke the Plant: A Remarkable Journey of Groundbreaking Scientific Discoveries and Personal Encounters with Plants.* Berkeley, Calif.: North Atlantic Books.

Goldenberg, Shifra Z., and George Wittemyer. 2020. "Elephant Behavior Toward the Dead: A Review and Insights from Field Observations." *Primates* 61 (1): 119–28.

Goodall, Jane. 2006. "Epilogue: The Dance of Awe." In *A Communion of Subjects: Animals in Religion, Science and Ethics*, edited by Paul Waldau and Kimberly Patton, 651–56. New York: Columbia University Press.

_____, Marilyn Kroplick, Debra Merskin, Carrie P. Freeman, Marc Bekoff, et al. 2021. "Joint Open Letter to the Associated Press Calling for a Change in Animal Pronouns—Animals Are a Who, Not a What." https://www.idausa.org/assets/files/assets/uploads/pdf/openletterapstylebook.pdf.

Goodenough, Ursula. 2023. *The Sacred Depths of Nature: How Life Emerged and Evolved*. 2nd ed. New York: Oxford University Press.

_____, and Paul Woodruff. 2004. "Mindful Virtue, Mindful Reverence." *Zygon* 36 (4): 585–95.

Hutto, Joseph. 2014. *Touching the Wild: Living with the Mule Deer of Deadman Gulch*. New York: Skyhorse Publishing.

Jensen, Derrick. 2016. *The Myth of Human Supremacy*. New York: Seven Stories Press Publishing AG.

McCue, Laura M., William R. Cioffi, Michael R. Heithaus, and Lynne Barrè. 2019. "Synchrony, Leadership, and Association in Male Indo-Pacific Bottlenose Dolphins (*Tursiops aduncus*)." *Ethology* 126 (7): 741–50.

Ramp, Daniel, and Marc Bekoff. 2015. "Compassion as a Practical and Evolved Ethic for Conservation." *BioScience* 65 (3): 323–27.

Rilke, Rainer Maria. 1934. *Letters to a Young Poet*, rev. ed. Translated by M.D. Herter Norton. New York and London: W.W. Norton.

Rizzolo, Jessica, and Gay Bradshaw. 2021. "Nonhuman Animal Nations: Transforming Conservation into Wildlife Self-Determination." *Society and Animals* 29 (4): 393–413.

Rosner, Mary. 1994. "Values in Doing and Writing Science: The Case of Barbara McClintock." *Journal of Advanced Composition* 14 (2): 475–94.

Rue, Loyal. 2011. *Nature Is Enough—Religious Naturalism and the Meaning of Life*. Albany: State University of New York Press.

Schaefer, Donovan O. 2015. *Religious Affects: Animality, Evolution, and Power*. Durham, N.C.: Duke University Press.

Smolker, Rachel A., Janet Mann, and Barbara B. Smuts. 1993. "Use of Signature Whistles During Separations and Reunions by Wild Bottlenose Dolphin Mothers and Infants." *Behavioral Ecology and Sociobiology* 33 (6): 393–402.

Smuts, Barbara. 1999a. "Living with Animals." Commentary in *The Lives of Animals*, edited by J.M. Coetzee, 107–20. Princeton, N.J.: Princeton University Press.

_____. 1999b. "Sanctifying the Cosmos." Review of *The Sacred Depths of Nature* by Ursula Goodenough. *Scientific American* 280 (5): 100–02.

_____. 2001a. "Coming Home." *Natural History* 110: 26–30.

_____. 2001b. "Encounters with Animal Minds." *Journal of Consciousness Studies* 8 (5): 293–309.

Swimme, Brian, and Thomas Berry. 1992. *The Universe Story: From the Primordial Flaring Forth to the Ecozoic Era—A Celebration of the Unfolding of the Cosmos*. New York: HarperCollins.

Swimme, Brian Thomas, and Mary Evelyn Tucker. 2011. *Journey of the Universe*. New Haven, Conn.: Yale University Press.

Tobias, Michael Charles, and Jane Grey Morrison. 2017. *Anthrozoology: Embracing Co-existence in the Anthropocene*. Cham: Springer International.

Treves, Adrian, Francisco J. Santiago-Ávila, and William S. Lynn. 2019. "Just Preservation." *Biological Conservation* 229: 134–41.

Tucker, Mary Evelyn. 2011. *Worldly Wonder* (The Second Master Hsüan Hua Memorial Lecture). Chicago and La Salle, Ill.: Open Court.

Watts, David P. 2020. "Responses to Dead and Dying Conspecifics and Heterospecifics by Wild Mountain Gorillas (*Gorilla beringei beringei*) and Chimpanzees (*Pan troglodytes schweinfurthii*)." *Primates* 61 (1): 55–68.

Webb, Christine, Becca Franks, Monica Gagliano, and Barbara Smuts. 2023. "Un-Tabooing Empathy: The Benefits of Empathic Science with Nonhuman Research Participants." In *Conversations on Empathy: Interdisciplinary Perspectives on Imagination and Radical Othering*, edited by Francesca Mezzenzana and Daniela Peluso, 216–34. Abingdon and New York: Routledge.

Weil, Simone. 2002. *Gravity and Grace*. Oxfordshire: Routledge.

Wels, Harry. 2013. "Whispering Empathy: Transdisciplinary Reflections on Research Methodology." In *What Makes Us Moral? On the Capacities and Conditions for Being Moral*, edited by Bert Musschenga and Anton van Harskamp, 151–65. Dordrecht: Springer.

Other Recommended Resources

Websites and Videos

Chimpanzee Waterfall Displays: Dr. Jane Goodall and the Jane Goodall Institute USA. 2011. "Waterfall Displays." Video. January 6. https://youtu.be/jjQCZClpaaY.

Elephants with Body of Dead Conspecific: National Geographic. 2016. "Rare Footage: Wild Elephants 'Mourn' Their Dead." Video. September 2. https://youtu.be/Ku_GUNzXoeQ.

Journey of the Universe Video. www.journeyoftheuniverse.org.

Journey of the Universe Course. www.coursera.org/learn/journey-of-the-universe?.

Doing Science Differently

Despret, Vinciane. 2016. *What Would Animals Say If We Asked the Right Questions?* Minneapolis: University of Minnesota Press.

Haraway, Donna. 2007. *When Species Meet*. Minneapolis: University of Minnesota Press.

Waal, Frans de. 2016. *Are We Smart Enough to Know How Smart Animals Are?* New York: W.W. Norton.

Religious Naturalism

Hogue, Michael Stephen. 2010. *The Promise of Religious Naturalism*. New York: Rowman & Littlefield.

Raymo, Chet. 2008. *When God Is Gone, Everything Is Holy: The Making of a Religious Naturalist*. Notre Dame, Ind.: Sorin Books.

Religious Naturalist Association. https://religious-naturalist-association.org.

Stone, Jerome A. 2008. *Religious Naturalism Today: The Rebirth of a Forgotten Alternative*. Albany: State University of New York Press.

About the Contributors

Dave Aftandilian is Associate Professor of Anthropology, member of the leadership team for the Compassionate Awareness and Living Mindfully (CALM) Program, and founding Director of the Human-Animal Relationships (HARE) Program at Texas Christian University. He is the editor or coeditor of four books, including *What Are the Animals to Us? Approaches from Science, Religion, Folklore, Literature, and Art* (Tennessee, 2007); *City Creatures: Animal Encounters in the Chicago Wilderness* (Chicago, 2015); and *Grounding Education in the Environmental Humanities: Exploring Place-Based Pedagogies in the South* (Routledge, 2019).

Barbara R. Ambros is Professor of East Asian Religions in the Department of Religious Studies at the University of North Carolina, Chapel Hill. Her publications include *Bones of Contention: Animals and Religion in Contemporary Japan* (University of Hawai'i Press, 2012) and a special issue of *Religions* titled "Buddhist Beasts: Reflections on Animals in Asian Religions and Culture" (coedited with Reiko Ohnuma, 2019). She is working on a monograph about life releases in early modern Japan.

Geoffrey Barstow received his Ph.D. in Tibetan studies from the University of Virginia and is now Associate Professor of Religious Studies at Oregon State University. He is the author of *Food of Sinful Demons: Meat, Vegetarianism, and the Limits of Buddhism in Tibet* (Columbia, 2018) and editor of *The Faults of Meat: Tibetan Buddhist Writings on Vegetarianism* (Wisdom, 2019). His research focuses on the history of vegetarianism on the Tibetan plateau, asking questions about how animals were viewed, how they were treated (e.g., eaten), what that can tell us about Tibetan Buddhism, and how Buddhist ideas about animal ethics might impact broader philosophical discussions.

Beth A. Berkowitz is Ingeborg Rennert Chair of Jewish Studies and Professor in the Department of Religion at Barnard College. She is the author of *Execution and Invention: Death Penalty Discourse in Early Rabbinic and Christian Cultures* (Oxford, 2006); *Defining Jewish Difference: From Antiquity to the Present* (Cambridge, 2012); and *Animals and Animality in the Babylonian Talmud* (Cambridge, 2018). She is coeditor of *Religious Studies and Rabbinics: A Conversation* (Routledge, 2017). Her area of specialization is classical rabbinic literature, and her interests include animal studies, Jewish difference, and Bible reception history.

Matthew Calarco is Professor of Philosophy at California State University, Fullerton where he teaches courses in Continental philosophy and animal and environmental ethics. He is the author of several books in animal studies and related fields, including most recently *The Boundaries of Human Nature* (Columbia University Press, 2022).

Christopher Carter is Associate Professor of Theology and Religious Studies at the University of San Diego and an Ordained Elder in the United Methodist Church. He is the author of *The Spirit of Soul Food: Race, Faith, and Food Justice* (Illinois, 2021) and coeditor of *The Future of Meat Without Animals* (Rowman & Littlefield, 2016).

Andrea Dara Cooper is Associate Professor and Leonard and Tobee Kaplan Scholar in Modern Jewish Thought and Culture in the Department of Religious Studies at the University of North Carolina, Chapel Hill, where she teaches a range of courses on religion and culture, the history of Judaism, gender, and philosophy. Her research interests include Jewish thought, cultural and literary theory, critical animal studies, and post-Holocaust ethics. She is the author of *Gendering Modern Jewish Thought* (Indiana University Press, 2021).

Allison Covey is Assistant Teaching Professor in the Ethics Program at Villanova University. She teaches moral philosophy and Christian moral theology, specializing in animal and environmental ethics. Covey holds a Ph.D. in systematic theology from the University of St. Michael's College at the University of Toronto as well as an M.A. in theological studies (scripture) and an M.A. in pastoral studies from the University of St. Thomas in Houston. Prior to entering academia, Covey spent more than a decade in pastoral ministry.

Barbara Darling is Senior Professor of the Practice of Religion at Wheaton College in Norton, Massachusetts, where she teaches courses in Religion and Animals, Religion and Ecology, and others. She is also a member of Wheaton's Network for LGBTQ+ Inclusion, Support, and Advocacy; and of its Diversity, Equity, Access, and Leadership (DEAL) Senate. She serves on the Advisory Group for the Yale Forum on Religion and Ecology and has edited several books in the Boston University Studies in Philosophy and Religion series, including *Can Virtue Be Taught?* (Notre Dame, 1994), *Courage* (Notre Dame, 2002), and *Responsibility* (Notre Dame, 2007). Barbara's house rabbit animal companions, Daisy and Teddy Charlie, fill her life with joy.

Becca Franks is Assistant Professor of Environmental Studies at New York University where she is the director of WATR-lab and co-director of the Wild Animal Welfare Program. The core question driving her work is: How can we advance our understanding of animals in response to the urgent demands of the Anthropocene?

Monica Gagliano is Research Associate Professor of Evolutionary Ecology at Southern Cross University, where she directs the Biological Intelligence lab funded by the Templeton World Charity Foundation. She pioneered the new research field of plant bioacoustics, extended the concept of cognition to plants, and is the author of *Thus Spoke the Plant* (North Atlantic, 2018).

Vincent Goossaert 高萬桑 (Ph.D., EPHE, Paris, 1997) is Professor of Daoism and Chinese religions at École Pratique des Hautes Études (EPHE), Université PSL. His research deals with the social history of Chinese religion in late imperial and modern times. He is coeditor of *T'oung Pao*, a leading journal in sinology established in 1890. His recent publications include *Making the Gods Speak: The Ritual Production of Revelation in Chinese History* (Harvard University Asia Center, 2022), *Heavenly Masters: Two Thousand Years of the Daoist State* (University of Hawai'i Press & Chinese University Press, 2021), and *Vies des saints exorcistes: Hagiographies taoïstes, 11ᵉ-16ᵉ siècles* (Paris, Les Belles Lettres, 2021).

Aaron S. Gross is Professor of Religious Studies at the University of San Diego. He specializes in studying Jewish modernity, animals and religion, and food and religion, with a subspecialty in studying South Asian traditions. He is a past President of the Society for Jewish Ethics and the founder of the nonprofit advocacy groups Farm Forward and Better Food Foundation. He is the author of *The Question of the Animal and Religion: Theoretical Stakes, Practical Implications* (Columbia University Press, 2014) and coeditor of *Feasting and Fasting: The History and Ethics of Jewish Food* (NYU Press, 2019), among other works.

James Hatley is Professor Emeritus in Philosophy and Environmental Studies at Salisbury University in Maryland. In the last decade he has authored a series of essays responding to philosophical and religious questions emerging in a time of human-caused mass species extinction, many of which were written in collaboration with the Extinction Studies Working Group founded by Australian anthropologist Deborah Bird Rose. Hatley is also the author of a study on the Holocaust titled *Suffering Witness: The Quandary of Responsibility after the Irreparable* (SUNY, 2000), as well as coeditor of two collections of essays focusing respectively on the thought of Emmanuel Levinas and Maurice Merleau-Ponty. Currently Hatley spends much of his time in Montana, where he continues to advocate on behalf of all living kinds, particularly through encouraging public engagement in practices of contemplative ecology and creaturely liturgy.

Laura Hobgood is Professor and holder of the Paden Chair in Environmental Studies and Religion at Southwestern University. She has published several books, including *A Dog's History of the World: Canines and the Domestication of Humans* (Baylor, 2014) and *Holy Dogs and Asses: Animals in the Christian Tradition* (Illinois, 2008), along with numerous articles and book chapters focused on animals and religion. In addition to teaching, researching, and writing, Laura volunteers with her partner as a dog foster for municipal shelters and orphan squirrel rehabilitator for wildlife rescue, as well as riding a bicycle as much as possible.

Linda Hogan, Professor Emerita of English and Ethnic Studies at the University of Colorado at Boulder, is a Chickasaw author of numerous works, including, most recently, *The Radiant Lives of Animals* (essays; Beacon), which received a National Book Foundation Award for Science Literature, and *A History of Kindness* (poetry; Torrey House). She has received many fellowships, grants, and awards, including from the Lannan Foundation, the Guggenheim Foundation, and the National Endowment for the Arts. Her novel *Mean Spirit* was a Pulitzer Finalist, and the novel *Solar Storms* was a New York Times Notable Book. Her first book of essays, *Dwellings: A Spiritual History of the Natural World*, has become a classic in environmental literature. Her poetry books, *Rounding the Human Corners* and *The Book of Medicines*, were both Pulitzer nominees. In addition, she has published several other collections. She is currently working on Sacred Indigenous Traditions for The Fetzer Institute and a new collection of essays on animals she has known.

Mark A. Krause is Professor of Psychology at Southern Oregon University and has served as associate editor for *Animal Behavior and Cognition*, consulting editor for *Journal of Comparative Psychology*, and is coauthor of *Introduction to Psychological Science* (Pearson Canada, 2020). He is coeditor of the book *Evolution of Learning and Memory Mechanisms* (Cambridge, 2022). He has researched learning and memory in snakes, birds, chimpanzees, and humans.

Adrienne Krone is Assistant Professor of Environmental Science & Sustainability and Religious Studies at Allegheny College. She has a Ph.D. in American religion from Duke University, and her research focuses on religious food justice movements in North America. Her current research project is an ethnographic and historical study of the Jewish community farming movement.

Sarah May Lindsay (she/her) has a Ph.D. in sociology from McMaster University. Her main research areas include human-nonhuman animal relations, human and nonhuman animal shelters and housing, nonhuman companion animals, nonhuman animal use and abuse (abolitionism/liberationism), environmentalism and social movements, disability, deviance, and speciesism. She works from the intersectional perspective of Critical Animal Studies and Vegan Sociology, leveraging progressive pedagogy for social change. Her doctoral research focused on companion, "service," and "support" animal co-sheltering policies and practices at women's emergency shelters in Ontario, Canada. Recent publications include a journal article on the "problem" of multispecies families in women's shelters and a co-authored introductory chapter on the connectivity of Critical Animal Studies and Critical Disability Studies.

Seth B. Magle is Director of the Urban Wildlife Institute at the Lincoln Park Zoo in Chicago, and also Executive Director of the Urban Wildlife Information Network, a global alliance of researchers in dozens of cities working together to study urban animals. He holds a Ph.D. in ecology from Colorado State University and has published over 50 articles on urban wildlife species ranging from prairie dogs to rats to birds. His vision is to help create a world in which cities are a critical part of the conservation of biodiversity.

Alan Santinele Martino (he/him) is Assistant Professor in the Community Rehabilitation and Disability Studies program in the Department of Community Health Sciences at the University of Calgary. His main research interests are in critical disability studies, gender and sexualities, and qualitative and community-based research (particularly using participatory and inclusive research methodologies). His work has been published in multiple journals, including *Disability Studies Quarterly, Canadian Disability Studies Journal,* and *Culture, Health and Sexuality,* as well as edited volumes on disability and/or sexualities studies.

Katharine Mershon is Assistant Professor of Philosophy and Religion at Western Carolina University. Her research and teaching span the archival and philosophical spaces of the modern Americas, with a particular focus on religion in non-traditional spaces and materials. She is currently working on a book project entitled "Dogs Save: Stories of Canine Redemption in American Culture" (under contract with Columbia University Press).

Robert W. Mitchell is Foundation Professor of Animal Studies and Psychology at Eastern Kentucky University, where he created the interdisciplinary Animal Studies undergraduate major, the first of its kind, in 2010. He has studied diverse species—dolphins, apes, monkeys, sea lions, dogs, and humans—and his edited books examine deception, pretending, imagination, self-recognition, anthropomorphism, and spatial cognition in relation to animals and children.

Eric D. Mortensen is the John A. Von Weissenfluh Professor of Religious Studies and Chair of the Department of Religious Studies & Ethics at Guilford College, where he teaches courses on Tibetan & Himalayan, East Asian, and comparative religions. His research focuses on animal divination, folk stories of monsters and invisible villages, and other topics in the religio-folkloric traditions of the Tibetans of Gyalthang. He was an ensemble member in the 1991 international tour of the theatrical production of Martha Boesing's *Standing on Fishes*, a play about and involving the Council of All Beings.

Todd Ramón Ochoa is a cultural anthropologist and Associate Professor of Religion in the Department of Religious Studies at the University of North Carolina, Chapel Hill. Ochoa has written extensively about animal sacrifice in his books, *Society of the Dead: Quita Manaquita and Palo Praise in Cuba* (California, 2010) and *A Party for Lazarus: Six Generations of Ancestral Devotion in a Cuban Town* (California, 2020).

Margaret Robinson is a two-spirit Mi'kmaw scholar, raised in the Eskikewa'kik district of Mi'kma'ki. She works as an Associate Professor at Dalhousie University where she holds the Tier 2 Canada Research Chair in Reconciliation, Gender, and Identity. She is a member of Lennox Island First Nation, in the district of Epekwitk.

Nerissa Russell is Professor of Anthropology and member of the Cornell Institute of Archaeology and Material Studies (CIAMS) at Cornell University. She is a zooarchaeologist who studies human-animal relations through animal remains from archaeological sites, mainly from early farming societies in Eastern Europe and Southwest Asia. She is the author of *Social Zooarchaeology: Humans and Animals in Prehistory* (Cambridge, 2012).

Donovan O. Schaefer is Associate Professor of Religious Studies at the University of Pennsylvania. He is the author of *Religious Affects: Animality, Evolution, and Power* (Duke University Press, 2015) and *Wild Experiment: Feeling Science and Secularism after Darwin* (Duke University Press, 2022).

Barbara Smuts, Professor Emerita of Psychology at the University of Michigan, studies canine evolution and social relationships among domestic dogs. She is interested in how many conventional views of other animals often negatively influence our treatment of them and how such views can be altered.

Sarra Tlili is Associate Professor of Arabic literature at the University of Florida in the Department of Languages, Literatures, and Cultures. Her main areas of research are animal and environmental ethics in Islam, Qur'anic stylistics, and tradition and modernity in Arabic literature. Her publications include *Animals in the Qur'an* (Cambridge, 2012), "All Animals Are Equal, or Are They? The Ikhwān al-Ṣafā's Animal Epistle and its Unhappy End," and "From Breath to Soul: The Quranic Word *Rūḥ* and Its (Mis)interpretations."

Kenneth R. Valpey is a research fellow of the Oxford Centre for Hindu Studies and a fellow of the Oxford Centre for Animal Ethics. He is the author of *Cow Care in Hindu Animal Ethics* (Palgrave Macmillan, 2020).

Lina Verchery is a filmmaker and scholar of Buddhism who teaches at Victoria University of Wellington | Te Herenga Waka in Aotearoa New Zealand. A trained ethnographer, her areas of research and teaching include contemporary Chinese Buddhism and Buddhist monastic life, as well as the intersections of Buddhism and art, interspecies ethics, and environmental anthropology. She holds a Ph.D. in Buddhist Studies from Harvard

University and an M.Div. in Buddhism from Harvard Divinity School. An award-winning filmmaker, her documentary films about Buddhism and connected topics have been screened in festivals and on television networks around the world.

Christine Webb, Lecturer and Research Associate in Harvard University's Department of Human Evolutionary Biology, studies social behavior and emotion in our close primate cousins. Her latest work also engages critically with questions in animal and environmental ethics, particularly in deconstructing anthropocentric biases in scientific research with other species.

Index

Note: Page numbers in *italics* indicate illustrations; **boldfaced** page numbers indicate tables.